Frescoes of the Skull

Works by Samuel Beckett
Published by Grove Press

Cascando and Other Short Dramatic Pieces
(*Words and Music; Eh Joe; Come and Go; Film* [*original version*])

Collected Poems in English and French

The Collected Works of Samuel Beckett (twenty-two volumes)

Company

Endgame

Ends and Odds
(*Not I; That Time; Footfalls; Ghost Trio; Theatre I; Theatre II; Radio I; Radio II*)

Film, A Film Script

First Love and Other Shorts
(*From an Abandoned Work; Enough; Imagination Dead Imagine; Ping; Not I; Breath*)

Fizzles

Happy Days

How It Is

I Can't Go On, I'll Go On: A Selection from Samuel Beckett's Work

Krapp's Last Tape and Other Dramatic Pieces
(*All That Fall; Embers* [*a play for radio*]; *Acts Without Words I and II* [*mimes*])

The Lost Ones

Malone Dies

Mercier and Camier

Molloy

More Pricks Than Kicks

Murphy

Poems in English

Proust

Stories and Texts for Nothing

Three Novels
(*Molloy; Malone Dies; The Unnamable*)

The Unnamable

Waiting for Godot

Watt

Frescoes of the Skull

The Later Prose and Drama of Samuel Beckett

James Knowlson and John Pilling

Grove Press, Inc., New York

First Evergreen Edition 1980
First Printing 1980
ISBN: 0-394-17610-3
Grove Press ISBN: 0-8021-4293-1
Library of Congress Catalog Card Number: 79-6153

LIBRARY OF CONGRESS CATALOGING IN PUBLICATION DATA

Knowlson, James.
  Frescoes of the skull.

  Reprint of the 1979 ed. published by J. Calder, London.
  Bibliography: p. 287
  Includes index.
    1. Beckett, Samuel, 1906–   —Criticism and interpretation. I. Pilling, John, joint author. II. Title.
[PR6003.E282Z765 1980]   848'.91409   79-6153
ISBN 0-394-17610-3 (pbk.)

Manufactured in the United States of America

Distributed by Random House, Inc., New York

GROVE PRESS, INC., 196 West Houston Street, New York, N.Y. 10014

Contents

For Elizabeth and Poppy

Acknowledgements

We are grateful, above all, to Samuel Beckett for generous permission to quote from his published and unpublished works and to the Librarian and Archivist of Reading University Library for permission to quote from manuscripts deposited in the Beckett Archive. The authors are also grateful to the holders of the copyright to Samuel Beckett's writing in the United Kingdom, Messrs Faber and Faber and John Calder (Publishers) Ltd. and Calder and Boyars for permission to quote from his work.

James Knowlson wishes to thank several directors, producers, actors and actresses for helping to make his knowledge of Beckett's plays much closer to first-hand; among these are: Donald McWhinnie, Patrick Magee, Madeleine Renaud, Jean Martin, Roger Blin, Alan Schneider, Pierre Chabert, Walter Asmus, Dame Peggy Ashcroft, Billie Whitelaw and Tristram Powell.

John Pilling would like to thank Peter Murphy for stimulating, in particular with respect to *How It Is*, any number of ideas that would otherwise have remained still-born, and Stephen Wall for invaluable advice on the style and content of the section dealing with the three *Still* texts.

On the prose side of this book, written by John Pilling, the section on *Still, Sounds* and *Still 3* appeared previously in *Essays in Criticism*, XXVIII, no. 2, April 1978. On the drama side, written by James Knowlson, an earlier version of the short *Come and Go* section was previously published in *Gambit International Theatre Magazine*, vol. 7, no. 28, 1976, as was the penultimate chapter 'Beckett and John Millington Synge'. Part of the *Krapp's Last Tape* chapter adapts an article that appeared in the *Journal of Beckett Studies*, no. 1, Winter 1976 and the chapter on *Happy Days* borrows a few pages from the Afterword to the Faber and Faber bilingual edition, *Happy Days / Oh Les beaux jours* (1978), ed. J. Knowlson. All the other chapters are unpublished.

Introduction

Almost all great writers have had to suffer neglect at certain moments in their careers, usually at the outset (when their language is condemned as either too *outré* or too derivative) and again when they have moved beyond the work or works that have made them famous, and entered upon a 'late' period, characterized by an extremely personal and idiosyncratic use of language, 'to set', in T.S. Eliot's words, 'the crown upon a lifetime's effort'. In the case of Samuel Beckett this paradigm is partially confirmed and partially negated, for whilst Beckett has only gradually (and in some cases grudgingly) been accorded classic status, there has recently been considerable critical activity, on both sides of the Atlantic, devoted to demonstrating that in this case, despite the inherent difficulty of his work, the artist has not escaped the critics in pursuit of him. There is no doubt an element of compensation here, designed in some way to make up for the years of penury and disfavour that came before the fame and fortune. But there is also an eminently natural desire to explicate what are, at any rate superficially, forbiddingly inaccessible texts which may never be fully explained to everyone's satisfaction. It may be that, with works of such density and uniqueness, there is a need to develop a correspondingly original kind of criticism, which will not depart so far from tradition as to become esoteric, but which will not be afraid to be unconventional when the need arises. Something of this kind is attempted here, although it will be clear that the approach is nothing like as unconventional as it might have been. The business of evolving a language more appropriate and adaptive has been considered a matter secondary to the need for a coherent and integrated account of what 'late' Beckett is about, and where Beckett may be adjudged to have been successful (or unsuccessful) in emulating those works, like *Waiting for Godot* or *Molloy*, that first established him as a writer of stature and originality.

The omission of any detailed consideration of the 'mature' Beckett of the period 1940-1950 (in prose) and 1949-1956 (in drama) is, in other words, a deliberate and conscious act on the part of both authors, and is not in any way intended to diminish the public's growing sense that Beckett was at this time 'at the crest of a wave' as Krapp put it. Likewise, the inclusion of two studies that concern themselves mainly with Beckett's most substantial unpublished works is not intended to distract attention from areas of Beckett that are more rewarding or satisfying, especially when neither Beckett's first long prose work (*Dream of Fair to Middling Women*) nor his first play (*Eleuthéria*) are likely to be made available for public scrutiny in his lifetime. But it was felt that no account of 'late' Beckett could entirely ignore the originating impulses that led him to express himself first in prose and later, after a gap of sixteen years, in drama, without impoverishing and artificially isolating a body of work that abundantly testifies to Beckett's dictum that 'one is a victim of all one has written'. At the same time no attempt is made to read the late works by the light of the earlier or the earlier in terms of the later. For if one thing is certain where Beckett is concerned, there is no key that will unlock every problem thrown up by his work, no formula that will elucidate every aspect of his *oeuvre*.

This is one reason why there is no attempt at uniformity of style or method on our part, and why each major area of Beckett's enterprise has remained the preserve of the critic whose primary scholarly interest over many years has been in the one genre or the other. In both cases, however, there has been a desire to use, where relevant, unpublished material or rejected drafts that illustrate the genesis of the work in question, in the belief that this is one of the more profitable (and indeed inevitable) ways that 'second-generation' Beckett criticism can build upon the findings of the first generation. There has also been an attempt, on both sides, to offset the disadvantages of a divided focus by bringing the prose work and the drama as close together as is feasible, given the fundamental dissimilarity of modes, wherever this is relevant. By at all times submitting each section or chapter for the other's scrutiny, we have tried to compose a book that justifies the singularity of its title.

The title itself, *Frescoes of the Skull*, though an adequate description of any one of Beckett's works, is peculiarly appropriate to his 'late' period, in which an always cerebral artist has been engaged in an unprecedented archaeological investigation, or better, 'onto-speleology', as Beckett himself describes it. Beckett's shapes may seem a long way from the cave-paintings of Lascaux or Les Eyzies, and they can hardly hope to outlast them. But they are in their own way quite as remarkable and testify to Beckett's continuing dedication to an art that is both 'totally intelligible' and 'totally inexplicable'.

Key to Abbreviations and Editions cited

KLT	*Krapp's Last Tape and Embers*, London, Faber and Faber, 1959.
	Lessness, London, Calder and Boyars, 1970.
	The Lost Ones, London, Calder and Boyars, 1972.
MPTK	*More Pricks than Kicks*, London, Calder and Boyars, 1970.
M	*Murphy*, London, John Calder, 1963.
OE	*Our Exagmination Round His Factification for Incamination of Work in Progress*, London, Faber and Faber, 1936.
	Pas suivi de quatre esquisses, Paris, Editions de Minuit, 1978.
P	*Play and Two Short Pieces for Radio*, London, Faber and Faber, 1964.
PTD	*Proust and Three Dialogues with Georges Duthuit*, London, John Calder, 1965.
	Sounds and *Still 3* in *Essays in Criticism*, XXVIII, April 1978, pp. 155-157.
SR	*Six Residua*, London, John Calder, 1978 (includes *From an Abandoned Work*, *Enough*, *Imagination Dead Imagine*, *Ping*, *Lessness* and *The Lost Ones*).
TFN	*Texts for Nothing*, London, Calder and Boyars, 1974.
TN	[Three Novels] *Molloy*, *Malone Dies*, *The Unnamable*, London, John Calder, 1959.
W	*Watt*, London, John Calder, 1963.
WFG	*Waiting for Godot*, London, Faber and Faber, 1965.

also abbreviated:

F & F	Federman, R. and Fletcher, J., *Samuel Beckett: His Works and His Critics*, Berkeley and Los Angeles, University of California Press, 1970.

Conversion Table to American Editions

References in the following table are normally to the Grove Press *Collected Works of Samuel Beckett* (New York, 1970). 'From an Abandoned Work', 'Enough', 'Imagination Dead Imagine' and 'Ping' are referred to in *First Love and Other Shorts*, Grove Press (New York, 1974). 'He is barehead', 'Horn came always', 'Afar a bird', 'I gave up before birth', 'Closed place', 'Old earth', 'Still' and 'For to end yet again' are referred to in *Fizzles*, Grove Press (New York, 1976). 'Three Dialogues with Georges Duthuit' appear in *Samuel Beckett, Twentieth Century Views*, ed. M. Esslin, (Prentice-Hall Inc., New Jersey, 1965). The page numbers in the Grove Press edition of *The Lost Ones* (New York, 1972) are identical with the Calder and Boyars edition (London, 1972). *Lessness* is not published separately in book form by Grove Press; references therefore are to the Calder and Boyars edition (London, 1970). '. . . but the clouds . . .' is not printed in the Grove Press, *Ends and Odds* (New York, 1976); references therefore are to the Faber and Faber edition (London, 1977). At the time of going to press, *All Strange Away* is published only in Great Britian in a trade edition. 'Sounds', 'Still 3', 'As the story was told' and 'La Falaise' are not published in American editions.

4 *Proust*, 62.
5 *Murphy*, 109; *ibid.*, 4; *ibid.*, 2.
6 *Molloy*, 13-14.
7 *Murphy*, 56; *Proust*, 56.

11 *Murphy*, 112.

15 *Proust*, 67.

20 *MPTK*, 56-58.

21 *Molloy*, 173.

22 *MPTK*, 83; *ibid.*, 143.

29 *Happy Days*, 44.

30 *Endgame*, 58.

31 *Happy Days*, 43.

32 *Proust*, 70.

33 *WFG*, 9; *ibid.*, 49.

34 *Proust*, 49.

36 *Malone Dies*, 1-2.

37 *Cascando and Other Short Dramatic Pieces*, 13; *The Unnamable*, 179.

45 *Proust*, 17; *Stories and Texts for Nothing*, 75; *ibid.*, 76; *ibid.*, 76.

46 *Stories etc.*, 79; *ibid.*, 78; *ibid.*, 79; *ibid.*, 82.

47 *Stories etc.*, 83; *ibid.*, 82; *ibid.*, 81; *ibid.*, 83, 84; *ibid.*, 82; *ibid.*, 83; *ibid.*, 85.

48 *Stories etc.*, 87; *ibid.*, 90; *ibid.*, 91-92.

49 *Stories etc.*, 93; *ibid.*, 94; *ibid.*, 78; *Proust*, 49; *Stories etc.*, 95.

50 *Stories etc.*, 96; *ibid.*, 96; *ibid.*, 97; *ibid.*, 98; *ibid.*, 99; *ibid.*, 98-99; *ibid.*, 95-96; *ibid.*, 99; *ibid.*, 95; *ibid.*, 99.

51 *Stories etc.*, 102; *ibid.*, 101; *ibid.*, 101; *ibid.*, 102-103; *ibid.*, 103; *ibid.*, 101; *ibid.*, 104; *ibid.*, 104; *ibid.*, 104; *ibid.*, 103; *ibid.*, 102; *ibid.*, 105; *ibid.*, 102; *ibid.*, 102.

52 *Stories etc.*, 103; *ibid.*, 104; *ibid.*, 107; *ibid.*, 107; *ibid.*, 110; *ibid.*, 110; *ibid.*, 108; *ibid.*, 107; *ibid.*, 112.

53 *Stories etc.*, 111; *ibid.*, 111-112; *ibid.*, 112; *ibid.*, 113; *ibid.*, 112-113; *ibid.*, 113; *ibid.*, 114; *ibid.*, 114; *ibid.*, 113-114; *ibid.*, 115.

54 *Stories etc.*, 115; *ibid.*, 111; *ibid.*, 118; *ibid.*, 118; *ibid.*, 119; *ibid.*, 117.

55 *Stories etc.*, 118; *ibid.*, 121; *ibid.*, 121; *ibid.*, 123; *ibid.*, 124; *ibid.*, 125.

56 *Stories etc.*, 125; *ibid.*, 125; *ibid.*, 127-128; *ibid.*, 128; *ibid.*, 128; *ibid.*, 128-129; *ibid.*, 128; *ibid.*, 130.

57 *Stories etc.*, 130; *ibid.*, 127; *ibid.*, 131; *ibid.*, 134.; *ibid.*, 134; *ibid.*, 134.

58 *Watt*, 77; *Stories etc.*, 135; *ibid.*, 139; *ibid.*, 138; *ibid.*, 138; *ibid.*, 139; *ibid.*, 137; *ibid.*, 137; *ibid.*, 138-139; *ibid.*, 139; *ibid.*, 139; *ibid.*, 138; *ibid.*, 137; *ibid.*, 138; *ibid.*, 139.

59 *Stories etc.*, 140; *Three Dialogues*, 21; *Stories etc.*, 139; *ibid.*, 137.

61   *How It Is*, 61; *ibid.*, 84.
62   *How It Is*, 34; *Watt*, 124; *How It Is*, 11.
63   *Molloy*, 47; *ibid.*, 34.
64   *How It Is*, 7; *ibid.*, 7; *ibid.*, 9; *ibid.*, 10; *ibid.*, 16; *ibid.*, 11; *ibid.*, 31; *ibid.*, 10; *ibid.*, 28-32; *ibid.*, 11.
65   *How It Is*, 30; *ibid.*, 11; *ibid.*, 15-16; *ibid.*, 10-11.
66   *How It Is*, 16; *ibid.*, 16; *ibid.*, 17; *ibid.*, 18; *ibid.*, 18; *ibid.*, 38; *ibid.*, 21.
67   *How It Is*, 14; *ibid.*, 21; *ibid.*, 22; *ibid.*, 76-77; *ibid.*, 27-32; *ibid.*, 27; *ibid.*, 32; *ibid.*, 29; *ibid.*, 30; *ibid.*, 31; *ibid.*, 32; *ibid.*, 28.
68   *How It Is*, 8; *ibid.*, 8; *ibid.*, 8; *ibid.*, 35; *ibid.*, 25; *ibid.*, 36; *ibid.*, 18; *ibid.*, 16; *ibid.*, 35; *ibid.*, 44-45; *ibid.*, 45; *Watt*, 117; *Endgame*, 84; *How It Is*, 143.
69   *How It Is*, 36; *ibid.*, 40; *ibid.*, 43; *ibid.*, 77; *ibid.*, 86; *ibid.*, 51; *ibid.*, 47; *ibid.*, 47; *ibid.*, 14; *ibid.*, 42; *ibid.*, 46.
70   *How It Is*, 13; *ibid.*, 48.
71   *How It is*, 21; *ibid.*, 21; *ibid.*, 16; *ibid.*, 52; *ibid.*, 52; *ibid.*, 59-60; *ibid.*, 113-115.
72   *How It Is*, 60; *ibid.*, 61; *ibid.*, 62; *ibid.*, 62.
73   *How It Is*, 47; *ibid.*, 46; *ibid.*, 62; *ibid.*, 83; *ibid.*, 11; *ibid.*, 62; *ibid.*, 62; *ibid.*, 62; *ibid.*, 69; *ibid.*, 76; *ibid.*, 76; *ibid.*, 132; *ibid.*, 83; *ibid.*, 83; *ibid.*, 87.
74   *How It Is*, 94-95; *ibid.*, 42; *ibid.*, 41; *ibid.*, 14; *ibid.*, 46; *ibid.*, 56; *ibid.*, 63; *ibid.*, 56.
75   *How It is*, 81; *ibid.*, 37; *ibid.*, 129.
76   *How It Is*, 130; *ibid.*, 130; *ibid.*, 131; *ibid.*, 33; *ibid.*, 10; *ibid.*, 17; *ibid.*, 17; *ibid.*, 36; *ibid.*, 33; *ibid.*, 39; *ibid.*, 14-15.
77   *How It Is*, 115; *ibid.*, 92; *ibid.*, 129; *ibid.*, 27; *ibid.*, 129; *ibid.*, 146; *ibid.*, 7; *ibid.*, 67; *ibid.*, 129.
78   *How It Is*, 61; *ibid.*, 37; *ibid.*, 37; *ibid.*, 38; *ibid.*, 60; *ibid.*, 113; *ibid.*, 132; *ibid.*, 135.
81   *Krapp's Last Tape and Other Dramatic Pieces*, 25.
82   *Krapp*, 25; *ibid.*, 26; *ibid.*, 26.
83   *Krapp*, 25; *ibid.*, 12; *ibid.*, 28.
84   *Krapp*, 23; *Proust*, 3.
85   *Krapp*, 24; *ibid.*, 25; *ibid.*, 26; *ibid.*, 26-27; *ibid.*, 26; *ibid.*, 16.
86   *Krapp*, 19; *ibid.*, 25; *ibid.*, 22, 27.
87   *Krapp*, 15; *ibid.*, 19; *ibid.*, 19.
88   *Krapp*, 21; *ibid.*, 28.
89   *Krapp*, 22-23; *ibid.*, 16; *ibid.*, 19; *ibid.*, 24.

90 *Krapp*, 25; *First Love, etc.*, 43.
93 *Krapp*, 22.
94 *Happy Days*, 33; *ibid.*, 37.
95 *Happy Days*, 11; *ibid.*, 52; *ibid.*, 60; *Malone Dies*, 6.
96 *Happy Days*, 35; *Krapp's Last Tape, etc.*, 116.
97 *Happy Days*, 54; *ibid.*, 34.
99 *Proust*, 14; *Happy Days*, 39; *The Unnamable*, 179.
100 *Happy Days*, 52-53; *ibid.*, 28; *ibid.*, 40; *ibid.*, 49; *ibid.*, 62.
101 *Happy Days*, 20-21; *ibid.*, 21; *ibid.*, 21.
102 *Happy Days*, 27; *ibid.*, 51.
103 *Happy Days*, 38; *ibid.*, 42-43; *Endgame*, 32-33.
104 *Happy Days*, 31; *ibid.*, 16; *ibid.*, 34.
105 *Happy Days*, 40; *ibid.*, 34.
106 *Happy Days*, 18; *ibid.*, 15; *ibid.*, 24; *ibid.*, 33.
107 *Happy Days*, 50-51; *ibid.*, 54; *ibid.*, 60; *ibid.*, 50.
108 *Happy Days*, 62; *ibid.*, 9.
109 *Stories, etc.*, 82-83.
112 *Cascando, etc.*, 54.
113 *Cascando, etc.*, 54; *ibid.*, 53.
114 *Cascando, etc.*, 45.
115 *Cascando, etc.*, 49; *ibid.*, 48; *ibid.*, 48; *ibid.*, 47; *ibid.*, 47; *ibid.*, 50; *ibid.*, 46; *ibid.*, 47; *ibid.*, 48.
116 *Cascando, etc.*, 57; *ibid.*, 50; *ibid.*, 47; *ibid.*, 50; *ibid.*, 51; *ibid.*, 47; *ibid.*, 51; *ibid.*, 53; *ibid.*, 54; *ibid.*, 55.
117 *Cascando, etc.*, 57; *ibid.*, 59; *ibid.*, 53; *ibid.*, 52; *ibid.*, 53; *ibid.*, 61.
118 *Cascando, etc.*, 53.
125 *Cascando, etc.*, 70.
127 *WFG*, 57A; *Happy Days*, 11.
133 *Fizzles*, 27; *ibid.*, 26; *ibid.*, 32; *ibid.*, 11; *Molloy*, 13; *Fizzles*, 44; *ibid.*, 25; *ibid.*, 44; *ibid.*, 7-8; *ibid.*, 14; *Murphy*, 73; *Molloy*, 13; *Fizzles*, 10; *ibid.*, 21-22; *ibid.*, 44; *ibid.*, 15.
134 *Fizzles*, 15; *ibid.*, 38; *ibid.*, 32; *ibid.*, 20; *ibid.*, 27; *ibid.*, 14; *ibid.*, 21.
135 *Fizzles*, 43; *ibid.*, 44; *ibid.*, 44; *ibid.*, 20; *ibid.*, 27; *ibid.*, 22; *ibid.*, 14; *ibid.*, 15.
140 *How It Is*, 22.
141 *Proust*, 6.
145 *First Love, etc.*, 63.
146 *First Love, etc.*, 63; *ibid.*, 63; *ibid.*, 63; *ibid.*, 65.

147 *First Love, etc.*, 63; *ibid.*, 65; *ibid.*, 65.
148 *First Love, etc.*, 65-66; *ibid.*, 66; *ibid.*, 66; *ibid.*, 66.
149 *Stories, etc.*, 131.
151 *First Love, etc.*, 53.
153 *First Love, etc.*, 53; *Murphy*, 215; *First Love, etc.*, 53-54.
154 *First Love, etc.*, 56; *ibid.*, 58; *ibid.*, 60; *MPTK*, 19; *First Love etc.*, 54, 60.
155 *First Love, etc.*, 56; *ibid.*, 58; *ibid.*, 60; *Proust*, 50; *WFG*, 34A; *Proust*, 55; *First Love, etc.*, 59.
156 *First Love, etc.*, 57; *ibid.*, 58; *ibid.*, 59.
162 *How It Is*, 41.
169 *First Love, etc.*, 69.
170 *First Love, etc.*, 69; *ibid.*, 69.
171 *First Love, etc.*, 69; *ibid.*, 70; *ibid.*, 72; *ibid.*, 72; *ibid.*, 72.
177 *Fizzles*, 48; *ibid.*, 50-51.
178 *Fizzles*, 50; *ibid.*, 50; *First Love, etc.*, 39; *Molloy*, 39-40; *Watt* 15.
185 *Proust*, 70.
186 *Fizzles*, 55.
187 *Fizzles*, 55; *ibid.*, 55-56; *ibid.*, 56; *ibid.*, 56; *ibid.*, 56.
188 *Fizzles*, 56; *ibid.*, 56; *ibid.*, 57; *ibid.*, 58; *ibid.*, 58; *ibid.*, 59.
189 *Fizzles*, 59; *ibid.*, 59-60; *ibid.*, 60; *ibid.*, 60-61.
191 *Stories, etc.*, 81.
197 *The Unnamable*, 94; *ibid.*, 153; *Ends and Odds*, 14.
199 *The Unnamable*, 26.
200 *Ends and Odds*, 22.
201 *Ends and Odds*, 15; *ibid.*, 15.
202 *The Unnamable*, 26; *Ends and Odds*, 22.
203 *The Unnamable*, 30; *Ends and Odds*, 18.
204 *Ends and Odds*, 15; *ibid.*, 16; *ibid.*, 18; *ibid.*, 15.
206 *Stories, etc.*, 107; *Ends and Odds*, 22.
207 *Ends and Odds*, 31.
208 *Ends and Odds*, 28; *ibid.*, 37.
210 *Ends and Odds*, 37; *ibid.*, 28.
211 *Proust*, 2; *ibid.*, 2; *ibid.*, 3; *Ends and Odds*, 28.
212 *Ends and Odds*, 29; *ibid.*, 28-29; *ibid.*, 37; *ibid.*, 32; *ibid.*, 37; *ibid.*, 37; *Endgame*, 57.
213 *Ends and Odds*, 33; *ibid.*, 31; *Endgame*, 68; *Ends and Odds*, 31; *ibid.*, 32; *ibid.*, 34.
214 *Ends and Odds*, 30-31; *ibid.*, 32; *ibid.*, 33.
215 *Ends and Odds*, 33; *ibid.*, 36; *ibid.*, 32; *ibid.*, 36.

216 *Happy Days*, 18; *Ends and Odds*, 33.
217 *Ends and Odds*, 36; *ibid.*, 29; *ibid.*, 31; *ibid.*, 36.
218 *Ends and Odds*, 37; *ibid.*, 35; *ibid.*, 29; *ibid.*, 37.
219 *Ends and Odds*, 34; *ibid.*, 37; *ibid.*, 34; *ibid.*, 31; *ibid.*, 34; *ibid.*,
     31; *ibid.*, 37; *ibid.*, 29.
222 *Krapp's Last Tape, etc.*, 83.
223 *Ends and Odds*, 47.
224 *Ends and Odds*, 44; *ibid.*, 45; *ibid.*, 46; *ibid.*, 46.
225 *Ends and Odds*, 46; *ibid.*, 47; *ibid.*, 46.
226 *Ends and Odds*, 48, *ibid.*, 45; *ibid.*, 49.
227 *Ends and Odds*, 44; *ibid.*, 46.
228 *Ends and Odds*, 46; *Krapp's Last Tape, etc.*, 24.
229 *Ends and Odds*, 76.
230 *Ends and Odds*, 79; *ibid.*, 77; *ibid.*, 72.
231 *Stories, etc.*, 103.
232 *Ends and Odds*, 100; *ibid.*, 92; *ibid.*, 100; *ibid.*, 97; *ibid.*, 100;
     ibid., 94; *ibid.*, 84.
233 *Ends and Odds*, 89; *ibid.*, 90; *ibid.*, 94; *ibid.*, 100.
243 *Proust*, 67; *ibid.*, 67; *ibid.*, 6; *ibid.*, 6-7.
244 *Proust*, 11; *ibid.*, 60; *ibid.*, 56; *ibid.*, 41; *ibid.*, 56; *ibid.*, 56; *ibid.*,
     64; *ibid.*, 64; *ibid.*, 4; *ibid.*, 4; *ibid.*, 15; *ibid.*, 59; *ibid.*, 57; *ibid.*,
     52; *ibid.*, 57.
245 *Proust*, 48; *ibid.*, 62; *ibid.*, 18; *ibid.*, 47; *ibid.*, 60; *ibid.*, 23.
246 *MPTK*, 143.
248 *Proust*, 60.
249 *Murphy*, 47.
251 *Endgame*, 22.
252 'Three Dialogues', 20; *ibid.*, 21.
255 *Proust*, 71.
262 *WGF*, 42.
264 *Endgame*, 18; *ibid.*, 11; *Krapp's Last Tape, etc.*, 41.
269 *WFG*, 49A; *Happy Days*, 45.
282 *Ends and Odds*, 46.

Two from the Trunk

Dream of Fair to Middling Women

Beckett began his first long prose work, *Dream of Fair to Middling Women*, in 1932; it was never finished. Despite the extensive summary of its contents which Raymond Federman prints as part of the appendix to his *Journey to Chaos: Samuel Beckett's Early Fiction* (Berkeley and Los Angeles, University of California Press, 1965), despite the more or less complete sections from the novel that have been published, and despite the citation of phrases from it to support interpretations in the many critical studies of Beckett, it inevitably retains, for those who have not read the complete text, the mysterious and fascinating aura of the unknown. Whether this aura could survive the text being made generally available is doubtful but, as it may never be published, the aura is not likely to diminish. There is, of course, something very ironic in the way a text that Beckett very wisely abandoned as self-indulgent and out of control should have become a matter of scholarly interest, but it is one of the perennial disadvantages of celebrity that a writer to a large extent becomes, in Auden's phrase, his admirers. In the case of *Dream of Fair to Middling Women* there are at least two good reasons why the work will continue to be required reading for Beckett scholars. The first is that it contains much of the material that was later incorporated into *More Pricks than Kicks*; the second is that it presents, not always very clearly, but in a more consecutive form than is available to us elsewhere in Beckett, his views on what art can and cannot do, and what he, as artist, sees himself as doing. However dead Beckett may consider the work to be (he claims to be unable to remember it in detail, and to have no copy), these are powerful reasons for considering it as still alive.

We have grown accustomed, in recent years, to thinking sophisticatedly about narratives, postulating the existence of a 'second self' and such like intermediaries, and drawing diagrams to explain (or explain away) how 'narrator' and 'narrated' interact. These techniques are of little assistance where *Dream* is concerned, since the figure whose voice dominates all the others despises from the start the material he might be expected to shape, and suggests throughout that shape is of little interest to him now that he has ceased to believe himself the Cézanne of his trade, 'very strong on architectonics' (*Dream of Fair to Middling Women*, p. 159 of the typescript in the Reading University Library Beckett Archive, MS. 1227/7/16/9; all further references are to this copy). Indeed to try and summarize the plot of *Dream* is even more profitless than is usual with Beckett; this is no doubt because the young Beckett was determined to avoid 'the vulgarity of a plausible concatenation' (*PTD*, 81-82). The longer one reads, the less likelihood there is of something coherent emerging, and, defeated by its inconsequential mode of developing, we are likely to start reaching for terms like 'picaresque' or other such conveniently disarming but misleading labels. There is even less point in our thinking up labels where *Dream* is concerned than where more finished, and more refined, fictions of Beckett are under our scrutiny: *Dream* is a work designed to elude definitions of any kind. It does not even, like *Murphy*, take the trouble to suggest that, behind the events being recorded, there is some ordering genius who might be capable (or interested enough) to step in halfway through and restore things to their proper places. There is no benevolent figure standing behind *Dream* ready to catch it, if it should fall; the figure who does occupy that position is seemingly determined that fall it should.

The first 'section' (too inconsequential to be called a 'chapter') focusses the author's disgust with his material in a manner calculated to outrage even the least fastidious sensibility. In the first of its two brief paragraphs, the hero, Belacqua, pedals frenziedly 'down a frieze of hawthorn' on his bicycle until halted by the prospect of a defecating horse: the writing of *Dream* will be a similar excretion of waste matter, without any of the consoling lyricism of Proust, whom the hawthorn irresistibly summons up. The second paragraph, a perfect triumph of *non sequitur*, lasts just long enough for the idea of purposeless movement to lodge in our minds before it peters out. This is Beckett's way of cutting Proust's (or any self-conscious writer's) lucubrations on childhood to an absolute minimum, pouring implicit scorn on the practice, and yet contriving to satisfy, if only obliquely, our demands for some 'background' against which the other events may figure. There is, then, considerable deliberation in the 'unfinishedness' of this opening section.

The second (of the three) sections, all hundred and twenty pages of it, introduces us immediately to the erotic possibilities indicated by the title. Belacqua is 'in love from the girdle up' with a music student who has departed Dublin for Vienna, and 'the supreme adieu' (obscurely prefiguring the 'supreme caress' that Murphy muses on; *M*, 77) has just occurred. It is characteristic of his suspicion of 'the lyrical loinstring' (10) that Beckett should disdain the chance to write about their farewell, and typical of his penchant at this time for literary put-downs that he should suggest in passing that only a writer like Mallarmé could possibly be interested in such things (27). Beckett is obviously striving here to avoid all sentimentality. Not until *Murphy*, three years later, did he have the confidence to describe a farewell that is not only 'memorable' (*M*, 7) but, in its eccentric way, moving.

Beckett exploits, in these early pages of *Dream*, a fairly simple principle of contrast. After the flurried movement of the brief first section, we are pulled up short and asked to consider the stasis that has kept the young Belacqua rooted to the spot. This is obviously a stasis not occasioned simply by his loved one's departure, since the whole business of amatory relationship is regarded as rather tiresome, something one only lets oneself in for when one is insufficiently vigilant or, as here, unlucky enough to have encountered an attractive female (compare Murphy and Celia). Beckett makes clear, however, that the real satisfaction of thinking (as distinct from the false satisfactions of love) can only be fully achieved when one is alone and when one has ceased to move. This involves Beckett in explaining how Belacqua's mind defends itself against a hostile external world by making systematic adjustments — the first of such explorations and confrontations in Beckett: 'having fixed the technique, he sat on working himself up to the little teary ejaculation, choking it back in the very act of emission, waiting with his mind blank for it to subside . . . The cylinders of his mind abode serene' (3). Belacqua is obviously seeking a kind of safety valve that will enable him to find reality once again pleasant, but it is no ordinary pleasure (as the narrator of *Murphy* would say, 'pleasant was not the word'; *M* 6) and the metaphor of onanism which Beckett uses at this point alerts us to how isolated and solipsistic a world we are entering. Despite the physicality of the metaphor, the whole drift of this passage suggests that there has been some kind of split between mind and body, which cannot be easily reunited. Belacqua regards being 'entombed and enwombed' in the mind with as much satisfaction as Murphy after him, but as with Murphy 'the impudent interpolation of the world's ghastly backside' and the reminder that he cannot so mould reality as to 'pump up a few poor tears' (4) when it pleases him so to do, are things he finds exceedingly disagreeable. In view of the fact that these speculations have been prompted by contemplating the departure of a woman, it is clear that, fifteen years later, Molloy has acquired a certain wisdom: 'From things about to disappear I turn away in time' (*TN*, 12).

As far as the mind-body problem is concerned (and also, as we soon find out, as far as the sexual problem is concerned) Belacqua is against a 'solution of continuity', but forced to recognize that his own mind, despite his desire to disappear into it, itself operates with a certain causal remorselessness. The love-ache and the pang occasioned by his 'insubordinate mind' are, he finds, chained together by an 'ergo' (4). The psychological effect of discovering that 'sons of Adam' are not only isolated from the world, but also doomed to have minds that are unfree, is to sink Belacqua into a profound 'transcendental' gloom which the narrator is quick to assure us will not resolve itself into a 'conclusive proposition' but will at least allow the suffering figure to escape further misery by falling asleep:

> now in the very process of his distress at being a son of Adam and afflicted in consequence with a mind that would not obey its own behests was being concocted a gloom to crown his meditation in a style that had never graced the climax of any similar series in his previous experience of melancholy. A positively transcendental gloom was brewing that would incorporate the best and choicest elements in all that had gone before and made its way straight in what at first would have the appearance of a conclusive proposition. Needless to say it would be nothing of the kind. But considered in the penumbra of a clause on which to toss and turn and whinge himself to sleep it could scarcely have been improved on. (4-5)

Reality, having already proved truculent and unmanageable, now turns positively aggressive, in a scene with a 'wharfinger' which is the first of many such encounters with so-called authority in Beckett. This 'funny-sad' scene, which contains more pathos than Beckett will later allow himself, is couched in terms that remind us, rather heavy-handedly, that Belacqua is in an unremittingly secular situation, with no possibility of being granted the 'indulgence, absolution or remission' (6) that he has been optimistically hoping for. The human condition, we infer, is irremediable, and can only be palliated by disappearing into the world of sleep. Beckett models his description of Belacqua falling asleep on Joyce's Sinbad passage, but despite his invocation of St Julian of Norwich and the Russian clown Grock, a truly Joycean universality is beyond him:[1]

> he was crowned in gloom and had a wonderful night. He groped, as one that walks by moonshine in a wood, through the grateful night to the impertinent champaign of the morning. Sin is behovable but all shall be well and all shall be well and all manner of thing shall be well. *Inquit Grock* . . . (7)

In a sense, *Dream* will never get beyond this point, as the narrator seems to know only too well. His pretensions to shaping a story have come to grief (as they will again as the 'dream' continues) in the sheer complexity of the human character. Beckett discusses these matters openly and (as later in *Murphy*) is quite prepared to admit that some of his 'flat' characters are as fully comprehensible as any other author's. The problem for Beckett is that he is interested in characters so obscure as to be effectively nobody, or characters like Belacqua who, in their best moments, seek to be nobody. Even a fictional work as unconventional and eccentric as this can only reduce and simplify such figures. To illustrate this point Beckett hypothesizes a figure he calls Nemo, who materializes at various points in *Dream* without exerting any meaningful influence on the work as a whole, and thereby exemplifies the Beckettian philosophy he has been designed to convey. Beckett has recourse here to a musical analogy so important that we shall have to return to it later — the claim that Nemo is 'a regrettable simultaneity of notes' (8) — thereby consolidating the feeling generated throughout this disquisition that language is an utterly inadequate medium anyway.

What is remarkable about *Dream* is that, despite the flurry of information and activity that make the surface of the prose so turbulent, most of the basic elements of Beckett's later aesthetic nevertheless emerge. The 'real presence' for instance is unequivocally damned as 'a pest because it did not give the imagination a break' (9); this is obviously what lies behind Mr Kelly's anguished plea, so poignantly expressed in *Murphy*, to be spared the beastly particulars of Celia's story (*M*, 13; cf. *PTD*, 74).

Beckett does not seek, in *Dream*, to dramatize ideas by mediating them through character, since character has already been identified as an impossibly complicated matter. Beckett merely presents his own ideas in all their unvarnished and unpremeditated awfulness. Accordingly we learn (to our inestimable advantage when faced with such puzzling phenomena as the disappearing Watt of part four of *Watt*) that it is 'the object that becomes invisible before your eyes . . .[which] is the brightest and best!' (9-10). Since, by this time, this is very much what Belacqua has become, we must be content that Belacqua, at least, has been able to achieve some kind of satisfaction from the enterprise in which he has been more or less innocently involved by Beckett.

Beckett's ideas in *Dream* are too manifold to be coherently expressed: having rigorously eschewed the temptation to dwell on the feelings of Belacqua whizzing by train across Europe to join his loved one, Beckett is seduced into a digression on the pointlessness of background information that we have already registered as a natural corollary to his remarks on character, and a necessary inference from the brief section one. However Beckett does not pay much attention to his own criticisms. A somewhat lack-lustre satire on German culture and a passage describing the Smeraldina's physical grossness (both of which should by rights have come under the stigma of background information) are only put into focus (without ever taking on much point) by the passage describing Belacqua's awe at the radiance of his loved one's face. It is a measure of Beckett's prose style at this time that he can oscillate between these extremes of attraction and repulsion in one paragraph, but it is also of course, part of his purpose to bring the two into opposition. It is a way of surreptitiously dramatizing what he is all the time seeking to avoid: his theme. The thought of the body, for instance, moves him to emotional out-pourings of revulsion; but as his scrutiny focusses on her head the prose becomes brutally clear, lucid, chaste. 'The face was authentic Madonna' is how Beckett puts it, doubtless because it enables him to get in as much of the Florentine Renaissance[2] as an encounter in Vienna will allow.

It is precisely this 'transcendental' side to his personality that explains Beckett's interest in astronomy (inherited with such mixed results by Murphy). Indeed, Beckett feels that the night sky is superior even to music as an image of the essence of existence, because it is more beautiful, emptier of content (or what conventional narrative would regard as content) and, for all we know, infinite. Beckett sees the sky as an image of the relationship between the art object and the creative mind, and it is no wonder that he was so sensitive to Kant's emotional response to the stars in his *Critique of Aesthetic Judgment*. The art surface, in Beckett's opinion, has an 'astral incoherence' but there is behind it, as behind the walls of Belacqua's room, a rat that fidgets, which can only be the mind seeking an escape into being, 'flowering up and up through darkness to an apex' (14-15). The reference at this point is to Dionysus the Areopagite and gives the discussion a more conventionally mystical colouring than Beckett is perhaps comfortable with. In *Dream*, Beckett is forced to realize that he is a '*mystique raté*', a 'dud mystic' in fact (166). The writing at this point, despite its scientific metaphors, is imprecise in a way Beckett would shudder at now, so that what are really very remarkable ideas suffer seriously from the manner of their trans-mission: 'The tense passional intelligence, when arithmetic abates, tunnels, skymole, surely and blindly . . . through the interstellar coalsacks of its firmament in genesis, it twists through the stars of its creation in a network of loci that shall never be co-ordinate' (14).

It might be said, as Beckett said of those who did not admire Denis Devlin's poetry, that 'To cavil at [this] . . . as over-imaged . . . is to cavil at the probity with which the creative mind has carried itself out'.[3] But Beckett is not always creative in *Dream*, and since he has no real programme (unlike Murphy, or Murphy's narrator) to which his narratorial endeavour might usefully be applied, the plea of probity never enters our minds.

Whilst Beckett manages to give the surface of *Dream* the 'astral incoherence' that he thinks of as necessary to the art work, he cannot seemingly prevent his character Belacqua from involvement in an incoherence that is all too familiarly terrestrial: sexuality. Having cast himself somewhat unwillingly in the role of helpless sacrificial victim, Belacqua finds himself plunged 'in a gehenna of sweats and fiascos and tears and an absence of all douceness' (16) from which nothing, seemingly, can extricate him. Try as he may to invest the Smeraldina with a literary veneer, she insists on involving him in erotic activity. In one of the most explicit passages of this kind in the whole of his *oeuvre*, Beckett shows how Belacqua is studiously seeking to dissociate himself from a sexual commitment that can only increase his feeling of rage and ruin his perilous equilibrium:

> So he would always have her be, rapt, like the spirit of a troubadour, casting no shade, herself shade. Instead of which of course it was only a question of seconds before she would surge up at him, blithe and buxom and young and lusty . . . It is a poor anger that rises when the stillness is broken . . . the poor anger of the world that life cannot be still, that live things cannot be active quietly . . . (20-21)[4]

Even the most obvious defence against sexual activity, conversation, has the unfortunate side-effect of returning one to the world that sexual ecstasy has (at least temporarily) carried one away from. At the same time, however, it is conversation that allows one to exhibit one's intellectual brilliance. Although the dialogues in *Dream* are much less crisp and pointed than those in *Murphy* and much more diffuse than the exchanges in the better stories of *More Pricks than Kicks*, at least Belacqua can keep the Smeraldina at bay by talking to her. This is almost impossible with the Syra-Cusa, the second of these 'fair to middling women' (as the title ungallantly has it), because she is determinedly unintellectual: she thinks so little of Belacqua's gift to her of an edition of Dante that she leaves it behind in a café. Beckett performs a character assassination on the Syra-Cusa worthy of Wyndham Lewis, from which point she ceases to play a significant part in this narrative (though she is resuscitated for an appearance in *More Pricks*):

> She was never even lassata, let alone satiata; very uterine; Lucrezia, Clytemnestra, Semiramide, a saturation of unappeasable countesses . . . Her eyes were wanton, they rolled and stravagued, laskivious and lickerish, the brokers of her zeal, basilisk eyes . . . and the body like a coiled spring, and a springe, too, to catch woodcocks. And hollow. Nothing behind it . . . She was always on the job, the job of being jewelly. (44)

With the third 'fair to middling' woman by contrast, conversation is unavoidable, and even desirable. The Alba is of Irish extraction, and a figure of some note in the Dublin society of her day, not least because she is an educated lady (who knows at least the spines of several books), but more particularly because she is not above gratifying her admirers to the best of her ability, provided they recognize themselves as social and/or intellectual inferiors. She is the most conventionally beautiful of the three, partly thanks to nature and partly by dint of laborious preparation before parties, and less complicatedly rapacious than the Smeraldina or the Syra-Cusa, which is no doubt what induces Belacqua to accompany her home (as in 'A Wet Night') when the party at the Frica's begins to show signs of disarray. The Alba is the first woman in the novel with a sufficiently complex psychology for Beckett to interest himself in her mind rather than, as in the previous two cases, to confine himself largely to the external features of the female physiology. This is an important area of *Dream* because it helps to explain how Beckett in later writings has been able to create moving studies of the female personality. (Celia, in *Murphy*, was only three years away.) In one passage in particular, which occurs at the end of one of the Polar Bear's intellectual harangues, we are offered the chance to see how the Alba can retire, Belacqua-fashion, into her mind, in search of the spring that will keep her sufficiently in touch with the tumult of the outer world to destroy it and thereby construct an area that she can inhabit freely and peacefully without interruption: 'she had been spent and almost, it seemed to her and to many that knew her, extinguished by her days . . . She had been spent in day winning. Poor in days she was light and full of light. Rich in days she was heavy and full of darkness. Living was a growing heavy and dark and rich in days. Death was black wealth of days' (147). The oppositions are more schematic than in later Beckett, but they are nevertheless a genuine attempt, one of the most impressive before *Murphy*, to articulate the relationship between ordinary quotidian reality and the higher realities of rich darkness and transfigured light. The Alba, like Murphy after her, 'reviled the need, the unsubduable tradition of living up to dying, that forced her to score and raid thus the music of days' and seeks — in this respect (as her name, which means 'dawn' suggests) strikingly unlike Murphy, who is more interested in darkness — 'to abide, light and full of light, caught in the fulness of this total music of days' (148). The situations of the Alba and Murphy are not, however, finally unlike each other, for the Alba daydreams of a time when she can be 'alone, unlonely; unconcerned, moored in the seethe of an element in which she had no movement' (148), which is a state very similar to that of Murphy's third zone, only intermittently achieved, in which 'he did not move, he was a point in the ceaseless unconditioned generation and passing away of line' (*M* 79). It is symptomatic that Beckett leaves this description of the Alba's aims without subjecting it to the withering mockery so often found elsewhere in *Dream*, and it is an index of how important these aims are to Beckett that the pompously intellectual Polar Bear begins to fidget in the face of something he cannot contain within his hidebound traditional categories. Later, in a typically oblique and rather more back-handed compliment to the Alba, Beckett goes so far as to suggest that in some ways she is a good deal more mature and commendable than the restless Belacqua: 'she does not really care about moving . . . she puts not her trust in changes of scenery, she is too inward by a long chalk, she inclines towards an absolute moral geography, her soul is her only *poste restante*. Whereas he does care, he prays fervently to be set free in a general way, he is such a very juvenile man. But he will get over all that' (157). If there is a lingering criticism of the Alba here, and a lingering admiration for Belacqua's quest for freedom, this is because Beckett throughout *Dream* is criticizing himself, before he has actually allowed himself to create anything. In *Murphy* he is prepared to confine his narrator to occasional ironic shafts that do not ultimately threaten the developing drama of the narrative, and Celia's inwardness and reluctance to move (which she inherits from the Alba as much as Murphy) are impressive in direct proportion to how little she understands her needs and how unselfconscious her actions are. The Alba is only too conscious that if she allows herself to be amorously involved, she cannot but make it 'a mess and tangle' (146). But involvement is, strictly speaking, impossible, since Beckett (following Proust) sees the relationship between man and woman as one which illustrates the 'profound antagonism latent in the neutral space that between beings victims of real needs is as irreducible as the zone of evaporation between damp and incandescence' (170-171).

Antagonism is perhaps the wrong word for Belacqua, since he remains largely passive in the area of erotic activity, and therefore forces the woman to make most of the running. Beckett suggests indeed — in a passage that no doubt explains why the young Beckett was so attractive to women — that it is precisely Belacqua's inactivity that makes him so desirable and enigmatic a figure. This enables Beckett to criticize both the predatory females that mill around Belacqua and also Belacqua himself, who is longing for a Limbo 'purged of desire' (38) but always succumbing, insufficiently passive, in each of his three relationships, for one reason or another. The Smeraldina 'rapes' him one afternoon and their relationship 'goes kaputt' (15). His relationship with the Syra-Cusa remains platonic but involves him in some unpleasantly active avoidance of involvement. The hours Belacqua spends alone with the Alba have a veil drawn over them. But the shambling figure who emerges in the rain of the small hours at the end of *Dream* is much more likely to have been overcome by Bacchus than by Eros — the blue-stocking Alba has a fondness for bottled beer.

It is clear even from the unfinished *Dream* that Beckett did not intend to leave his anatomy of womankind at this point, and in *More Pricks than Kicks* Belacqua, before inexplicably ending up as the late husband of the Smeraldina, conducts *amours* at various times with such resolutely Irish colleens as Ruby Tough and Lucy (whom he marries) and Thelma bboggs (whom he also marries). However, *Dream* would obviously have become even more unmanageable if Beckett had gone on, Chaucer-fashion,[5] to link tale to tale with Belacqua as the only common denominator. Beckett clearly entertained the idea of a neater, more formal arrangement, as we see from his dismissal of the Syra-Cusa, immediately prior to the thumb-nail sketch of her already quoted:

> Why we want to drag in the Syra-Cusa at this juncture it passes our persimmon to say. She belongs to another story, a short one, a far far better one . . . she remains, whatever way we choose to envisage her, hors d'oeuvre. We could chain her up with the Smeraldina-Rima and the little Alba, our capital divas, and make it look like a sonata, with recurrence of themes, key signatures, plagal finale and all. From the extreme Smeraldina and the mean Syra you could work out the Alba for yourselves, you could control our treatment of the little Alba. (43)

It is abundantly clear that Beckett is striving for what he would later call 'a new form'[6] which does not allow straightforward and simple-minded inferences on the part of the reader. But the very fact that he entertains conventional structures as a possibility indicates his uncertainty at this time. The admission, if only in passing, that a short story might be a better mode for the essentially plotless writing Beckett is pursuing, is of great interest in view of the subsequent *More Pricks than Kicks*.

As any extensive quotation immediately reveals, stylistically *Dream* is too various to be wholly satisfying. Beckett is obviously using *Dream* as a kind of practice-pad on which to try out certain styles, and even, perhaps, as a way of getting out of his system all the other styles of other writers he has been attracted by. It is not enough, however, to say, as critics generally do, that the book is Joycean in style, and leave it at that. Even if the evidence were not more complex than this description suggests, we might object that Joyce wrote in several distinctively different styles throughout his career, and that no one style of his can be given such a simple label. Joyce is certainly the writer most in Beckett's mind, as, given the deep respect and affection Beckett had for Joyce, is almost unavoidable. But Beckett is himself aware of how many different Joyce styles there are, and he makes no attempt to emulate or imitate all of them. In the paragraph which concludes the party sequence (and later 'A Wet Night') and which pokes gentle fun at the conclusion to Joyce's 'The Dead'[7] we have, in fact, an example of Beckett consciously standing aside from Joyce and defining for himself what his own area will be. The resolutely untranscendental and monotonous rain of Beckett is a long way from the chill and mysterious yet strangely tranquil snow of Joyce. It is, in fact, the Joyce of *Dubliners* that matters most to Beckett in *Dream*, for while Beckett's 'meanness' is not always as 'scrupulous' as Joyce's, and whilst the desire to write 'a chapter in the moral history of my race' is alien to Beckett's temperament, the satire on Dublin's literary pretensions stems from an impulse similar to that which led Joyce to expose the tawdriness of Irish culture in a story like 'A Mother', and the wearily detailed descriptions of parts of Dublin remind one of the foot-loose and pointless peregrinations of the people Joyce saw as in the grip of a kind of paralysis. Although much of the story is set on the Continent, it is Dublin — from tram-conductor to witty Jesuit priest — that dominates *Dream*. And yet one never feels that Dublin is of quite such consuming interest to Beckett as it so obviously was for Joyce, and consequently the characterizations of particular locales are less resonant and powerful.

Beckett obviously regarded the later Joycean styles of *Portrait*, *Ulysses* and *Finnegans Wake* as so uniquely adapted to Joyce's own special aims that it would be pointless to imitate them, however much (as 'Dante . . . Bruno . Vico . . Joyce' shows) he admired them. Beckett was, however, clearly intrigued by the sheer bravado of some of Joyce's most extreme experiments, and at two different junctures in *Dream* (the moment of arrival in Vienna, and the occasion of a slight sexual indisposition of Belacqua's — the first published as 'Sedendo et Quiescendo', the second as 'Text'[8]) — he tries his hand at a kind of post-*Ulysses* pastiche, partly perhaps to convince himself finally that this kind of thing is not for him, and partly just to let off steam, and to demonstrate his imitative powers. These passages are in some ways more obscure, because less disciplined, than even the knottiest passages of late Joyce, and there is no organizing principle which will make all things grist to the mill in the way Joyce almost miraculously can. It is no surprise that Beckett soon wearies of his literary coat-trailing, and it is unfortunate that the publication of 'Sedendo et Quiescendo' has suggested that the whole work is written in the same bizarre manner.

For whilst much of the writing in *Dream* is equally bizarre, it is strikingly Beckettian in its manner. Beckett's main stylistic interest is in exploring the possibilities of the sentence — not only the 'formal declarative sentence' much prized by Kenner,[9] and its near relative, the lapidary apophthegm or epigram (refined by the time of *Murphy* into a vehicle of great comic power) — but also the sentence that seems not to know how to come to an end, destroying the reader's expectations and impinging more deeply on his nervous system, so that the point Beckett is seeking to make can emerge from the rhetoric and surface detail.[10] It is not therefore a prose that can be hurried; it is, like Wyndham Lewis's, not a prose that flows. There is a certain stiffness about it (found again, slightly modified, in *Murphy* and *Watt*) that derives from Beckett's uncertainty about what he is really trying to do, and a certain *hauteur* and mandarin aloofness that is ultimately self-congratulatory and unsatisfying. The irony is that Beckett was well aware, as the *Proust* book indicated, that 'style is more a question of vision than technique' (*PTD*, 87-88) and yet in *Dream* he obviously felt forced to exploit technique precisely because his vision was so dramatically occluded. Even *Murphy*, for all its wonderful qualities, cannot always claim to have a style perfectly fitted to its contents (the lyricism can be cloying, and the documentary realism can be a little flat), though it is, obviously, overall a distinct improvement. Looking further ahead, whatever else may be wrong with *Watt*, we certainly cannot complain that it is seriously vitiated by its style.

Dream must have alerted Beckett to the fact (not fully realized in his earliest stories[11]) that he would never be able to write a prose which observed traditional rules of decorum, and that even if he were to become sufficiently confident to propose his own rules of decorum to supersede them, he would soon be disobeying them also. It is a feature of *Dream*, as of its successor *More Pricks than Kicks*, that Beckett is greatly attached to the literary, philosophical or cultural reference (used primarily to offset and aggrandize the basically tawdry goings-on he is concentrating on), and also deeply attached to the phrase that explores (or explodes) the possibilities of metaphor. This last is so pervasive in *Dream* that it threatens at times to throttle altogether the purely informational aspect of the narrative. In *Murphy* the touch is lighter, and in *Watt* Beckett has the habit under strict control, but metaphor remains a problem for him occasionally even in the more desiccated and more severely functional later texts.

It is in this respect, indeed, that *Dream* is especially confused, making it something of an irony that Beckett should characterize the true poet's mind as 'clear' (78). The descriptions of the effect women have on Belacqua, and the descriptions of the state of absence Belacqua seeks to permanently inhabit, are written in an excited and over-imaged style not far removed from the excrescences of Beckett's first published story 'Assumption'. Beckett alludes to this habit late on in the work, without convincing us (or indeed himself) that he is at all interested in the public response to literature: 'The multiplication of figure to the detriment of style is forced upon us by our most earnest desire to give satisfaction to all customers' (164). Nevertheless this 'multiplication of figure' in *Dream* is especially important, since it reveals for the first time how Beckett is using images to structure a long prose work. They are, interestingly enough, the kind of image patterns that will later be very distinctive characterizing features of his writing. [12]

The main image cluster he employs is the one that is perhaps at the base of all Beckett's thinking: the opposition between, and interaction of, light and darkness. In later works Beckett is often content to explore the relationship without necessarily postulating an 'objective correlative' that embodies an aspect of one or the other, but, in *Dream*, Beckett is much more conventionally engaged in seeking out such correlatives in order that he may hang his philosophizings upon them, and it is clear, from the moment we find him preferring the face of the Smeraldina (with its madonna-like 'radiance') to her rather less entrancing physique, that there will be no shortage of metaphorical attributions of this kind. Belacqua is not attracted by the 'glare of her flesh' because it threatens to 'dazzle' him (38), and involves him in the blinding light of being revealed for what he is. Wanting only to gaze into her eyes (a desire which the Smeraldina, typically, cannot understand), Belacqua justifies himself by telling her, 'I'm a classicist . . . didn't you know?', but the Smeraldina remains unimpressed and cannot offer him the solace he requires. It is a mark of how much more attractive the Alba is that Belacqua has no need to explain to her the satisfactions she offers; and the narrator, indeed, records them with something like reverence:

> It was the magic hour . . . when Night has its nasty difficult birth all over the sheets of dusk, and the dark eyes of the beautiful darken also. This

was the case now with the Alba, furled in her coils upon the settee, the small broad pale face spotted in a little light escaped from the throttled west. Her great eyes went as black as sloes . . . Pupil and white swamped in the dark iris gone black as night (135).

The Alba's power over Belacqua is of the kind that can almost turn the twilight of a predominantly crepuscular novel into the 'white night' of Dostoevsky's Petersburg: 'Then lo! she is at the window, she is taking stock of her cage. Now under the threat of night the evening is albescent, its hues have blanched, it is dim white and palpable, it pillows and mutes her head' (155). Belacqua is so spellbound by this that he can only murmur in admiration at the way the Alba has become the 'Spirit of the Moon'. But his experience with the Smeraldina has taught him that 'the neighbour is not a moon, slow wax and wane of phases, changeless in a tranquillity of changes' (21) and Beckett guides Belacqua therefore away from the moon of Dante and the Romantics and towards the more unequivocal pleasures of darkness.

Perhaps the most important exploration of the relationship between light and darkness occurs when Belacqua (an inveterate star-gazer in the Murphy manner) is impressed by the 'abstract density' of the night firmament as an image of the creative mind. 'It is the passional movements of the mind charted in light and darkness', Beckett writes; 'the inviolable criterion of poetry and music, the non-principle of their punctuation, is figured in the demented perforation of the night colander' (14). This is a much fuller statement of the aesthetic of incommunicability that Beckett had hinted at in his monograph *Proust* and much more complex (though less memorable) than the formulation in *Three Dialogues with Georges Duthuit*. The immersive, centripetal, contractive activity of the artist in *Proust* is now seen, more graphically, as 'the mind suddenly entombed, then active in an anger and a rhapsody of energy, in a scurrying and plunging towards exitus . . . invisible rat, fidgeting behind the astral incoherence of the art surface' (14). The condition of mind of which Beckett is speaking is intended to be eminently tangible, and as substantial as the images of 'cup', 'funnel' and 'tunnel' can make it. That Beckett's imagery can work wonderfully well even at this early stage is demonstrated by a passage describing how Belacqua is miraculously offered the chance to live in a meaningful way at last:

He lay lapped in a beatitude of indolence, that was smoother than oil and softer than a pumpkin . . . He moved with the shades of the dead and the

> dead-born and the unborn and the never-to-be-born, in a Limbo purged
> of desire. They moved gravely, men and women and children, neither
> sad nor joyful. They were dark, and they gave a dawn light to the darker
> place where they moved. They were a silent rabble, a press of much that
> was and was not and was to be and was never to be, a pulsing and
> shifting as of a heart beating in sand, and they cast a dark light. (38-39)

This 'dark light' derives not from Milton's 'darkness visible' but from
Corneille's *'obscure clarté'* in *Le Cid* (which Beckett studied as an
undergraduate). But the idea is essentially his own, for the light is
accompanied (as in the residua of the 1960s) by an extraordinary pulse
'as of a heart beating in sand', which directly prefigures the strange
noises later Beckett narrators hear in their heads, and which later
Beckett plays seek to somehow appease, defeat, enshrine, or merely
endure. The concept is so appealing to Beckett that it completely
disarms his very strong ironic instinct. 'If that is what is meant by
going back into one's heart,' writes Beckett, 'could anything be better,
in this world or the next?' (39).

What Beckett has described here, for the first time, is the moment
when, with 'the mind its own asylum at last' (compare Murphy), 'live
cerebration' — 'real thought and real living, living thought' — can
reprieve the mind from its exposure to 'the glare of understanding'
(39). It is a priceless moment, and thoroughly relished by Beckett, and
much more impressive than the earlier attempt to define the 'real
poise . . . on the crown of the passional relation' because Belacqua is
not, as there, merely 'prattling on' (24). Unfortunately this moment is
extremely precarious, short-lived and, once lost, difficult (if not
impossible) to regain. *Dream* is quite explicit that, far from living
normally like this, the common lot of man (even of the apparently
unflappable Nemo) is to be forced to confront an immensely
menacing and aggressive universe: 'Behind him, spouting and
spouting from the grey sea, the battalions of night, devouring the sky,
soaking up the tattered sky like an ink of pestilence. The city would be
hooded, dusk would be harried from the city' (25). However
narcissistic Belacqua becomes, and however much he cultivates
indifference, the world is always on the point of engulfing him and
drowning his individuality. Drowning is, in fact, the image that
dominates the 'Assumption'-like paragraph from *Dream* which was
most readers' introduction to *Dream* in John Fletcher's *The Novels of
Samuel Beckett*. Beckett's later attitude to the sea (e.g. in 'The End',
Molloy, Embers) is much more ambigous, but, in his early writing, it

represented a threat to these moments of mental illumination. Not even Beckett's inevitable allusions to Lautréamont, Victor Hugo and Rimbaud (122) can make it seem other than an apocalyptic horror for Belacqua.

In *Murphy* and later works, Beckett consolidates the imagery of light and darkness with an elaborate image-pattern based on the vocabulary and experience of music; and *Dream* was also an important trial-run in this area. Beckett is not seeking to bring literature and music closer together; in a sense he sees them as essentially at war with one another. Since this is so flatly in contradiction to the received idea of the Symbolist aesthetic (which Beckett is still occasionally seen as representing), it is worth stressing that for Beckett, as he made clear in *Proust*, music is a form that is not attended with the same problems of expression as literature has, and hence the one cannot be assimilated to the other. As we have seen, when Beckett introduces the Syra-Cusa figure, he scorns the introduction of musical analogies in a way that ought perhaps to put us on our guard about extending Molloy's phrase 'the long sonata of the dead' into a description of the trilogy as a whole. It is clear from the unpublished story 'Echo's Bones' (c. 1934) that Beckett regards the mind as being the repository and initiator of all the most soothing blandishments, 'a Limbo of the most musical processes'. But in writing novels, as he discovers in *Dream*, he is faced with the distressing fact that language interferes with these sonorous harmonies:

> observe what happens in [the] event . . . of our being unable to keep those boys and girls up to their notes . . . We call the whole performance off . . . it tails off in a horrid manner . . . The music comes to pieces. The notes fly about all over the place, a cyclone of electrons. And then all we can do, if we are not too old and tired by that time to be interested in making the best of a bad job, is to deploy a curtain of silence as rapidly as possible. (100)

In practice, this 'curtain of silence' involves making what Beckett calls 'these territorials' jump to a less sublime melody. But this, as Beckett reflects sadly a few pages later, involves the artist in an unavoidable secession from the ideal. Beckett embeds this insight in a discussion of how his 'real' characters are essentially beyond his control:

> They flower out and around into every kind of illicit ultra and infra and supra. Which is bad, because as long as they do that they can never meet . . . Belacqua drifts about, it is true, doing his best to thicken the tune, but harmonic composition properly speaking, music in depth on

the considerable scale is, and this is a terrible thing to have to say, ausgeschlossen. (104)

If we think of the way Murphy and Celia 'meet' and the very considerable harmonies that *Murphy* as a novel establishes, it is clear that we would do better to think of *Murphy* not as a tentative and only partially achieved essay in what the later novels approach more experimentally, but rather as the conventional success that Beckett needed to give him the substance against which his unique reductive procedures could operate. It is one of the prime virtues of *Dream* that in passages like the one quoted above, it makes us see *Murphy* as not so much the beginning of a career as the end of one part of it.

There is much in *Dream* that we can safely ignore, either because Beckett later deals with it more profoundly, or because he is already growing out of it almost at the moment of writing. In the first category we might place the description of Alba watching Belacqua disappear into the gloom (156), which is a Romantic type-situation Beckett only frees himself from in chapter eight of *Murphy*, with the image of *Murphy* multiplied in the children's masquerade which is all Celia is left with at their final parting. Or we might point to the way the death of a minor character (the figure Nemo who is Belacqua's *alter ego*, and a devout Narcissist) reflects on the pointlessness of the major character (Belacqua not being purposeful enough to be a devout anything), a technique prefiguring the contrast between the suicide of the old butler in *Murphy* and Murphy's accidental demise. At one point in *Dream*, in the midst of an Eliotic discussion of bangs and whimpers, Beckett entertains the idea that a 'bang' would be an excellent way of finishing off Belacqua, but reserves this fate for Murphy three years later.

In the category of tricks that Beckett is already growing out of, we find the interpolation of conversations and events long past or somewhere in the future, verbal exchanges that seem to suffer a kind of elephantiasis under our gaze and get further and further from having any real point, and an excessive reliance on learned analogy to get out of any hole. There is considerable pleasure to be derived from the story of Belacqua and his boots (as funny as any of the later accounts of Beckett heroes' difficulties with their necessary accoutrements), and also from the scene between the Polar Bear and the Jesuit priest which reappears in 'A Wet Night' in *More Pricks than Kicks* (*MPTK*, 62-63), and which provided Beckett with the necessary practice in aggressive comic dialogue that bore such fruit in the Neary and Wylie exchanges in *Murphy*. But the exchanges between Jean du Chas and the Polar Bear on the subject of the latter's pullet (quoted by Lawrence Harvey[13]) and between Belacqua and the Alba regarding the Frica's forthcoming party can only be considered as early (and largely unsuccessful) attempts at conveying the complexity of the relationship between man and woman and man and man which *Murphy* handles so much more sensitively.

There can be no final judgment on *Dream* because it is, in the end, only a large, unfinished torso. Beckett obviously felt its successful features could survive transplantation into the stories of *More Pricks than Kicks*. But some of the less successful features are also, of course, incorporated wholesale, so that *More Pricks* is, even at its best moments, a deeply divided work. In some ways *Dream* is a more attractive text, for all its immaturity: it lacks the professional competence of *More Pricks than Kicks*, but it shows more signs of the genius that is soon to emerge. It is, for all its defects, a remarkably courageous work for Beckett to have written, quite unlike anything being written at that time, and more ambitious than most things that have been written since. If in the end we cannot resist the temptation to apply the vernacular of the title to the contents as a whole, we must remember that it was necessary for Beckett to write a 'fair to middling' prose work in order that he should be able to write the so much more than 'middling' *Murphy*.

Notes

1. Cf. *Ulysses*, London, The Bodley Head, 1960, p. 871. The quotation from St. Julian pre-dates Eliot's more celebrated use of it. Grock is the presiding genius of *Dream*.
2. Beckett visited Florence in 1927.
3. 'Denis Devlin', *transition*, no. 27, April-May, 1938, p. 293.
4. Beckett later (*Three Novels*, p. 127) associates anger with Flaubert. Belacqua, however, 'shrank always from the *mot juste*' (166).
5. As John Fletcher pointed out (*The Novels of Samuel Beckett*, London, Chatto and Windus, 1964, p. 16), the title is a mixture of Chaucer (lines from whose *Legend of Good Women* form the epigraph) and Tennyson.
6. In the interview with Tom Driver first published in *Columbia University Forum*, IV, Summer 1961, pp. 21-25; quoted from L. Graver and R. Federman, eds., *Samuel Beckett: the Critical Heritage*, London, Henley and Boston, Routledge and Kegan Paul, 1979, p. 219.

7. As first pointed out by R. Cohn, *Samuel Beckett: The Comic Gamut*, New Brunswick, New Jersey, Rutgers University Press, 1962, pp. 33-34; *More Pricks than Kicks*, p. 87.

8. 'Sedendo' is in *transition*, no. 21, March, 1932, pp. 13-20; 'Text' in *New Review*, no. 2, April, 1932, p. 57, but most accessible in Cohn, *The Comic Gamut*, p. 308.

9. Hugh Kenner, *Samuel Beckett. A Critical Study*, new edition, Berkeley and Los Angeles, University of California Press, 1961, p. 91.

10. Proust is not necessarily a strong influence here; for the relationship between the two writers see my 'Beckett's *Proust*' in *Journal of Beckett Studies*, no. 1, Winter 1976.

11. Particularly perhaps in 'A Case in a Thousand', but also in 'Assumption'. It may well be that 'Echo's Bones' (c. 1934) made him realize that the short story was not his *métier*. Only after the war did he return to the genre.

12. We might, indeed, see them as the 'bits of twine' that are holding together this 'ramshackle, tumbledown . . . bone-shaker' of a book (*Dream*, p. 124).

13. L. Harvey, *Samuel Beckett, Poet and Critic*, Princeton, New Jersey, Princeton University Press, 1970, pp. 333-36. Jean du Chas is the central figure in Beckett's spoof lecture 'Le Concentrisme' (R.U.L. MS 1396/4/15); compare Walter Draffin, in *More Pricks than Kicks*, as the author of an unfinished work titled *Dream of Fair to Middling Women* (*More Pricks than Kicks*, p. 153).

Eleuthéria

Eleuthéria was written in French from January to March 1947 (almost two years before *En attendant Godot*) and has never been published, performed or translated into English. It is one of the 'trunk manu-scripts' that Beckett once said almost outnumber the published works.[1] However, it differs from other unpublished dramatic writing — at least from that about which anything is so far known — in being complete, and in having been released in 1947-49 for circulation among Paris theatre producers, first by Jacoba van Velde, who, as Toni Clerkx, acted for a time as Beckett's agent in France, and then by Suzanne Dumesnil, now his wife.[2] The play was even announced as forthcoming by Les Editions de Minuit before being withdrawn by its author. His adamant opposition to its publication continues right up to the present day.

Why, we may ask, is Beckett so determined that *Eleuthéria* should neither be published nor produced, when with so many other *inédits* he has eventually relented? Clearly the main reason is that he is only too aware that it is severely flawed as a piece of dramatic writing, in ways that will become apparent as we proceed. It is also likely, however, that he felt that autobiographical tensions and remi-niscences were insufficiently distanced in the play for him to feel comfortable to see it appear in print. Even without the intimate revelations of Deirdre Bair's recent biography concerning the turbulence of Beckett's own relationship with his mother, one could already sense something of the author's personal involvement in the irritations that were provoked by Madame Krap's busy efforts to prise her ironically named son, Victor, from his room and involve him, by fair means or foul, in the 'normal' activities of gainful employment, love, marriage, doing and being. The following extract from the dialogue between Victor's mother and father, among many others, shows signs of this annoyance:

> MR K.   You played the anxious mother.
> MME K.   I *am* terribly anxious.
> MR K.   First pleading, then tearful. (*Silence*.) For the hundred and fiftieth time. (*Silence*.) You begged, you shouted, you wept.

(copy of typescript, R.U.L., p. 42, see note 1; my translation throughout)

Similarly, Victor's dream of his father on the diving-board telling his son to plunge in after him, irrespective of the boy's fear of drowning, is of little dramatic relevance. Unlike the related episode in *Embers*, which is more closely integrated into the thematic structure of the play, the only justification for this occurring in *Eleuthéria* is that Beckett wished to exorcize a disturbing personal reminiscence.[3]

Victor, the 'anti-hero' of *Eleuthéria*, frequents Beckett's own immediate neighbourhood in Paris, living characteristically for a martyr to existence, in the Impasse de l'Enfant Jésus (a cul-de-sac leading off the rue Vaugirard not far from Beckett's old flat in the rue des Favorites), and wandering, when he needs food, as far afield as the 'dustbins of Passy' to the rue Spontini.[4] Beckett allowed allusions to the Vaucluse and to Monsieur Bonelly's wine (drunk during the war in Roussillon by himself, Suzanne and their friends) to stand, however, in the French *Godot*, and no doubt the irony of the Parisian street names in *Eleuthéria* still gives him a modicum of pleasure. However, he must certainly have felt uneasy about the way in which central issues, such as whether or not life is worth living and the validity or otherwise of suicide or euthanasia, emerge as deeply felt personal questions. In his more mature plays, Beckett's characters dogmatize less and lay his heart on their sleeve with less evident signs of surgery than most of the characters in *Eleuthéria* do.

Another likely reason for Beckett's unwillingness to publish *Eleuthéria* is that, increasingly, the later works have overtaken it and made it appear uncharacteristically clumsy and over-explicit, of interest primarily as a source-book or as a point of comparison. There is no doubt that it anticipates many features of the later plays. The name, Victor Krap, has the same excremental associations as that of Beckett's later protagonist in *Krapp's Last Tape* and Monsieur Henri

Krap, the father of Victor, is found in the company of the equally unpleasantly named Madame Meck (mec = pimp), Madame Piouk (puke), and Olga Skunk; a Roumanian patient of Dr. Piouk is also mentioned, named Verolesco, who believed that he was suffering from syphilis! Henri Krap is, indeed, as John Spurling suggests, a prototype of Beckett's later 'heroes', adding the dry wit of Mr. Rooney in *All that Fall* to Hamm's talent as a *poseur*.[5] The three women, Mesdames Krap, Meck, and Piouk, look forward to Flo, Vi and Ru in *Come and Go* in their repeated concern for each other's appearance and health; in addition, like the woman of the later short play, two of them, Violette and Marguerite, have flower-inspired Christian names. Olga Skunk possesses some of the characteristics of the stenographer in *Radio II* (*Pochade radiophonique*) and the role of Tchoutchi, the Chinese torturer, who threatens Victor with his pincers, is comparable to that of the silent Dick, who wields a noisy whip in the same radio play. The Glazier addresses his son, Michel, in a manner reminiscent of Vladimir talking to the messenger boy at the end of the two acts of *Waiting for Godot*, while managing to indulge in banter and by-play with the glass-cutter and the mastic that also anticipate Clov's antics in *Endgame* with his step-ladder and telescope. The man sitting alone on a bed in his room echoes the situation of the television play, *Eh Joe*. There is an especially close relationship between *Eleuthéria* and *Embers*, in which father and son are again linked and in which the subject of suicide or euthanasia is never far from the surface. Even the Auditor's gesture of 'helpless compassion' in *Not I* is prefigured when, leaving Victor's room, Jacques raises his hands and allows them to fall helplessly to his side.

But the most striking affinity is with *Endgame*, where the dialogue between Hamm and Clov has the same mixture of intimacy, cynicism and cruelty that is found in *Eleuthéria* in the relationships between Mr. Krap and his wife, the same decrepit and his servant, Jacques, and the Glazier and his son. Exchanges between Henri Krap and his wife vacillate sharply from one extreme to another. One moment he is threatening to kill her; the next, he is recalling, with some tenderness, her attempted abortion of their son:

MR K.   How often did you try to get rid of him?
MME K.   Three times.
MR K.   And it had no effect.
MME K.   Only sickness.
MR K.   Only sickness! (*Pause*.) Then you said — let's see — what was that beautiful sentence you used?

MME K.   What beautiful sentence?
MR K.   Yes, let's see now — *since he's there* — ?
MME K.   *Let's keep him, since he's there.*
MR K.   That's it! That's it! *Let's keep him, since he's there!* We were on
         the water . . . I stopped rowing. The water rocked us.
         (*Pause.*) It rocked him too. (44-5)

It is in highly ambivalent passages like this that an authentic dramatic
voice can already be detected.

Despite Beckett's continued opposition to the play's publication, it
would be wrong to imagine that *Eleuthéria* is entirely lacking in the
qualities that characterize *Waiting for Godot* and *Endgame*. The French
is fluent and idiomatic throughout, and shows a keen sensitivity to
tone and register. Whole sketches of the dialogue move along rapidly
and smoothly in short, crisp *répliques*, interspersed with a judicious
use of silence. The text is enlivened by word-play and wit, and, above
all perhaps, by surprise and conflict. Compared with *Waiting for Godot*
there is, of course, a much larger number of characters in *Eleuthéria*:
seventeen as compared with five. Yet the problem of retaining interest
in an essentially static drama remains similar in the two plays. A
comparison of the different ways in which Beckett sought to solve this
problem goes some way towards explaining why *Godot* was to be such
a resounding success and why *Eleuthéria* should have been withheld as
a defective work. But it also points to the importance of *Eleuthéria* both
as an experimental work in its own right and as a forerunner of the
later plays.

In *Waiting for Godot* Beckett drew on the theatrical tradition of the
vaudeville, which he had enjoyed in the films of Charlie Chaplin,
Laurel and Hardy, Buster Keaton, Ben Turpin and Harry Langdon.
Beckett was able to show that vaudeville, as well as being vital, could
also be extremely flexible. And the blend of serious concerns,
vaudeville speech-rhythms and visual 'gags' worked successfully for a
number of reasons. First of all, a tragi-comic ambivalence has always
been part of the clown's appearance and humour. He is, in other
words, already much closer to Beckett's view of humanity than are the
middle-class occupants of the salon in *Eleuthéria*. Secondly, as Martin
Esslin pointed out in a review of the Schiller-Theater *Godot*, the
vaudeville tradition anchored Beckett's figures firmly in a down-to-
earth, yet theatrical reality, while allowing them to be concerned with
wide-ranging, sometimes metaphysical considerations, as well as
representing humanity in a more universal way.[6] Pratfalls or verbal

banter could, therefore, be incorporated into a more allusive set of references, yet still retain their original, physical and comic impact.

It might seem at first as if Beckett was trying to do something similar in *Eleuthéria* with the traditions of boulevard comedy and melodrama. But the situation is, in reality, very different. In *Godot* he was not parodying the vaudeville; he was merely adapting it to serve his own purposes. In *Eleuthéria*, on the other hand, he falls rather awkwardly between two stools. For the nature of his theme, expressed through Victor's desire to escape from the world means that Beckett as author has too little authentic interest in the world of 'le boogie-woogie', as the Glazier calls it, for telling parody. At the same time he is forced, by his very choice of setting and characters, to create it in enough detail to attempt at least to hold our interest by peopling it with just the sort of creatures that Victor would be reluctant to join. In the first act, therefore, Beckett tends to rely more on parodying the mechanics of bourgeois comedy than on parodying the characters themselves, whom he sketches in with only the thinnest of caricatural lines. Paradoxically perhaps, the play only begins to come alive with the arrival of the world-weary, indeed almost moribund Henri Krap, who introduces an authentic note of complexity of thought and unpredictability of behaviour. Previous to this the play has been concerned with superficially amusing, but soon tedious devices: frequent accelerated comings and goings of the servants, Jacques and Marie; much stage-business with a visiting-card, tray, and drinks (port and tea); numerous exaggerated greetings and trivial pleasantries; and a social chit-chat which is undercut by repeated references to suffering and is animated by frankness and egocentricity carried to the point of rudeness. It is interesting to observe how much more amusing such exaggerated greetings and embraces or irritated, impolite remarks can be when they are placed in the context of the clown tradition to which *Godot*'s 'tramps' belong. In *La Cantatrice Chauve*, with a similar setting and in a similar context of parody, Eugène Ionesco carried such devices much further towards frenzy and eventual collapse. But Ionesco has a recognizable anti-logical stance that makes the knowledge that almost anything might happen in the English salon of the Smiths part of a thoroughly consistent, surrealist approach to the world. In *Eleuthéria*, on the other hand, one feels that the unpredictable behaviour of some of the characters or their incongruous remarks have been introduced only as surprise elements to enliven an otherwise rather dreary series of exchanges. It is only in the relationships between Mr. Krap and his wife and between the Glazier and his son that surprisingly swift changes of attitude or mood come to be an acceptable part of that volatile, highly ambivalent view of human love or friendship that was later to characterize *Godot*, *Endgame* and *Happy Days*. Introducing surprising language or actions into a conventional setting is much less effective than the opposite technique which was adopted by Beckett later in *Happy Days*, where some of the dramatic force derives from apparently normal speech and behaviour occurring in highly unusual circumstances. Beckett had shown that, when genuinely interested in his subject, as with the world of the Dublin *literati* in *More Pricks than Kicks* in the early thirties, he had a keen eye and a sharp ear for parody and satire. After *Eleuthéria*, with the exception of the odd unpublished theatre fragment, he was not to attempt parody in any systematic way again until *Play*, where by setting the parodied phrases in a strange purgatorial state, he was able to modify considerably reactions to them.

The second act of *Eleuthéria* is probably the least successful of the three. Victor is brought into the arena for the first time in person after being continually (and fairly conventionally) talked about in the first act of the play. He is a faceless character who can impose his presence only through non-existent characteristics. He does not listen; he does not even try to understand: consequently, he forgets what he is told from one moment to the next and is totally uninterested in the wishes, needs or ideas of anyone else. He is both unwilling and unable to justify his voluntary exile from life. The negative nature of his character means that he can only function with minimal dramatic success as a figure harassed by the pleas and demands of others and buffeted by the force of their reasoning. As a victim of the constant interference of his family and their friends, he might conceivably have inspired some sympathy. But he does not seek any, since he is totally convinced that he is right in rejecting life as part of a search for inner freedom. Consequently, he eludes our sympathy and escapes our understanding. For even though the wish for some form of clarification, definition, even explanation of Victor's motives is mocked within the drama itself, it is nonetheless a very real factor in the failure of the play to retain dramatic interest. In the novel, Beckett is able to cover up the essential indigence of his nay-saying heroes (Belacqua or Murphy, for example) by an ironic narration that lends colour and complexity to what is basically a pallid, simplistic outlook. In the drama, there is no ironic or biased intermediary and a character must either speak for himself or others will speak against him. If one compares Beckett's method in *Eleuthéria* with that adopted in his later plays, one finds in *Godot* or in *Happy Days*, for example, that it was to be the situation in which his characters were placed or the world as a whole that was to appear as strange, mysterious, faceless and unknowable, rather than the main characters themselves. The tramps may be waiting for an elusive, unknowable Godot, but they possess positive, human characteristics. Winnie recognizes in her barren world that 'here all is strange' (*HD*, 33), but she invites sympathy as well as understanding by her human weaknesses, as well as by her display of courage in such appalling circumstances. By contrast, Victor's facelessness and apathy in *Eleuthéria* can only result in a decided reduction of dramatic interest.

Since Victor is such a dead weight dramatically, much has to depend on the other characters, especially on the Glazier (who is on stage almost throughout the second act) and also on the inventiveness of the visual by-play, or on the quality of the writing. From all three points of view, the second act fails, although the failure is neither uniform nor entirely without interest. As far as the other characters are concerned, Beckett is to some extent saddled with the puppets of the first act, who come in turn to visit Victor after the death of his father, the one really interesting creation of the previous act. One of them, Dr. Piouk, has strong views on the matter of suicide but allowing him the opportunity to expound them means that there is too much of a break between Victor's personal 'drama' on the one hand and the philosophical issues that arise out of it on the other. The new character of the Glazier is a utility figure, an amalgam of several different roles: an investigator, a practical man of action, a father figure, a representative of rationalism and, consequently, a lover of shape in human affairs. It is, however, worth noting, that in creating the various characters, Beckett is concerned with establishing echoes and patterns that are not at all unlike those found in his later plays. The Glazier, for instance, is explicitly linked on several occasions with Victor's father. His son, Michel, seems at first to be contrasted with the recluse, Victor, but he soon displays similar tendencies to lethargy, ignorance and isolation. In addition, there are several hints of martyrdom, as allusions are made to the circumstances and the time scheme of the Passion of Christ.

An attempt is made to keep up the momentum of the first act by introducing various items of stage 'business'; there are constant comings and goings once again: Victor loses his shoe, his glass, and the bill for his room; the Glazier and his son conduct a lively if lengthy series of exchanges concerning the glass-cutter, the mastic, the ruler, and the lock; and, finally, Joseph's efforts to remove Victor by force result in the wrestler being knocked out by the Glazier's hammer. As this summary suggests, the play has something of the frenetic rhythms and horse-play of knockabout farce. And when the Glazier threatens to repeat the attack with the hammer (and the chisel) on Dr. Piouk, his wife comments that 'this is becoming like a melodrama' ('ça tourne au mélo[drame]', 75). The dramatic rhythms are too stumbling, however, for successful farce or melodrama and too often the text appears almost as limp as does its central protagonist. What is conspicuously lacking is that density of dramatic texture that, in Beckett's later plays, results from a tragi-comic blend of tones or from the multi-levelled nature of many of the statements.

There are numerous self-conscious theatrical allusions in *Eleuthéria*. In the first act, Henri Krap comments, for example, that 'From the dramatic point of view my wife's absence means absolutely nothing' (17). He goes on to ask Dr. Piouk how he envisages his role in the evening's entertainment; 'And you, my dear sir,' answers Dr. Piouk, 'is your own role settled then?' (24). In the second act, in reply to Madame Meck's question as to the meaning of the play, the Glazier answers 'It aims to distract and entertain the public, Madame' (53). In *Waiting for Godot* and *Endgame*, such theatrical allusions are used more sparingly and are usually voiced with a touch of irony. 'What is there to keep me there?' asks Clov in *Endgame*, Hamm replying succinctly, 'The dialogue' (*EG*, 39). In later plays, such self-conscious references disappear as participation in a ritual (as in *Krapp's Last Tape*) or explicit role-playing (as in *Play* or *Film*) becomes an integral part of the dramatic situation. In the later miniature dramas of the 'seventies, the situation has become so drastically deprived and artificial that self-conscious theatricality would introduce yet another level of reference to complicate unduly an already strange and disturbing experience.

It is ironic, however, in the case of a play that has never been performed, that *Eleuthéria* should be of interest for its self-conscious attitude towards the audience. Victor shows that he is fully aware of the 'otherness' of the audience on his first appearance at the beginning of the second act when, addressing the spectators directly, he seems to be on the point of explaining his conduct to them. But at the end of the play, instead of doing this, he pointedly turns his back on them as he settles down to sleep, cutting the spectators too out of his isolated world, as he has done with everyone else in the drama. In the third act, the audience has its own self-elected representative, 'le commissaire du peuple' as he describes himself, who climbs down from a stage-box on to the stage to comment on and attempt to resolve, after his own fashion, the vagaries of a dramatic situation that does not coincide with his notion of the clear-cut drama that he feels he ought to be watching. Beckett was never to use this Sheridan-Pirandello type of device again in his theatre. Instead, in *Happy Days*, the puzzled judgement of the audience, trying to make what semblance of sense it can of Winnie's strange predicament, is incorporated into the fabric of the play in the person of Mr Cooker or Shower. In Winnie's narrative, this observer asks his wife the kind of questions that the spectators may have been formulating for some time: 'What does it mean? he says — What's it meant to mean?' (*HD*, 32). In other plays, explanations are withheld (or simply cannot be provided) to answer similarly crucial questions, while other information which appears much less vital to the satisfaction of the audience's curiosity is offered. We should not, however, be misled, as several critics have been, by Beckett's light-hearted comment that an empty theatre constituted more or less the ideal conditions for the presentation of his plays. Consciousness of an audience's expectations and its needs is implicit in all that Beckett has written for the stage, whether the presence or the independent role of that audience is acknowledged or not.

But the third act of *Eleuthéria* is more interesting than the rather obvious device of an intruding spectator might suggest. For once the Spectator has set foot upon the stage, he begins to experience himself those pressures towards shapelessness, softness and vagueness which have already been felt by others in the play. This results partly from his incursion into a dimension which is alien to his ordered, if rather tawdry existence. But it also derives from the contagious nature of Victor's own lack of definition. 'There you are like a kind of seeping (comme une sorte de suintement)' says the Glazier to Victor, 'For the love of God, take on a bit of shape' (62). In the course of his visit to his parents' home to see his dead father, Victor had explained himself to the servant, Jacques, in a way 'that was something like music' (97). (Here one may safely presume that it was the Schopenhauerian Idea incarnate, rather than the Leibnizian 'occult arithmetic' that Beckett had in mind, to adopt a distinction made by Beckett in *Proust* (see

PTD, 91-92.) But as soon as Victor is forced to formulate his thoughts verbally, the play begins to sprawl in all kinds of unlikely directions. Already, in the second act, the Glazier had admitted that 'we're all circling around something that has no sense. We must find a sense for it, or lower the curtain' (87). Interestingly, at one point in the final act, the stage directions suggest that Beckett is trying to create the impression that the play as a whole is grinding to a halt of its own accord, a first tentative attempt at the threat of total collapse and stasis that was to become a staple ingredient in *Waiting for Godot*. Almost as interesting is the way in which the Spectator's attempts to explain why he has stayed in the theatre at all leads to a comparison with a game of chess between two bad players:

> It's like watching a game of chess between two tenth rate players. Three quarters of an hour have gone by and neither of them has touched a piece. There they are like two half-wits gaping at the board; and there you are, even more half-wit than they, riveted to the spot, nauseated, bored to extinction, worn out, flabbergasted by such stupidity. Finally, you can't stand it any longer. You say to them: 'But for God's sake do this, do this, what are you waiting for, do this and its finished, we can go off to bed'. There's no excuse for you, it's against all the rules of good manners, you don't even know the blokes, but you can't help yourself, it's either that or hysterics. (103)[7]

As John Spurling has pointed out, this passage foreshadows the long drawn-out quality of *Endgame*, as well as its basic chess-board situation. But perhaps just as important as the failure of the players to end the game is the spectator's state of tense, even bored fascination. For it is surely one of Beckett's major achievements as a dramatist to have succeeded in conveying a sense of the weariness of waiting and the slow, difficult process of ending in such a way that boredom on the part of the spectator is not allowed to destroy the dramatic interest of the work. In *Eleuthéria* this does, in fact, happen on a number of occasions. But in the published plays it is rare, considering the challenging nature of the tasks that Beckett sets himself.

The third act of *Eleuthéria* reveals, in effect, an innovator searching for fresh ways of using the constants of the theatrical situation. If again we think ahead to *Waiting for Godot*, other parallels become clear. In *Godot*, the fundamental fact that all theatre is waiting — for something to happen or someone to arrive — is used by Beckett to create a central situation in which boredom and the avoidance of boredom have become key elements in preserving theatrical tension. Waiting in *Waiting for Godot* is not merely, or even primarily, a source of suspense. Part of the originality of the play lies in the concrete reality of the silence that has to be filled, so that comic talk and routines, in the words of one critic of the 1964 Royal Court production, 'take place not for their own sake, but as pitiful and momentary tricks for holding the terrible silence at bay'.[8] And, in *Godot*, that silence is experienced by the spectator as well as by the actor. The greater distance and objectivity of the spectator involves, of course, risk — for, as Tom Stoppard once stressed, unlike reading a book, once an audience leaves its seats it leaves for good[9] — but it also imposes on the action, dialogue and games a degree of complicity between actors and audience that may involve a degree of shared tedium or irritation or may become the necessary base for the laughter of release. So self-conscious lines like 'Come on, Gogo, return the ball, can't you, once in a way?' (*WFG*, 12) or 'How time flies when one has fun!' (*WFG*, 76) are laugh-lines based on complicity. And looking ahead another twenty years to *Not I* (1973), the spectator is brought there into a different, and more complex, form of complicity with what is being said. All of these variations on what one might term the 'theatrical relationship' have their origins in the experimentalism of *Eleuthéria*.

In a lengthy preliminary note to the play, Beckett describes in detail the lay-out of the set and indicates the nature and the limits of the 'marginal' action which accompanies the main action and which is made possible by the adoption of a split set. To one side is Victor's room, dirty, squalid, and almost empty except for a bed; to the other is an area of his parents' sitting-room, clean, elegant and heavily encumbered with furniture. There is no dividing wall and the two distinct *loci* share the same rear wall and window and the same floor. There is no very sharp distinction either between the two spaces of this dualist set, the change being established more by the contrast between emptiness and clutter and by the nature of the furnishings. At times even, actors in the two different spaces almost touch each other.

The set has been wrongly described by Beckett's biographer as divided into two equal halves.[10] In fact, Victor's room occupies three quarters of the stage and the Krap's sitting-room is contained within it like a kind of enclave. And so already in *Eleuthéria*, we find an early if more radical sketch for the later separate, and uneven, zones or 'territories' occupied or claimed by Beckett's stage characters. These separate areas clearly represent theatrically the solitary nature of each individual human consciousness. 'We are alone' Beckett had written in *Proust* in 1931, 'we cannot know and we cannot be known'. (*PTD*, 66) But they also focus on divisions between the characters or within themselves. 'Estragon is on the ground', Beckett said during rehearsals for his production of *Waiting for Godot* in Berlin, 'he belongs to the stone. Vladimir is light, he is oriented towards the sky'.[11] Hamm too has his own stage territory into which Clov shuffles from his kitchen only at Hamm's command. Winnie has her mound of earth which spreads out around her like a skirt, while Willie's home is his hole in the ground. A dualistic approach to life finds its literal embodiment in Krapp's zone of light and larger area of stage darkness. The setting in *Eleuthéria* is therefore not so different from Beckett's later plays as might at first have been supposed.

Yet the split stage does provide two quite separate, if related, sets of actions. Beckett clearly hoped that although contrapuntal actions would still register with the audience, movements in the 'marginal' action would almost come to be taken for granted and would be assimilated without the need for the spectator to effect constant switches of attention. It is difficult, however, to see how this device could have operated without being disconcertingly distracting. Yet the manner in which Beckett envisaged the split set is certainly not lacking in boldness and is nothing like as crude as has been suggested.[12] Subsequently, he probably came to recognize relatively early the problems arising from the use of such a device and was never to adopt so radical a division again.

In the first act, when the main action takes place in the Krap's sitting-room, the 'marginal' action is of the son, Victor, mostly immobile, but sometimes pacing restlessly from the front of the stage to the rear window or from the side door of his room to the invisible central barrier between these two distinct 'sites'. Beckett focusses on rhythm and pattern here with the same precise concern that he later brought to arranging the pile of bodies into an ordered heap in *Waiting for Godot* or to shaping Winnie's meticulously planned gestures in *Happy Days*. In the second act, the main action is set in Victor's room, with the 'marginal' action in the Kraps' sitting-room; this is mostly empty, except for a number of entries by the servant, Jacques, and a single visit by Victor to view his father's body. Only two sentences are uttered in the course of the 'marginal' action, one in each act. Beckett wrote indeed that most of the time the 'marginal' set consists of a 'site and a human being in stasis' (Preliminary note, 2).

Victor's room is looked at from a different angle in each act. In the first act it is placed to the left of the sitting-room; in the second, it is to the right. Consequently the focal point of the action remains the same, to audience right of the stage. In the preliminary note, Beckett adds that, in the third act, there is no 'marginal' action, since by then, according to the logic of the shifts, the Kraps' sitting-room would have fallen into the pit! It is interesting, however, and perhaps not entirely coincidental, that Beckett should have been experimenting with different angles of vision at almost the same time as Arthur Adamov was doing the same in *La Parodie* (also written in 1947).

Eleuthéria is Greek for freedom, and in his desire to free himself from both the external world and his own will, Victor Krap takes his place among Beckett's other potential escapees from the 'colossal fiasco' of existence, Belacqua and Murphy. When pressed for explanations, even when threatened with physical torture, he confesses 'The life that I lead? It is the life of someone who wants nothing to do with yours . . . I am convinced that at every level life is always the same burden' (113-114). Victor himself provides little specific evidence of what he most abhors in life, his only positive admission being his fear of being hurt. Yet more universal suffering and death constantly surface as inescapable elements of the life from which he retreats. For Victor's hatred extends further than the petty emotional dishonesty of the Krap or the Pioux households to encompass the very roots of existence. His answer is to attempt to withdraw from it all. Partly this is a response to the pointlessness of ceaseless activity in the light of the inevitability of death: 'The cow which, at the gates of the slaughter-house, realizes all the absurdity of pastures' (13). But it is also part of an uncompromising rejection of life itself. For Victor concludes that 'the simplest thing would be never to have begun', words that echo W.B. Yeats's version of *Sophocles's Oedipus at Colonnus*: 'Never to have lived is best, ancient writers say; / Never to have drawn the breath of life, never to have looked into the eye of day'.[13] Victor seeks his freedom, 'By being as little as possible. By not moving, not thinking, not dreaming, not speaking, not listening, not perceiving, not knowing, not wanting, not being able and so on. I believe my prisons were there' (116). In his renunciation of the world as will and his conscious cultivation of willlessness, Victor clearly reflects the central impulse in Schopenhauer's *The World as Will and Idea*. Yet the strength of the world-weariness is Beckett's own.

Intellectually, Victor eventually renounces his quest. 'One cannot be free', he says. 'I was mistaken. I can't live the life I lead any longer. I understood that last night when I saw my father. One cannot see oneself dead. That is theatre' (118), recalling Malone's 'I shall not watch myself die, that would spoil everything' (*TN*, 180). But offered the choice between assimilation into life as he knows it or the 'great departure' into death, he still clings, with whatever little justification, to his former isolation. But this is now expressed in terms of a new stoical acceptance of his imprisoned state:

> I'll tell you how I'll spend my life: in rubbing my chains together, one against the other. From morning to evening and from evening to morning. That little useless sound will be my life. I won't say my joy. My calm. My limbo. And you come and talk to me about love, and reason, and death! (*Pause.*) Go away, just go away. (128)

Victor's stance is both part of Beckett's own lengthy debate with himself on being and non-being and an element in a wider spectrum of responses to Henri Krap's question 'how can one live?', in a play where this issue is treated far less obliquely than in any of Beckett's later writings. The range extends from a bland, unthinking acceptance of the 'system of pensums and prizes' to, at the other extreme, Dr. Piouk's radical solution of suicide or euthanasia. His programme reads as follows:

> I would forbid reproduction. I would perfect the condom and other means of contraception and would make their use universal. I would create abortion corps under the control of the State. I would drown the new-born. I would favour homosexuality . . . I would encourage with all the means at my disposal recourse to euthanasia, without however making it obligatory. (33)

However logical Dr. Piouk's proposals may have seemed as a way of curtailing life, they must equally have struck Beckett as execrable as he wrote them down. After all, only a matter of months before, several of his friends (notably Alfred Péron and Paul Léon) had suffered and died during the war from similar extermination techniques.

Victor is offered a suicide pill by Dr. Piouk. And the choice in the doctor's mind is a simple one between choosing life or death. Suicide, offering an escape from the horrors of existence, is a temptation in *Eleuthéria*, as it was to be in Beckett's later plays from *Godot* to *Play*. Yet it is rejected by Victor as being irrelevant to his concerns and particularly to his search for freedom. For he recognizes that once dead, he would in all probability also have lost the consciousness to be aware of his own freedom. So Victor's response, though it constitutes a rejection of being as it is generally understood, is not , to his mind at least, a prescription for death. Victor's father works from similar attitudes.

> The mistake is to wish to live. It is not possible. For what is given is unsatisfactory in the life that is offered to us . . . It is a question of materials. Either there is too much and you don't know where to begin or there is too little and it's not worth beginning. And yet we still begin, because we are afraid of doing nothing. You even think sometimes that it will end; that happens too. Then you realize its only bluff. And so you begin again, with too much or too little. Why then can't we come to terms with a life that's only bluff? It must be our divine origin. They say to you, that's life, beginning and beginning again. But no it's only the fear of doing nothing. Life is not possible. (38-9)

But Mr. Krap senior not only pontificates interestingly about life, in a manner reminiscent of Clov in *Endgame* or the Opener in the radio play *Cascando* ('They say, That is not his life, he does not live on that. They don't see me, they don't see what my life is, they don't see what I live on, and they say, That is not his life, he does not live on that.' *Play and Two Short Pieces for Radio*, 43). He has discovered his own way of coming to terms with it. His logic is impeccable: since life is itself bluff, pretence is the only adequate response to it.

> Finding life impossible and the great remedy to this repugnant, either out of shame or cowardice, or precisely because he is not really living, what can man do to avoid the madness — oh a discreet, reticent enough form of madness — that he has been taught to fear? (*Pause.*) He can pretend to live and pretend others are alive. (40)

At the end of the play, Victor does not even bother to pretend. He opts to stay in his room, a voluntary exile, condemning himself to a form of incarceration in liberty. For a *living death* seems, absurdly, yet conclusively, preferable to the other paths open to him. In this way, the example of Victor anticipates the consistently unsatisfactory nature of all the alternatives open to future Beckett protagonists. 'You must go on, I can't go on, I'll go on' says, nonetheless, the narrator of *The Unnamable* (*TN*, 418). And Beckett's characters follow this impulse rather than Victor's turning his back on life and on the audience. By comparison, those who choose to endure life, like Estragon and Vladimir, Mr. Rooney, Winnie, or even Krapp, seem far more courageous than Victor, whose stance on life, however unusual, is no more dramatically compelling than his featureless mask had been.

Notes

1. Conversation with J. Knowlson, c. 1974. The original autograph notebooks are in the University of Texas Library (Austin); an original typescript is at Dartmouth College Library. A xerox copy is in Reading University Library, MS 1227/7/4/1, and references in the text are to this copy.
2. D. Bair, *Samuel Beckett. A Biography*, New York, Harcourt Brace Jovanovich, 1978, pp. 361-4, 367.
3. D. Bair, *op. cit.*, pp. 16-17.
4. This is because Passy is a well-to-do area and the left-overs are likely to be correspondingly tasty there; confirmed by S. Beckett, 3.xii.78.
5. J. Fletcher and J. Spurling, *Beckett. A Study of his Plays*, London, Eyre Methuen, 1972, pp. 51-2.
6. *Journal of Beckett Studies*, no. 1, Winter 1976, pp. 99-100.
7. The translation in this instance is taken from J. Fletcher and J. Spurling, *op. cit.*, p. 50.
8. *The Times*, 31 December 1964.
9. T. Stoppard, 'Playwrights and Professors', *The Times Literary Supplement*, no. 3, 684, 13 October 1972, p. 1219.
10. D. Bair, *op. cit.*, p. 361. She also describes the play as a 'serious traditional three-act play'! (p. 362).
11. W.D. Asmus, 'Beckett directs Beckett', *Theatre Quarterly*, vol. V, no. 19, 1975, p. 21.
12. In *Beckett. A Study of his Plays*, John Spurling speaks of 'a vertical splitting of the proscenium rectangle' (p. 48).
13. W.B. Yeats, *Sophocles's Oedipus at Colonnus*, in *Collected Plays of W.B. Yeats*, London, Macmillan and Co., 1960, p. 561.

Post-Trilogy Prose

Texts for Nothing

Beckett's *Texts for Nothing* (1950-52) have suffered at the hands of critics unable or unwilling to grant that they are any more than rejected passages from *The Unnamable* (1949-50), or meditations on problems already considered in more depth in that work. It is easy to see why this state of affairs has come into being, since Beckett himself, in one of his few interpretative comments on his own work, has stressed the close connection of the two, and indicated that the *Texts* did not achieve what he had hoped for: 'The very last thing I wrote (he said in 1956) . . . was an attempt to get out of the attitude of disintegration, but it failed'.[1] It is abundantly clear that the *Texts* offer little that would allow Beckett to move from disintegration to integration, and also clear that they are not his most brilliant or compelling works. But Beckett's aesthetic at this time was predicated upon failure and the unavoidability of failure, and he has always been more interested in disintegrative forms than integrative ones, so we should not, as certain critics have done, assume that the *Texts* are a failure *tout court* and dismiss them in favour of more finished, or more accessible, works. They may not represent an escape from the *impasse* of *The Unnamable*, but Beckett is not so in love with the printed word as to have published them as mere adjuncts to that work. The *Texts* deserve the more extended treatment they have so far been denied, and in this way their intrinsic interest and individuality can be conclusively demonstrated.

Perhaps some of the neglect they have suffered is attributable to the title Beckett gave to them, which seems to confirm that they are worthless and empty of significance. This has not been helped by the information that John Fletcher, in his influential study of Beckett, was the first to provide, namely that the title is derived from the musical term *mesure pour rien*, meaning 'a bar's rest', and hence, in literary terms, 'a group of words conveying nothing'.[2] Other critics have stressed that in music a bar's rest may be an essential part of the musical whole, but have clearly felt that literature is too substantial a medium to permit the interstices of utterance to occupy the foreground, or concentrated on the musical elements in the *Texts* to the exclusion of other, more interesting, matters. It would be foolish, in any case, to allow the title of the work, whose oblique musical reference will be lost on most readers, to dictate our own feelings about it as it manifests itself on the page, and especially ill-advised to accede to the author's apparent condemnation of his work when the author is as severely self-critical as Beckett habitually is. The title is actually a good deal less dismissive than, for instance, the sobriquet 'fizzles' that Beckett, with some justice, applied to his abandoned prose of the early 1960s.

The other barrier to seeing the *Texts* plain is the temptation to treat them all as of equal status, without recognizing that some of them imply critical changes of direction in Beckett's work, and that some of them are indeed failures by any criteria. There is a temptation in almost all the critical accounts of Beckett to treat each work, or each section of each work, as equally interesting, which has done much to discredit the critical literature on Beckett and to bring it close to hagiography. The failure to recognize the variations in texture and quality between and within the individual *Texts* does a disservice to the collection as a whole, and makes it impossible to perceive the distinctive contribution to Beckett's enterprise that the best, and the best parts, of the *Texts for Nothing* make. At the same time only a reading that explores each individual text can hope to lay bare the dense strategies that are operating in each case and, after a general consideration of the milieu of the *Texts*, this is the procedure that will be followed here.

In the light of Beckett's recent experiments with shorter fiction, it is easy to see the *Texts* as the first instances of an impulse that later came to dominate his practice in fiction and drama. For the primary differences between the *Texts* and *The Unnamable*, which helps to account for almost all the other disparities between them, is obviously the reduction of format that enables Beckett to delimit the area of his investigations, and to concentrate on specific problems that got shelved, or simply lost, in the turbid prose of *The Unnamable*. Thus each text sets itself a particular task, and stays as far as possible within its confines, as indeed the word 'text', in the sense of 'a statement on which one dilates', goes some way towards suggesting. It is a characteristic of almost all the *Texts* to circle back to their point of origin, after a consideration of related issues, in an attempt to complete a truncated opening, or to end with as much finality as can be mustered in the light of the self-questioning that has been going on. There is more concession made by Beckett here, in other words, to traditional formal requirements than is possible in the 'residua' that followed a decade later. The *Texts* are much less shapeless than they at first appear, and, by and large, less shapeless than *The Unnamable* from which they derive. It is, as elsewhere in Beckett, the sense of a wild and whirling content battering and eroding an increasingly fragile but resistant formal barrier that gives the *Texts* their exciting and astringent tension and prevents them from being merely inchoate and diffuse.

Beckett refers to the formal constraints he is impelled by in the frequent reminders that reason has not yet departed from him completely, and accedes to the demands of form by planting repeated elements, or elements which are reiterated with minor variations, at key points in the text. This aligns the *Texts* with the prose that went before it rather than with the brief residua that have come after it, and it is no surprise to find references to Molloy, Malone and Pozzo scattered through the series. But there are many indications also that the *Texts* are a forward-looking work, amongst which one cannot help but be struck by the prefigurations of *How It Is* (the mud of *Text 1*, the suggestion of a life 'above in the light' in *Text 2*, the interest in justice in *Text 4* — which contains the phrase 'I say it as I hear it' — the 'unwitnessed witness of witnesses' in *Text 12*), the prefigurations of *From an Abandoned Work* and 'Afar a bird' in *Text 5*, and the oblique prefiguration of the couple walking hand in hand of *Enough* at the end of *Text 1*. The *Texts for Nothing* occupy a genuine median point between *The Unnamable* and the works that have come after them, and represent a striving for a new language quite as idiosyncratic and exploratory as any of the more obviously experimental writings. In *Text 2* indeed, Beckett indicates that the turbulent flood, the 'babble' of *The Unnamable*, is something he has had to leave behind in a situation where everything has been much more severely reduced and 'words are stopping too'.

The unique form of the *Texts* is a reflection of their uniqueness of subject matter. There is little attempt made here to tell a narrative in the manner which the speaker of *The Unnamable* finds himself unable to resist, and hence much less temptation to invent 'vice-existers' and subsume the self under the rudimentary biography of someone else. Hence there are none of the set-pieces of *The Unnamable*, and little of the centrifugal energy so characteristic of that work. The *Texts* are centripetal, and move much closer to (though never actually arriving at) solipsism. As Richard Coe has observed, the relationship between Self and Others has been changed from one in which all beings 'move more or less in the same dimensionless void' to one in which the Self occupies an 'underground' position relative to the Others 'above in the light'.[3] The attitude towards evidences of selfhood alters accordingly, since there is now a great gulf fixed between the 'I' and those who, throughout the trilogy, bore witness to its existence. This explains why the 'I' is floundering from one sentence to the next, with even less consistency of purpose than the narrator of *The Unnamable*. There is nothing that may be regarded as stable here, not even the obsessive inquisition that tends to take one of two or three basic forms. Each strategy which the voice engages in, in order to settle decisively the question of whether or not it is substantial, founders because there is no external, ratifying element that will guarantee its substantiality. The more the shadowy self becomes aware of this, the more desperate it becomes, until the point where it resigns itself to solitude and awaits the demise of all voices whatever. Whatever 'shifts' (as the Unnamable would call them) the Self adopts, they tend to increase the instability that the Self is suffering from, and to involve it in more and more labyrinthine discriminations, quicksands and whirlpools of extraordinary intransigence and tenacity. Whilst there remained in *The Unnamable* a sense of progress, of problems posed and partially reduced, in *Texts for Nothing* all is regress, especially those 'shifts' which seem to offer routes away from regress.

This is why the linguistic surface of the *Texts*, as unique as their form and their subject matter, is like a landscape suffering a multiplicity of stress fractures before our eyes. There is much greater tonal oscillation between adjacent elements than may be found in *The Unnamable*, and the reliance on gestures of cancellation is much more dominant. The sentences are mostly short, as if perpetually on the verge of petering out, or being throttled into inexistence. The imagery is more local, more unexpected, more various. The 'labours of poetical excavation' (*PTD*, 29) throw up disarming and disturbing outcrops of a kind of lyricism that has been largely absent from Beckett's repertoire since he gave up writing in English. Beckett is moving in the *Texts* towards the 'bits and scraps' of atomized material that he will attempt to organize in *How It Is* and the residua, but he is without any principle of organization, and hence can only (as he himself testified) go on disintegrating. Despite his remarks to Israel Shenker that 'in my work there is consternation behind the form, not in the form'[4], in *Texts for Nothing* the 'consternation' seems to be very much in the form. It is with consternation that the *Texts* begin:

> Suddenly, no, at last, long last, I couldn't any more, I couldn't go on. Someone said, You can't stay here. I couldn't stay there and I couldn't go on . . . How can I go on, I shouldn't have begun, no, I had to begin . . . I could have stayed in my den, snug and dry, I couldn't. My den, I'll describe it, no, I can't.
>
> (*Texts for Nothing*, London, Calder and Boyars, 1974, p. 7: all further references are to this edition.)

But notwithstanding this unpromising beginning, somehow a discourse emerges, in which a location ('quag, heath up to the knees, faint sheeptracks . . .') and a population ('we seem to be more than one, all deaf') are brought into tenuous relationship. At the same time an effort to take up an attitude ('I am far from all that wrangle') is strenuously made. The speaker's situation is at once revealed to be an essentially *post mortem* one, in which time and space have become impossibly confused: 'I am down in the hole the centuries have dug . . . They are up above, all round me, as in a graveyard' (8). There is only the memory of categories that once were meaningful, exposed now in all their arbitrariness: 'often I could answer, An hour, a month, a year, a century, depending on what I meant by here, and me, and being, and there I never went looking for extravagent meanings, there I never much varied, only the here would sometimes seem to vary' (8). The 'here' has become as invariable as the 'now' will soon be seen to be; the 'unending suck of black sopping peat' is of a piece with the unending 'evening' on which the subsequent *Texts* lay emphasis. But at this early stage the speaker refuses to accept the absolute disjunction between 'up there' and 'down here', partly because he is still a prey to tormenting memories of life above, and partly because he sees this as the only way to preserve an integrated self that will not be subject to fragmentation. *Text 1* is the only one of the *Texts for Nothing* in which such an integration seems possible, and ends with a nostalgic memory of childhood which stresses the harmonious intermingling of elements in essence disparate:

> I was my father and I was my son, I asked myself questions and answered as best I could . . . or we walked together, hand in hand, silent, sunk in our worlds, each in his worlds, the hands forgotten in each other. That's how I've held out till now. And this evening again it seems to be working, I'm in my arms, I'm holding myself in my arms, without much tenderness, but faithfully, faithfully. (11)

This irrational childhood synthesis that brought the protagonist such calm (as he admits openly in the novella, 'The Calmative') is a far cry from the irrationality that does not lend itself to synthesis: 'All mingles, times and tenses, at first I only had been here, now I'm here still, soon I won't be here yet . . .' (10). But for the moment such a synthesis still seems possible, and the end of the text is almost peaceful: 'Sleep now, as under that ancient lamp, all twined together, tired out with so much talking, so much listening, so much toil and play' (11). Of course, despite the tranquillity of this conclusion, there are clear indications that it cannot last. The Joe Breem narrative is now seen for what it is, 'a comedy, for children'. The adult self obviously cannot solace itself with a structure beginning unhappily and ending happily, because beginning and ending are now all muddled up ('All mingles'), and stories, as the end of *Text 3* will prove, have lost their efficacy. Stories cannot be repeated *ad nauseam*, as when in childhood the child knows narratives by heart. In the subsequent *Texts* there are sudden resurrections of the narrative spirit, but all immediacy and vibrancy has been surrendered, and the longer the series wears on the less likelihood there is of this resource being reconstituted. In the first of the *Texts for Nothing* Beckett has staved off the realisation of his essential poverty, but it becomes impossible for him to delude himself much longer, and the split has widened by the time he begins the second *Text*.

Text 2 is a largely diagnostic exercise, and suffers from a plainness and straightforwardness that seem out of place in these murky latitudes. Each of the three memories that form the bulk of the text — Mother Calvet, Verger Joly, Piers encountering the Graves brothers — has a certain charm and even humour, but none of them is as compelling as the memories of *Text 1*, and no obvious relationship is established between them. The sense of failure is much stronger here than in *Text 1*, 'the subject dies before it comes to the verb' (13) and the pronoun 'I' is conspicuous by its absence, occurring only once, at the end of the text. The two worlds of 'above' and 'below' are now estranged completely and the speaker is quite without the resources that would re-establish commerce between them. He attempts to reduce the world 'above' to the status of a stimulus that will obliterate the world 'below' ('one last memory, it may help, to abort again', 14) but cannot free himself of its substantiality ('If only it could be wiped from knowledge. To have suffered under that miserable light, what a blunder', 13). Unfortunately the world 'below' cannot be said to offer an attractive alternative: 'Here you are under a different glass, not long habitable either, it's time to leave it . . . Go then, no, better stay, for where would you go, now that you know?' (12). But it is the strategy of *Text 2* to make the 'here and now' as 'habitable' as it may reasonably be expected to be, and the speaker is gradually brought round to an awareness of its advantages: 'Here at least . . . no talk of a creator and nothing very definite in the way of creation. . . . A pity hope is dead. No. How one hoped above, on and off. With what diversity' (14, 15). At the same time the status of the 'here and now' remains disturbingly uncertain, as if the speaker has lost the certainties of 'above' (which he still remains drawn to) and found nothing to replace them with: 'it's changing, something must be changing, it must be in the head, slowly in the head the ragdoll rotting, perhaps we're in a head, it's as dark as a head before the worms get at it, ivory dungeon' (13). The resigned finality of the emotional and broken sentences that end the text may suggest that a new and more definitive kind of knowledge is at hand, but it is hardly the 'end rent with stifled imprecations' (14) that has been prophesied, and there has been too much uncertainty about the world 'below' for it to seem a viable alternative to the 'endurable' world above. One feels at the end that certain issues have been dodged in the second *Text*, as the opening sentence of the third one seems to confirm.

Text 3, the longest and most diffuse, is orientated towards the future, as *Text 2* was orientated towards the past. It is a predictive text, announcing its subject matter ('there's going to be a story') and indicating its eccentricity in relation to what has gone before ('there's going to be a departure'). It begins in a mood of confidence and certainty that sounds impressive, but is ultimately seen to be hollow:

> Yes, no more denials, all is false, there is no one, it's understood, there is nothing, no more phrases, let us be dupes, dupes of every time and tense, until it's done, all past and done, and the voices cease, it's only voices, only lies. (16)

Only a massive effort of will can sustain this vision, but beneath it all the suspicion grows that it is futile anyway, and really beside the point: 'What matter how you describe yourself, here or elsewhere, fixed or mobile, without form or oblong like man, in the dark or the light of the heavens, I don't know, it seems to matter, it's not going to be easy' (17-18). In the end it turns out to be all too easy to construct a plausible enough existence with a companion to soften its hardships, but it proves impossible to transfer this consoling image to the 'here' and hence 'get into my story in order to get out of it'. It begins to break upon the speaker's consciousness that his 'departure' has been a derogation of responsibility towards the 'here' and no departure at all in experimental terms. For the second text running Beckett ends in a mood of finality, but with the problem of getting 'something to happen here' further from being solved than it had previously been: 'There is no flesh anywhere, nor any way to die . . . Here, nothing will happen here, no one will be here, for many a long day . . . And the voices, wherever they come from, have no life in them' (20-21). This powerful conclusion goes some way towards redeeming a text that has simply marked time and deferred a real 'departure'. But 'there's no way to go on' from this point, and the next *Texts* are much more challenging precisely because they are genuine attempts at coming at the problem in an unprecedented way.

Text 4 is concerned with the impossibility of 'departure', and yet contains within it the very striking departure of changing the nominative 'I' into an accusative 'he', who enjoys to the full the opportunity of 'accusing' the 'I' of several crimes done in 'his' name, and who thus begins the strain of legal imagery that dominates the next few Texts. There is much subtle criticism embedded in this harangue, which is almost vituperative enough to be seen as a 'malediction' in the manner of *Endgame*'s Hamm:

> He protests he doesn't reason and does nothing but reason, crooked, as if that could improve matters. He thinks words fail him, he thinks because words fail him he's on his way to my speechlessness, to being speechless with my speechlessness, he would like it to be my fault that words fail him, of course words fail him. He tells his story every five minutes, saying it's not his, there's cleverness for you . . . there's profundity for you, he has me who say nothing say it's not me. (22-3)

The aggrieved tone is so carefully and compellingly caught here, however, that the 'me' begins to amount to a substantial personality and hence to what *The Unnamable* would call a 'vice-exister'. But the 'he' cannot strictly accuse the 'I' because the linguistic element 'I' no longer denominates anything that must necessarily exist. Ultimately the 'I' seems to have benefited from the accusations to the point of seeing where previous errors have been made:

> a story is not compulsory, just a life, that's the mistake I made, to have wanted a story for myself, whereas life alone is enough . . . What counts is to be in the world . . . so long as one is on earth . . . you may even believe yourself dead on condition you make no bones about it . . . there are moments, like this moment, when I seem almost restored to the feasible. (24)

There are a series of what one cannot forbear from calling deadly ironies here. For although the text has identified 'where I'd go, if I could go . . . who'd I be, if I could be' it has been clear from the start of the text (and indeed from the start of the series) that the plane of the feasible has been irrecoverably lost and did not offer satisfaction anyway. The feasible cannot be re-constituted, because the irrational has usurped its premises (its premisses as well). Restoration to the feasible can only now be temporary, and can only interfere with the Self's ability to adopt a substantial and substantiating voice. At the end of *Text 4* therefore the 'I' is left in a state of suspension more desolate even than that with which the text began its inquisition: 'I wait for me afar for my story to begin, to end, and again this voice cannot be mine' (25). 'Life alone' would be 'enough' if it could be uttered in an account — 'my story' — that was not a fiction. Without it 'life alone' is loneliness, and self-lessness that cannot be remedied. In the following text the loneliness is peopled once again with what *Text 1* called 'all my little company' (10), and a different kind of account is, with difficulty, rendered.

Text 5 is an examination (an aptly judicious one, as it turns out) of the image-making faculty that has been at the root of Beckett's enterprise in the previous texts. It is Beckett's most trenchant analysis thus far in his career (and only superseded by *How It Is*) of an idea so basic to him that it figured centrally in his first book *Proust: 'Pues el delito mayor . . . es haber nacido'* (*PTD*, 67). We need not, in other words, seek analogues in Kafka, from whom Beckett has been careful to distinguish himself. There is a literalism in Kafka that is quite foreign to *Text 5* which concerns 'the silence of quite a different justice, in the toils of that obscure assize where to be is to be guilty' (26). The assize is indeed so obscure that no image, not even the highly charged image elaborated here, can fully represent the

condition of the Self. This is why Beckett stresses later on the infinite
variability of the imagistic method, and remembers nostalgically the
sky and the earth and the sea which belong 'to the same family' of
uninvented things: 'Who are all these people, gentlemen of the long
robe, according to the image, but according to it alone, there are
others, there will be others, other images, other gentlemen' (27). At
the same time the image inevitably contains some portion of the truth,
and refuses to let the speaker languish into insouciance ('Insidious
question, to remind me I'm in the dock', 27). The net result is that *Text
5* is more nakedly confessional than those that have preceded it, and
reads throughout like a considered statement that might be acceptable
to a court of law or, as the speaker hopes, 'before the justice of him
who is all love' God (28). But in order to tell 'the whole truth' the
speaker must play all the roles, as when (in *Text 1*) 'I was my father and
I was my son', and this proves wearying and (unlike the child's
inspired synthesis of roles) ultimately self-gratifying:

> It's tiring, very tiring, in the same breath to win and lose, with
> concomitant emotions, one's heart is not of stone, to record the doom,
> don the black cap and collapse in the dock, very tiring, in the long run,
> I'm tired of it, I'd be tired of it, if I were me. It's a game, it's getting to be
> a game . . . (29)

The images that throng the speaker's head are now seen to be
predatory phantoms that prevent real feelings coming into being.
This is why the confessional mode reverts to the accusatory mode of
the previous text:

> It's they murmur my name, speak to me of me, speak of a me, let them go
> and speak of it to others, who will not believe them either, or who will
> believe them too. Theirs all these voices, like a rattling of chains in my
> head, rattling to me that I have a head. (29)

So tenacious are these aggressive phantoms in their quest to provide
the 'I' with a Self ('They want to create me', 30) and so wearied is he
by taking on factitious roles, that the speaker can only resign himself
to being tormented by them permanently: 'That's where the council
will be tomorrow . . . It will be another evening . . . but it will be the
same night . . . ' (29). His vigilance, 'ears straining for a voice not from
without' (26) is 'in vain' (30) because he cannot finally adjudicate
between the image from without ('before my eyes') and those from
within ('in my helpless head, where all sleeps, all is dead, not yet
born', 26). The session has indeed been 'calm, on the whole' (30), but

only because the inquisition has been insufficiently inquiring. The tiredness at the end is something which this speaker will ultimately have to atone for ('it falls, it's noted') 'under a different glass', as *Text 2* says.

Text 6 offers no relief from the weariness. 'If my head could think I'd find a way out' (32), the speaker tells us, but his head is now afflicted with 'wretched acoustics . . . the merest scraps, literally' (31). 'The attempt to comprehend' the moment of vacancy ('the intervals between these apparitions', 31) gets cluttered up with imagistic considerations (keepers, male nurses, ghouls, coons) that confuse the issue, and confer a fake multiplicity and substantiality on what is changeless and uncertain: 'look at me, a little dust in a little nook, stirred faintly this way and that by breath straying from the lost without. Yes, I'm here for ever, with the spinners and the dead flies, dancing to the tremor of their meshed wings . . .' (32). The occasional appearance of a butterfly, 'quick dead' (33), only confirms the speaker's sense of how long he has been unborn and how remote his own death is. The phantoms seek to make him 'frantic with corporeality' (31) and he still longs for 'a form of life, ordained to end, as others ended and will end, till life ends' (34). But he has realized that 'this unnamable thing that I name and name and never wear out' (34) is only words, and that there are no 'intervals' of non-being that can be enshrined in them. The reciprocation that was once possible (in childhood) between subject and object has disappeared for good, and been replaced by a hermetic 'farrago of silence and words, of silence that is not silence and barely murmured words' (34):

> I can see me still, with those [eyes] of now, sealed this long time, staring with those of then, I must have been twelve, because of the glass, a round shaving-glass, double-faced, faithful and magnifying, staring into one of the others, and seeing me there . . . staring back sightlessly . . . (33)

Now the mirror has shattered into fragments, and the eyes are beginning to burn with tears. Even at the end, when the speaker rallies, as if remembering that 'a little resolution is all that is needed to come and go under the changing sky' (32), his 'high hopes' are undercut. 'I give you my word' (35) is not so much an assurance as a confession of his spuriousness. It is a natural reaction to the recognition that 'there is no one here, neither me nor anyone else' (32) to want to populate some elsewhere with creatures who possess a past, a present and a future. But it is not possible: 'what elsewhere can there be to this infinite here?' (32). The nostalgia for history, 'that slime where the Eternal breathed and his son wrote' (33), has to be conquered and wiped out. It is the product of believing that there is 'some other thing beside this thing' (34) (compare *Play*) and hopelessly futile.

Notwithstanding this, the seventh text is an essay in retrieval of the kind that has already been attempted without conspicuous success. At this mid-point in the series, preparatory to accepting the Self's non-being and concentrating on the words that break its silence, the protagonist is undertaking one final quest in the world above for conclusive evidence of having existed: 'I'd like to be sure I left no stone unturned before reporting me missing and giving up' (36). One feels here the accuracy of Beckett's realization that 'the French work brought me to the point where . . . I was saying the same thing over and over again'[5] for, however much the speaker may console himself ('This tone is promising, it is more like that of old', 36), *Text 7* is one of the least adventurous of the series, relying on a cluster of motifs (departure, a paradigmatic archetype, an enclosed location) which advertise their poverty: the station is a terminus, the paradigm is a 'vile parrot', the waiting-room has a 'quarter-glass self-closing door'. The speaker's reluctance to entertain the notion of some more decisive course of action ('one must not hasten to conclude, the risk of error is too great', 39) is balanced by his realization that 'personally I have no more time to lose' (39). But this realization comes much too late to get the speaker out of the 'trough of all this time' (37) that he is languishing in. Even before the text is really under way the inquiry is already foundering: 'it's passing, lighter than air, like a cloud, in moonlight, before the skylight, before the moon, like the moon, before the skylight' (36). But the voice persists with its ruminations nonetheless, and the text gets uttered, as it were, in spite of itself.

Text 8 is one of the climaxes of the series, but it is a melancholy comment on how little progress has been made since *The Unnamable*, which it closely resembles. The speaker is hoping, Unnamable-fashion, 'to wear out a voice' and inhabit the resultant silence: 'I'll be silence, I'll know I'm silence, no, in the silence you can't know, I'll never know anything' (41). Although this quite clearly refers us back to the last page of *The Unnamable*, we do not feel here quite the same headlong recklessness driving the voice on into an inconceivable future. This is not just because the sentences are shorter and less breathless, but because the text as a whole is more decisive than those that have preceded it. Certain truths of his situation are now fully recognized by the speaker and accepted for what they are: 'Only the words break the silence, all other sounds have ceased . . . It's an unbroken flow of words and tears. With no pause for reflection . . . it's for ever the same murmur, flowing unbroken, like a single endless word and therefore meaningless' (40). This sudden access of wisdom is the consequence of two crucial changes in the psychology of the speaker. Firstly he has almost freed himself from the tyranny of time and memory: 'I begin to have no very clear recollection of how things were before . . . and by before I mean elsewhere, time has turned into space and there will be no more time, till I get out of here. Yes, my past has thrown me out, its gates have slammed behind me . . .' (40-1). Secondly he has almost freed himself from the tyranny of reason and discrimination: 'I say no matter what . . . without reason, no matter what, without reason . . . I don't know what all that means, day and night, earth and sky, begging and imploring . . . that looks like a contradiction, it may be for all I know . . . The mistake I make is to try and think . . .' (41). This freedom, however, turns out to be a form of enslavement: 'I'm a mere ventriloquist's dummy, I feel nothing, say nothing' (42). Although the craving for a genuine freedom, the re-unification of a bifurcated personality, remains the primary desideratum — 'Me, here, if they could open, those little words, open and swallow me up, perhaps that is what has happened. If so let them open again and let me out . . . to try and be one again. Or if I'm guilty let me be forgiven . . .' (41) — the bifurcation between Self and Other is so extreme that it cannot be remedied. The only positive advance is that the speaker is now prepared to acknowledge some commerce between Self and Other: 'that other who is me . . . it's as him I must disguise myself till I die, for him in the meantime do my best not to live . . .' (42). This is no doubt why a vision of 'insignia [that] advance in concert, as though connected by the traditional human excipient' (43) follows. But this is a vision, unfortunately, that can only be maintained by 'a final effort of will' which summons up a bowler hat that is 'a sardonic synthesis of all those that never fitted me' (43). It will not fit the speaker this time either; he cannot go 'out . . . and be one again' and show that the sardonicism is misplaced. It might be done if 'no were content to cut yes's throat and never cut its own' (42) but this is not possible, as the conclusion demonstrates by its very syntax: 'No, the answer is no. For even as I moved . . . I would know it was not me, I would know I was here, begging in another dark, another silence, for another alm . . .' (44). The 'vacancy' (in the double sense of emptiness and unoccupied position) is 'tempting' (43) but not achievable. The words with which the text began, and which now constitute the text, prevent a true vacancy establishing itself. And not even silence can be considered vacant any longer (the most important of the crucial discoveries that the speaker makes in *Text 8*): 'If I were silent I'd hear nothing. But if I were silent the other sounds would start again, those to which the words have made me deaf or which have really ceased' (40). None of the subsequent texts will come as close to synthesis again, but at many points the speaker will regress to a state of ignorance more rudimentary than the qualified wisdom he has achieved in *Text 8*, so we cannot forbear from granting this text the kind of major status that so many of the others wilfully forego.

Text 9 is one of the most confused, and confusing, of the series, except insofar as, by virtue of the discoveries made in *Text 8*, everything has boiled down to the speaker's ability to say something about his condition, as distinct from doing anything to ameliorate it. This is actually the principal ironic underpinning to the text, since it is at no time concerned with the possibility of *experiencing* the 'way out' but only with the possibility of being *able to say it*. The difficulty here is that the 'avalanche' of 'wordshit' (46) needs no encouragement from the speaker, and is burying him slowly whether he will or no, rendering it impossible for him to complete the 'first step on the long travelable road' (46) towards the graveyard he longs for and is haunted by. Unlike *Text 11*, which manages to complete its truncated opening utterrance against all odds, *Text 9* has to remain content with the hypothesis of what would obtain in the unlikely event of being able to utter. The speaker is conscious throughout of how thoroughly hypothetical the whole thing is, and is not slow to latch on to the advantages that accrue from treating the hypothetical as actual: 'here are my tomb and mother, it's all here this evening, I'm dead and getting born, without having ended, helpless to begin, that's my life. How reasonable it is and what am I complaining of?' (47). The irrationalism of the previous text has been forgotten here, and replaced by a kind of rationalism that operates without reference to personality: 'there is reasoning somewhere, moments of reasoning, that is to say the same things recur . . . It's mechanical . . .' (45). This mechanical rationalism threatens to throttle the flow of the prose, but reveals itself, as it does so, as paradoxical and contradictory: 'What variety and at the same time what monotony, how varied it is and at the same time how, what's the word, how monotonous. What agitation and at the same time what calm, what vicissitudes within what changelessness' (46). However desiccated this formalism may seem, it offers more than the confusion that gradually comes to dominate the text and leaves the speaker without any idea where he is, and so without any chance of attaining the 'elsewhere' that would ratify his image of the road towards the grave. For in this world of words the question of the body has shrunk to 'a minor point, a minor point' (49) and physical movement has become merely an aesthetic problem, 'sequency of thought, and felicity of expression' (49). The speaker can only imagine himself ('borne by my words' as he punningly puts it) in movement, and only find solace in the imaginings of others, the words of Dante emerging from the *Inferno* with which *Text 9* concludes. A real emergence from his own *Inferno* is as far away as ever.

Text 10, than which only the penultimate text is shorter, explores not only the possibility of 'giving up' the quest — not surprisingly, in view of the confusion generated by *Text 9* — but also the possibility of making a quest of 'giving up' itself. The only way this can be achieved is by a narrowing of perspective, a concentration on the enclosed space of the skull: 'the heart's not in it anymore, nor is the appetite what it was. So home to roost [the head] comes among my other assets, home yet again, and no trickery involved . . .' (50). But there *is* some trickery involved, for the speaker discovers that his head is not so perfectly sealed that he is not subject to the delusory 'first aid' of thinking that his situation is remediable: 'one day I shall know again that I once was, and roughly who, and how to go on, and speak unaided, nicely, about number one and his pale imitations. And it is possible . . . that at the close of the interminable delirium . . . I may not be reproached with having faltered' (51). The only way he can make 'giving up' into 'going on' is to give up everything, including the cherished dream of being 'a perfect sphere hermetically closed to the without', an idea that Murphy, too, was forced to abandon. And the only way to do this is to round on the words that, since *Text 8*, have been intruding on his 'intervals', and to subject them to the withering critique that he has previously reserved for himself: 'No, no souls, or bodies, or birth, or life, or death, you've got to go on without any of that junk, that's all dead with words, with excess of words, they can say nothing else, they say there is nothing else . . .' (51-2). What exactly he will replace words with remains as yet only a dream, but it is a dream that he almost makes reality at the end of the text. 'A voice

of silence, the voice of my silence' can be heard indistinctly behind the
mysterious union of 'I' and 'he' that suddenly seems a possibility once
more:

> I'll go to sleep, so that I may say, hear myself say, a little later, I've slept,
> he's slept, but he won't have slept, or else he's sleeping now, he'll have
> done nothing, nothing but go on, doing what, doing what he does, that
> is to say, I don't know, giving up, that's it, I'll have gone on giving up,
> having had nothing, not being there. (52)

This is close to the 'calm and silence . . . which saying I don't break'
that has become the main aim of the speaker, but 'this evening it's too
late, too late to get things right' (52) and the speaker can only
mesmerize himself into unconsciousness. There is no 'calmative' like
that which retained enough of its tranquillizing power to bring down
the curtain on *Text 1*, the last time sleep was possible. And the chance
of achieving a 'voice of silence' is lost through weariness, as the chance
of synthesis was lost through weariness in *Text 5*.

In the next text, *Text 11*, the rigmarole continues and resolves itself
once more (literally resolves itself, as it turns out) into naming the
unnamable rather than, as in *Text 10*, accepting the inability to do so.
The text preserves the semblance of form by struggling through to a
final statement, but it is a good deal less conclusive than it looks, since
the time of 'those who knew me' can never actually arrive. Time has
not actually become space, as *Text 8* suggests it will, but it has ceased
to flow normally and it has passed the speaker by: 'It's time that can't
go on at the hour of the serenade . . . and time devours on, but not me,
there we have it, that's why it's always evening . . .' (53-4). It is
profitless to dream of 'what evenings they were then' because time has
become purely mental ('in the head, like a minute time switch', 54)
and fluid to the point of disappearance ('like a patch of sea, under the
passing lighthouse beam, a passing patch of sea under the passing
beam' 54). Memory has lost its authenticity and become conflated
and arbitrary: 'caput mortuum of a studious youth . . . and chewing . . .
a lesson . . . in the old head done with listening, there I am old, it
doesn't take long . . .' (54). Only if the Self regained control of its voice
could it put back meaning into time and constitute itself as being. But
the voice that maunders on is 'headless' (54) and is not addressed to
anyone: 'I don't speak to him any more, I don't speak to me any more,
I have no one left to speak to . . .' (56). At the same time the speaker is
visited by moments of revivified reason, which hold out the hope to
him that he can organize his language into statements that will confer

existence on him: 'I speak, a voice speaks that can be none but mine, since there is none but me . . . I'm saying it now, I'll be saying it soon, I'll say it in the end, then end, I'll be free to end, I won't be any more . . .' (56). Here the quest changes from the desire to complete the opening utterance and shifts in the direction of discovering something truly decisive ('a new no, to cancel all the others . . . that none says twice') that will guarantee a perfect absence. But this 'new no' is much too ardently desired to be the real negation sought for, and still appears in tandem with a 'yes' that keeps the dialectics going. It is indeed 'still the same old road . . . up yes and down no' (53) that it has always been in *Texts for Nothing*. The minor triumph of finishing the sentence that has initiated the text and brought it into being is possible only because true absence is impossible: 'And that is why . . . when comes the hour of those who knew me, it's as though I were among them . . . among them watching me approach, watching me recede . . .' (57). To be 'between two parting dreams' is to occupy the middle ground between them. The conclusion is certainly heroic under the circumstances, and moving too, but in the end it helps things not a whit, as the speaker's disappointed comment 'that is all I can have had to say' quite clearly indicates.

Text 12, the shortest, is once again concerned with 'memory and dream' but alters the focus of the analysis by presenting the 'I' as an aspect of the 'he' that *Text 11* had lost contact with. This is a way, perhaps the only one, of achieving some kind of synthesis, however imprisoning an existence 'in the dungeons of this moribund' (59) may be. It fails disastrously, however, because: 'there are voices everywhere, ears everywhere, one who speaks saying, without ceasing to speak, Who's speaking?, and one who hears, mute, uncomprehending, far from all, and bodies everywhere . . .' (59). With such a multiplicity of entities this new 'he', who seems to possess infinity (like God), is actually only the most recent of an infinite series at the end of which an 'unwitnessed witnesser of witnesses' must be presumed to stand: 'what's to be said of this latest other, with his babble of homeless mes and untenanted hims, this other without number or person whose abandoned being we haunt, nothing. There's a pretty three in one, and what a one, what a no one' (59). The sarcastic tone comprehensively dissipates the traces of the God of negative theology that cluster round this 'other'. It is a more economical version of Lucky's tirade, and quite as devastating. The only 'blessing' which the speaker can expect is from negative linguistics, which enable him to speak (as Watt found) of nothing 'as if it were something' (*W*, 74): 'what a blessing it's all down the drain, nothing ever as much as begun, nothing ever but nothing and never, nothing ever but lifeless words' (60).

Text 13 is perhaps the most demanding, but certainly the most impressive of the series, and in no way deserves the obloquy visited on it by Beckett when he dismisses it as a 'coda worthy of the rest' (63). It is a kind of coda certainly, formally distinct from what has gone before, but playing variations occasionally, in a quite independent way, upon material that has formed the substance of the work as a whole: the absence of time ('to speak of once, is to speak of nothing', 62), the absence of space ('here is empty, not a speck of dust, not a breath', 63), the need for an ending ('the extinction of this black nothing and its impossible shades', 64), the persistent impression that there is something substantial ('there's a voice without a mouth, and somewhere a kind of hearing, something compelled to hear, and somewhere a hand . . .', 61). There are even strange moments of confidence such as have occurred in previous texts: 'once you've spoken of me you can speak of anything' (61).

> It has always spoken, it will always speak, of things that don't exist . . . True, there was never much talk of the heart, literal or figurative . . . the heart is gone, no one feels anything, asks anything, seeks anything, says anything, hears anything, there is only silence. (62-3)

In the end, with a voice that is 'weaker still' (61) (weaker even than it was at the end of *Text 12* or *Text 10*), Beckett turns to the self-cancelling device of contradiction as the nearest thing to the 'new no' which he has yet to find: 'it's true and it's not true, there is silence and there is not silence, there is no one and there is someone, nothing prevents anything' (63). But far from ending 'on a castrato scream' as this text predicts (62) (and as the desperateness of the speaker's position justifies) Beckett creates, with consummate care, a manner that makes it seem as if it is indeed the silence speaking, with no human agency to prompt it. There is nothing quite so breathtakingly adventurous and compelling throughout the length and breadth of *The Unnamable* as this 'voice murmuring a trace' (61) interspersed with the comments of someone who has almost disappeared ('these are the expressions it employs' (62) . . . 'yet another locution', 63).

The *Texts for Nothing* are not brought to a factitious end, or indeed to a strict end at all. It is only a temporary 'silencing of silence', although it seemed to Beckett (as late as 1956) as if he had done nothing worthwhile since writing them. The miraculous thing in *Text 13* is that silence is made to speak without surrendering its silence:

> And were there one day to be here, where there are no days, which is no place, born of the impossible voice the unmakable being, and a gleam of light, still all would be silent and empty and dark, as now, as soon now, when all will be ended, all said, it says, it murmurs. (63-4)

These final words are not heroic, like the words which bring *The Unmamable* to a halt, but quiet, tremulous, teetering on the verge of non-existence. They are perhaps as close as Beckett has ever come to writing which is 'expressive of the impossibility to express', an idea from which Beckett disassociates himself. But they are best described in Beckett's own words at the end of the third dialogue with Duthuit:

> I know that all that is required now . . . is to make of this . . . fidelity to failure, a new occasion, a new term of relation, and of the act which, unable to act, obliged to act, he makes, an expressive act, even if only of itself, of its impossibility, of its obligation. (*PTD*, 125)

Between 1949, when Beckett despised this course of action, and 1952, when he composed the thirteenth *Text for Nothing*, he had been forced to change his mind and find a new 'fidelity' to failure. The 'end sheets' of *Text 13* bear traces of the 'infant languors' (63) of something new that has just been born. 'If speaking of me one can speak of life', says the voice at the beginning, with the caution characteristic of the sequence as a whole; but the adjacent utterance is quite unequivocal: 'and it can' (61). It is fitting that the last of these neglected texts should show Beckett on the way to conquering the 'attitude of disintegration' that is everywhere evident in them. It does not make the achievement of *How It Is* any less miraculous. But it does something much more important: it makes *How It Is* possible.

Notes

1. In the 'interview' with Israel Shenker, first published in *New York Times*, 6 May 1956; reprinted in L. Graver and R. Federman, *Samuel Beckett: the Critical Heritage*, London, Henley and Boston, Routledge and Kegan Paul, 1979, p. 148.
2. J. Fletcher, *The Novels of Samuel Beckett*, London, Chatto and Windus, 1964, p. 196.
3. R. Coe, *Samuel Beckett*, Edinburgh and London, Oliver and Boyd, 1964, p. 80.

4. In the interview with Israel Shenker, *op. cit.*, p. 148.
5. *eo. loc.*

How It Is

There are times when even the most seasoned reader of Beckett, faced with the forbidding prospect of confronting *How It Is*, must be tempted to adopt the narrator's wry critique of 'the peace that passeth understanding' and say of *How It Is* that it is 'just one of those things that pass understanding there are some' (*How It Is*, London, John Calder, 1964, p. 68; all further references are to this edition). But there is no need for such a judgment to be a pejorative one, if we remember Moran's wise passiveness before the dance of the bees that greets his return home after failing to find Molloy: 'Here is something I can study all my life, and never understand'. But it is also Beckett's most intimate and passionate achievement ('little book all my own the heart's outpourings', 92) and, for anyone who penetrates its daunting exterior, surprisingly simple and straightforward. 'My work', Beckett wrote to Alan Schneider a short time before he began to make preliminary sketches for the novel, 'is a matter of fundamental sounds (no pun intended) made as fully as possible'.[1] It is easy with hindsight to accuse Beckett of being disingenuous here — *Comment c'est* is, after all, a pun on *commencer* (or *commencez*) and Pim's fundament is much in evidence — but it is clear that the work is as fundamental a sound as Beckett has ever made, a work beside which the 'fizzles' are indeed little more than attempts to 'break wind noiselessly'. If there are very good reasons why *How It Is* cannot be expected to please as wide an audience as *Godot* or *Murphy*, there are equally good grounds for believing that, like another magisterial work (to which Beckett owes much), it will 'fit audience find, though few' (*Paradise Lost*, VII, 31) in anyone prepared to submit themselves to the rigour of reading it.

Beckett has made the reading of *How It Is* as arduous as the experience portrayed within it and as obsessive as the labour with which he worked on it. Even a casual reader cannot help but be struck by the sheer strangeness of the printed pages that comprise what the French original (though not the English translation) innocently describes as a 'novel'. It is a much more strenuous and prolonged exercise in 'de-familiarization' than any of Beckett's subsequent prose works can match, and yet a work which reveals its guiding principles with a disarming casualness that makes even *Molloy* seem insinuating by comparison. The narrator's elaborate humility before Heraclitus the Obscure (38) reminds us that — though Watt might disagree — 'obscure keys' may be less useful, in opening obscure locks, than simple ones (cf. *W*, 122). An enquirer's 'why is it . . . ?' is continually being rendered pointless by the narrator's imperturbable demonstration of 'how it is'.

For a book whose action (or hypothesized action) takes place in 'primeval mud impenetrable dark' (12), *How It Is* is remarkably crystalline, with each phrasal unit identifying itself as a separate item and each of the 'three parts' distinguished by different rhythms of speech and silence and different thematic concerns. It has the same clarity and decisiveness as Leopardi's poem *A se stesso* (long a favourite of Beckett's), from which he took the epigraph for his first book *Proust* and to which *How It Is* forms a kind of gloss. '*E fango è il mondo*' wrote Leopardi; for Beckett too, the world has become *fango*, mud. But the parallel with Leopardi extends further, for it is clear that Beckett is, like the gloomy Italian, addressing his remarks to himself, *a se stesso*, in the absence of anyone with whom he might communicate more normally. The 'invocation' with which the work begins is not, as in Milton, addressed to Urania and the Muses, but to himself, so as to announce his 'vocation', call himself into existence and constitute himself at the centre of the work. Beckett's opening is both splendidly direct and disconcertingly oblique, with the phrase 'tell me again finish telling me' interpretable as both a self-addressed injunction (the product of the 'voice once without . . . then in me') and also as a remark addressed to an Other (from whose discourse 'I quote' and 'say it as I hear it'). Even the tone of voice is ambiguous, a strange mixture of urgency and weariness, according to whether one regards the 'me' as subject or object of the utterance. Beckett's 'beginnings' are usually less innocent than they appear, but it is doubtful if he has ever been more subtle in embodying the essence of what follows than at the opening of *How It Is*.

But the opening of *How it is* is, like Molloy's 'beginning', posterior to the events that are described in the 'novel' proper: 'I quote a given moment long past . . . on from there that moment and following'. Despite the 'losses everywhere' that make this narrative even more 'ill-said ill-heard ill-recaptured ill-murmured' than Sam's account in *Watt*, it is 'preferable' to have it 'recorded . . . somehow somewhere', both 'as it stands' (as a finished sequence) and 'as it comes' (as the sequence about to unfold). It is not therefore perverse to begin a work purporting to record 'how it is' with the words 'how it was'; for we are confronted on the first page with the fragmentary 'scraps of an ancient voice' and on the last page we are reminded 'that's how it was'. This ancient voice, or 'what remains of it', faces the same problem Molloy faced, a decade previously: 'My life, my life, now I speak of it as of something over, now as of a joke which still goes on, and it is neither, for at the same time it is over and it goes on, and is there any tense for that?' (*TN*, 36). Molloy discovers that there is not, for despite his penchant for the 'mythological present' (*TN*, 26), he is continually reverting to the imperfect and other past tenses. In *How It Is* Beckett discovers that there is a way of dealing with 'my life' as 'something over . . . which still goes on', and that it is more than merely a question of tense that is involved. In *How It Is* each verset has its own brief existence and yet contributes to a sequential unravelling of material. By eroding the substantiality of the paragraph (which remains the staple of the trilogy, notwithstanding Molloy's, and the Unnamable's disregard for normal distribution), Beckett contrives to make each verset seem both an end in itself and part of a greater whole. The French title could hardly be more apt here, for the book is always beginning again and ending again a few words later, and hence the speaker's life seems very much like 'something over . . . which still goes on'.

It would be misleading, however, to suggest that *How It Is* has only one solution to Molloy's problem, for it is a work that decisively solves Beckett's difficulties with that 'double-headed monster Time' that have tormented him for so long. Time has ceased to be the almost exclusively temporal issue that it was in *Texts for Nothing*. It is not so much in *Text 8* as in *How It Is* that time may truly be said to have 'become space', for each verset occupies its own space on the page, and behind each utterance — as we are continually reminded — lie 'vast *tracts* of time' (my italics). Purely temporal specifications are

therefore attended with more than the usual difficulty that attaches to
the Beckett hero's struggles with what preceded what and what came
after; in *How It Is* there is no stability of tense enabling us to repose
securely in an ordered pattern of existence. The 'past moments old
dreams' (7) are 'fresh like those that pass' (7) and at the moment of
being remembered seem not so much past and old as present and now.
Beckett concludes the first 'image' in part one with a finality that
severs the present decisively from the past:

> . . . saying to myself you're no worse and was worse

> I pissed and shat another image in my crib never so clean since (9)

But increasingly, in the knowledge that 'the images will cease' (11),
Beckett uses the present tense to show how great the nostalgia for the
former life, 'above in the light', can be. This enables him to create a
composite 'image of the moment' (17) which is both real and unreal,
enduring and evanescent, an image of how it is, if not quite an
accurate statement of how it was.

Beckett sees the 'image' as a category distinct from the categories of
'dream' and 'memory'. But even the images cannot really be said to
utter 'how it is', for — as the reference to tins suggests — they have no
more substance than celluloid, and will have to be abandoned:

> that's all it wasn't a dream I didn't dream that nor a memory I haven't
> been given memories this time it was an image the kind I see sometimes
> see in the mud part one sometimes saw

> with the gesture of one dealing cards and also to be observed among
> certain sowers of seed I throw away the empty tins they fall without a
> sound (11)

The image of the sower here may make us think of the moment in
Enough when the narrator says, 'Stony ground but not entirely' for,
despite such details as 'sheep like granite outcrops' (34) and despite the
strangely mechanical movements that dominate the images — the
table gliding 'from light to darkness to light' (11), the biting and
swallowing of the 'love-idyll' (31-35) — there is a vibrancy about the
images that makes life in the mud seem ponderous and impoverished.
This is partly because the mental projector is subject to sudden
accelerations of tempo:

> I don't move her anxiety grows she suddenly leaves the house and runs
> to friends (11)

> suddenly yip left right off we go . . .

> suddenly we are eating sandwiches . . . (33)

But these abrupt alterations are congenital to the psyche of the Beckett hero, as *From an Abandoned Work*, with its sudden rages and bursts of speed, reminds us. In *How It Is* Beckett suggests that sudden spurts are forced upon him by the rudimentary syntax he is working with: 'suddenly like all that was not then is I go . . . sudden series subject object subject object quick succession and away' (12). The 'quick succession' with which the unpunctuated words of *How It Is* break upon us conceals the slow and patient labour that Beckett has expended in bringing the words into existence. The locomotor ataxy which afflicts his protagonist's attempts at movement ('semi-side right left leg left arm push pull') is a severely decelerated analogue of the accelerated images, reminding us that the mechanism of syntax, when it becomes an object of scrutiny, is as miraculous and complicated as the phenomenon of walking. In *How It Is* Beckett is moving away from the visual and towards the verbal, which is why the 'images' have to cease; he becomes less concerned with *seeing* how it is and more concerned with *saying* how it is. The act of writing on Pim's back supersedes the celluloid fantasies of 'before Pim'. The tins that make no sound (silent movies) can only express 'how it was' not 'how it is'; despite his persistent erosion of the surface of the text with silence, Beckett's obsession in *How It Is* is very obviously with language.

It remains important, however, to take cognizance of 'how it was' and to see what role the images play in the overall scheme of *How It Is*. The images of part one represent not just a profound nostalgia for a world of light in which colour and contour are restored to prominence, but also a deep need to people the solitude with relationships that once were meaningful. The central figure in the most poignant images is a woman, as later with Pam Prim in hospital in part two, and in the case of the third image (16-17), and possibly the second (11), the woman is Beckett's own mother.[2] As in the first image, where a child peers 'through my spy-glass sidelong', there is no reciprocity between the woman and the protagonist. In the second, the woman's initial perception ('all is well he is working') modulates into a realization that all is far from well, at which point she abandons her aloofness and runs to friends, her failure to 'call me by my name' the indirect cause of the speaker's 'death'. In the third, the woman plays the role of educator, as the protagonist later will in relation to Pim, but (again as with Pim) there is no real harmony in the relationship:

> . . . she closes her eyes and drones a snatch of the so-called Apostles'
> Creed I steal a look at her lips

> she stops her eyes burn down on me again I cast up mine in haste and
> repeat awry (17)

The protagonist knows 'even then' that the religion of his mother
cannot solace him; the 'huge head hatted with birds and flowers', the
smothering verbena, and the nightshirt that 'whelms' him are more
substantial than 'the sky whence cometh our help'. But the child sees
at the same time how ridiculous and constricting these insignia of
bourgeois convention can be, and knows that everything (not just the
eyes of his mother that 'burn with severe love') 'with time shall pass
away'. Beckett conflates past and present by abolishing the image and
thus reminding us of the brevity of life, for scarcely any time has
passed since the suggestion that things will 'pass away'. He is careful
to let the scene speak for itself and thus increase the vividness of the
memory, so that the disappearance of the image is something of a
shock: 'that's all it goes out like a lamp blown out' (17). But the next
verset glosses the image implicitly, with its allusion to the poem 'je
suis ce cours . . .' of 1948: 'the space of a moment the passing moment
that's all my past' (17). In the poem Beckett's life is 'the space of a door
that opens and shuts', brief and mechanical and repetitive. In the
novel Beckett's life is as brief as his mother's, and no more repeatable
than hers.

In the fourth image the little boy has become 'a small old man' (20)
with his head in his hands, overcome by the misery of the world. But
the image is brief, cut short by an act of appropriation that will allow
Beckett to develop the tears and laughter that are the 'heart' of his
work. It would be wrong to imagine that in *How It Is* we find
'deterioration of the sense of humour fewer tears too' (20). The
anguished plea to Thalia for 'a leaf of thine ivy' (42) is followed
immediately by a hilarious reference to Abraham's bosom and the
work as a whole has more instances of wild humour[3] than any other
book of Beckett's.

The fifth image is similarly brief and therefore aptly compared to
'rags' (23) since it is never in any sense as substantial as the second or
the third image. The mention of the hand that keeps a yellow crocus
in sunlight by tweaking the string that connects the two items
contrasts with the hand that Beckett has insistently referred to some

pages earlier; the one is involved, like the writing hand, in a mechanical operation, the other 'free' to approach the face and draw a 'curtain' across the eyes (15). But once again the items called up by the image ('long' in time (22) but short in space) perish and vanish, reminding us implicitly that it is *ars* as well as *vita* that is *brevis*.

The sixth image (24) is briefer still, and invites comparison with the image of Pam Prim in hospital in part two (85). But there the colour white predominates, whereas here the protagonist is struck by analogies between the moments of darkness above and the impenetrable darkness below. The seventh image (30-35), by far the longest, offers a picture of adolescent appetitiveness that is both touching and revolting, 'fine' (30) and 'very pretty' (35) in its way but also 'not like that' as well, and ultimately too picturesque and euphoric to be confused with real life ('it doesn't happen like that'). Beckett is reworking here the situation of the poem 'Arènes de Lutèce' against a distinctively Irish background of 'emerald grass' and the Leopardstown racecourse (32), with the steeples of Dun Laoghaire (33) that feature in so many Beckett works. Of all the images this gives the protagonist the greatest pleasure, but at the cost (as with Krapp) of reminding him how appallingly lonely he is: '. . . I realize I'm still smiling there's no sense in that now been none for a long time now' (34). Like Krapp, the protagonist seeks obsessively to call back this image of happiness, but unlike Krapp he realizes that the image (like the previous ones) must be made to disappear if the speaker is to come to terms with his solitude:

> . . . perhaps we shall come back it will be dusk the earth of childhood glimmering again streaks of dying amber in a murk of ashes the earth must have been on fire when I see us we are already at hand
>
> it is dusk we are going tired home I see only the naked parts the solidary faces raised to the east the pale swaying of the mingled hands tired and slow we toil up towards me and vanish
>
> the arms in the middle go through me and part of the bodies shades through a shade the scene is empty in the mud the sky goes out the ashes darken no world left for me now but mine . . . (35)

This 'last' image (31) — there are only fragments of image thereafter — cures the protagonist of the desire to revisit the past and makes him realize that these nostalgic excursions are increasing rather than decreasing his suffering. The 'mingled hands' make one think of the banished Adam and Eve leaving paradise for the fallen world, and the earth on fire suggests the cities of the plain that were given over (as in

Proust's great work) to fleshly lusts and lecheries. The protagonist of
How It Is is exorcizing these appetites just as earlier he was exorcizing
his appetite for alimentary sustenance ('I'll never die of hunger', 8), but
the images and dreams that he calls up give him 'food for thought' and
the knowledge that (given his complete loss of appetite there is
'something wrong there', 8). There is 'something wrong' with all the
images, and what is wrong with them is that they recall to life a figure
who is intent on being dead: 'ah these sudden blazes in the head as
empty and dark as the heart can desire then suddenly like a handful of
shavings aflame the spectacle then' (38). The visual 'spectacle'
obviously does not provide the same solace as the sound of a clinking
tin: 'not a sound and I listen not a gleam and I strain my eyes . . . my
only season [cf. the poem 'vive morte ma seule saison'] . . . a tin clinks
first respite very first from the silence of this black sap' (27). Beckett is
preparing us here for the sounds that dominate part two, as the
'spectacles' (the images and the 'big scene of the sack' 39) have
dominated part one. The heart, no doubt the one appropriated from
the figure in the fourth image (20), has only one desire left, to be
'empty and dark'. But the head refuses to be 'dead' (18) and keeps
performing the 'little miracle' (39) that the Occasionalist philosophers
thought only God could perform.

It is thanks to this little miracle that the protagonist can 'live on'.
But it is only a little miracle and it is therefore no surprise to find the
'ancient voice' changing it to 'lived on', to remind us firstly that it once
provided sustenance which is now no longer needed, and secondly
that it is a thing of the past which he has now very sensibly abandoned.
The dream of Jesus which occurs when the protagonist falls 'asleep
within humanity again just barely' (50) is not the only 'image not for
the eyes made of words not for the ears' (51); all the images are
diaphanous and insubstantial. The head still requires a 'pillow' of
those 'old words' that Watt was in such great need of (*W*, 115). At this
point Beckett repeats the 'old words' of Hamm at the end of
Endgame ('old stancher, you remain', *EG*, 53), in order to remind us
that fiction (the fiction of Pim, as it turns out) is a way of 're-
integrating the matrix'[4] that has been severed by being born. But
fiction necessarily consists of 'old words'. Not until part three will
new words begin to fill the space left vacant by the images of part one,
and confirm that 'there is more nourishment in a cry nay a sigh torn
from one whose only good is silence . . . than sardines can ever offer'
(157). Until that time the narrator cannot constitute himself in any

meaningful way. He is a 'tenement of naught' (40), whose 'imprecations' make 'no sound' (45), lukewarm (or 'luke', 48) like those in Dante's 'outer hell'. Only if he can succeed in 'saying something to myself' — 'a little pearl of forlorn solace' — will he be able to turn his tenement of naught into what Donne called a 'dialogue of one'.[5]

Part two of *How It Is* shows how these solaces — 'marguerites from the latin pearl' (85) — are thoroughly 'forlorn' and ultimately only 'lies' (94). Yet the speaker is as intent as the Winnie of *Happy Days* on finding part two 'a happy time in its way' (57), and it is the only moment in the book when the speaker's appalling loneliness appears to disappear. It may be perverse of the speaker to think of part one (before Pim) as a 'golden age' in which 'I was young I clung on on to the species . . . the human' (52), but in part two (a decidedly more iron age) we are faced with an anguished self-laceration in which he 'clings on', quite literally, to the human species (through the figure of Pim), and yet almost forfeits the right to be considered human. The 'losses of species' (52) are not confined to part one, with its allusions to alpaca llamas (15) and the natural historian Haeckel (47); in part two the speaker commits atrocities of an inhuman kind on a figure as helpless and confused as himself (who is, in fact, himself). Pim is not the kind of 'other' who can provide the 'comfort' wished for at the end of part one; he is merely the self in its role of victim responding to the self in its role of tormentor. The 'species' are in this sense indeed lost, no longer distinct, and the 'loss of species' is an essential pre-condition to realizing that the self, however manifold in aspect, is solitary in essence. The focus in part two is on one single substantial delusion — the figure of Pim, a projection mistaken for an 'other' — whereas in part one the delusions (as represented by the 'images') were multiple and insubstantial. The mangled quotation of Dante's most celebrated line at the end of part one — 'abandoned here effect of hope' (52) — seems designed to remind us that the abandonment of the images (and images generally) is essential if anything resembling hope is to be restored. But it also serves to remind us of how 'abandoned' the protagonist is, and it hangs, like Dante's warning, at the portals of a dreadful inferno (part two, with Pim). It is only in the second part that the speaker realizes that 'others' are a fabrication designed to solace the solitary ˙self, and that the hope of company will have to be eternally abandoned.

Part two of *How It Is* is Beckett's most sustained attempt to demolish the distinction between subject and object that has intrigued him all

his life. In 'Sanies 1' (in *Echo's Bones*) and the fourth *Text for Nothing*
Beckett stresses the fact that the self is an object as well as a subject
and that — once it has cast itself in the 'accusative' role — it cannot be
other than guilty: guilty of not-being, guilty of not being the subject.
In part one of *How It Is* the speaker hypothesizes five categories of
'others' who have made him into an object and borne witness to his
existence. The culmination of this idea occurs when the speaker offers
himself as a subject ('I'), an object ('me') and an objective subject ('he'):
'if they see me I am a monster of the solitudes he sees man for the first
time and does not flee before him . . .' (14). Beckett's irony is multiple
here, for he is able to attack those critics who, 'knowing nothing of my
life', invent pretentious magazine headlines ('a monster of the
solitudes' indeed!) and at the same time stress the humaneness of his
enterprise ('he sees man for the first time . . .'). He is also, of course,
alerting us to the 'monster' his protagonist will become in part two
when *he* 'sees man for the first time' (or thinks he does) in the form of
the self-projection Pim.

It would be incorrect to assume from this, however, that Beckett's
attitude to 'others' is the same as Sartre's in *Huis clos*. For Beckett hell
is not so much other people as oneself; the truly infernal experience is
to be immured in one's own consciousness with one's own illusory
companions. At the end of part one, just prior to the crucial conjur-
ation of a fictitious 'other' (the arrival of Pim) Beckett reminds us that
'in adversity others what comfort' (53), and demonstrates that only an
irremediably solitary self could take much comfort from thinking of
itself as 'me sole elect'. At the same time we realize that 'others' are not
merely, and not necessarily, a 'comfort', for they make demands on us
that we cannot satisfy and provoke us to acts of violence that we
cannot undo. In trying to account for the voice which seems so
'ancient' that it can hardly belong to him, the protagonist is driven to
postulate generations of Krams and Krims who care only for making
an accurate transcription of the protagonist's suffering and are
uninterested in trying to ameliorate it. Later on, in trying to account
for the justice or otherwise of the world as he visualizes it, the
protagonist is driven to postulate a single and omnipotent Other of
Godlike proportions, whose mercy seems thoroughly arbitrary and
random and who is quite as inhuman as his minions Kram and Krim.
But it is revealed in part three that these ideas of an Other are ways in
which the isolated Self conceals from itself 'the issueless predicament
of existence'[6], and this is why there is so much violence and inhu-

manity in the central episode of part two, the encounter with Pim.

The speaker has yet to realize that he is thoroughly alone, and yet has to be seen to succumb to the desire for company. This is why part two concerns itself with two issues which part one considers have 'ceased to be of interest' (23): the question of 'who is speaking' (23) and the struggle to attain selfhood ('is it me is it me', 18). For despite the protagonist's false humility — 'my part now the utility man's' (58) — and his elaborate withdrawals — 'how I can efface myself behind my creature' (58) — most of part two is devoted to the demonstration that the victim (Pim) and the tormentor (Bom) are one and the same person. In this regard, of course, the two questions which part one regards as no longer relevant ('who is speaking?' and 'is it me?') are still not relevant, for if there is only one person there it must be 'me' and if a voice can be heard it must be 'mine'. But these are conclusions that the protagonist does not wish to reach, indicative as they are of his utter loneliness and introversion. The exchange of names that initiates the relationship between the 'utility man' and his 'creature' offers abundant testimony of how the protagonist's reluctance to relinquish the idea of a companion is balanced squarely against his implicit acknowledgement that Pim is nothing but a wish-fulfilment:

> . . . he had no name any more than I so I gave him one the name Pim for more commodity more convenience . . .

> . . . . . .

> when this has sunk in I let him know that I too Pim my name Pim there he has more difficulty a moment of confusion irritation it's understandable . . .

> . . . . . .

> the one I'm waiting for oh not that I believe in him . . . he can call me Bom for more commodity that would appeal to me m at the end and one syllable the rest indifferent (66-67)

It is clear, despite the speaker's exaggerated indifference to the problem of naming, that this is a matter of some concern to him; later indeed, in part three, his concern increases to manic proportions with all possible permutations of Pim, Bom and Bem (122-24) considered, and 'commodity' and 'convenience' forgotten. But at the same time all names are plainly arbitrary in a situation where there is really only one person, and where that person is, like his predecessor, un-namable. The protagonist erects his personal preference into a rule —

'm at the end and one syllable the rest indifferent' — and shows considerable inventiveness in fitting Kram, Krim, Pam Prim and even a dog called Skom Skum within this rubric; but all these instances only serve to obscure the self that lies behind them. It may be true that the controlled proliferation of proper names ending in 'm' makes reading *How It Is* 'more convenien[t]' for the reader. But the transformations are taking place in an area adjacent to the real problem: the one syllable word with 'm' at the end that is crucial — 'am' — is not a proper name at all. The name Pim, like the name Bom, makes the protagonist 'less anonymous . . . less obscure', but only on a superficial level, and neither is of much assistance in stating 'how it is', which is essentially an 'anonymous' utterance of the verb 'to be', without reference to Pims and Boms. Beckett brilliantly conveys both the necessity and the absurdity of these strange monosyllabic projections; and treats them with more variety than he is able to bring to bear on later important monosyllables (the 'ping' of *Ping*, for example). But this may be because in *How It Is* the idea of 'life', however minimal, remains a possibility. The first name the protagonist scores on the backside of his victim (not 'Pim' but 'BOM', as if to bring his name closer to the object it is written on) has a substantive quality that elevates it above all the previous material in the book and, as the narrator quickly realizes, it 'oblige[s] me to have had a life' (67), even if it is only 'a life I'm said to have' (67). *Ping*, by contrast, or *Imagination Dead Imagine* are works in which there is 'no trace anywhere of life' in the sense in which the word is used in *How It Is*.

The double discourse of *How It Is* — the staple unpunctuated prose and the occasional capitalized elements — dramatically illustrates Beckett's inability to believe in anything enduring and substantial. At the end of parts two and three the capitalized elements are swamped by a flood of yesses and noes that break upon the 'Roman capitals' (69) like waves. Beckett is commenting here, as elsewhere, on the relationship between head and heart, for the 'capitals' are (as the etymology of the word suggests) products of intellection, like the 'capitals' that decorate a pillar, whereas 'yes' and 'no' are much more 'fundamental sounds'. Beckett's attitude to the device of capitalization suggests that he is more than a little antagonistic to what most readers of *How It Is* would regard as its most striking feature. The 'Roman capitals' are, despite their novelty, only another version of what Beckett calls, in *Text 11* as here, 'the old road' (68), the old Roman road in fact, without the chevrons (53) and zigzags (52) that the modern road (and modern fiction) has. 'There are times', Beckett wrote in 1938 in a parody of Stendhal, 'even in Europe, when the road reflects better than the mirror'[7], but by the time of *How It Is* the Roman road is as anachronistic as any of the other appurtenances of culture. The 'stoic love' (69) that the protagonist refers to is actually a species of self-love; it may be 'stoic' of the self-as-victim to endure it, but it is hardly 'stoic' of the self-as-tormentor to enjoy it. There is a marked absence of the Stoic ethic of *apatheia* in the relationship between Pim and Bom, however 'classical' or 'decadent' the cruelty may seem. (It is interesting to note, by the way, that the 'yellow book' that makes one think of the 'Nineties is 'not the voice of here', 91.) The Pim-Bom symbiosis is in fact, like the mud, 'primeval' (12), primitive, barbarian, the product of emotional needs, and not (like Stoicism) a sophisticated code of conduct. Beckett is not, despite appearances, the 'stoic comedian' that Hugh Kenner (among others) thinks he is; he is a modern tragicomedian as the subtitle to *Waiting for Godot* suggests. The 'Roman capitals' are 'fables' (69) of 'the old road' (68); the 'new life', by contrast, like Celia's for Murphy, 'must be true' (69). The 'life in common' with Pim is an 'orgy of false being' (76) as pointless as the orgies of the Rome of the Decadence. In the end there is indeed 'only one kind of talk here' (84); even the capitalized sections are enunciated in the 'midget grammar' (84) of the lower case portions.

The encounter with Pim towards which part one has pointed so assiduously — a technique reminiscent of that in *Murphy* which suggests that 'section six' will solve all difficulties — remains the centre of *How It Is*, in emotional as well as structural terms. In part three, just before the demolition of the structure, the speaker is prepared to countenance any rearrangement of material predicated upon the inviolability of the encounter at the centre: 'on condition that by an effort of the imagination the still central episode of the couple be duly adjusted' (144). 'Still central', of course, in the sense of 'always' rather than 'tranquil' and 'always' central because the encounter is an education for the protagonist as much as it ever is for Pim. Bom (if we may call him that) has to learn that 'here all self to be abandoned' (91) if 'how it is' is to be objectively stated, and also that to 'say nothing when nothing' (91) is not only possible — as it was not in *Texts for Nothing* — but necessary. Pim has indeed 'finished me' (95), as the opening versets of part three conclusively show. After Pim, and Bom's treatment of him, the substantial self has become, like the bones of

Echo without Narcissus, mere voice:

> . . . I've seen myself quite clear ever since nothing left but voice

> . . . nothing left but words . . . (103-4)

Part two of *How It Is* is Beckett's most intransigent critique of 'how it is' in a world given over to violence and timidity. For behind the essentially private struggle between Pim and Bom lurks the essentially public issue of dominance and subordination, free-will and determinism. The suffering of the Bom-Pim figure is beyond the remedies and consolations of culture, which have become fragments that will not shore up the ruins of personality. Culture is very much a matter of 'how it was' for this figure: 'the humanities *I had* my God and with that flashes of geography' (47); 'the anatomy *I had*' (my italics in both cases). At the same time he cannot deny that his culture has made him what he is: 'it's not said where on earth I can have received my education acquired my notions of mathematics astronomy and even physics they have marked me that's the main thing' (45). They have marked him indelibly, of course; he can only rid himself of 'categories of being' (15) — later identified as 'useful necessary beautiful' (51) — by handing them on to another, and marking him likewise. The 'dream' of hearing 'a human voice' that will absolve him of his loneliness founders in violence and self-delusion. Part two of *How It Is* is certainly 'more fertile in vicissitudes and peripeteias' (62), but the 'early days . . . prior to the script' are more 'heroic', and the golden age of part one, where Bom travelled hopefully against tremendous odds, is more 'heroic' still.

It would be wrong, of course, to see part two in exclusively cultural terms, just as it would be wrong to see it as a kind of gloss on Kafka's *In the Penal Colony*, which it superficially resembles. It is not a piece of special pleading when Beckett tells us that the Pim-Bom relationship is not 'sadism pure and simple' (70) and reminds us: 'what but words could be involved in the case of Pim'. Beckett's humour is as evident here as in the violent education of Molloy's mother, and more carefully controlled, as when the speaker thinks to himself 'if I have to learn Italian obviously it will be less amusing' (63) — a remark which not only brilliantly encapsulates the problems everyone faces since Adam said 'goo to a goose' (*OE*, 20) and the problems Beckett himself faced as a student of Italian at Trinity, but suggests at the same time that Dante's grim masterpiece — which contains sufferings infinitely worse than those inflicted on Pim by Bom — will inevitably be on the syllabus. The critique of culture in part two, the fascination with 'the savage economy of hieroglyphs' (*OE*, 15) very obviously lies behind the dominant feature of part three, mathematical calculation.

Here Beckett tries to do what he accused Descartes, in the notes to *Whoroscope*, of doing: proving God 'by exhaustion'. Beckett knows that such a strategy cannot be successful, and has already provided a gloss on the futility of such an exercise in part two: '. . . Krim says his number's up so is mine . . . quick all numbers up it's the only solution' (84). The absurd calculations of part three demonstrate with unanswerable finality that this is indeed the only solution, however equivocal it may seem. (Beckett is revivifying a dead metaphor for death and seems almost to be recommending, von Hartmann fashion, universal suicide.) Mathematics appears to offer the kind of refuge in which suffering may be subsumed into abstract patterns, but it is exposed here as a myth which is quite as illusory as the religion it has supplanted. Beckett registers his aggrieved disappointment in the phrase 'I always loved arithmetic it has paid me back in full' (41). The calculations may seem to be 'correct' (they are superficially more correct than Sam's calculations regarding the Lynch family); they even provide much-needed relief from the reiteration that there is 'something wrong there'. But the more complicated the calculations become, the more remote they are from the protagonist's real situation, from 'how it is'. In this respect they are like all the other false constructs that part three of *How It Is* reveals to be 'all balls'.

It becomes clear in part three, as the versets dwindle to a trickle of single phrases, that all ideas of order, however consoling, must be finally abandoned in the face of the 'mess' of existence.[8] The imagination is not, of course, as 'spent' as the speaker would have us believe; if it were truly exhausted, there would be no 'formulation' whatever, 'present' or otherwise. The 'alternations of history prophecy and latest news ' (141) are indeed 'refreshing' in their way, however derisory it may be to introduce temporal constraints into an essentially timeless continuum. Even a narrative as rudimentary as this cannot subsist without subdivisions of some kind, and 'the idea of the three books' is not in fact 'set aside' quite so decisively as it might have been. It is difficult not to feel that Beckett is comparing his triadic structure with the four books of *Finnegans Wake* which allowed Joyce to present a cyclical Vichian view of time and — without of course going so far as to take Joyce to task — presenting an alternative, atomistic one. By comparison with Joyce's book, *How It Is* is truly 'in

danger of being incomplete' (142) and from the perspective of Vico it
is arguable that 'of our total life it states only three quarters' (142). But
it succeeds by saying in its stead that 'of the four three quarters of our
total life only three lend themselves to communication' (143) and is
therefore 'equally defendable' on its own terms. Beckett simplifies the
elaborate paraphernalia of Joyce's compendious account and
substitutes something less removed from the common experience of
humanity.

There are moments when we detect the presence of a writer who
knew too much about history to theorize about it, the Apollinaire of
'Le Pont Mirabeau', the haunting refrain from which lies behind 'time
passes I remain' (36). There are moments too, when Beckett offers us
his own hilariously mangled version of the consoling Vichian system:
'abject abject ages each heroic seen from the next when will the last
come when was my golden every rat has its heyday . . .' (10). In the
absence of at least two of Vico's four Ages — the Theocratic and the
providential *ricorso* to the Theocratic — it is natural that the speaker
should cling to the idea of the Heroic and the Human that are (to
modify Beckett's own extravagant metaphor at Vico's expense; *OE*, 4)
the meat of the Vichian sandwich. But the only Golden Age for
Beckett is (as the truncated phrase in the above quotation suggests)
one in which history (and narrative) may be brought to an end.
Beckett's atomism is essentially apocalyptic. It is indeed 'thanks to the
sack that I keep dying in a dying age' (18), for the sack (as Ruby Cohn[9]
has shown) will go on providing him with material for continuance for
as long as he chooses to rely on it. It is the sack which keeps him
'variable' (18) as distinct from definitive. It is only a sleep as absolute
as that of death which may be regarded as a 'good' thing (40).

We can hardly forbear from recalling here Goya's celebrated
(though ambiguous) dictum that 'the sleep of reason brings forth
monsters'. And yet for Beckett, who is less Enlightened, the monsters
come forth when he emerges from sleep: 'if ever mute laugh I wake
forthwith catastrophe' (36). The real courage of part three is that
Beckett awakes to face catastrophe and take comfort from what
catastrophe can offer. In his words, the 'eyes that dare open stay open'
(94) as Mr Kelly's eyes in *Murphy* did not, and as even the eyes in *For to
End Yet Again* have difficulty doing. There are moments in part one
where mortality is something to be feared: 'I call it [the hand] it doesn't
come I can't live without it I call it with all my strength it's not strong
enough I grow mortal again' (16). But by the time of part three

'growing mortal again' has become something to be desired and 'all these words' are seen to be 'too strong almost all a little too strong' (124).

It is helpful here to remember that in *Dream of Fair to Middling Women* Beckett confessed to a 'strong weakness' for the caesura that gives a line of Racine its power.[10] In *How It Is*, by contrast, Beckett is more interested in the 'weak strength' that will allow him to repose in something more final than a caesura. It can hardly be coincidental that, in a conversation of 1962, Beckett told Lawrence Harvey of how he hoped to develop a 'syntax of weakness' more serviceable even than the 'métier qu'insinue plus qu'il n'affirme'[11] that he relied on in the writings of 1947-50. For a 'syntax of weakness' to properly emerge words have to be recognized as the 'truant guides' (101) they are, and the violence at the end of *How It Is* may stem from Beckett's reluctance to accept this. Within twenty pages of the end he reminds us 'we're still talking of my life' (141) when we are in fact talking of his death and experiencing a verbal *rigor mortis*.

The end of *How It Is* is Beckett's gloss on Milton's paradise regained and Proust's time regained; it represents 'humanity regained' (30), and involves rejection of 'a past a present and a future something wrong there' (141). There is an immense relief in reaching the 'end of quotation' that marks the termination of fictional life and the inception of 'how it is'. The violence of the demonstration that all has been false conceals the fact that it is a precondition of establishing what is true. The inscriptions with which *How It Is* concludes signify not so much the arrival of another tormentor as the resolution of the dichotomies and trichotomies that have prevailed up to this point. Despite its overtones of crucifixion (and in a sense because of them) the end of *How it is* is a kind of birth, with its own distinctive labour pains. In acknowledging the voice as 'mine yes not another's' (160) whereas at the start it was 'in me not mine' (9), the speaker finds his own voice at last and becomes the 'different man more universal' (74) that he had earlier despaired of becoming. The last verset begins with a subjective cry ('good good') and ends with an objective statement ('how it is'). But the two are really indistinguishable by now. 'Narrator' and 'narrated' cannot here be separated. Beckett's writing here, to adopt his emotional defence of Joyce, is 'not about something: *it is that something itself*. The realization that 'this solitude when the voice recounts it' is the 'sole means of living it' (141) is superseded by the realization that, when the voice stops recounting it, there is a way of departing from life altogether.

The end of *How It Is* is moving beyond words, yet only words. The 'script' (67) of a life has been uttered and made permanent by print. Almost alone among Beckett's works *How It Is* makes the distinction between manuscript and published text seem somehow irrelevant; it possesses the immediacy and personality of the former and the clarity and objectivity of the latter, and shows — to use Beckett's words on his friend Arikha's experiments in another medium — the 'deep marks' of 'what it is to be and be in face of'. It must strike any sympathetic reader of *How It Is* as consummately ironic that, speaking of his translation from the French, Beckett felt that the English language had seduced him, as in the days before he adopted French, into saying more than he meant to say.[12] For it is precisely the infinite suggestibility of *How It Is* that gives its 'marks' a depth and subtlety that few, if any, of Beckett's other works can equal.

Notes

1. Letter of 29 December 1957 to Alan Schneider; *The Village Voice*, March 19, 1958, p. 15.
2. The third 'image' describes a well-known photograph of Beckett, reproduced in *Beckett at Sixty*, London, Calder and Boyars, 1967, opposite p. 24.
3. E.g. The Paolo and Francesca allusion (40), the autobiographical (?) reminiscence (41), the philosophical *hauteur* of the disquisition on sponges (43), the absurd dignity of Bom (67), the parody of the Trinity (122), sudden scatological intrusions (144), bizarre clichés (147), etc.
4. Quoted from the unpublished story 'Echo's Bones' (c. 1934) in the L. Harvey Collection, Dartmouth College Library, Hanover, New Hampshire.
5. J. Donne, 'The Extasie', line 74.
6. 'MacGreevy on Yeats', *Irish Times*, 4 August 1945, p. 2.
7. Quoted from the unpublished essay 'Les Deux Besoins' (c. 1938) in the L. Harvey Collection, Dartmouth College Library, Hanover, New Hampshire.
8. See the interview with Driver; L. Graver and R. Federman, *Samuel Beckett: the Critical Heritage*, p. 219.
9. See R. Cohn, 'Comment c'est: de quoi rire', *French Review*, XXXV (May, 1962), pp. 563-9.
10. For Beckett's affinities with Racine, see V. Mercier, *Beckett/Beckett*, New York, Oxford University Press, 1977, pp. 74-84.
11. 'La peinture des van Velde ou le monde et le pantalon', *Cahiers d'Art*, 20-21, 1945-6, p. 354.
12. See Raymond Federman, 'Samuel Beckett's Fiction since *Comment c'est*', *L'Esprit Créateur*, Vol. XI, no. 3, Fall 1971, p. 28.

Drama after *Endgame*

Krapp's Last Tape

Beckett first heard the Irish actor, Patrick Magee, reading some extracts from *Molloy* and *From an Abandoned Work* on the BBC Third Programme in December 1957. He was impressed and moved by the distinctive cracked quality of Magee's voice which seemed to capture a sense of deep world-weariness, sadness, ruination and regret. Two months later, he began to write a dramatic monologue for a character who was described in the first draft as a 'wearish old man' with a 'wheezy ruined old voice with some characteristic accent'.[1] For some time, in fact, the play was simply referred to by Beckett as the *Magee Monologue* until, several versions later, he conferred on the failing old man the harsh sounding name of 'Krapp' with unpleasant e.cremental associations that lead its owner and the watching audience back to a decaying, disgusting, yet still demanding body with which Krapp has tried in vain to come to terms all his life. 'What's a year now?' Krapp asks himself, as he sets down on magnetic tape an annual retrospective review of his sixty-ninth year: 'The sour cud and the iron stool' (*Krapp's Last Tape and Embers*, Faber and Faber, London, 1959, 17; all further references are to this edition). For Krapp's present concerns revolve around the gratification of those very bodily appetites that, earlier, he had resolved should be cut out of his life. Eating bananas and drinking whisky have become for him habitual ways of filling in the time. Of the physical activities that he once considered excesses, only sex has come to play a reduced part in his lonely existence. But all of them have become mechanical actions from which Krapp derives little comfort.

Concerning what had once seemed important to Krapp, Martin

Held, who played the role in the 1969 Schiller-Theater Werkstatt production directed by Beckett, reported the author as saying at rehearsal 'Krapp sees very clearly that he's through with his work, with love and with religion'.[2] The dreams that he once cherished of becoming a successful writer and producing an *opus magnum* had led only to the derisory 'Seventeen copies sold, of which eleven at trade price to free circulating libraries beyond the seas. Getting known' (17). A solitary visit to church as an old man has resulted in the bathetic 'Went to sleep and fell off the pew' (18). Of Krapp's former love-life, once quite active, all that remains is a recorded account of some moments spent with a girl on a lake.

The 'Last Tape' of the title suggests clearly enough that death is somewhere close at hand, a feeling echoed — rather too blatantly for Beckett in recent years — in Krapp's croaking efforts to sing Sabine Baring Gould's evening hymn 'Now the day is over'. In the 1969 Schiller-Theater production Krapp cast several anxious glances over his left shoulder, in case death itself should be waiting for him in the surrounding darkness. Beckett explained to Martin Held in Berlin that 'Old Nick's there. Death is standing behind him and unconsciously he's looking for it'.[3] In the copy of the play corrected by Beckett for the 1973 Royal Court revival, this action was referred to in a marginal note as a 'Hain',[4] the allusion being to a poem by Matthias Claudius, set to music by Schubert, in which Death says 'Be of good courage, I am not wild, you will slumber gently in my arms'.[5] The content of this 'last tape', recorded live towards the end of the play, is summed up by Krapp himself as a lot of 'drivel' (18) and the empty bleakness of his present existence contrasts starkly with the eager hopes and lofty aspirations that are captured in the various *memorabilia* recorded on earlier tapes by the younger versions of himself. From being a positive, purposeful form of stocktaking, recording and listening to the tape-recorder have now become a mechanized habit, a birthday treat and a ritual action in the old man's barren life. So Krapp returns obsessively to brood, with despairing fascination, on his earlier description of the moments spent with the girl in the punt on the lake or to listen, accidentally and with impatience, to fragments of an account of his vision recorded on the same tape. This vision had once seemed so significant that it needed to be set down as a key moment for future recall, but now he cannot bear to listen to it in its entirety, so painful is the gulf between a past experience that seemed to offer a key to possible fulfilment and a present of failure, emptiness, and meaninglessness.

The Krapp who is seen by the audience walks laboriously across the stage and lacks manual dexterity. He is near-sighted, hard of hearing, irascible and impatient in his behaviour. Like most of Beckett's characters (Molloy, Malone, Hamm, Dan Rooney) he is at a point of advancing physical and intellectual decline. Even his power to use words which once constituted the focal point of his activity as a struggling writer has gradually failed, so that the meaning of words like 'equinox' and 'viduity', which he once pronounced naturally, if pompously, has now to be searched for in a voluminous dictionary. Krapp's only verbal pleasure derives from the child-like relish he experiences in lengthening the vowel sound in 'spoool', a moment he describes later as the 'Happiest moment of the past half million' (17). The tape-recorder has become the sole companion of his solitude and the tapes are addressed as if they were recalcitrant children ('ah! the little rascal', 'ah! the little scoundrel' 10). With the words they contain, they represent the only form of contact that Krapp can achieve in a depleted, almost totally isolated existence that, ambiguously, he has sought out and yet dreads ('Past midnight. Never knew such silence. The earth might be uninhabited', 18).

The spectacle of an old man indulging in morbid reflections on his former glories or regretting his past failures is, of course, common in European dramatic literature. Several obvious examples spring to mind: the monologue of Don Dièue in Pierre Corneille's *Le Cid*, Shakespeare's Lear, or even the old servant, Firs, who brings Chekhov's *The Cherry Orchard* to a characteristically barren conclusion with the words 'Life has gone by as if I'd never lived . . . I'll lie down. There's no strength left in you; there's nothing, nothing, Ah, you . . . job-lot!'.[6] Yet by adopting the mechanical device of the tape-recorder (instead of the writer's traditional means of recording experience, the notebook or diary, together wth its theatrical or cinematic equivalent, the monologue or flash-back) Beckett has created a directness of confrontation between a man's various selves that produces an effect radically different from earlier dramatic portrayals of a man commenting on his own past life.

As so often in Beckett's theatre, the dramatic idea is simple and bold. The juxtaposition between the old man's physical appearance and the confident, even arrogant, voice that was his thirty years before — a voice that characterized his whole outlook at the time — both intensifies and modifies the pathos of Krapp's present state. For

decline, loss, failure and disillusionment are shown concretely and
the spectator himself becomes the active agent, listening and
observing, and able to assess the vastness of the distance that separates
the sixty-nine year old Krapp from his former self. Moreover, the
lyrical quality of some of Krapp's earlier recorded words becomes
more sharply poignant because of the sensation that we are eaves-
dropping on a strange encounter between a pathetic old man and a
stranger whom he knows was once himself. A gesture included in the
performance of Martin Held epitomized this moving contrast, as
Krapp cupped a gnarled hand on the table by the side of the tape-
recorder, as if he were once again caressing the girl's body as a visual
accompaniment to the sensual words of the recording, 'I lay down
across her with my face in her breasts and my hand on her' (16).

The central dramatic situation of *Krapp's Last Tape* combines
therefore direct theatrical experience of regret, loneliness, and
disappointment at life with conflict, distance and incongruity. This
particular combination of elements was already present in Beckett's
discussion in *Proust* (1931) of the lack of congruence between the time-
state of aspiration and the time-state of attainment in man: 'We are
disappointed,' wrote Beckett, 'at the nullity of what we are pleased to
call attainment. But what is attainment? The identification of the
subject with the object of his desire. The subject has died — and
perhaps many times — on the way. For subject B to be disappointed
by the banality of an object chosen by subject A is as illogical as to
expect one's hunger to be dissipated by the spectacle of uncle eating
his dinner' (*PTD*, 13-14). Yet Krapp demonstrates precisely this very
natural, if illogical, form of disappointment. And it seems likely that
Krapp's Last Tape may have sprung directly from a renewed meditation
on the poisonous ingenuity of that cancer 'Time'. which changes and
deforms man, facing him with so bitter a human dilemma. This seems
to me far more likely than the alternative suggestion that Heine's
poem *Der Doppelgänger* might be a source for the genesis of the play.[7]

But the stage image contains elements that were never part of the
original idea as it had been expressed in *Proust*. For example, the
device of the tape-recorder allows Krapp to bring to the judgement of
his former selves a lucidity and a contempt which goes some way
towards forestalling the sentimentality that might seem, almost
inevitably, to lie at the heart of so dramatic and potentially moving a
confrontation. ('Just been listening to that stupid bastard I took
myself for thirty years ago, hard to believe I was ever as bad as that',

16.) The pithy, sometimes macabre humour with which Krapp describes his present plight also serves as a counter-balance to sentimentality. ('Fanny came in a couple of times. Bony old ghost of a whore. Couldn't do much, but I suppose better than a kick in the crutch', 17.) In fact, Krapp brings to the contemplation of his own past a characteristic blend of longing and loathing. With Beckett's approval, it would seem, in the first production, Magee stressed in Krapp a bitter lack of resignation. And so expressions like 'I told her I'd been saving up for her all my life' (17) or 'All that old misery . . . Once wasn't enough for you' (18) emerge as searing indictments of a distant, yet still disturbing past or of an empty, disastrous present. Krapp's recourse to a form of mechanized memory-bank serves to underline the unbridgeable gulf which exists between the essentially ephemeral, unreal quality of his daily life — which, on another level, is, of course, only too monotonously, depressingly real — and the dream of absolute being which constantly haunts Beckettian man; 'Be again, be again' (18) repeats Krapp. In watching *Krapp's Last Tape* we come to experience not only the particular sadness of an individual lifetime of faded aspirations and frustrated ideals but the unreality of all past human experience that can necessarily only exist in the memory.

Another means of blunting the sentimentality that could so easily have dominated the play and, at the same time, of avoiding too overtly realistic a portrayal of Krapp as an old degenerate and 'tippler', was to cast him, initially at least, in the role of the clown. So Krapp wears ill-fitting clothes and, in early productions, big dirty white boots, and his white face and purple nose pave the way for the banana-skin routine that is borrowed directly from the circus-ring, or from vaudeville and silent-screen comedy. Krapp's slapstick play reflects, of course, in caricatural form his bodily concerns and certain dominant patterns in his behaviour: his persistent addiction to a fruit that he believes harmful in his state of constant constipation, his plans for a 'less . . . engrossing sexual life' (12) which are negated in advance by the sexual innuendo of the banana protruding obscenely from his mouth and waistcoat pocket, and, finally, his general physical clumsiness and vacuity of manner. But, as in *Endgame*, the comic business is placed near to the opening of the play with the intention of prompting an ambiguity of response on the part of the spectator, so that neither the comic nor the pathetic aspects of Krapp's appearance and predicament are lost. Yet the balance is a delicate one to preserve and

Beckett has had second thoughts on how far the clownish elements in Krapp's physique, dress and behaviour should be stressed. Even in the first 1958 Royal Court production, the purple nose of the drinker-clown was much toned down and has since been entirely deleted by Beckett. And, as I have discussed in greater detail elsewhere,[8] in Beckett's 1969 Schiller-Theater production, the banana-skin routine was promptly followed by several pieces of additional action in which Krapp shuffled to his cubby-hole to fetch ledger, tins and tape-recorder. This triple journey established an image of Krapp as a weak, tired, failing old man which counterbalanced the image of the clown first encountered by the audience.

Krapp's relations with women figure prominently in the play — in his younger days with his mother, Bianca, the 'girl in a shabby green coat, on a railway station platform', the girl with eyes 'Like . . . chrysolite!' (14), as well as the woman in the punt on the lake, and in his old age with Fanny, the 'bony old ghost of a whore' (17), and his fantasy woman, Effie, the heroine of Fontane's well-known nineteenth-century novel, *Effi Briest*. But all of Krapp's 'affairs' are described in terms of mingled regret, relief, and unsatisfied longing. Even the momentary harmony that was achieved with the girl in the punt was attained only after they had agreed that 'it was hopeless and no good going on' (16-18).

The black and white imagery that runs through the entire play suggests that Krapp's inability, even his unwillingness, to find happiness with a woman arises out of a fundamental attitude towards life as a whole that affects most aspects of his daily living. Krapp is only too ready to associate woman with the darker side of existence and he clearly sees her as appealing to the dark, sensual side of man's nature, distracting him from the cultivation of the understanding and the spirit. Krapp's recorded renunciation of love is then no mere casual end of an affair. The words of Sir Philip Sidney's sonnet apply strikingly to Krapp's situation: 'Leave me ô Love, which reachest but to dust / And thou my mind aspire to higher things'.[9] In Krapp's case, earthly love is not renounced for the greater love of God, as it was in the Petrarchan tradition. Instead, the renunciation of love forms part of an ascetic quest that rejects the world as an inferior creation and shrinks away from the material element of the flesh to concentrate upon the spiritual or the pneumatic. Krapp is clearly following here in a Gnostic, even a specifically Manichean tradition,[10] with its abstention from sexual intercourse and marriage (so as not to play the

Creator's game), its rift between God and the world, the world and man, the spirit and the flesh, and its vision of the universe, the world and man himself as divided between two opposing principles, the forces of darkness constantly threatening to engulf the forces of light. There are numerous indications in the play that Krapp has attempted to separate the light from the darkness in his life in order to rise above the dark side of his nature and liberate the light of understanding which (in Gnostic thinking) is regarded as being imprisoned in an envelope of matter. The new light above Krapp's table is seen, for instance, as a great improvement by Krapp because it forms a clearer division between the light and the dark. As a result, Krapp believes he can move out into the darkness, before returning to the zone of light with which he would wish to identify his essential self, but which, ironically, takes him back to the excremental associations surrounding his name: 'I love to get up and move about in it [the darkness], then back here to . . . (*hesitates*) . . . me (*Pause.*) Krapp' (11).

But Krapp's den is an artificially created setting and the point about God's world outside this refuge is that there is no such clear division between the light and the darkness. Separating one from the other in his life and in his relations with others is a much more difficult, painful, and morally isolating business. For the world had appeared, and still does appear, to Krapp in the form of a bewildering mixture of light and dark. As Beckett said in a rare published interview with Tom Driver, 'If there were only darkness, all would be clear. It is because there is not only darkness but also light that our situation becomes inexplicable . . . where we have, at one and the same time, darkness and light, we have also the inexplicable'.[11] Even the women with whom Krapp has been involved at different times are portrayed, disquietingly, in both light and dark images. Bianca is white by name, but they live together in Kedar (or, in Hebrew, Black) Street. Conversely, the nurse whom he admires at a distance is a dark young beauty with an incomparable bosom, who pushes a black pram, 'most funereal thing' (14) — linking characteristically birth and death — but she wears a uniform that is all 'white and starch' (14). And although Krapp's fantasy woman is placed in the Northern light-filled setting of Fontane's novel, her name 'Effie' links her with that of Fanny, the whore, with whom she is ostensibly contrasted, by announcing her physical function, recalling as it does also Beckett's remark that one should 'eff the ineffable'.

It is clear that for Krapp the central issue in his life is one of coming to terms with a fundamental dualism, either by attempted separation or by reconciliation. Krapp's account of the experience of the vision is heard only in fragmentary form, yet enough is played back for it to be apparent that what is being described there is the belief that light and darkness have at least been reconciled. The natural setting for the experience ('in the howling wind . . . great granite rocks the foam flying up in the light of the lighthouse and the wind-gauge spinning like a propeller', 15) reflects metaphorically the storm and night that Krapp has been striving to keep under in his life and his work, as well as the light of the understanding by which he has tried to be guided. He will henceforth draw on the darkness, but he sees this darkness as lit up by the 'fire in me now' (19). 'Storm and night' are seen as mysterious, wild, uncontrollable, exciting elements that can be reconciled with the experience of light only by regarding them as irrational compared with rational. As shown elsewhere,[12] it is certainly in this way that Beckett himself regarded the vision, for, in the 1969 Berlin *Krapp* production notebook, Beckett explained that 'Krapp decrees physical (ethical) incompatibility of light (spiritual) and dark (sensual) only when he intuits possibility of their reconciliation as rational-irrational. He turns from fact of anti-mind alien to mind to thought of anti-mind constituent of mind'.[13] The two warring elements remain then identified as sensual and spiritual, are independent and even incompatible, but reconciliation is effected at the level of the intellect. However, as Beckett commented, although ethically correct, Krapp is guilty of intellectual transgression, for (and this is a Gnostic belief) it is the duty of the intellect to separate the light from the dark and not to reconcile the two.

The issue of separating or reconciling the light and the dark also forms the underlying infra-structure of the episode with the girl in the punt, which, significantly, immediately follows the experience of the vision recorded on the tape. Since Krapp first winds the tape so far forward that we only hear the end of the episode, it appears that the harmony they achieved results from a purely physical union. However, when the tape is wound back and replayed, the sense of the passage is markedly changed.

> — upper lake, with the punt, bathed off the bank, then pushed out into the stream and drifted. She lay stretched out on the floor boards with her hands under her head and her eyes closed. Sun blazing down, bit of a breeze, water nice and lively. I noticed a scratch on her thigh and asked her how she came by it. Picking gooseberries, she said. I said again

I thought it was hopeless and no good going on and she agreed, without opening her eyes. (*Pause*.) I asked her to look at me and after a few moments — (*Pause*.) — after a few moments she did, but the eyes just slits, because of the glare. I bent over her to get them in the shadow and they opened. (*Pause. Low*.) Let me in. (*Pause*.) We drifted in among the flags and stuck. The way they went down, sighing, before the stem! (*Pause*.) I lay down across her with my face in her breasts and my hand on her. We lay there without moving. But under us all moved, and moved us, gently, up and down, and from side to side. (15-16)

In this unashamedly lyrical passage, the girl is prevented from opening her eyes by the fierce glare of the sun and it is only when the man creates shade for her that her eyes open. Rather as he has done when alone in his 'old den', Krapp has therefore created a separate area, in this case a zone of shade, which makes the temporary union that they attain possible. It would seem that once Krapp has equated woman with darkness and the irrational, he is able to establish and accept contact with a woman from whom he has resolved to part anyway, thus avoiding any possibility of continued physical entanglement.

Bianca, the dark nurse, and the girl in the punt all have eyes that have fascinated Krapp at different moments in his life. Bianca's eyes are said to be 'very warm' and 'incomparable' (12); the dark nurse has eyes 'Like . . . chrysolite!' (15), echoing Othello's words 'If heaven would make me such another world / Of one entire and perfect chrysolite / I'd not have sold her for it'.[14] If this preoccupation with the eyes of women recalls the image of the eye in the work of the Metaphysical poets or Proust's narrator's fascination with the mystery discerned in Albertine's eyes, Beckett tends to widen the resonance of the image by showing the girl's eyes not merely as windows on to the soul but as mirrors too, reflecting and uniting all the contrarities of a divided cosmos, 'Everything there, everything on this old muckball, all the light and dark and famine and feasting of . . . (*hesitates*) . . . the ages!' (17). That is at least what he sees there from his vantage point at the end of his sixty-ninth year. It was not however something that he had recognized thirty years earlier.

Krapp ended the recording made at the beginning of his thity-ninth year on a high note of buoyant optimism, acknowledging that, although happiness was something that he would perhaps never attain, this was more than compensated for by the fact that there was within him a fire that made mere happiness appear totally irrelevant. Throughout the play, fire and light have been used to distinguish the understanding and the spirit. Yet these inspired words are listened to at the end of the play by a weary and a disillusioned Krapp, an old man who is still enslaved by those strong physical appetites that, for so long he has tried to subjugate, and in whom the fire of the understanding has now dwindled to a few dying embers. The old fire that was in him has now been transformed into the 'burning to be gone' of his old age (17). The final confrontation between the younger and the older Krapp evokes, then, more than mere sadness at the inevitable decline that occurs in man. For Krapp shows us a man who is torn by conflicting forces and whose life has been ruined by this conflict. Moreover, as Beckett made clear to the San Quentin Drama Workshop, although Krapp recognizes the terrible mistake he made in following what he took to be a vision, he also sees that whatever decision he had made would have led to failure. For Krapp in the company of 'a good woman', 'patting the bottoms of the third and fourth generations', as the narrator of *From an Abandoned Work* put it (*SR*, 14) would have felt equally sure that he had frittered away his life. Beckett told Pierre Chabert that he had once thought of writing a play on just such a situation, arriving at the same sense of failure and solitude.[15] In fact, Henri Krap in *Eleuthéria* was already, to some extent, that 'other' Krapp who had married and had a son.

The old polarities of light and darkness are reflected in *Krapp's Last Tape* in numerous images of, on the one hand, light, fire, breeze and clear water and, on the other, darkness, heat, mist and vapour. The greater number of what Beckett called the light and dark emblems in the play do not occur, however, in isolation but are explicitly integrated. Even the death of Krapp's mother, which would seem to represent only the final corruption of the flesh, still hints at integration, for, as Beckett pointed out, 'if the giving of the black ball to the white dog represents the sacrifice of sense to spirit the form here too is that of a mingling'.[16]

Explicit integration of the light and the dark occurs also in the setting, the stage props, and in the costume of Krapp. In the Schiller-Theater 1969 production, it was in this area in particular that Beckett chose to emphasize the dualistic theme of the play.

In subsequent productions, it seemed at first as if he were trying to counter a tendency to over-emphasize Manichean elements. In fact, it was only Krapp's outward appearance that was made less explicitly, perhaps even for Beckett less crudely, the focal point of the Manichean oppositions. Since the 1973 Royal Court production with Albert

Finney as Krapp (which was directed by Anthony Page but to which Beckett contributed suggestions), instead of wearing the black waistcoat and grimy white shirt that are referred to in the text, Krapp has been dressed in a dark coloured dressing gown and has worn old plimsolls or slippers. In both set and props, however, the light and dark oppositions have been preserved, even extended with the inclusion of Krapp's shadow on the back of his cubby-hole, the use of an opaque, black material for its curtain, the swinging of the overhead lamp against which he bumps his head, bathing it first in light then in darkness, and the emphasis on the darkness on the stage as an area into which he glances, walks or throws the banana skins.

What is most important about the light and dark emblems in the play is that Krapp was unable to see them in terms other than those of opposition. He can choose only between absolutes of black or white. And his choice results in total self-isolation. He is a prisoner of his own dreams and fantasies, in a world that might just as well have been 'uninhabited'. Critics have been tempted to regard the play in almost equally absolute black and white terms, either as indicating the impossibility of happiness or as providing an object lesson, pointing one in the direction of a more positive approach to life.

A determinedly positive over-view of the play would suggest that behind the fragmentation shown between Krapp's different selves, there was a unity that he was unable himself to see but that we could discover in his common characteristics and, above all, in his own *blindness* to unity. The episode with the girl in the punt is seen in this view as a living example of a fusion that Krapp rejected in favour of his lonely, and ultimately sterile, artistic mission. And yet if such a reconciliation of opposites is tempting, it is, as Beckett suggested to Chabert, also taunting: Would that unity have been preserved?; does the nature of life allow such harmony?; what in any case would it have led to? — to adopt Ionesco's image, a future of egg production? These are a few of the many questions that Krapp's experience raises but will certainly not solve. And the fact that different views ranging from the rosy-hued to the black (or, to use Clov's term, 'dark grey', which is closest to my own) are all possible, indicates more the intractable nature of the problem than any deficiencies in the drama. In fact, of all Samuel Beckett's plays, *Krapp's Last Tape* seems to fuse most successfully a moving human situation with philosophical issues that lead one directly into judgements on the nature of existence. And the fact that the images are carefully chosen and patterned to suggest a dualistic view of the world does not here inhibit the apparent spontaneity of the verbal flow. It is important to stress that dualism is not a skeleton to which flesh has to be added. It is *itself* that flesh. What is experienced is, then, a form of poignant theatre poetry, not a mere representation of philosophical ideas. For, even more perhaps than *Waiting for Godot* or *Happy Days*, *Krapp's Last Tape* provides a central dramatic confrontation that is simple and moving. This ensures that the issues remain at a human and accessible level.

Notes

1.   The first known autograph version is contained in the *Eté 56* manuscript notebook in Reading University Library, MS 1227/7/7/1. It is headed *Magee Monologue* and is dated 20.2.58.
2.   'Martin Held talds to Ronald Hayman', *The Times Saturday Review*, 25 April 1970.
3.   *eo. loc.*
4.   Beckett's corrected copy of the 1970 Faber and Faber reprint is in Reading University Library, MS 1227/7/10/1. References to the 'Hain' are on pp. 11, 14 and 19.
5.   See M. Claudius, *Sämtliche Werke*, Munich, 1968, p. 87.
6.   A. Chekhov, *Plays*, New York, Hartsdale House, 1935, p. 135.
7.   J. Fletcher and J. Spurling, *Beckett. A Study of his Plays*, London, Eyre Methuen, 1972, p. 91.
8.   J. Knowlson, *'Krapp's Last Tape*: the Evolution of a Play, 1958-1975', *Journal of Beckett Studies*, no. 1, Winter 1976, pp. 50-65.
9.   *The Poems of Sir Philip Sidney*, ed. W.A. Ringler, Jnr., Oxford, Oxford University Press, 1962, p. 161.
10.   See K. and A. Hamilton, *Condemned to Life. The World of Samuel Beckett*, Grand Rapids, Michigan, W.B. Eerdmans, 1976, pp. 51-58.
11.   'Beckett by the Madeleine', *Columbia University Forum*, IV, Summer 1961, quoted from L. Graver and R. Federman, *Samuel Beckett: the Critical Heritage*, London, Henley and Boston, Routledge and Kegan Paul, 1979, p. 220.
12.   J. Knowlson, *Light and Darkness in the Theatre of Samuel Beckett*, London, Turret Books, 1972.
13.   Reprinted in facsimile in J. Knowlson, *Light and Darkness*.
14.   Beckett has written in this quotation in the corrected copy in Reading University Library, MS 1227/7/10/1.
15.   P. Chabert, 'Samuel Beckett metteur en scène', *Revue d'Esthétique*, 10/18, Paris, 1976, p. 226.
16.   See facsimile in J. Knowlson, *Light and Darkness*.

Happy Days

The relationship between Winnie in *Happy Days* and Krapp in the earlier play is rather like that of non-identical twins who have chosen quite different paths in life. The two plays were written in English within three years of each other and, as with *Not I* and *That Time*, Beckett has been unwilling to see them produced on the same theatrical bill.

Krapp created a prison for himself by choosing at the age of thirty-nine to plumb the darkness of his own being in an attempt to create an *opus magnum* in which light and dark would be reconciled. A partial consequence of the vision that inspired this choice was his past and present isolation ('the earth might be uninhabited', *KLT*, 15). His solitary den is the physical manifestation of that imprisonment and, although he is attracted like a moth to the zone of light around his table, the darkness that surrounds him is no more his now than it was thirty years ago. Winnie's own prison has grown insensibly around her in the form of the mound of earth which restricts her movements and threatens to overwhelm her entirely. Her world is light-filled but the light is just as hellish as Krapp's darkness had come to be and evokes extinction just as unequivocally. Krapp chose solitude but makes companions of his recorded voices; Winnie chose a companion and needs to talk to him in order to confirm her own existence. Krapp once spoke optimistically, as one who believed that he knew the path he should follow, but now he finds his previous state of conviction either laughable or painful. Winnie, on the other hand, remains an incurable optimist, in spite of the prevalent pressures towards degeneration and decline that cruelly distort her attempts to rise

above her predicament. Krapp once used words with the sureness of a
creative writer, but his linguistic achievement has now been reduced
to an infantile playing with sounds. Many of Winnie's words are
second-hand, lifted from the world of everyday clichés, traditional
pieties, and a culture based on a collection of verses similar to *Familiar
Quotations*. Yet at times — and many more times than one might think
— she over-reaches herself to express, sometimes obliquely, more
sensitive or more profound concepts or emotions.

Yet if Winnie and Krapp have followed divergent paths, they have
more in common than their imprisoned state or their fear of solitude.
The light and dark dualism of *Krapp's Last Tape* is paralleled in *Happy
Days* by the elemental contrast of earth and air. As Krapp had sought,
in Gnostic fashion, to escape from the world of sense and matter, only
to finish his life abjectly in his 'old rags', a dispirited, regretful old
wreck, so Winnie aspires to soar weightlessly over the earth by the
exercise of her will and the strength of her optimism ('she is like a bird'
commented Beckett).[1] Her dream is that she will 'simply float up into
the blue . . . And that perhaps some day the earth will yield and let me
go, the pull is so great, yes, crack all round me and let me out' (*Happy
Days*, London, Faber and Faber, 1962, p. 26; all further references are
to this edition). Instead, the earth tightens its grip increasingly on her,
and images of aspiration, movement upwards and potential release are
negated by a dominant impulse and movement downwards, as
Winnie sinks, or is sucked down, into what promises to be her tomb
('ah earth you old extinguisher', 28). Like Krapp, then, Winnie
aspires to more than the facts of her mortal existence will allow her to
attain.

The clash between Winnie's responses and the harsh conditions of
her desolate situation is as essential to the dramatic force of the play as
the conflict between the two selves of Krapp had been earlier.
However, before the effects of this clash can be assessed, we need to
look rather more closely at the different elements involved. Winnie
and Willie survive like two castaways in a barren, uninviting
landscape. Their home is the mound of earth which is often designed
as the central point in an expanse of reddish, or grey, baked,
undulating terrain set under an orange to flame coloured sky. Several
features of this bleak world seem to have been inspired by Daniel
Defoe's *Robinson Crusoe*. In an early manuscript version, Winnie kept a
track of the passing days by referring to notches on a tally-stick
exactly as Crusoe had done.[2] In the finished play, Winnie prays to

God (in the first act) and shades herself from the fierce heat of the sun, again like Crusoe. She also utilizes her possessions with a resourcefulness, economy and care that is worthy of Defoe's frugal hero. Moreover, Winnie's frequent recourse to the phrase 'great mercies' or 'tender mercies' echoes Crusoe's own expressions of pious gratitude for the good things that Providence seemed to have held back and released for his use.

Yet Beckett's two castaways inhabit a much stranger and less easily circumscribed world than Crusoe's 'Island of Despair'. For as Winnie's trunk, and later her head alone, projects from the mound of earth, or as Willie's hand emerges from his hole by its side, one is reminded rather of the damned in Dante's *Inferno*, whose limbs protrude from the frozen lake or the livid stone. Several references in the text intensify these apparently infernal associations, in particular the 'blaze of hellish light' (11), the parasol bursting into flames, and the great heat which has already scorched the surrounding grass and which now threatens to char Winnie's own flesh and that of her husband. As an alternative to the searing heat which they must endure, Winnie can only conceive of an equally harsh but opposite extreme: 'It might be the eternal cold . . . Everlasting perishing cold' (39). And, characteristically, she is duly grateful for the heat rather than the cold and 'the eternal dark . . . Black night without end', judging that it was 'Just chance, I take it, happy chance' (45) that it was not otherwise. Extreme heat, extreme cold, and eternal darkness are, of course, the precise characteristics of traditional portrayals of Hell. The ferryman, Charon, in Dante's *Inferno*, for instance, is ready to transport Dante and Virgil across the Styx 'Into eternal darkness, thereto dwell / In fierce heat and in ice' (Canto III, v.87-88, Cary translation). One thinks, in any case, of Beckett's own way of describing Giordano Bruno's principle of identified contrarities: 'minimal heat equals minimal cold' (*OE*, 6).

But Winnie's world is *not* the Hell of Dante or of Milton. In both Heaven and Hell, all must be static and resolved. 'Hell', wrote Beckett in the essay on Joyce's 'Work in Progress', 'is the static lifelessness of unrelieved viciousness. Paradise the static lifelessness of unrelieved immaculation' (*OE*, 22). Winnie could truthfully repeat Malone's words from *Malone Dies*: 'I feel at last that the sands are running out, which would not be the case if I were in heaven or in hell' (*TN*, 184). For however unchanging and apparently endless Winnie's existence might appear to be, change *is* present in the shape of decline, degeneration and deceleration. For Winnie and Willie are not so much the last survivors of a giant holocaust, such as a nuclear explosion, or of a sudden and dreadful natural disaster, as the victims of a slow process of running down: dentifrice, universal 'pick-me-up', lipstick, and Willie's vaseline are all depleted and in danger of running out. Winnie's bag is still there in the second act, but she is unable to reach it and so can no longer make use of the articles it contains. Progressively the earth is depriving Winnie of her powers and her resources, straining to the utmost her ability to adapt to 'changing conditions' (28). Most important of all, words themselves, which are essential to the maintenance of her being, seem likely to become useless, as Willie's long silence in the second act suggests that, one day, as Winnie realizes, there will be no one at whom they may be directed. One recalls, in this context, Ada's words to Henry in the earlier radio play, *Embers*: 'You will be quite alone with your voice, there will be no other voice in the world but yours' (*Krapp's Last Tape and Embers*, 33).

In many ways, however, Winnie's world is still recognizably that of the 'earthball', even though it too is affected by the prevalent entropy — it has almost dried up in the fierce heat of the sun and, by the second act, might conceivably have lost its atmosphere. The ritual gestures which she performs in the first act to keep going through her day are of the most everyday kind: brushing her teeth, looking in the mirror, putting on her lipstick, donning her hat, singing her song, recounting her stories, and, above all, talking to, or rather at Willie. Yet, paradoxically, all of this occurs in a world where living in time, and perhaps even dying, have already been confined to the 'old style'.

We appear, then, to be witnessing, as so often in Beckett's writing, an extension of life, close enough to our own to permit a considerable degree of recognition, sympathy and understanding and yet merging into a characteristically Beckettian form of purgatory. But it is a purgatory that is radically different from the 'conical purgatory' of Dante. For culmination and fulfilment are totally excluded from Beckett's stage world, just as they are from the purgatory which he ascribed to James Joyce in the essay on the 'Work in Progress'. Although Winnie's predicament is physically far more serious at the end of the play than it was at the beginning, we have no assurance that it has yet reached any terminal point.

The strange, purgatorial features of this stark world are to some extent domesticated by the force of Winnie's buoyant optimism, by her essentially creative use of language, and by the ritualized nature of her habits. She possesses, in fact, a whole gamut of well-tried techniques for converting the strange into the familiar, the unknown into the known, and the distasteful into the acceptable. For her possessions, her gestures, and her words (whether her own or those of others, in the shape of quotations from her 'classics') are all ways of asserting her will and spirit and of convincing herself that she can, after all, understand and cope with a reality that becomes increasingly inexplicable and intolerable as the play proceeds. Like the figure in *The Unnamable*, or Mouth in *Not I*, Winnie hears sounds or cries in her head. But although these sounds are described as 'like little . . . sunderings, little falls . . . apart' (40), she still regards them as a boon, and another way of helping her to get through her 'day'. Even her stories are partly ways of objectifying the sense of mystery that must represent a challenge to her rationalistic approach to existence or, as in the case of Mildred and the mouse, of giving oblique expression to the fear, violence, and suffering that, in Beckett's view, seems to be an unavoidable accompaniment to procreation, birth and being.

Exactly how far Winnie succeeds in convincing herself that she understands, can cope, and that 'all is well' is left a matter of deliberate uncertainty. But there is no doubt at all that she *is* aware, and increasingly so as the play goes on, that things elude her, and that, in spite of all her determined efforts to remain cheerful, 'sorrow keeps breaking in', as she concedes at one point (27), a distorted quotation of Dr. Johnson, 'cheerfulness was always breaking in'. These chinks in her armour are revealed by the tiny qualification of a remark, by a break or faltering in her voice, or by the swift erasure of a smile. One consequence of this failure to come to terms totally with sorrow is that Winnie's determined cheerfulness and resilience appear far less glib and trite than they would otherwise be. Indeed, as a result, the role of Winnie (and the play as a whole) gains a greater level of emotional depth, which is often experienced in the theatre but which, perhaps surprisingly, has managed to elude many academic critics.

Once again it is worth noting that Beckett is not only bringing together two conflicting elements. He is also using the independent response and judgement of the spectator as an important mediating factor in the drama. For just as the spectator was given the task of assessing the gap that separated the older Krapp from his younger self, so, in *Happy Days*, he registers the discrepancy that exists between the harsh realities of Winnie's existence and her incongruous 'look on the bright side' philosophy. But Winnie's situation deteriorates rapidly with the second act and she shows visible signs of distress and a growing awareness of the nature of her plight. As a result, the ironic contrast to which the spectator is asked to respond shifts accordingly. His response can also be altered, of course, by the emphasis that is given to this shift of balance by the actress playing the part of Winnie. Madeleine Renaud's performance as Winnie, for example, however good, failed, it seemed to me, at the highest level because it remained too consistently lyrical and sentimentalized and did not fully reflect the growing terror and desperation of the second act. As a result, this act seemed too much like a replay of the first, when it both echoes and differs radically from it, prompting at this stage a response more akin to chilled horror than pathos. The National Theatre, London, 1975 production, with Dame Peggy Ashcroft as Winnie, caught this change much more accurately.

Happy Days of all Beckett's plays, and Winnie of all Beckett's stage characters, have provoked the most active hostility from critics. One of the most common criticisms is that, by choosing as his heroine a woman whose most natural means of expression is the cliché, Beckett imposes drastic limitations on his writing so that, in the trenchant words of one of the most hostile of commentators, 'Winnie doesn't interest Beckett at all but she has an enormous amount to say and almost all of it is extremely boring to listen to'.[3] Another objection to the play is that it is more of a script for acting than a written text.[4] Hostile criticism should not, however, blind us to the fact that in the United States of America, Britain, France, Germany and Ireland it has been widely acclaimed by audiences in the theatre. It would, of couse, be absurd to deny that its success has depended to some extent on factors such as the surprise, power and suggestiveness of the image of Winnie confined to her mound of earth or of Willie's final and long-awaited front of stage appearance. Clearly the interplay of word and gesture, sound and silence, the comic value of visual 'gags', and the orchestration of movements and facial expressions with words have also had an important contribution to make. However, Beckett's stated intention to 'write a play that would live through its text alone'[5] cannot, in my view, be held to have foundered because of the triteness or the boring nature of its heroine's chatter or because it was conceived in a mixture of visual and verbal terms. In fact one could argue, as Beckett himself did of Proust's description of Saint-Loup's telephone call to his grandmother, that his virtual monologue makes a work like Jean Cocteau's *Voix Humaine* seem 'not merely a banality, but an unnecessary banality' (*PTD*, 26). For Winnie touches, however lightly, on many of the central problems that have concerned Western philosophy at least since Descartes: the relationship of the mind and the body; the autonomous existence of 'things' or their dependence on the human consciousness; the power and the limits of the will; the absence or failure to care of any divine Creator; and the status of past experience and its relationship with the present. But Winnie scales such dizzy 'heights', as she calls them (30), intuitively. She experiences these issues as puzzling enigmas, rather than as problems susceptible of solution. So philosophical speculations seem to arise naturally enough out of her specific situation and are expressed in and through carefully structured, yet living, credible human speech and actions. The spectator is, therefore, involved at several levels simultaneously: at a direct, human level, responding emotionally and imaginatively to Winnie's physical presence, predicament, words and actions; and at an intellectual level, recognizing in her busy chatter fears and feelings, as well as ideas, which lie, often obliquely expressed, behind her words. This technique has the advantage of avoiding for the most part the over-explicit. Its ambiguity and its openness seem well suited to express the vision of a world which eludes definition and reduction to closed systems of any kind and is characterized above all by mystery and bewilderment.

In *Happy Days*, Beckett brings together two of his most important themes, integrating them far more closely into the dramatic situation than in any of his previous plays. First is the need for a witness to validate one's own existence. Second is the compulsion to go on saying words 'as long as there any' (*TN*, 418). Bishop Berkeley's dictum 'to be is to be perceived'[6] here takes the form of Winnie's desperate need for a witness who, if he cannot actually *see* her, will be there as an 'Auditor' to *listen* to her words, even at times to respond to them.

Winnie turns towards Willie literally hundreds of times in the course of the first act and, on most occasions, contrives to see him, although not without difficulty or discomfort. Since she is unable to move her head, however, in the second act, she can neither look at him nor view herself in her mirror. Her own visual perceptions become, therefore, increasingly reduced as the play goes on and, like Malone with his inventory, she is able to list, in her case exhaustively, the elements that fall within her field of vision: the bag, the sunshade, the earth and the sky, and her own body. Of that she can see only:

The nose. (*She squints down.*) I can see it . . . (*squinting down*) . . . the
tip . . . the nostrils . . . breath of life . . . that curve you so admired . . .
(*pouts*) . . . a hint of lip . . . (*pouts again*) . . . if I pout them out . . . (*sticks
out tongue*) . . . the tongue of course . . . you so admired . . . if I stick it
out . . . (*sticks it out again*) . . . the tip . . . (*eyes up*) . . . suspicion of
brow . . . eyebrow . . . imagination possibly . . . (*eyes left*) . . . cheek . . .
no . . . (*eyes right*) . . . no . . . (*distends cheeks*) . . . even if I puff them
out . . . (*eyes left, distends cheeks again*) no . . . no damask. (39)

But Winnie needs to know that she is being observed and, adopting a
phrase with an ironic Biblical resonance, she asks Willie: 'Could you
see me, Willie, do you think, from where you are, if you were to raise
your eyes in my direction? (*Turns a little further.*) Lift up your eyes to
me, Willie, and tell me can you see me, do that for me, I'll lean back as
far as I can. (*Does so. Pause.*) No? (*Pause.*) Well never mind' (23). [7] Since
the possibility of Willie seeing her seems unlikely, Winnie's need to be
observed is transposed into the feeling that 'someone is looking at me.
I am clear, then dim, then gone, then dim again, then clear again, and
so on, back and forth, in and out of someone's eye' (31). Repeated in
the second act, where it also seems to offer Winnie reassurance, this
feeling does little but pose questions to the audience. For who, after
all, can be 'looking at [her] still, caring for [her] still?' (37). A
hypothesized God-observer? Willie himself? Or just the hundreds of
eyes from the audience, who are even less able to do anything to help
Winnie in her plight than her husband can do. Winnie's statement
illustrates how closely the issue of perception has come to be woven
into both the dramatic situation and the thematic structure of the
play.

The two visitors in Winnie's first story are given the names of
Shower and Cooker and, as Ruby Cohn has pointed out, [8] both point
to their role as observers by recalling the German words *schauen-
kucken* meaning 'look'. The story externalizes, therefore, Winnie's
need to be observed, although its significance cannot, of course, be
confined to this. In the first act, Winnie dreamed that one day Willie
might come round to the front of the mound and let her eyes 'feast'
on him. But when eventually he does this at the end of the play, her
cry that he should 'feast [his] old eyes' on her (46) results in a much
more fraught experience. It is Willie's look that terrifies her. For, at
this stage, the look not only confirms her existence; it also threatens it,
pecisely because it belongs to the Other, and so is alien and outside
her control. Similarly, Beckett suggested in the course of the 1971
Schiller-Theater production that, when Willie sinks down with his

face to the ground, it will not be clear whether this is because of weakness or because of Winnie's gaze.[9] For instead of merely 'feasting', the look also judges, and perhaps condemns.

Yet the dominant mode of perception in the play is the ear rather than the eye. Winnie addresses Willie constantly in both acts and puts dozens of questions to him, even though her queries frequently elicit no reply and have to be answered by herself. 'If only I could bear to be alone, I mean prattle away with not a soul to hear' (18) she comments. But this is exactly what she cannot bear. On several separate occasions she explains the precise logic upon which her reassurance depends:

> Not that I flatter myself you hear much, no Willie, God forbid. (*Pause.*) Days perhaps when you hear nothing. (*Pause.*) But days too when you answer. (*Pause.*) So that I may say at all times, even when you do not answer and perhaps hear nothing, something of this is being heard, I am not merely talking to myself, that is in the wilderness, a thing I could never bear to do — for any length of time. (18)

As a result, words are crucial to maintaining Winnie's existence as an autonomous being. The situation is even more desperate for her than it was for the tramps in *Waiting for Godot* since, in the second act, she cannot be sure that her husband is even alive to listen to her. Objects provide her with things to do but, above all, they give her something to talk about. Similarly, she does not just perform actions; she also comments avidly upon them. And commentary often seems to be more important to her than the familiar everyday actions themselves. Willie's own role is primarily to stimulate and to listen to Winnie's words. The all-important words 'And now?', repeated constantly throughout the play and often addressed to Willie, particularly in the second act when he is silent, lead not just to what she might do next to fill in her 'day' but to what she should *say*. For Winnie recognizes that, of all her time-fillers, words have become her most precious commodity. She once even makes it clear that she is thinking of performing some action only with the intention of economizing on her words. And, at one point, existing is equated by her with talking: 'That is what enables me to go on, to go on talking that is' (18).

Words are for Winnie, first and foremost, items in a survival kit. But they also allow her to try to understand and assert control over reality. Her optimistic clichés are the most obvious signs of her faith in words to triumph, partially at least, over what might otherwise appear unbearable. There is a strong sense that Winnie is struggling with the help of words to tame an elusive, mysterious reality. Events such as the bursting into flames of the parasol (or its equally puzzling, predicted reappearance later) challenge her ability to understand and cope with what is happening to her. But ultimately they fail to confound or terrify her only because, at one level at least, she is able *through language* to accept them as part of a world in which the mysterious and the inexplicable appear as the norm. So the repeated phrase 'here all is strange' becomes for Winnie yet another message of comfort rather than a betrayal of bewilderment or terror. It is clear that Winnie is confronting the absurd with an armoury that consists only of her optimism and a language of clichés and second-hand terms. This attempt to impose some meaning on a meaningless world with worn-out words appears at once pathetically inadequate and rather admirable. At the very least, it makes Winnie's compulsive chatter appear far less trivial than it would otherwise be; at the most, it invests her with a muted form of brave heroism.

Language works, then, something of a miracle for Winnie. But it also leads her to the very edge of the abyss. This is partly because, while recognizing the importance of words to her continued survival, she also knows that the time will come when words must fail, either in the sense that they will run out before the end is reached, as was foreseen in the second of the *Texts for Nothing*,[10] or that there will be no one there to whom they may be addressed.

> Oh no doubt the time will come when before I can utter a word I must make sure you heard the one that went before and then no doubt another come another time when I must learn to talk to myself a thing I could never bear to do such wilderness. (*Pause.*) Or gaze before me with compressed lips. (*She does so.*) All day long. (*Gaze and lips again.*) No. (*Smile.*) No no. (*Smile off.*) (22)

But words fail in another sense, as the following passage reveals:

> There is so little one can say, one says it all. (*Pause.*) All one can. (*Pause.*) And no truth in it anywhere. (*Pause.*) My arms. (*Pause.*) My breasts. (*Pause.*) What arms? (*Pause.*) What breasts? (*Pause.*) Willie. (*Pause.*) What Willie? (*Sudden vehement affirmation.*) My Willie! (*Eyes right, calling.*) Willie! (*Pause. Louder.*) Willie! (*Pause. Eyes front.*) Ah well, not to know, not to know for sure, great mercy, all I ask' (38)

Winnie's 'vehement affirmation' 'my Willie!' is a desperate attempt to insist that the possessive pronoun *does* mean something in a world in which words fail to confer meaning as well as comfort. Winnie shows that she is acutely aware of this more radical failure of words to identify or evoke any reality:

> I speak of temperate times and torrid times, they are empty words. (*Pause.*) I speak of when I was not yet caught — in this way — and had my legs and had the use of my legs, and could seek out a shady place, like you, when I was tired of the sun, or a sunny place when I was tired of the shade, like you, and they are all empty words. (29)

For if the play is partly about the power of words to create meaning, it is also concerned with their ultimate failure to encompass the mystery and chaos of being. Winnie's account of the visit of the Shower (or Cooker) couple illustrates how inappropriate it is to seek for meaning in such a situation:

> What's she doing? he says — What's the idea? he says — stuck up to her diddies in the bleeding ground — coarse fellow — What does it mean? he says — What's it meant to mean? — and so on — lot more stuff like that — usual drivel — Do you hear me? he says — I do, she says, God help me — What do you mean, he says, God help you . . . And you, she says, what's the idea of you, she says, what are you meant to mean? Is it because you're still on your two flat feet, with your old ditty full of tinned muck and changes of underwear, dragging me up and down this fornicating wilderness. (33)

But this encounter also reveals that it is existence itself and not just Winnie's special predicament that is being depicted as mysterious and beyond rational explanation. So Winnie's need to talk, yet her awareness of the failure of her words to do all she wants them to do, is part of the larger theme of the quest for, yet absence of, meaning in existence. 'We're not beginning to . . . to . . . mean something?' Hamm had asked incredulously in *Endgame*, prompting Clov to break into derisive laughter and to reply 'Mean something! You and I, mean something! . . . Ah, that's a good one' (*EG*, 27).

However banal much of what Winnie says might appear to be, her talk has a resonance and an emotional range that again makes one doubt how it may accurately be described as trite or boring. Certainly hundreds of words are expended on the most humdrum activities: combing her hair, doing her nails, cleaning her spectacles, inspecting her gums, and reading the words on the medicine-bottle label or on the handle of her tooth-brush. Some of these actions merely fill in the time for Winnie but many point to the theme of physical decline and decay and suggest that a more universal form of entropy is operating as lipstick and medicine both run out. Using the technique of the 'shaggy-dog' story, Winnie spins out her decipherment and interpretation of the inscription on the tooth-brush ('guaranteed, genuine, pure') over the whole of the first act. Yet by allowing Winnie

to lavish as much care on these few words as if they were crucial lines
in the Dead Sea Scrolls, Beckett is able to effect a neat parody of the
human quest for knowledge in a world dominated by suffering and
death. Moreover, Winnie's puzzlement over the term 'hog's setae'
leads eventually to a definition of a 'hog' — when what the audience
actually wants defined is the word 'setae' — as a 'castrated male swine
reared for slaughter', which reflects ironically on the fate of man in
general as well as on that of Willie in particular.

It might seem again, at first, as if the verbal and the visual humour
of the first act is present solely in order to lighten the text or to reflect
Winnie's optimistic outlook. In reality, many of the jokes pick up
more serious themes and participate in a whole network of parallels,
echoes and allusions. Willie's pun on 'formication' for example (after
the appearance of the ant carrying an egg) is linked most immediately
by Winnie to the derisory nature of God's creation: 'How can one
better magnify the Almighty by sniggering with him at his little
jokes, particularly the poorer ones' (24). But it is also one of many
sexual references or innuendos that originate sometimes with
Willie — the pornographic postcard, his '*sucked* up', possibly his
'opening for smart youth' and sometimes, in spite of her surface
Puritanism, with Winnie's memories, which are crammed full of
sexual images:

> My first ball! (*Long pause.*) My second ball! (*Long pause. Closes eyes.*) My
> first kiss! (*Pause . . .*) A Mr Johnson, or Johnston, or perhaps I should
> say John*stone*. Very bushy moustache, very tawny. (*Reverently.*) Almost
> ginger! (*Pause.*) Within a toolshed, though whose I cannot conceive. We
> had no toolshed and he most certainly had no toolshed. (*Closes eyes.*) I see
> the piles of pots. (*Pause.*) The tangles of bast. (*Pause.*) The shadows
> deepening among the rafters. (15)

And it is sex which is responsible for the continuation of the life that
plunges man inevitably into suffering. The sexual innuendos
contrast, then, with images of sterility or 'discreation'.[11] 'What a
blessing nothing grows', says Winnie feelingly, 'imagine if all this
stuff were to start growing' (27).

On several occasions in the text the verbal graphically (and
comically) evokes the visual, after the manner of the radio play. For
example, Winnie encourages Willie to rub in his vaseline in order to
protect him from the sun, adding the evocative phrase 'now the other'.
No futher commentary is needed. Winnie's accompaniment to
Willie's difficult re-entry into his hole is almost as successful as a piece
of comic writing as the verbal evocation of Mrs. Rooney being

squeezed into Mr. Slocum's car in *All that Fall*. But in neither case are the ingredients merely humorous. In *Happy Days* Winnie's evocation of what sounds suspiciously like a breech birth is one of a whole series of images that evoke a desire to return to the womb or suggest, as the story of Milly and the mouse was to do later, the violence of sexual violation, procreation and birth.

Sorrow, regret, and loss intrude repeatedly into Winnie's chatter. Her quotations, for instance, introduce into her meditations, unnoticed it would seem to Winnie herself, 'woe' and the transitoriness of earthly things, and, on a number of occasions, they provide a telling *memento mori*.[12] A single word or phrase will often deepen a whole sequence of apparently trivial remarks or will hint at a level of experience customarily by-passed by Winnie's particular brand of optimism. A short passage selected almost at random will illustrate clearly how this is done:

> One cannot sing just to please someone, however much one loves them, no song must come from the heart, that is what I always say, pour out from the inmost, like a thrush. (*Pause.*) How often have I said, in evil hours, Sing now, Winnie, sing your song, there is nothing else for it, and did not. (*Pause.*) Could not. (*Pause.*) No, like the thrush, or the bird of dawning, with no thought of benefit, to oneself or anyone else. (31)

The phrase 'in evil hours' introduces an awareness of sorrow that belies the would-be consoling tone of the extract, in which Winnie is seeking to explain to her own satisfaction why Willie should be unwilling or unable to repeat his hoarse rendering of the musical-box tune, the Waltz Duet from the *Merry Widow*.

And the partial quotation from the first scene of *Hamlet* (Marcello's 'Some say that ever 'gainst that season comes / Wherein our Saviour's birth is celebrated / The bird of dawning singeth all night long') with its reflection of birth, salvation and continuous song adds a sadly ironic dimension to Willie's and Winnie's own inability to sing. On other occasions, memories 'float up' of times when, for instance, Winnie remembered herself as 'young and . . . foolish . . . and beautiful . . . possibly lovely . . . in a way . . . to look at' (27). Here cliché shades into a delicate concern for finding the appropriate epithet which, when set against the physical realities of her present plight, becomes more moving in the theatre than the words in themselves might suggest. There are times when Winnie shows that she is capable of envisaging her future fate with great clear-sightedness. And this insight produces its own form of savage, yet chilling lyricism: 'the happy day to come when flesh melts at so many degrees and the night of the moon has so many hundred hours' (16).

One of the chief strengths of *Happy Days* is the sharpness of its internal dramatic contrasts. Sometimes these contrasts, however well integrated, seem a little too artificial to be either moving or comic, as with that of an old, decrepit Willie reading out aloud two incongruous newspaper announcements, 'Wanted bright boy' and 'opening for smart youth'. More often they arise more naturally and provoke an unusual ambivalence of response. For instance, Winnie looks more than a little absurd in her 'small, ornate, brimless hat' (14). And yet as she frees a strand of hair from under it and muses 'Golden you called it, that day, when the last guest was gone (*hand up in gesture of raising a glass*) to your golden . . . may it never . . . (*voice breaks*) . . . may it never . . . (*Hand down. Head down. Pause. Low.*) That day. (*Pause. Do*) What day?' (20), the contrast between 'then' and 'now' is direct and moving. The dramatic effectiveness of the moment at which Winnie takes the revolver out of her bag depends hardly at all on recognizing the word-play on Browning as both a gun and a poet (and the quotation from Browning's poetry) but hinges rather on the incongruous presence of the gun among these other feminine articles and on the contrast between nostalgia and the actual threat of suicide:

> You'd think the weight of this would bring it down among the . . . last rounds. But no. It doesn't. Ever uppermost, like Browning. (*Pause.*) Brownie . . . (*Turning a little towards Willie*) Remember Brownie, Willie? (*Pause.*) Remember how you used to keep on at me to take it away from you? Take it away, Winnie, take it away, before I put myself out of my misery. (*Back front. Derisive.*) *Your* misery. (26)

The musical box song may seem extremely sentimental when read. But in its dramatic context it is, first, rather grotesquely comic, as Willie sings it hoarsely without the words. Then, at the end, when sung by Winnie, it manages to sound moving, a pale reflection of Proust's 'Vinteuil' phrase, but capturing something of the yearning which transcends the banality of its words.

Contrast extends to the most minute details of mood, voice, speed, and rhythm. For example the monotony of using a single voice most of the time is broken by giving Winnie several distinct voices, which contrast one with the other — the narrative tone in the Shower/Cooker story, the voice of Mr Shower and that of his female companion, and the little girl voice for part of the Mildred and the mouse story. For Winnie impersonates others as well as inventing stories and, like the protagonist of *That Time*, makes up whole stretches of dialogue with herself in order to survive. The pace, rhythm and volume of her chatter is also determined by the need for contrast and variety. So Beckett directs that a section of the text is to be delivered in a garbled fashion, while, as Winnie holds up her parasol and considers how she has adapted to 'changing conditions', there is a maximum slowing down of pace. That the pace of the second act is generally slower is indicated by the increased frequency of the stage direction 'long pause' and of the ringing of the bell. Time is discontinous in this play and moments in the present are often separated drastically from each other as well as from moments in the past. Winnie's puzzled statement: 'Then . . . now . . . what difficulties here for the mind. (*Pause.*) To have been always what I am and so changed from what I was. (*Pause.*) I am the one. I say the one, then the other' (38), applies just as much to present time as it does to past. Winnie's volatility of mood as well as the fragmentation in her thought and speech may then be attributed to her time experience.

It has sometimes been suggested that the second act of *Happy Days* is an irrelevance. Nothing could be further from the truth. For the existence of two acts renders a whole series of dramatic contrasts possible as well as numerous subtle modulations of mood. Most crucial is, of course, the basic contrast in situation. For Winnie's deprivation has become so much greater in the second act, her resources have become more seriously depleted and her awareness of the physical discomfort and actual pain of her situation is more explicit: the bell 'hurts like a knife' (40); 'my neck is hurting me' (44) she admits; and she screams loudly, as Mouth did in *Not I*, in accompaniment to her story of Milly screaming in the nursery. There are times too in the second act when Winnie's automatic reflex responses fail to function, as she asks the question 'What is that unforgettable line' and is unable to answer with any line of consoling verse. Her reasoning becomes so much more desperate there, as she tries to convince herself with an astounding reflection of Cartesian logic that Willie is actually still there to listen to her:

> I used to think that I would learn to talk alone. (*Pause.*) By that I mean to myself, the wilderness. (*Smile.*) But no. (*Smile broader.*) No no. (*Smile off.*) Ergo you are there. (*Pause.*) Oh no doubt you are dead, like the others, no doubt you have died, or gone away and left me, like the others, it doesn't matter, you are there. (37-38)

The humour of the opening of the play and the word-play and

innuendos of the first act are now things of the past. Winnie's optimistic clichés remain with her by force of habit, but they are used less frequently and in a more isolated form. In any case, the repetition of these same words and phrases ('that is what I find so wonderful' and 'great mercies, great mercies' in particular) in so dire a predicament inevitably means that the irony becomes so sharp as to be at times almost unbearable. In addition, the second act has acquired its own more appropriate recurring phrases of reassurance, 'some remains' or 'a part remains', terms which are used first concerning the reason, then are applied by Winnie to her physical looks; 'does anything remain?' (46) she asks. When Willie finally does make his appearance at the end of the play, so that it seems as if he were indeed answering her plea from the first act, Winnie is seen to be sharp and shrewish, counter-balancing her earlier show of affection for her 'poor dear Willie' (10). In consequence, a much fuller, more ambiguous picture of the relationship of the couple is given, introducing an ambiguity which characterizes also Willie's closing attempts to reach Winnie, either to kiss her or to kill her or himself.

If one looks at the challenge offered to the dramatist by the choice of setting, situation and characters in *Happy Days*, it undoubtedly appears as Beckett's boldest piece of dramatic writing to date. *Not I*, *That Time* and *Footfalls* are after all so much shorter that it makes the retention of dramatic interest a much less daunting task, even taking into account the greater degree of reduction found in the most recent plays. A list of the ingredients in *Happy Days* sounds like a deliberate accumulation of difficulties: a woman who talks to herself for most of the play and who, having lost her mobility before it begins, loses the use of her upper limbs before the second act; a husband who is invisible, except for the sight of the top of his head for a short time, who makes only one front of stage appearance in the play's closing moments, and who speaks only forty-eight words in the first act and a single word 'Win' in the second; no possibility of any other characters coming on stage; no change of set; and only the most banal of everyday props. Yet perhaps Beckett's most impressive achievement, in my own view, is to have taken a very common-place woman, a creature of habit *par excellence*, capable only of speaking in a common-place language, and from this to have created in *Happy Days* a work of searing power that has been compared (and not entirely unreasonably) with Aeschylus's *Prometheus*. One of the most revealing of the critical remarks that followed the opening of the French production was that

which spoke of it as a play which recalls 'the immobility of the great
sacred theatrical works, in which human speech sufficed to fill and
animate the theatrical space, and which consisted entirely of the
essential realities to which these texts return one: Time, Space, and
the Word'.[13] Perhaps alone among Beckett's major plays, *Happy Days*
has, in my own view, been widely underestimated. It may be that,
eventually, it will come to be regarded as one of his finest pieces of
writing for the theatre.

Notes

1. R. Cohn, *Back to Beckett*, Princeton, New Jersey, Princeton University
    Press, 1973, p. 189.
2. In typescript 1, Ohio State University Libraries, Columbus, Ohio,
    Winnie speaks of how she would count the number of times she had to
    establish that her husband could hear her: 'The tally-sticks, don't you
    remember the tally-sticks Edward [Willie], they must be lying about
    somewhere still, every thirtieth notch, then every fifteenth. (*Pause.*)
    Then weekly' (p. 8). Cf. 'Upon the Sides of this square Post I cut every
    day a Notch with my Knife, and every seventh Notch was as long again
    as the rest, and every first Day of the Month as long again as that long
    one; and thus I kept my Kalendar, or weekly, monthly, and yearly
    reckoning of Time'. *The Life and Strange Surprizing Adventures of Robinson
    Crusoe*, Oxford, Blackwell for Shakespeare Head Press, 1927.
3. R. Hayman, *Samuel Beckett*, London, Heinemann, 1968, p. 58.
4. A. Alvarez, *Beckett*, London, Fontana/Collins, 1973, p. 108.
5. R. Cohn, *Back to Beckett*, p. 178.
6. Used by Beckett in the form *esse est percipi* to preface *Film* (1964).
7. Cf. 'I will left up mine eyes unto the hills, from whence cometh my
    help', Psalm 121, v.1 and 'Unto thee lift I up mine eyes, o thou that
    dwellest in the heavens', Psalm 123, v.1.
8. R. Cohn, *Back to Beckett*, p. 182. See also Elin Diamond, 'The
    Fictionalizers in Beckett's Plays', in R. Cohn, ed., *Samuel Beckett a
    Collection of Criticism*, New York etc., McGraw-Hill Inc., 1975, p. 115.
9. *Glückliche Tage*, Schiller-Theater production notebook, R.U.L. MS
    1396/4/10.
10. Cf., 'But they are failing, true, that's the change, they are failing,
    that's bad, bad. Or it's the dread of coming to the last, of having
    said all, your all, before the end, no, for that will be the end, the end of
    all, not certain', *TFN*, 13.
11. A term used by D. Alpaugh of *All that Fall* in 'The Symbolic Structure
    of Samuel Beckett's *All that Fall*', *Modern Drama*, IX, December 1966,
    p. 328.
12. The role of Winnie's quotations, her song and her stories is much more

fully discussed in my bilingual edition of *Happy Days/Oh les beaux jours*, London, Faber and Faber, 1978, pp. 108-111 and in S.E. Gontarski, *Beckett's Happy Days. A Manuscript Study*, Columbus, Ohio, Ohio State University Libraries, 1977, pp. 59-73.

13.   Gilles Sandier in a review in *Arts*, 935, 6-12 November 1963.

Play

Play is in several respects a key work in Beckett's dramatic canon. In spite of its many obvious affinities with earlier plays — *Endgame*, for instance, in which Nagg and Nell confined to their dustbins clearly anticipate the figures set in urns in *Play*, or *Happy Days*, in which Winnie's natural mode of expression, like that of the three speakers in *Play*, is the cliché — *Play* looks forward to some of the most important and more experimental features of the miniature dramas of the 1970s.

Earlier in Beckett's theatre, light had been a more or less constant factor, grey in *Endgame*, 'blazing' in *Happy Days*, and used spatially in *Krapp's Last Tape* to create a zone of light separate from the darkness. But *Play* reveals the dramatic effectiveness of a rigorously and rhythmically controlled interplay of light and darkness, produced in this case by the spotlight switching rapidly from one head to another and so governing the dramatic tempo of the play. For, in principle at least, the actors take their cue from the light and not from the other actors. This sharp intercutting of speeches by means of light was never again used in exactly the same form by Beckett. But the principle of intercutting itself becomes a major structural device in *That Time*, and the idea of a single spotlight picking out a human head (or, as it was to become almost ten years later, a mouth) first arose soon after Beckett had finished writing *Play*.[1] *Play* also demonstrated how a rapidly delivered text could, despite its difficulties, rivet the attention.

Although Beckett had been involved on a number of occasions with productions of his plays in Paris and London, ever since Roger Blin's first production of *En attendant Godot* in 1953, it was only in the course of rehearsing *Play* in February to March 1963 with Jean-Marie Serreau in Paris and, immediately afterwards in March to April with George Devine in London, that Beckett came to be so intensely preoccupied with the effects that could be obtained by varying the intensity and the speed of both speech and lighting in the repeat of the play. George Devine was widely recognized as an expert on lighting techniques and Beckett worked very closely with him on this aspect of the production.[2] Later, a meticulous concern for the dramatic shapes as well as the effects that could be derived from variations in sound and lighting levels characterized *That Time* and, even more strikingly, *Footfalls*. As the production notebooks show, this same concern was to figure prominently in Beckett's own Berlin productions of *Endgame*, *Krapp's Last Tape*, *Happy Days* and *Waiting for Godot*, as well as *That Time* and *Footfalls*. It can therefore be said with some certainty that *Play* laid the foundations for Beckett's later emphasis on a subtle choreography of sound and silence, light and darkness, movement and stillness.

The title of *Waiting for Godot* describes a state and names its enigmatic, unseen cause; *Endgame* alludes to a game of chess; *Krapp's Last Tape* evokes excrement as a man's name and endows him with a tape-recorder; *Happy Days* recalls an ironic greeting. By comparison *Play*, like *Film*, seems to be Beckett's most explicit and plainly descriptive title. In one sense, this is exactly what it is. Three stock characters, a man, his wife, and his mistress are involved in an only too familiar triangular relationship. Clandestine meetings, domestic squabbles, partings and recriminations have long formed the staple diet of much domestic drama or light comedy. Once again here they are only too clearly the stuff of a 'play'. *Play* is also what it says it is in the sense that the three characters speak only when they are illuminated by that most theatrical of devices, the spotlight. And yet placing the figures in receptacles like funeral urns, situating them in a kind of purgatorial after-life, making the spotlight into an 'inquirer' and the three figures into 'victims', compelled to go over again and again the events of their previous relationship, clearly sets both the figures and the events into a very different perspective. *Play* seems then like 'play' in another sense — concerned as it is with such a trivial, ludicrously squalid affair or 'pastime' — that of a parody of both life and theatre. 'I know now,' says the man, 'all that was just . . . play' (*Play and Two Short Pieces for Radio*, Faber and Faber, London, 1964, 16; all further references are to this edition), as he refers back to the incidents of his past life. One is reminded of Plato's words that 'we should keep our seriousness for serious things and not waste it on trifles, and that, while God is the real goal of all beneficent serious endeavour, man . . . has been constructed as a toy for God . . . All of us then, men and women alike, must fall in with our role and spend life in making our *play* as pefect as possible'[3]. And yet as M's subsequent question suggests ('And all this [their present plight] when will all this have been just play?', 16-17), if all is indeed regarded as 'play', in limbo as in life, this will still not wipe out the pain as well as the absurdity from either. There is, in fact, not a scrap of comfort to be gained from the drastic change that has taken place. Even W2's apparently optimistic 'At the same time I prefer this to . . . the other thing. Definitely. There are endurable moments' (15) is less optimism than a sour assessment of what has gone before. For this is, after all, only one small segment in a larger spectrum of emotional responses to their situation and is repeated in any case over and over again.

In his director's notes for the Old Vic production of *Play*, George Devine compared the inquisitorial light to a 'dental drill'.[4] And it is certainly far more of an 'instrument of torture', to use Billie Whitelaw's picturesque phrase,[5] than an Opener like that which urges on Voice and Music in *Cascando* and takes an interest in what they reveal. But, as with the beam of light in *Not I*, the torture for the three figures caught up in this inquiry (as distinct perhaps from that of the actors playing the parts) comes not from the actual pain caused by the light as from its persistent piercing of the darkness and prevention of any possible peace. The light is both within the strange stage world to which the three figures are confined and outside the drama that it brings into existence, since, as spectators and listeners, we depend on it as on the conductor of an orchestra and, at the same time, recognize it for what it is, *viz*: a spotlight. Beckett seems to have been concerned in rehearsals with reducing this more objective, mechanical side of the light (which cannot, for obvious reasons, be entirely avoided) and playing up more the 'human' side. For in writing to Devine about variations in speed and intensity, he suggested that 'the inquirer (light) begins to emerge as no less a victim of his inquiry than they and as needing to be free, within narrow limits, literally to act the part, i.e. to vary if only slightly his speeds and intensities'.[6] But the role of the light is even more ambiguous, for it has also been seen as 'a metaphor for our attention (relentless, all-consuming, whimsical)'[7] and as a way of 'switching on and switching off speech exactly as a playwright does when he moves on from one line of dialogue on his page to the next'. [8] Neither of these analogies conflict, of course, with the more human qualities of Beckett's modified 'inquirer'.

In the stage directions relating to the voices in the opening Chorus, Beckett wrote that they should be 'faint, largely unintelligible'(9). Although it is the rapid tempo of the play and audience laughter that prevents the remainder of the text from being understood in full the first time round, George Devine recognized that this play was treating language in a way that was significantly different from Beckett's earlier plays, except for Lucky's monologue in *Waiting for Godot*. For Devine made the following observations in his director's notes: 'words not as conveying thought or ideas but as dramatic ammunition — cf. light . . . words have no significance or meaning whatsoever — just "things" that come out of their mouths — the best dramatic use — the constant shock treatment . . . Tonelessness — speaking to themselves — no attitude to an audience — pointless to have tone on constant repetition'. [9] There is, of course, nothing here or in the play itself (which does not entirely conform to Devine's commentary on it) that one would not already find in Artaud's *The Theatre and its Double*, which we know Beckett had read, [10] or in Ionesco's essay 'Expérience du théâtre', printed in the *Nouvelle revue française* in 1958, which he may well have looked at. But what is striking about Beckett's theatricalism is that he adopts such distinctive devices only when they accord closely with his themes and when they can be integrated into a highly personal dramatic vision.

The 'faint, largely unintelligible' voices of the Chorus provide a surprise and a shock at the opening of the curtain. If the words are to be followed at all, the spectator needs to bring the highest level of concentration to bear immediately on what he hears. The rest of the play is then able to capitalize on this heightened concentration. But the Chorus also manages in a matter of seconds to establish a sense of ritual, each voice intoning a statement which proceeds quite independently of the others. For, instead of choral unison, what we are offered is three separate monologues, which appear on first hearing to be related only rhythmically one to another, as Beckett's layout of the phrasing shows and the actors' delivery would make quite clear. In addition, the Chorus provides markers which separate the second part (or, as Beckett termed it, the 'Narration') [11] from the third part (or the 'Meditation'). It also indicates the end of the first and second run-throughs of the play.

As their lack of individual names suggests, the three figures in *Play* (M, W1, and W2) are not three-dimensional characters. Any attempt to analyze them as if they are would be absurd. The stereotype predominates: a virile male who wants the best of both worlds, domestic bliss and extra-marital spice; a possessive, shrewish wife; and a concerned, yet demanding 'other woman'. In fact, they have only enough individuality to be described, in Barbara Bray's words, as 'people in all their funny, disgraceful, pitiable fragility and all the touchingness, in spite of everything, of their efforts to love one another, and endure'.[12] The settings reek of deliberate cliché: the morning room of a large house set among lawns; a butler, Erskine by name; the mistress posed by an open window, indulging in the traditional pastime of idle mistresses, doing her nails or stitching; a private detective set on the adulterous trail; and a possible escape from it all to the Riviera or 'our darling Grand Canary' (12). This all belongs, of course, to the artificial world of melodrama and romance embodied in romanticized fiction and echoed in a style of theatre parodied neatly by Tom Stoppard in *The Real Inspector Hound* (1968).

The parody extends from that of postures, actions and attitudes to finely etched parody of word, phrase and syntactical construction: 'Judge then to my astoundment' (11), 'as I was sitting stricken' (11), 'Fearing she was about to offer me violence, I rang for Erskine' (11), 'How could we be together in the way we are, if there were someone else' (11), '[I had] not much stomach for her leavings either' (13). These examples are borrowed from all three speakers, although it is the wife who is most extravagantly endowed with clichés.

Yet the humour of *Play* is not simply that of parodied romance and 'finely enamelled cliché'.[13] It has a much sharper edge than cliché is ever normally allowed. For among the stiffly genteel remarks, other more violent responses occur which, although they are almost as cliché-ridden, contrast sharply and incongruously with them. This conflict between two opposing sets of clichés not only provokes a sense of mixed amusement and shock but also brings one, however fleetingly, into closer touch with something approaching genuine emotional torment. The violence is expressed in animal or bird images, which, although lacking in freshness, still appear more vividly real than the glossy, novelettish world in which the adulterous affair took place. The mistress tells how the wife 'burst in and flew at me' (10), 'I smell you off him, she screamed, he stinks of bitch' (11); the man 'slinks in' (11) like a dog to confess his guilt; and, according to the wife, his mistress 'had means, I fancy, though she lived like a pig' (19). The description of the mistress by W1 is in terms more appropriate to a grotesque monster than a desirable woman, 'Pudding face, puffy, spots, blubber mouth, jowls, no neck, dugs you could . . . calves like a flunkey' (13). The wife regularly uses verbs of smell and gutter level nouns when she speaks about her rival, 'a bitch' (11), 'a common tart' (13), 'a slut' (14), 'give up that whore . . . or I'll slit my throat' (10). The best example of humourous disparity of language is found in the man's 'At home, all heart to heart, new leaf and bygones bygones. I ran into your ex-doxy, she said one night, on the pillow, you're well out of that. Rather uncalled for, I thought. I am indeed, sweetheart, I said, I am indeed. God what vermin women. Thanks to you, angel, I said' (14).

As George Devine pointed out in a dispute with Kenneth Tynan, *Play* cannot be understood in purely literary terms.[14] And the theatrical dimension means that these elements of parody, cliché, and verbal incongruity register rapidly, and only partially. For if the momentum of the production is to be maintained and there are to be no laughter pauses — as there were none in the British première or in the Royal Court 1976 revival — it will prove impossible to seize the whole of the text the first time round. Beckett was, however, clearly aware that, though much of the detail of this second part was missed or overlooked on first hearing, it would swim into focus during the *reprise*. As with the musical *reprise* that was included in some of Haydn's string quartets (which Beckett much admires), response to the 'Narration' inevitably differs on the second run-through of the text. Themes already sound familiar, detailed variations are more easily recognized, and ordered patterns or more subtle echoes can be discerned in the composition. But also with *Play*, experience shows that reception changes from one of keen, but amused attention in the course of the first hearing to a more sombre appraisal of the tormented plight of the three figures during the second.

The median blackout, the simultaneous use of spots on all three heads and the lowered strength of both light and voice mark the opening of a third section of the play which already displays a torment arising partly out of the situation itself but also out of their imaginings of a life on earth of which they are not part. There is still humour, but it is in the form of irony rather than parody: 'There is no future in this' (16), 'things may disimprove, there is that danger' (16), 'perhaps they have become friends' (17). Images and attitudes persist from the

'Narration', but in a modified, muted, reduced form. They will now be 'kissing their sour kisses' (18) speculates the mistress, while the wife pictures her rival still sitting by a window, gazing now at the olives, waiting for him to return; she tries hard to be precise in the most appropriate cliché selected for the occasion, 'Shadow stealing over everything. Creeping. Yes' (20). Since individual statements are shorter in this part, the light cuts more rapidly from face to face and the impression is of a more frenzied pace. It is only in the 'Meditation' that. the inquisitorial light comes to be addressed directly by its victims. Attitudes liable to have been applied once to the man are now transferred to the light. The wife's 'get off me' (16) and her 'you will weary of me' (15) and the mistress's 'go away and start poking and pecking at someone else' (16) echo tired or irritated reactions to a lover. This is part of a desperate need to anthropomorphize the light. For while it may be supposed capable of possessing human feelings of curiosity, pity, understanding, satisfaction or even weariness, there is some hope that unbroken darkness, silence and peace might be reached in the end. But while the motives and purpose of the light remain unknowable, release seems horrifyingly remote. M's last question 'Am I as much as . . . being seen?' (22) assumes, then, an overriding importance.

The three figures retain a certain individuality of response to both the purgatorial situation and the 'hellish half-light'. W2 hopes that madness might provide her own form of release from torment, M seeks darkness and peace, and W1, more desperately, tries to discover what must be done or said to rid herself of the light. But more important than this is the fact that, rather like a fragmented musical round song, with each voice starting at a different point on the score, the three sets of statements follow the same basic patterns. The three voices can therefore be traced as they move through similar emotional responses to the light and imaginings of the other two left on earth, to speculations as to what is causing their torment and the possibilities of it ever ending. But these related statements do not coincide in time. Instead, they echo what another voice has recited earlier and, as in *That Time*, contrast or interrelate in more complex ways with the surrounding statements. Sometimes, since the range of their pre-occupations is so limited, the lines of their statements converge briefly, only to move quickly apart again as they follow their own path. The impression is that of a clockwork mechanism, in which all the cogs are wound up so that they move inexorably on but coincide only momentarily one with another. Yet within the broader patterns of movement, there are intricate variations in tone, colour, intensity and pace, as the following series of responses will show:

W1.   Hellish half-light.

Spot from W1 *to* M.

M.   Peace, yes, I suppose, a kind of peace, and all that pain as if . . . never been.

Spot from M *to* W2.

W2.   Give me up as a bad job. Go away and start poking and pecking at someone else. On the other hand —

Spot from W2 *to* W1.

W1.   Get off me! (*Vehement*.) Get off me! (16)

The identical repeat of the whole play reveals the three characters caught up for eternity it would seem in an endless repetition of story and inquisitorial ritual: the mechanism, in fact, never running down. However, in the course of rehearsing the French translation, *Comédie*, with Jean-Marie Serreau in Paris, an alternative version of the *da capo* which incorporated an important element of variation was adopted and developed further in the London Old Vic production. In brief, the changes consist of, first, a slight weakening of both the light and the voices in the first Repeat and even more so in the fragment of the second Repeat, the variation ranging in strength from A (the strongest) to strength E (the weakest). Secondly, an abridged Chorus is adopted for the opening fragment of the second Repeat. Thirdly, there is a breathless quality in the voices from the beginning of Repeat 1, which increases to the end of the play. And fourthly, the actual order of the speeches at the opening of the Repeat is changed. In the letter to George Devine of 9 March, Beckett describes the new arrangements for the Repeat as 'dramatically more effective'.[15] But it is also clear that what is involved is a distinct evolution in his way of conceiving the replay. For he writes of 'the impression of falling off which this would give, with suggestion of conceivable dark and silence in the end, or of an indefinite approximating towards it.[16] This view of the *da capo* brings the dramatic form of *Play* much closer to that of Beckett's earlier plays in which things are gradually running down and in which stasis, although it seems remote, nonetheless seems ultimately possible. Modifications to the order of the replies confers, of course, a degree of freedom on the inquirer-light. Variation in order seems, in fact, to have replaced Beckett's earlier idea of introducing into the Repeat 'a quality of hesitancy, of both question and answer, perhaps not so much in a slowing down of actual débit as in a less confident movement of spot from one face to another and less immediate reaction of the voices'.[17] A consequence of this change is that the light seems to be as much caught up in this unexplained ritual as the figures themselves are. It does not function, then, only by prompting them into speech, but is itself prompted like them to enact and reenact a role within this strange, purgatorial world.

A further effect of the repetition is to torment us, the spectators, as well as the victims of the light. For, as my co-author has pointed out elsewhere, 'one feels that the light should have been able to un-scramble the essentials more successfully the second time around. We are as much passive sufferers of the light as the heads are'.[18] But if we did think we were there to unscramble what we hear, by the end of the second repeat we have come to recognize our mistake. We are there simply to observe and witness, as 'they' were there to respond, and as the light is there to elicit these responses. There is no more question of understanding why this should be so than there is of supplying the 'reasons unknown' that would account for man's 'wasting and pining' in Lucky's monologue in *Waiting for Godot*.

If, as Deidre Bair supposes,[19] biographical issues and tensions lie at the source of *Play*, they are soon transformed into a complex work which, while being rich in humour and humanity, still possesses its own special brand of repeated torment. If the later miniature dramas of the 1970s go back for inspiration to the world of *The Unnamable*, the technical dramatization of that world owes much to *Play*. The inheritance is clear enough: a rapidly delivered monologue, a head picked out by a spotlight from the surrounding darkness, fading lighting effects, and the intercutting of several voices. But there are deeper affinities too. *Play* brought together (without the help of a tape-recorder) different time states, as both *Not I* and *That Time* were to do, and treated them all as infernal. It also mapped out a world of apparently infinite time and space in which figures talk or wander restlessly, just as troubled there as they were in life. This world looks forward naturally enough to the various levels of ghostly existence that are found in *Footfalls* and in the television plays, *Ghost Trio* and *. . . but the clouds . . . .* In *Play*, visual and verbal elements function as one and are sufficiently vital to hold the attention, a virtue which, as we shall see, not all of the miniature dramas possess. More compelling than any of its progeny except *Not I*, and certainly more approachable than all of them, *Play* stays in the mind as much for its human as for its infernal characteristics. Perhaps for this reason alone it will survive the test of time as a piece of theatre worthy to figure alongside *Waiting for Godot*, *Endgame*, *Krapp's Last Tape*, and *Happy Days*.

Notes

1. In the 'Kilcool' manuscript, dated Paris, Dec. 1963, Beckett envisaged a 'woman's face alone in constant light'. Trinity College, Dublin MS. 4664, p. 10. Rosemary Pountney first pointed out to me the connection between 'Kilcool' and *Not I* and *That Time*.
2. As a letter from Beckett to George Devine, dated 9.3.64, shows; see J. Knowlson, ed., *Samuel Beckett: an Exhibition*, Turret Books, London, 1971, p. 92.
3. *The Collected Dialogues of Plato*, ed. E. Hamilton & H. Cairns, Pantheon Books, New York, 1961, *Laws*, VII, 803c, p. 1375.
4. *Samuel Beckett: an Exhibition*, p. 91.
5. *Journal of Beckett Studies*, no. 3, Summer 1978, p. 86.
6. *Samuel Beckett: an Exhibition*, p. 92.
7. H. Kenner, *Samuel Becket: A Critical Study*, new edition, University of California Press, Berkeley and Los Angeles, 1968, pp. 210-211.
8. J. Fletcher and J. Spurling, *Beckett. A Study of his Plays*, p. 107.
9. *Samuel Beckett: an Exhibition*, p. 91.
10. Letter to J. Knowlson, 11.iv.72.
11. M. Esslin, 'Samuel Beckett and the Art of Broadcasting', *Encounter*, Sept. 1975, p. 44.
12. B. Bray, 'The New Beckett', *The Observer*, 16 June 1963.
13. H. Kenner, *Samuel Beckett*, p. 211.
14. I. Wardle, *The Theatres of George Devine*, Jonathan Cape, London, 1978, pp. 207-208.
15. *Samuel Beckett: an Exhibition*, p. 92.
16. *eo.loc.*
17. *eo.loc.*
18. J. Pilling, *Samuel Beckett*, Routledge and Kegan Paul, London, 1976, p. 90.
19. D. Bair, *Samuel Beckett: A Biography*, New York, Harcourt Brace Jovanovich, 1978, pp. 481-482.

Come and Go

. . . for the coming is in the shadow of the going and the going is in the shadow of the coming, that is the annoying part of it .[1]

In this short 'dramaticule', written in English in 1965, which varied in length on publication from 121 to 127 words,[2] three women, Flo, Vi and Ru, 'ages indeterminable', sit side by side on an almost invisible bench placed in the centre of the stage, in a zone of soft light. In turn, each woman makes a single exit and an entrance, moving silently out into the surrounding darkness and returning once more into the light. During her absence, the other two express first concern and then horror at her present condition and future fate. The question put by each in turn concerning the third absent friend ('Does she not know?') varies little in form and, on each occasion, prompts an answer that in its archaic, Biblical phrasing contains the name of God (e.g. 'God grant not').

Deliberately, the essential item of information is left unstated in words. Instead, it is whispered, unheard by the audience, into the ear of a horrified companion. The appalled response of the one receiving the news indicates clearly enough that the gossip concerns the imminent death of the friend who has just left them, giving them the opportunity for this exchange of dark confidences. An earlier, and a much longer version of the play, entitled *Good Heavens*, had, much less successfully, made this more explicit, even spelling out the terminal date of the third friend's incurable ailment ('Three months. At the outside . . . Not a suspicion. She thinks it is heartburn').[3] The unspoken nature of the condemnation in the final version is more powerful precisely because it is less explicit. For while it leaves a mystery unresolved, it also tends to lead one beyond the particular illness of an individual woman to embrace the fate of all mankind.

That the earlier title *Good Heavens* was not merely exclamatory but was also a bitter indictment of God's mercy is suggested by the dark tone of the finished play and by the way in which the response to the whispered news 'Oh' is rendered in the French translation by, in turn, 'Misère', 'Malheur' and 'Miséricorde'. The published title *Come and Go* (*Va et vient*) not only picks up the movements of the characters entering and exiting. It also points to the brevity of life, recalling, as *Breath* was to do, Pozzo's 'the light gleams an instant, then it's night once more'. But, as with the title of *All that Fall*, *Come and Go* may also echo the words of a psalm, 'The Lord shall preserve thy going out and thy coming in from this time forth, and even for evermore' (Psalm 121, verse viii).

The opening line of the play 'When did we three last meet?' recalls, of course, the meeting of the three witches in *Macbeth*. But Beckett's three women look back on an unfulfilled past, as well as forward to a doomed future — their own rather than that of any other person in the drama. No particular period of past time is alluded to, although with their rather precise, archaic mode of speech and the sombre uniformity and muted colouring of their drab costumes they seem like middle-class ladies from the recent past. Their names, Flo, Vi and Ru recall flowers (Flora, Violet and Rue), the latter reminding one of Ophelia's madness scene with Laertes in *Hamlet*.[4] Superficially they may make us think of the Three Graces as they link hands, but, more precisely, they resemble in appearance the three mothers in Fritz Lang's '*M*', a film much loved by Beckett.[5]

Harking back to their childhood, when they would sit together on the log 'in the playground at Miss Wade's', the three women link hands as they used to do then, using the special way they had adopted among themselves, like initiates in some secret cult. Their hands form, in fact, the pattern of an unbroken chain, an emblem that, traditionally, has been used to symbolize eternity. As alike as possible in appearance, the three women are also united by a visual image that not only brings together past and present but throws into relief the ephemeral quality of the life of the individual by setting against it an evocation of togetherness and endlessness.

The austere patterning of word, silence and gesture that makes up this simple, yet moving, little play is brought to an enigmatic conclusion by another highly suggestive image. Flo's comment 'I can feel the rings' (when it is expressly stated that no rings are visible on their hands[6]), may relate to adolescent dreams of a love that has, presumably, never been realized or has led only to deception. For just as, when they were girls, they could only look forward with blind hope, now all they can do is look back in memory to their girlhood, comforting themselves, as Eugene Webb has suggested[7], with the illusion that they are wearing engagement or wedding rings. But both the theme and the dramatic structure of the play are dominated by images of circularity and recurrence, and once again the ring, the common symbol of eternity, sets up an internal conflict with the fate of mortals who are unable to escape from the ravages of the 'Time cancer'[8] that marks the log on which they used to sit with quite a different kind of ineradicable ring. As the Metaphysical poet, Henry Vaughan, wrote, for instance, in his poem, 'The World':

> I saw Eternity the other night
> Like a great *Ring* of pure and endless light,
> All calm, as it was bright,
> And round beneath it, Time in hours, days, years,
> Driv'n by the spheres
> Like a vast shadow mov'd, In which the world
> And all her train were hurl'd.[9]

The banal situation of two women gossiping darkly about a third not present has been transformed in *Come and Go* into a miniature dramatic piece of considerable formal beauty by means of a stylization of dress, movement, gesture and language that brings Beckett closer perhaps to the theatre of W.B. Yeats than at any other time in his plays, except for the ritualistic opening of *Endgame*. The three women sit motionless and in silence at the opening and the close of the play; movements, which are few in number and symmetrical, are performed slowly and deliberately, as one of the three figures drifts soundlessly away like a phantom into the darkness; and, except for the more human, anguished response to the terrible news concerning the third friend, the voices are as dull and colourless as are the costumes. Words seem to represent something of an intrusion into the silence that constantly threatens to become the dominant reality. The numerous marked silences are as essential to the impact of the play as are the sparse words or the repeated gestures. And yet the imposition of silence also throws into greater relief the few phrases that are allowed any resonance of their own: 'Dreaming of love', 'I can feel the rings' and the virtual refrain 'God grant not'. Finally, the criss-cross patterning of hands that links the three women physically as they are united in a common plight is moving in the theatre because it echoes the formal symmetry of the rest of the play, as well as expressing in a single image fraternal compassion and fragile mortality.

Beckett's technique in creating this short dramatic piece has been compared with the spare brush strokes that compose a Chinese painting, in which everything that is not essential is discarded for the sake of purity of line and economy of means.[10] Yet, as so often with Beckett's plays, this extreme purity and economy were not arrived at immediately or without difficulty. There were at least fifteen versions of the play up to its final stage. And it began its life in an early draft much less starkly with the two women left on stage exchanging sexual confidences to explain the apparent health and vigour of one of them, compared, of course, with the unhappy prognosis for the one absent. This sexual motif had also been introduced in an opening scene where all the three women were seen together. In this scene, inappropriately it now seems, Beckett had parodied the style of romantic-erotic novels, for purposes of ironic contrast and comic deflation. One of the women read out aloud a passage from such a novel, 'Hermione rose at last from the steaming sweet-smelling foam and stood all pink and dripping before the great cheval-glass, inspecting her luscious forms. Caressingly she passed her hands . . .'[11] In later versions, the sexual motif is entirely removed so that, instead of basking complacently in a present contentment that is then immediately revealed as bitterly false, Beckett's three women focus on the fact of their mortality and the final version comes to have its present economy and symmetry of form. The mood has also been changed and the published text is imbued with a deep melancholy that gives it the force of a *memento mori*. Thematically, the play seems to be closely linked with Schopenhauer's view of the reunion of friends:

> If two men who were friends in their youth meet again when they are old, after being separated for a life-time, the chief feeling they will have at the sight of each other will be one of complete disappointment at life as a whole; because their thoughts will be carried back to that earlier time when life seemed so fair as it lay spread out before them in the rosy light of dawn, promised so much — and then performed so little. This feeling will so completely predominate over every other that they will not even consider it necessary to give it words; but on either side it will be silently assumed, and form the groundwork of all that they have to talk about.[12]

This same groundwork underlies Beckett's miniature drama, but the theme is suggested rather than stated, sensed behind the words rather than contained within them. This is true also of that sharp awareness of the tragic inevitability of death that Beckett shares with so many major dramatists. For Beckett's focus of interest in this play lies not so much in the unarguable fact of human mortality itself, as in shaping word, movement and silence into an aesthetic pattern that transforms so morbid a theme into a 'dramaticule' that, although a minor work when read, can seem almost as compelling in performance as some of Beckett's longer, and thematically more complex, plays.

Notes

1. *Watt*, p. 56.
2. Premièred in German at the Schiller-Theater Werkstatt, Berlin in January 1966 and directed by Deryk Mendel with Lieselotte Rau, Charlotte Joeres, and Sibylle Gilles, the play was first published in French in 1966. An English version was published in 1967 by John Calder to whom it is dedicated. For a detailed analysis of the manuscript · and published versions see Breon Mitchell, 'Art in Microcosm: The Manuscript Stages of Beckett's *Come and Go*', *Modern Drama*, 19, no. 3, September 1976, pp. 245-260, although Mitchell did not at the time know about the Reading *Good Heavens* manuscript.
3. R.U.L. MS 1227/7/16/5.
4. A detail owed to Breon Mitchell and, independently, to Hersh Zeifman.
5. D. Bair, *Samuel Beckett: A Biography*, p. 242.
6. *Come and Go*, p. 10, 'No rings apparent'.
7. E. Webb, *The Plays of Samuel Beckett*, London, Peter Owen, 1972, p. 119.
8. *Proust and Three Dialogues*, p. 18.
9. H. Vaughan, 'The World' in *The Works of Henry Vaughan*, Oxford, Clarendon Press, 1914, vol. 2, p. 466.
10. J. Fletcher and J. Spurling, *Beckett. A Study of his Plays*, p. 116.
11. R.U.L. MS 1227/7/16/5.
12. A. Schopenhauer, *Studies in Pessimism*, selected and translated by T. Bailey Saunders, London, 1908, p. 14.

Breath

Breath has either been treated too reverentially, surprising though this may seem,[1] or has been considered a rather weak joke, unworthy of serious attention. Like most of Beckett's work it is a mixture of the comic and the serious. Beckett himself wittily described it in a version of the French translation, *Souffle*, as a 'farce in five acts'. Its humour stems largely from the way it deliberately fails to satisfy audience expectations. It does this, of course, simply by being what it is, a thirty second play without characters and without words. Certainly, as written, it would have disappointed the audience of the erotic review, *Oh Calcutta*, for which it was composed. For in this context both the title and the contents of *Breath* seemed keenly ironic and, in the eyes of the show's producers, unsuitable until Kenneth Tynan, or someone else,[2] tried to improve on the joke by adding 'naked people' to the miscellaneous rubbish that littered the stage. Predictably, Beckett prevented any further use elsewhere of his travestied script.

Five seconds of faint light on the rubbish; a faint and brief vagitus or birth-cry; the inspiration of breath and a slow increase of light; a corresponding expiration of breath and a parallel slow decrease of light; another brief cry followed by silence. The text is skeletal enough. Considered as a non-verbal equivalent to Pozzo's 'They give birth astride of a grave; the light gleams an instant, then its night once more' (*WFG*, 89) or as a more subdued version of Winnie's 'bob up out of dark — . . . blaze of hellish light' (*HD*, 11), *Breath* is neatly self-sufficient. Yet it is surely only memorable because of its *succès de scandale*. For Pozzo's words make up only one line on a much larger canvas, whereas however admirably shaped *Breath* may be, its dramatic interest and impact must be judged as severely limited.

If it was regarded at first by some critics as a logical terminal point in Beckett's writing for the theatre, it is now clear that its main interest is that, in the wake of *Play*, it points forward to the miniature dramas of the 'seventies. This is not so much because of its actual brevity, as because of its meticulous interplay of light, sound and silence, its balanced variations in lighting strength, its formal symmetry, and its use of amplified sound, adopted later in *Not I* and *Footfalls* (live) and in *That Time* (recorded).

The three plays of the 'sixties (*Play*, *Come and Go* and *Breath*) offered Beckett the opportunity of exploring further the technical possibilities of the theatre and brought him into much more active participation in actual production, not only with *Play*, as we have seen, but also with *Come and Go*, which he directed himself in Paris in February 1966. And if *Breath* has very little to add to what Beckett had already said with more resonance in his longer plays, it is worth remembering that it still has a modest part to play in the growing simplification and economy of his later drama.

Notes

1. Misplaced reverence was accorded to the play when it was played several times over in the course of a Beckett evening at the Oxford Playhouse, on 8 March 1970 in aid of the Samuel Beckett Theatre Appeal.
2. See D. Bair, *op. cit.*, pp. 602-603.

Ends and Odds in Prose

Ends and Odds in Prose

In the days when Beckett believed that the artist was bound to fail, he went to great lengths to ensure that only those writings of his which had failed 'successfully' should find their way to the general public. It was with some reluctance that he gave his French publishers permission to bring out *Mercier et Camier* and *Premier Amour* some twenty-five years after they had been consigned to a drawer and forgotten, and he only gave permission to his English publishers to reprint his first full-length fictional work almost forty years after its first, extremely unsuccessful, appearance. In recent years, as his attitude to the 'art of failure' has changed radically, Beckett has been content to release either rejected drafts of works that had 'fizzled out' or early drafts of works that he later refined into something more satisfying.

Beckett's tremendous generosity in this regard — in gifts to libraries, in waiving copyright fees, in his willingness to let little magazines publish *inédits* — has enabled the new generation of Beckett critics to write more authoritatively about the nature of the Beckettian creative process, and to devote more attention to manuscript variants than is usually possible in an author's lifetime. But it has also perhaps had the effect of putting commentators on their guard and discouraging them from offering general criticisms, when it is always possible that there exist typescripts in Beckett's personal files that will disprove their contentions. It ought also to be said that many readers are suspicious of Beckett's tendency, since 1968, to bring out very brief texts in severely limited illustrated editions at prices beyond the reach of even fairly well-heeled collectors, if only to make perfectly clear that this is not something he indulges in for personal gain, nor in order to protect himself from scrutiny, but in every case to benefit someone else, be it personal friend, or fellow-artist, or penurious private press proprietor. There is no better proof of this than the text *All Strange Away*, brought out in 1976 by the Gotham Book Mart in an edition of 226 copies, illustrated by Edward Gorey, the proceeds from which go to the widow of one of Beckett's closest personal friends, the actor Jack McGowran. The publication of this text, which Beckett rightly regarded as inferior to *Imagination morte imaginez* (the work which finally grew out of it) allows one to study more closely the mechanics of Beckett's 'residual' art, and makes us all beneficiaries of a private act of generosity.

Before looking at *All Strange Away*, however, it is important to come to terms with the deeply puzzling *Fizzles* (*Foirades* in the French), which were published only recently (1976), but which date from before *All Strange Away*.

1.   The *Fizzles*

In a letter to me, Beckett says that the *Fizzles* dated from after *How It Is*, and there seems a certain logic in his following the 'fundamental sound' of *How It Is* with six short texts that 'break wind noiselessly' and fizzle out shortly after they have begun. The fact that Beckett saw fit to publish them together with *Still* and *For to End Yet Again* also suggests that they are the first attempts at a minimalism that, in the last twenty years or so, has been Beckett's standard practice, in prose and drama. But this dating has been questioned, notably by J.D. O'Hara, who sees the *Fizzles* as throwbacks to the *Texts for Nothing*, and on first French publication (in the *Minuit* house magazine) there were indeed hints that they were written at the end of the 1950s rather than at the beginning of the 1960s. The confusion is worse confounded by the fact that, in the three separate editions (English, French and American), Beckett juggles with the order of the texts, as if in some doubt about exactly how they relate one to another, and to the much more important *Still* and *For to End Yet Again*. It seems safest, in the absence of hard and fast evidence, to attempt first a broad overview of the texts in question, and then to see what each individual 'fizzle' contributes to the problems of language and being that have always been at the heart of Beckett's enterprise.

Any experienced reader of Beckett will be struck, on reading the *Fizzles*, by the plethora of motifs that have been encountered before. 'Afar a bird', for instance, alludes to the end of *From an Abandoned Work* (*For to End Yet Again and Other Fizzles*, London, John Calder, 1976, p. 41: all further references are to this edition), and refers obliquely to *How It Is* ('someone divines me, divines us, that's what he's come to, come to in the end', 39-40). 'I gave up before birth' alludes to the end of *Malone Dies* (46), the basic situation of which seems also to lie behind 'Horn came always'. Horn, in that 'fizzle', is reminiscent of Gaber in *Molloy*, and the obsession in 'He is barehead' with moving in a straight line calls to mind Molloy's problems in part one of the same novel. The 'sounds . . . of fall' in 'He is barehead' (28) remind one of Molloy's 'world collapsing endlessly' (*TN*, 40); the 'childhood sea' of 'Old earth' (54) recalls the first *Text for Nothing*; the 'I-he' confusions of 'Afar a bird' and 'I gave up before birth' are similar to the fourth *Text for Nothing*.

But there are also a number of motifs that point forward, rather than backward, in time: the 'ruinstrewn land' of 'Afar a bird' (39) makes one think of *Lessness, For to End Yet Again* and *La Falaise*; the tree of 'Old Earth' points forward to *Sounds* and *As the Story Was Told*; 'still, standing before a window' (at the end of 'Old Earth' 54) is analogous to *Still*, which is also prefigured at the beginning of 'He is barehead' (25). 'He is barehead' contains the 'fancy' (30) of *All Strange Away*, the labyrinthine structures of *The Lost Ones*, and the faint, remote sounds that are referred to again in *Sounds* and *As the Story Was Told*. 'He is barehead' contains references to Murphy (who also 'never wore a hat', *M* 53; cf. *TN*, 11) and to the Brunonian maxima and minima of Beckett's 1929 essay on Joyce. There are also several literary references to Milton's *Samson Agonistes* ('a little further on' in 'He is barehead', 27), to Shakespeare's *Hamlet* (the 'journey . . . from which it were better I had never returned' in 'Horn came always', 35) and to the end of Dante's *Inferno* ('I see the sky' in 'Old Earth', 53-54), which Beckett also refers to in *Text 9* and *The Lost Ones*, section four.

The *Fizzles* are clearly, therefore, transitional works, full of what 'He is barehead' calls 'fresh elements and motifs' (30) but far from being liberated from elements and motifs that are, in Beckettian terms, comparatively ancient. But despite these transitional features, the *Fizzles* are surprisingly homogeneous and form, no doubt with a judicious sprinkling of hindsight, a genuine collection, with a number of points of contact between the separate texts. 'He is barehead', for instance, ends with 'these bones of which more very shortly, and at length' (30); and 'Afar a bird' and 'I gave up before birth' attempt to reduce the 'he' of the 'I-he' dichotomy to bones, in order that the 'I' may achieve independent, authentic being.[1] The 'body seen before' of 'Closed Space' (50) reminds us that the Murphy-like figure of 'He is barehead' is precisely a body we have seen before. There is a new sense of purpose about the self-addressed admonitions of the respective speakers: 'I won't go on about worms, about bones and dust' ('I gave up before birth', 46); 'I'll let myself be seen before I'm done' ('Horn came always', 33). Almost all the texts, as befits Beckett's attempt to 'break wind noiselessly' are concerned, to a greater or lesser degree, with sound and silence. There is, too, a pervasive concern throughout with the problems of beginning and ending, announced in the first sentence of *For to End Yet Again*, surfacing again in 'Afar a bird' ('I'll feed it all it needs, all it needs to end', 40), and reaching a kind of high water-mark in 'He is barehead' where 'with one thing and another little by little his history takes shape' (30).

Of the individual 'fizzles', only two ('He is barehead' and 'Old Earth') are really noteworthy, since 'Closed Place' returns to *The Lost Ones* material, and two of them ('Afar a bird' and 'I gave up before birth') are almost identical. 'Horn came always', with its mention of a 'session' (34), is mainly interesting in its anticipations of *As the Story Was Told*, which is a much more satisfying piece of work. It is surely symptomatic that the texts in which Beckett seeks to immure the 'I' inside a 'he'-figure ('Afar a bird' and 'I gave up before birth') and the text in which the 'I' is obscurely dependent on an external agent (the Horn of 'Horn came always') are markedly inferior to the text in which a narrative is entrusted to a mostly disinterested 'he' ('He is barehead'), and also to the text which seeks to remove dichotomies altogether ('Old Earth'). For immediately after the *Fizzles*, Beckett wrote the 'last person' narrative *All Strange Away*, and afterwards only once (in *Enough*) reverted to the first person.

'He is barehead' has an allegorical feel about it, as if Beckett is consciously employing the metaphor of a road to comment on the nature of the narrative that is being told. But it is an extraordinarily physical text as well, and reads at times as if the 'he' is striving to get born. Beckett is clearly here (as the remark about worms in 'I gave up before birth' confirms) more concerned with life than death, and the open air obviously offers more 'life-giving' properties than the subterranean passages the figure is stumbling through. This figure is at least striving to get born, whereas the 'I' of the later 'fizzle' freely admits to having given up before birth. But it seems almost as if the allegorical form of the story is precisely what prevents the achievement of real being, and by the time of 'Old Earth', with its positive approach ('it will be you, it will be me, it will be us'), it is apparently 'too late' (53). The 'long gaze' at the end of the text seems promising, but it is followed by 'gasps and spasms' that indicate 'another body' is being born (54). These are certainly the two most complex 'fizzles', no doubt because they are decisively oriented towards what 'Old Earth' calls 'moments of life' (53), which inevitably involves Beckett in the problem of 'being seen' (33). It cannot be irrelevant, in this connection, that 'Closed Place', in the original French, bears the title 'Se voir'. Beckett seems to be striving in the *Fizzles* for the 'ejaculation' which he told Lawrence Harvey would be the 'most perfect form of being', if it could ever be achieved.[2]

It is obvious that none of the *Fizzles* breaks wind quite as noiselessly as Beckett would wish, which is why no doubt he has applied this unflattering sobriquet to them. But there are signs, in both the two best pieces, that Beckett is on the way towards mastering the 'syntax of weakness'[3] that reaches its most impressive form in *Still*. The dislocated syntax of 'Old Earth' may seem at the furthest remove from the careful, almost pedantic, only momentarily ruffled, syntax of 'He is barehead'; but the overall effect is strangely similar, and they are both much mellower in tone than, for instance, 'Afar a bird' with its 'little panic steps' (41). The extraordinary statement in 'Horn came always' to the effect that 'What ruined me at bottom was athletics' (35), which seems at first reading a rather tasteless *jeu*, is no doubt intended to indicate to us that Beckett's 'late' period will be more a matter of stillness than of movement. Nothing could be better adapted to portraying this than the minimalist forms Beckett has chosen to adopt, and it cannot be accidental that he speaks, in 'He is barehead', of 'the minima, these two unforgettable' (30) when the volume does indeed contain two unforgettable 'minima' *Still* and *For to End Yet Again*. It is, in short, clear that the *Fizzles* are more than just prose 'ends and odds', and 'in view of their importance, contribute to enrich' (30) our understanding of Beckett's post-*How It Is* achievement.

2. *All Strange Away*

All Strange Away, by contrast, written a short time after the *Fizzles* in 1963-64, represents a decisive break with what has gone before and illuminates not only the text it has most in common with, *Imagination Dead Imagine*, but also the more forbidding *Lessness*, *Ping*, and *The Lost Ones*. It also serves to remind us (as we are in danger of forgetting, our love of pattern being almost more pervasive than Beckett's own) that the Beckettian equation is never simple, and that Beckett's 'briefs' in prose — all, with the exception of *Still* and *As the Story Was Told* written originally in French — owe their origin to one of his rare fictional excursions into his native English, the language he had apparently abandoned for good as a prose medium in May 1945, after three years wrestling with the 'precious and illuminating' material of *Watt*, which inspired in him such memorable 'fatigue and disgust'.

All Strange Away, as the bizarre title self-cancellingly indicates, is an exceedingly strange and elusive piece of writing, obviously composed in one of those periods of 'absence' that Beckett finds most 'fertile in peripeteias' (as *How It Is* puts it). It poses problems of comprehension much more severe than those posed by even the most difficult sections of *How It Is*, and makes the *non sequiturs* in *From An Abandoned Work* — the only comparable attempt at writing fiction in English since *Watt* — look like the 'vulgarity of a plausible concatenation'. Even with the benefit of hindsight we may not always feel certain of Beckett's drift, and repeated reading of the text may leave one more puzzled than one ever is by re-reading the (much shorter) residua. It is perhaps not too much to say that, without Beckett's information as to its date, and in the absence of one or two indelible pointers, its intransigently experimental manner could almost be considered contemporary with *For to End Yet Again*, and thus his most recent prose text (as indeed in one sense it is). Beckett seems to possess an uncanny sense of timing in releasing his work, so that even a text a decade old manages to seem stunningly contemporary.

All Strange Away is elusive partly because it suffers from irrelevancies blurring the development of its main argument. Longer than any of the late prose except *The Lost Ones*, Beckett approaches his material in a disarmingly uneconomical and haphazard way. It is not a text which, like *The Lost Ones*, insinuates a submerged principle of composition behind its apparent randomness; it exhibits, indeed, a desperateness and anguish that is quite foreign to *The Lost Ones* and the material connected with that text, and rare in Beckett's writing since *How It Is*. It opens, for instance, with a dogged attempt to fend off weariness in which the prime casualty is the image of the road so dominant in *From an Abandoned Work* and the best of the *Fizzles*.

> Imagination dead imagine. A place, that again. Never another question. A place, then someone in it, that again. Crawl out of the frowsy deathbed and drag it to a place to die in. Out of the door and down the road in the old hat and coat like after the war, no, not that again. (*All Strange Away*, p. 7, London, John Calder, 1979; all further references are to this edition.)

This is followed by what *The Lost Ones* would call a 'description of the place', brief, telegrammatic, periodically interrupted by self-addressed instances of admonition ('try for him there', 'try all', 'try that', 'look at that later') consolation ('all right', 'no matter') and commentary ('same reasoning', 'no good', 'no, can't do that'). The imperative mood that always surfaces in Beckett's most inquiring fictions is once again present, its immediacy diffused slightly by the introduction of a different register of speech, advertised (in a manner not unlike that of *How It Is*, but quite different from that of the *Texts for Nothing*) by the use of capital letters: 'Light off and let him be, on the stool, talking to himself in the last person, murmuring, no sound, Now where is he, no, Now he is here' (7). The *first*-person narratives of *How It Is* and the *Fizzles* have here been replaced (and, with the exception of *Enough*, permanently replaced) by a *last*-person narrative in which one is able to educe only a tone of voice, a strangely disembodied voice with none of the reassuringly familiar and substantial attributes one associates with first-person narrative generally, even the decidedly odd first-person narratives that were Beckett's prime concern at one time.

One of the most striking features of Beckett's protagonist 'talking to himself in the last person' is that soliloquy and solipsism are obliged to secede in favour of an inanimate inquisitor clearly not far removed (in time as in conception) from the 'hellish light' of *Happy Days* and *Play*, an inquisitor which more and more engages the protagonist's attention as the dominant feature of his world, calling it into being almost, as later the light will do in *Imagination Dead Imagine* and *The Lost Ones*. In *All Strange Away* Beckett is moving towards the situation that obtains in *Imagination Dead Imagine* and *The Lost Ones*, where his favourite antinomies, light and darkness, are seen at last not as mutually exclusive but as polarities forming reciprocal parts of the same system:

> Imagine light. Imagine light. No visible source, glare at full, spread all
> over, no shadow, all six planes shining the same, slow on, ten seconds on
> earth to full, same off . . . Hell this light from nothing . . . Sheets of black
> paper, stick them to the wall with cobweb and spittle, no good, shine
> like the rest . . . Black bag over his head, no good, all the rest still in light.
> (8-9)

At this point in Beckett's career there is no way he can achieve the
permanent refuge of darkness that seems a possibility in *Still*. A
condition of vigilance is what is required of the protagonist of *All
Strange Away*: 'Light flows, eyes close, stay closed, till it ebbs, no, can't
do that, eyes stay open . . .' (9)

Concomitant with this recognition that the world external to the
observer cannot be made to disappear is the impulsion, inherited by
the speakers of *Imagination Dead Imagine* and *The Lost Ones*, to construct
and measure a world obeying rudimentary geometrical rules. This is
in order to isolate and tame the creative problems encountered in
those fictions which were dominated by the image of journeying into
an infinite and unforeseeable future. It is a measure of how different
this work is from the post-war trilogy of novels that are often regarded
as Beckett's greatest works, and which are obliquely alluded to at the
very beginning of *All Strange Away*. 'To think I had lost almost all
faculties of mensuration', says Molloy; the protagonist of *All Strange
Away* has miraculously retrieved them. But his interest in measurement is not a simple matter of scientific accuracy; here it is somehow
bound up with the exercise of the imaginative faculty. Beckett
hereabouts resuscitates the category of Fancy which the great
Romantic poets considered decidedly inferior to Imagination,
reminding us implicitly that he is a good deal less interested in the
Sublime than they were.

Beckett concentrates attention, as in other works of this period
(*Film*, for instance) on the organ of vision, the eye:

> Falling on his knees in the dark to murmur, no sound, Fancy is his only
> hope. Surprised by light in this posture, hope and fancy on his lips,
> crawling lifelong habit to a corner here shadowless and similarly sinking
> head to ground here shining back into his eyes. Imagine eyes burnt
> ashen blue and lashes gone, lifetime of unseeing glaring, jammed open,
> one lightning wince per minute on earth, try that. (11)

The eyes here are clearly the successors of the eyes of *How It Is* ('I close
my eyes not the blue the others at the back') and prefigure the 'eye of

prey' of *Imagination Dead Imagine*. Later the imagination conjures up a companion pair belonging apparently to a woman, in order to allow the classic Beckettian opposition of observer and observed to come into being once again. This looks like the origin of the 'long lashes imploring' that occur at the end of *Ping*, where the sexual question has ceased to be important. But in *All Strange Away* the sexual question is very much at the centre of the text, as the imagination turns voyeuristic and predatory, and enjoys the vicarious pleasure of conceiving the frictional contact of a little body with its own semi-pornographic projections:

> Faces now naked bodies . . . two per wall, eight in all . . . eight no more, one per wall, four in all, say all of Emma. First face alone, lovely beyond words, leave it at that, then deasil breasts alone, then thighs and cunt alone, then arse and hole alone, all lovely beyond words. See how he crouches down and back to see, back of head against face when eyes on cunt, against breast when on hole, and vice versa . . . Imagine him kissing, caressing, licking, sucking, fucking and buggering all this stuff, no sound. (12-14)

Beckett relishes the fleshly more fully in this text than is usual with him. After the agonies of self-inflicted torment of *How It Is*, it is obvious that his attitude has slightly softened, at any rate as far as the female physique is concerned. The loathing that Molloy and Malone feel towards the females that have cursed them with existence (still partially present here in the four-letter words) has modulated here to something like fascination at the strangeness of a 'faint stir of hair', a 'cheekbone vivid white', and the 'puckered tip of left breast' (21), uncovered by this assiduous investigation.

Whereas in *How It Is* the narrator says it as he hears it, and finds reception and transmission are (relatively speaking) interference-free, in *All Strange Away* the dominant mood is one of uncertainty as to where the sounds derive from, who they are addressed to, and what strength they possess. Much of the time it is 'a sound too faint for mortal ear'; periodically it vanishes completely and 'a great silence' supervenes; finally Beckett becomes aware of the possibilities of systematizing the relationship between sound and light and thereby exorcizing his fascination with them:

> Such then the sound roughly and if no clearer so then all the storm unspoken unless sound of light and dark or at the moments of change a sound of flow thirty seconds till full then silence any length till sound of ebb thirty seconds till black then silence any length, that might repay hearing . . . (26)

Despite the narrator's 'great need for words', and at the same time
precisely because of it, his abiding impression in the middle of the text
is that 'here all sound most doubtful . . . none ever been but only silent
flesh' (27). The idea that 'in the end that is when all gone from mind'
(the origin of one of the most often repeated linguistic units in *Lessness*)
there still will be 'the faint rise and fall of breast the breath to whip up
to a pant' (the origin of one of the most memorable components of
Still) (27) is recorded by the speaker without any of the emotional
inflection that usually accompanies Beckett's realization that the body
can survive the death of the mind and go on suffering in its absence.
But it is clear from the way the recording voice reverts to the
observable and measurable realities of his imaginative projection that
the ideal absence, in which every perception and memory will be
'gone from mind', is still a long way off. In *All Strange Away*, Beckett is
still at the stage of trying to believe in the veracity of his perceptions,
as the title obliquely hints (compare 'all these strangenesses', *HII*, 24),
and trying to create a substantial world in which he can embody his
sense of what it is 'to be and be in face of'. This is why Beckett
alters quite wilfully the original impression of a rectangular world
first to a cuboid one and finally to the rotunda shape familiar to us
from *Imagination Dead Imagine*. Much incidental humour of the wild
kind that surfaces from time to time in *How It Is* results from these
changes, each of which forces the recording voice to re-imagine the
consequences for the female figure cramped cumbersomely into one
half of the available space as if awaiting a companion. The most
amusing section of all occurs towards the end of the first (and longer)
part of the text when the narrator suddenly realizes: 'tighter fit for
Emma . . . she still might be mathematically speaking more than seven
foot long . . . suddenly clear these dimensions faulty and small woman
scarce five foot fully extended . . .' (29-30). This is perhaps the last
faint flicker of the sense of humour deteriorating in *How It Is* and in
almost complete abeyance in the prose since *All Strange Away*.

In the second part, under the title 'Diagram', Beckett returns to his
imagined rotunda and attempts, this time with more conspicuous
success, to establish the condition of the female figure that inhabits it:

> . . . full glare, face on left cheek at a, long black hair gone, long black
> lashes on white cheekbone gone, glare from above for features on this
> bonewhite undoubted face right profile still hungering for missing
> lashes burning down for commissure of lids . . . (31-2)

At this point a decisive and frightening change takes place: '. . . when like say without hesitation hell gaping they part and the black eye appears . . .' (32). Whatever this black eye represents, the speaker is not (unlike Krapp, with his 'eyes of perfect chrysolite') tempted to dwell on it. Instead he moves on hurriedly to another item of anatomy:

> Glare now on hands most womanly clear and womanly especially right still loosely clenched as before but no longer on ground since corrected pose but now on outer of right knee just where it swells to thigh while left still loosely hitched to right shoulder ball as before. All that most clear. (32)

It is the urge to see even more clearly, to subject the figure to what *Still* calls 'close inspection', that involves Beckett in distorting the perception to the point where he has to call in his imagination in order to know what he is 'really' seeing. The observer, as Beckett stated with unanswerable finality in his study of Proust, 'infects the observed with his own mobility' (*PTD*, 17). His area of observation has shifted now to the hands of the female figure, as if he has suddenly remembered *How It Is*, where the speaker is obsessively interested in his own hands and the hands of others. The image he manages to conjure up is an arbitrary one, but one which finally, by imaginative projection, takes on sufficient reality for him to feel that its essential strangeness has been tamed and come to terms with:

> No real image but say like red no grey say like something grey and when again squeeze firm down five seconds say faint hiss then silence then back loose two seconds and say faint pop and so arrive though no true image at small grey punctured rubber ball or small grey ordinary rubber bulb such as on earth attached to bottle of scent or suchlike that when squeezed a jet of scent but here alone. So little by little all strange away. (33)

It is so much a feature of Beckett's world that his characters inherit the possessions of their predecessors that we might be forgiven for thinking this rubber ball was once owned by Mr. Rooney in *All That Fall*. The anxiety Mr. Rooney feels on having his ball returned to him is very similar to the anguish of this figure squeezing, with 'straining knuckles', and then relaxing her grip, and then squeezing again, as if to remove all traces of nervousness and tension from her crumpled frame.

There seems no reason why the 'close inspection', once begun, should ever come to an end. But Beckett wearies suddenly of what he later (in *Imagination Dead Imagine*) calls the 'eye of prey' and is struck by the pointlessness of 'all this poking and prying about for cracks holes and appendages' (34). He reverts instead to material already tried and tested, a description of the illuminated rotunda, the body's posture, and the changes each must undergo. Beckett is acknowledging here the obsessiveness of the imagination, and exhibiting, not for the first time, a reluctance to move outside the area of his primary and most compelling concerns. As his final rehearsal of the basic situation fails to bring him the satisfaction he would like, he suddenly becomes the prey of the desire for stasis and changelessness that has afflicted all his heroes since Murphy:

> All that if not yet quite complete quite clear and little change likely unless perhaps to complete unless perhaps somehow light sudden gleam perhaps better fixed and all this flowing and ebbing to full and empty more harm than good and better unchanging black or glare one or the other or between the two soft white unchanging . . . (36-7)

This changelessness which he so ardently desires remains a pipe-dream, as in *Lessness* later, where all references to 'changelessness' are pulled up short by the word 'dream' which follows it. And yet his desire for changelessness reminds him of the nearest thing to changelessness that normal life allows, the mysterious world of sleep and dream. This is a world with its own special vicissitudes and strangeness, and can never be known in the way the dimensions of the rotunda can be known. It is a world containing the whole range of basic human feelings, and a world more alive and vibrant than ordinary mundane reality. The prose quickens, and also softens, as Beckett subjects this world to observation:

> Sleep stirring now some time add now with nightmares unimaginable making waking sweet and lying waking till longing for sleep again with dread of demons, perhaps some glimpse of demons later. Dread then in rotunda now with longing and sweet relief but so faint and weak no more than weak tremors of a hothouse leaf. Memories of past felicity no save one faint with faint ripple of sorrow of a lying side by side . . . (37)

This is clearly the origin of the image of two tranquil figures at the end of *Imagination Dead Imagine*, but it is quite without the deathly calm that makes their repose so memorable. Here Beckett cannot free himself of his earlier, and somewhat erotogenic, interest in movement, and is driven to describe the way the female figure seeks out alternative postures for herself. The figure's writhing is shown to be futile, partly perhaps because she has no companion to make it less narcissistic:

> Clear further how at some earlier more callow stage this writhe again
> and again in vain through weakness or natural awkwardness or want of
> pliancy or want of resolution and how halfway through on back with
> legs just clear how after some time in the balance thus the fall back to
> where she lay . . . (38-39)

Beckett has always been interested in the suspended moment when
everything hangs 'in the balance', and later, in *Still*, he describes the
way the movement of the hand towards the face is momentarily
arrested. In *All Strange Away* the figure accepts its inability to escape
from the rotunda, or permanently alter its posture, with some of the
equanimity more strongly developed in *Still*: '. . . with disappointment naturally tinged perhaps with relief and this again and again till
final renouncement with faint sweet relief . . .' (39). Beckett contrives
here, as later in *Lessness*, to satisfy both his scepticism as to the
durability of relief and also his belief in the possibility of the figure's
torments being mitigated from time to time. He knows that if a total
state of absence can be 'maintained', relief will be forthcoming; but he
also knows that the longing for an even more complete absence
(however ridiculous such a longing may be) will remain:

> Sleep if maintained with cacodemons making waking in light and dark if
> this maintained faint sweet relief and the longing for it again and to be
> gone again a folly to be resisted again in vain. (39-40)

Faced with a situation where all sensory perception has become 'so
weak and faint no more than faint tremors of a leaf indoors on earth in
winter to survive till spring', Beckett tries to imagine what a complete
absence would be like: '. . . no light immeasurable turmoil no sound
black soundless storm . . .' (40). He has been granted glimpses of such
a world in previous works, but has been unable to sustain it. Here too
it remains impossible to attain, however much he may long to bring it
into being. The last sentences of *All Strange Away* show Beckett
striving to pare down the phenomena he has imagined to bare
essentials, repeating the words he has imagined the figure speaking
and reducing them to two propositions only, the conviction that
Fancy is dead[4] and the memory of two figures sleeping side by side.
As the end of the text approaches, Beckett tries out, for perhaps the
first time in his work, the 'erasure' technique that we find again at the
end of *Enough*, and as the long final sentence winds to its appointed
and inevitable end he preserves the sense of an ending (as later in *Ping*)
by introducing one new phrase amid a multitude of familiar elements:

> . . . henceforth here no other sounds than those say gone now and never

were sprayer bulb or punctured rubber ball and nothing ever in that
hand lightly closed on nothing any length till for no reason yet imagined
fingers tighten then relax no sound and to the same end slip of left hand
down slope of right upper arm no sound and same purpose none of
breath to the end that here henceforth no other sounds than these and
never were that is than sop to mind faint sighing sound for tremor of
sorrow at faint memory of a lying side by side and fancy murmured
dead. (43-4)

The idea that all sounds, even the vitally important sound of
breathing (compare *Breath* and *Still*), are only a sop to the mind intent
on the need to imagine something rather than nothing is juxtaposed
here with the idea that there has been real sorrow issuing in real sighs
and memories too powerful to have been entirely imaginary. Any
resolution of the problems arising in a text as complex as *All Strange
Away* would be alien to Beckett's practice, and could only be strident
and unsatisfying. Indeed, he is moving here towards a manner that
will allow him to achieve what the Unnamable called 'affirmations
and negations invalidated as uttered, or sooner or later', a manner not
achieved in the *Texts*, and only finally achieved in the radical new
departure of *Lessness*. The strain on his resources is visible in the way
he finds it necessary to lengthen his sentences to include more and
more material, as far as possible unpunctuated in order that no one
unit is seen to be subordinate to another. The heavy punctuation of
the first few pages of *All Strange Away* is gradually abandoned until by
the time of the 'Diagram' section the sentences begin to take on the
glazed and crystalline severity that one recognizes as the staple feature
of Beckett's late prose.

It would be difficult to overestimate the importance of *All Strange
Away*; it contains in embryo almost all the elements from which
Beckett was to construct the strange and yet compelling world of his
recent prose. If it offers less immediate rewards than *Enough* or
Imagination Dead Imagine and is more hybrid in manner than *Ping* or *The
Lost Ones* or *Lessness*, it is in its own way quite as uncompromising and
remarkable as any of the later texts, and offers us a wider emotional
range than most of them. This is partly explained by the fact that
Beckett is here experimenting with a manner and with material that
offers new possibilities at a time when he had been feeling, in the
Fizzles, the regressive pull of the old. In the subsequent works he
restrains his wildness and operates over more manageable areas; the
equanimity of *Enough* and the thudding monosyllables of *Ping* are the
result of paying prolonged attention to the individual component

parts of *All Strange Away* and investigating its 'residual' possibilities. But *All Strange Away* offers us what Beckett calls in *The Lost Ones* our 'first aperçu' of the way his imagination will be working in the 1960s and 1970s and has a freshness and immediacy about it that makes even its elusiveness attractive.

3. *Imagination Dead Imagine*

Imagination Dead Imagine is the residual precipitate of *All Strange Away*, and is a much more controlled piece of work, more coherent, more accessible, and (despite its apparent dryness) more moving. Instead of concerning himself, as in *All Strange Away*, with the volatile wilfulness of the creative faculty of imagination, Beckett contents himself, in *Imagination Dead Imagine*, with one imaginative projection only: the rotunda of the last part of *All Strange Away*, now populated by two figures lying back to back. This concentration on a single object enables Beckett to avoid the diffuseness of the earlier text and allows him to present a more considered view of the workings of the imagination than was ever possible in the turbulent flurry of *All Strange Away*. *All Strange Away* is a fascinating torso, but shapeless and prolix; *Imagination Dead Imagine* is a finished piece of work, as Beckett obviously realized when he published the latter and suppressed the former.

The residual text consists of a skeletal prologue, two distinct 'sightings' of the rotunda, and a melancholy epilogue, and possesses a formal perfection quite alien to its successors, *The Lost Ones* and *Ping*. The prologue, for all its brevity, is a distinct advance on the opening of *All Strange Away*, which reverts to the weariness and self-disgust of the *Texts for Nothing*. *Imagination Dead Imagine* begins with a refusal to accede to resignation which is rewarded by a sudden and magical intuition:

> No trace anywhere of life, you say, pah, no difficulty there, imagination not dead yet, yes, dead, good, imagination dead imagine. Islands, waters, azure, verdure, one glimpse and vanished, endlessly, omit. Till all white in the whiteness the rotunda. (*Imagination Dead Imagine*, *Six Residua*, London, John Calder, 1978, p. 35: all further references are to this edition.)

Beckett is now intent, it is clear, on expunging all external realities ('islands, waters, azure, verdure') and exploring the inner world of his own skull. The impulse to subject this interiorized world to accurate measurement, first manifested in *All Strange Away*, seems somehow more natural and less obsessive here, as if it had been engaged in as a matter of course rather than a matter of pressing necessity: 'No way in, go in, measure . . . Two diameters at right angles AB CD divide the white ground into two semicircles ACB BDA. Lying on the ground two white bodies, each in its semicircle. White too the vault and the round wall eighteen inches high from which it springs' (35). Beckett confirms the new clarity of his vision by demonstrating that the world he has conceived is a much more substantial one than anything in *All Strange Away*: 'Go back out, a plain rotunda, all white in the whiteness, go back in, rap, solid throughout, a ring as in the imagination the ring of bone' (35). This movement out and back has now lost all the thematic resonances it once had, and is now used simply to establish, as in a control experiment, whether the existence of the rotunda is spatially determined. Beckett repeats the movement a moment or so later: 'Go back out, move back, the little fabric vanishes, ascend, it vanishes, all white in the whiteness, descend, go back' (35).

The imperative mood that dominates the beginning of this text contrives to make these movements seem more like physical activities than mental strategies. But this is only a way of imaging cerebral adjustments in a manner that will guarantee their being apprehensible. There is, in any case, no danger of our interpreting a text as oblique as this in a severely literal way, when it is clear that Beckett is trying to identify the optimum conditions in which imaginative enterprise can flourish. The imagination is free to roam through space as it will, but runs the risk of losing, by diversifying its manoeuvres, the substantial object it has been fortunate enough to come upon.

Beckett stresses that the workings of the imagination are at once mysterious and determined, arbitrarily granted and yet controlled by specific determinants. The object can be 'rediscovered miraculously' (37) only if the imaginative mind adopts the privileged 'point of view' that has already proved beneficial ('there is no other', Beckett tells us). This bi-focal attitude allows Beckett to stress the imagination's consuming need for some talismanic object that it may work upon; but at the same time to stress the haphazardness that is an unavoidable concomitant of exercising the imaginative faculty at all. Beckett is also at pains to point out that the imagination can never operate in exactly the same way twice, and that it is always, in a sense, 'at the end of an era', as Wallace Stevens said.[5] Imagining has become, for Beckett, less and less a matter of exercising the will, and more and more a matter of waiting for the mercies vouchsafed by inspiration. It is only natural, therefore, for Beckett to feel at the end of this text that more has been lost than has been gained, since the miraculous perception of the rotunda cannot be retrieved by any conscious striving on his part, and can only be altered out of all recognition in the unlikely event of a third 'sighting' being permitted to occur. The more involved Beckett is in an active way, the more likely it is that he will unbalance the delicate equilibrium of forces that has created this bizarre and compelling vision.

In his first *aperçu* of the rotunda Beckett stresses the strangeness of the mechanisms that it contains, but is clearly impressed by the extreme systematization that obtains within it:

> . . . wait, the light goes down, all grows dark together, ground, wall, vault, bodies, say twenty seconds, all the greys, the light goes out, all vanishes. At the same time the temperature goes down, to reach its minimum, say freezing-point, at the same instant that the black is reached, which may seem strange. Wait, more or less long, light and heat come back, all grows white and hot together, ground, wall, vault, bodies, say twenty seconds, all the greys, till the initial level is reached whence the fall began. (35-6)

There is clearly an element of reciprocation here; the systematization of the mechanism is matched by the systematization of the prose. Beckett is not interested as yet in deciding which systematization is primary or which conditions the other. He simply presents the mechanism and the description of the mechanism as indissolubly bound together, in a state of relative equilibrium.

The second *aperçu* of the rotunda, after its 'absence in perfect voids', is much less tranquil and harmonious, although 'externally all is as before': 'But go in and now briefer lulls and never twice the same storm . . . In this agitated light, its great white calm now so rare and brief, inspection is not easy' (37). The prose is much less musclebound than previously, as if Beckett were intent on achieving a reciprocation similar to that achieved in the first *aperçu*. We begin to feel the pressure of great emotion behind the studiedly dispassionate description of the bodies: 'Sweat and mirror notwithstanding they might well pass for inanimate but for the left eyes which at incalculable intervals suddenly open wide and gaze in unblinking exposure long beyond what is humanly possible' (37). This is the germ of the style that dominates *The Lost Ones*, the long, unpunctuated sentence that openly courts awkwardness and wins through to a kind of resolution despite its angularities. Beckett is avoiding in *Imagination Dead Imagine* the formulaic strain that he has always found it difficult to resist, and adopting here a more supple syntax which will enable him to exploit the self-cancelling effects he has found even more irresistible since his adoption of French in 1945:

> Piercing pale blue the effect is striking, in the beginning. Never the two gazes together except once, when the beginning of one overlapped the end of the other, for about ten seconds. Neither fat nor thin, big nor small, the bodies seem whole and in fairly good condition, to judge by the surfaces exposed to view. The faces too, assuming the two sides of a piece, seem to want nothing essential. (37-8)

The tonal and syntactical fluctuations here suggest that the imagination is finding it difficult to sustain its scientific dispassionateness, and is becoming involuntarily embroiled in the lives of the figures it has summoned up. There is a gnawing sense on Beckett's part of the inadequacy of remaining content with the measurable superficies, and a growing willingness to draw inferences and attempt conclusions that have nothing to do with scientific evidence at all:

> Between their absolute stillness and the convulsive light the contrast is striking, in the beginning, for one who still remembers being struck by the contrary. It is clear, however, from a thousand little signs too long to imagine, that they are not sleeping. (38)

Suddenly the epilogue, as poignant and elusive as the prologue, destroys all trace of serenity and tranquillity. The merest touch of emotional warmth and nostalgic regret breaks all the tenuous barriers between the creative mind and the bodies it has created: 'Only murmur ah, no more, in this silence, and at the same instant for the eye of prey the infinitesimal shudder instantaneously suppressed' (38). If we are again reminded here of *The Lost Ones*, as the prose shrugs off its potential lugubriousness and pulses with life, we should not forget that *The Lost Ones* takes such moments in its stride, and has no difficulty in 'whispering the turmoil down'[6] again, whereas at the end of this text there is nothing but wreck and turmoil:

> Leave them there, sweating and icy, there is better elsewhere. No, life ends and no, there is nothing elsewhere, and no question now of ever finding again that white speck lost in whiteness, to see if they still lie still in the stress of that storm, or of a worse storm, or in the black dark for good, or the great whiteness unchanging, or if not what they are doing (38)

The imagination, robbed of its talismanic object after its predatory and illegitimate appropriation of the object's otherness, is left at the end without anything meaningful that will make sense of its continuing hypotheses. Beckett has been stimulated into activity by the fact that there is 'no trace anywhere of life', has been granted two miraculous visions of a private world, has tried to infiltrate this world and then recoiled from its severity, and been forced to remember at the end that 'life ends' and 'there is nothing elsewhere'. It is as dispiriting a conclusion as Beckett has ever allowed himself, with a cluster of negatives that makes even the 'screaming silence of no's knife in yes's wound' seem endurable.

In the absence here of any 'yes' that might be set against the 'noes' as at the end of *How It Is*, we may be tempted to think that Beckett's search for 'a new no, to cancel all the others' (as the eleventh *Text for Nothing* puts it) is over. But *Text 11* offers an ironic gloss on this idea, and stresses the impossibility of 'a new no' ever being found: 'a new no, that none says twice, whose drop will fall and let me down, shadow and babble, to an absence less vain than inexistence. Oh I know it won't happen like that, I know that nothing will happen . . .' (*TFN*, 57). The twice-repeated 'no' at the end of *Imagination Dead Imagine* leaves us with a kind of 'absence', but not one that could be described as 'less vain than inexistence'. It is too close to inexistence for that. The elliptical syntax of the last few phrases suggests finally that there is once more 'no trace anywhere of life', as at the beginning. The sharp point of 'no's knife' is at its most exquisitely painful at the end of *Imagination Dead Imagine*.

4. *Enough*

Enough has always posed something of a problem for commentators intent on making Beckett's development as neat as they would like it to be. Even after repeated rereading it seems to be a work without forbears or progeny, as unrelated to the texts that immediately surround it as *Still* would seem to be. Lacking the intensity that we have come to expect of Beckett's obsessive concentration on a limited number of motifs over many years, it gives the impression of having been conceived as a miniature rather than refined into a precipitate, as the other 'residua' were. It is better to think of *Enough* as 'residual' in Beckett's second sense of the word — 'in relation to whole body of previous work' — than as 'residual' in the more obvious sense — 'even when that does not appear of which each is all that remains'.[7] One is indeed invited by the first sentence of the text to treat it as 'residual' in this second sense, since 'All that goes before forget', whatever else it may mean, is obviously part of the rudimentary aesthetic that prefaces *Enough* rather than part of the narrative proper. (It is, of course, in flat contradiction to the exploration of the past undertaken in the narrative.) This opening is as striking as any in these post-*How It Is* texts (except perhaps the brisk 'Imagination dead imagine' that begins *All Strange Away*) and advertises the uniqueness of *Enough*, which Beckett claims to have composed 'aberrantly' between *Imagination Dead Imagine* and *Ping*. However, by placing *Enough* in pole position before the other residua (in both French and English collections), Beckett surely intends us to recognize not only its aberrancy, but also its unprecedentedness, and thereby announce his new creative manner. For although both *All Strange Away* and *Imagination Dead Imagine* are very different indeed from the works which preceded them, it is only in *Enough* that Beckett discovers the prose style that breaks decisively with what has gone before, the blend of passion and blandness, straightforwardness and obscurity, that is the hallmark of the comma-less writings of the late 'sixties and early 'seventies.

It would of course be misguided to place undue emphasis on an 'art and craft' that are by no means lucidly expressed at the beginning of *Enough* and are roughly dismissed as matters of little moment at the end of the first paragraph. But at the same time it would be foolish to ignore the implications of this strange beginning, and the parallel pair of utterances ('Too much at a time is too much . . . Too much silence is too much'[8]) are clearly in some way connected with Beckett's awareness that 'bits and scraps' can no longer be considered the basis on which to write a full-length work. (*The Lost Ones*, begun only eight days after the completion of *Enough*, can only have confirmed Beckett in this belief.) At the same time the uncertainty as to whether the silence is due to personal inadequacy ('my voice too weak at times. The one that comes out of me') or some malfunction in a mechanism impersonal to the speaker ('I don't see it but I hear it there behind me. Such is the silence') indicates that the kind of relationship basic to *How It Is* ('I say it as I hear it') has once again been replaced by an altogether more haphazard conception of the relationship between stimulus and transmission. *Enough* is quite unlike *How It Is* in the way it assumes that existence continues without reference to verbalization ('When the pen stops I go on . . . When it refuses I go on'), although the return to paragraphed prose — another index of *Enough*'s individuality — offers Beckett no opportunity of encompassing this insight as part of the very fabric of the text. Perhaps only in *How It Is* and *Lessness*, where paragraphs are kept separate from one another, do we feel that there are modes of being outside the language of the text, and these are both works (the latter especially) intent on demonstrating that there is literally nothing beyond the propositions that are being uttered. It may be that the irritation Beckett feels in describing the 'art and craft' testifies to his having no real solution to this conundrum. Although he retained paragraphing for *The Lost Ones*, Beckett has more and more relied on an undifferentiated mass, as in *All Strange Away* and *Imagination Dead Imagine*. *Enough* is in fact somewhat regressive in its reliance on paragraphs, however much this may increase its readability, and however much this subtle material may benefit from such a presentation.

There is also a partial regression in subject-matter in *Enough*, which is the last of Beckett's prose works to explore the 'I-he' dichotomy which dominated *Texts for Nothing* and seemed to have been exploded for good and all in *How It Is*. The 'I-he' relationship in *Enough*, however, is a much more tranquil one than that in the *Texts* and has none of the residual signs of a wrestling match that are to be found in 'Afar a bird' and 'I gave up before birth'. There is an identity of purpose about the 'I' and 'he' in *Enough* that virtually requires us to see them as aspects of the same personality, as they have not been since the end of *Text 1*, when the 'I' was able to be both his father and his son and hold himself in his arms:

> I did all he desired. I desired it too. For him. Whenever he desired something so did I. He only had to say what thing. When he didn't desire anything neither did I . . . When he was silent he must have been like me. When he told me to lick his penis I hastened to do so. I drew satisfaction from it. We must have had the same satisfactions. The same needs and the same satisfactions. (*Enough, Six Residua*, London, John Calder, 1978, p. 25: all further references are to this edition.)

The complete absence in this narrator of a normally-developed appetitive streak prefigures the extreme docility of the inhabitants of the cylinder in *The Lost Ones*. But the narrator of *Enough* is not quite so drastically 'vanquished' as the woman who enables the searchers to find their bearings and (despite a number of features apparently indicating the contrary) is not so feminine either. Whilst it is tempting to see *Enough* as a reflection of Beckett's renewed interest in women at the beginning of the 1960s (as manifested, for instance, in *Happy Days*, which some critics have seen as containing the germ of the narrative of *Enough*[9]), it is clear that Beckett desired to neutralize the sexuality of the figure who narrates *Enough*, however 'feminine' the tone of voice and the accoutrements (the 'old breasts' of the end, for example), of the speaker. When Beckett wants to portray women (as in *Happy Days* or *Come and Go*, or *Not I*, or '. . . but the clouds . . .') he portrays them without disguising the fact. Ruby Cohn writes of the narrator of *Enough* as an 'androgynous creature with feminine sensibility', which is eminently commonsensible (and gives rise to a sensitive reading of the text[10]), but this does not really answer the question of why Beckett should have striven for sexual indeterminacy in the figure that dominates *Enough*.

One is hard put, of course, in the absence of anything in the text which would account for it, to find an explanation for Beckett's seemingly wilful evasiveness here, and one may be tempted to see the narrator as an embodiment of the female principle rather than simply a female *tout court*. But perhaps a more profitable approach is to see *Enough* as an obliquely allegorical narrative (preparatory to a more elaborately and openly allegorical work like *The Lost Ones*) of the relationship between different aspects of the self which has been Beckett's main area of interest for many years. One may feel the presence of Beckett saying quietly, in the manner of the addenda to *Watt*, 'no allegories where none intended'. But at the same time this approach offers at least partial clarification of details that remain unexplained by more paraphrastic readings of the text.

Enough is pre-eminently a narrative of separation — what *How It Is* would call 'abandon' — containing at the same time (and conflating) the other two elements of *How It Is*, the 'journey' and the 'couple'. It is also a narrative from beyond the grave, like 'The Calmative', or *Play*, or *Not I*. The separation takes place at a time when the 'he' figure is close to death, and is associated, in the narrator's mind, with a loss of meaning that is a kind of death. This helps to account for one's feeling that this is a strangely 'romantic' kind of text for Beckett to be writing at this stage of his career, and means that we should not summarily dismiss (as perhaps we should like to do) 'romantic' readings of it. But the more one considers the narrator's first description of the separation, the more one's suspicion grows that the 'romantic' reading is reductive and misguided:

> One day he told me to leave him. It's the verb he used. He must have been on his last legs. I don't know if by that he meant me to leave him for good or only to step aside a moment. I never asked myself the question. I never asked myself any questions but his. Whatever it was he meant I made off without looking back. Gone from reach of his voice I was gone from his life. (25)

It is difficult to resist the feeling that this is a good deal more guileful and cunning than its innocent surface suggests. Is this not a veiled dramatization of a problem that Beckett had concentrated on more directly in previous 'I-he' situations? Is this banishment of one self by another so very different from similar excoriations of the self in *The Unnamable*, the *Texts* and *How It Is*? Is it not perfectly possible that Beckett has seen (as the very first words of *Enough* suggest) that he must write in an absolutely new way, and that he must therefore explore what happens when he banishes personality (in the accepted sense) from his work? Is it not symptomatic, finally, that *Enough* is the last Beckett text to make use of a narrator who can endure the dishonesty and spuriousness of substantializing himself in the text under the mask of 'I'?

So great is the concentration in *Enough* on the older self's obsession with speaking and imparting knowledge, and so strong is the sense of the younger self's inability to live without its mentor, that one is forced to regard the separation of the two as an impoverishment for both selves. The narrator, in a mood of almost unflappable equanimity, tries hard to look on the bright side, although the dark side has more often been, for Beckett, 'less trying to the eyes' (*M*, 147). But mournfulness keeps breaking in and colouring the narrative with darker tones:

> He must have been on his last legs. I on the contrary was far from on my last legs. I belonged to an entirely different generation. It didn't last. Now that I'm entering night I have kinds of gleams in my skull. Stony ground but not entirely. Given three or four lives I might have accomplished something. (25-6)

The narrator's resignation has obviously been conditioned by the older self who, though quite evidently 'on his last legs', has powers of endurance, and feelings of optimism, that make him seem heroic and impressive. The younger self, deprived of its mentor, is unable to record these moments without some wry commentary upon them:

> . . . alluding for the first time to his infirmity he said he thought it had

reached its peak. The future proved him right. That part of it at least we were to make past together . . . One day he halted and fumbling for his words described his vision. He concluded by saying he thought it would get no worse. How far this was not a delusion I cannot say. I never asked myself the question. When I bowed down to receive his communications I felt on my eye a glint of blue bloodshot apparently affected. (28)

At the same time the younger self recognizes its debt to the older self. Without the influence of the older self, the younger would have been reduced almost to nonentity, as now it is in danger of becoming once more: 'To those engulfed years it is reasonable to impute my education. For I don't remember having learnt anything in those I remember. It is with this reasoning I calm myself when brought up short by all I know' (30).

The younger self has indeed been 'brought up short' by all it knows, and is seeking by means of the narrative of *Enough* to reason itself into a condition of calm. This is why the tone of the work oscillates so strangely and unpredictably between the emotional and the dry, the puzzled and the confident, the informative and the arcane. For the duration of their corporate existence, the reality they passed through was something incontrovertibly substantial, despite the disparity in their respective abilities to interpret it. 'All was', as the narrator says (31), with one of those 'past tenses . . . always sorrowful' (*MPTK*, 18) that have always appealed to Beckett. This does not mean that the relationship was always a satisfactory one, of course. The narrator recalls certain aspects of the relationship with considerable asperity:

> If the question were put to me I would say that odd hands are ill-fitted for intimacy. Mine never felt at home in his. . . . With his upper hand he held and touched me where he wished. Up to a certain point . . . He murmured of things that for him were no more and for me could not have been. The wind in the overground stems. The shade and shelter of the forests. (26, 31)

This tone of plangent regret is perhaps the one invariable tone in *Enough*, subsuming and ultimately outlasting all the other elusive and quicksilver tones. And it is clearly the nostalgia for a unity irretrievably lost that drives the narrator to relate the narrative in this highly idiosyncratic way. The confusion of times and tenses that leaves us unsure, despite reiterations, of the exact order in which events took place — the narrator's use of 'then' is especially haphazard and lacks any kind of specificity — is a deliberate device intended to recapture the reality of an association that has now become a part of history, a fiction almost: 'I see the flowers at my feet and it's the others I see. Those we trod down with equal step. It is true they are the same' (28). The desire to reunite and become once more substantial and real lies behind the narrator's somewhat cavalier treatment of narrative materials: the oddly discordant permutation of other possibilities in the middle of the text, the wilful disregard for consistency ('I set the scene of my disgrace just short of a crest. On the contrary it was on the flat in a great calm', 30), the dramatic erasure of everything but the flowers at the end: 'Nothing but the two of us dragging through the flowers. Enough my old breasts feel his old hand' (31). There is both relief and sadness here. The narrator has failed to retrieve the older self and can only retrieve him at all through the medium of imagination. But if the fiction is elastic enough the narrator can take comfort from it, and believe that a reunification has taken place. Fiction seems finally to offer the only 'calmative' that is worth anything, however pale a simulacrum of the real calm it may be. The older self knew, in his 'fumbling' way, that 'anatomy is a whole'. The younger self has had a lifetime to realize the truth of this, and is 'wandering companionless' like Shelley's moon referred to in *Proust* (*PTD*, 68) and remembered by Vladimir in *Godot* (*WFG*, 52). It is hardly surprising that with the break-up of the couple that has dominated Beckett's fiction since *Watt* — a good deal longer, then, than the 'ten years' the narrator of *Enough* speaks of — in the next work, *The Lost Ones*, each of the inhabitants is seeking the 'lost one' he is 'lost' without. In *Ping* only the traces of this 'lost one' are left, and from *Lessness* onwards the emphasis falls on those who are entirely alone.

Beckett spoke long ago, in *Proust*, of 'the only Paradise . . . the Paradise that has been lost' (*PTD*, 74) but only in *Enough*, perhaps, do we feel that paradise is a possibility. It is, as many critics have pointed out, the most paradisial of Beckett's works, the only one that could be meaningfully described as Beckett's *Paradiso*: 'I don't know what the weather is now. But in my life it was eternally mild. As if the earth had come to rest in spring' (30). But the paradise described is less celestial and transcendent than Dante's. The older self seems to embibe, Antaeus-like, the strength to endure from the closest possible contact with the earth, and the earth is repeatedly prey to the 'sudden pelting downpours' that made Mercier and Camier's 'journey' in Ireland (or in *Les Bosquets de Bondy*) so miserable. The younger self is, as befits its fictional proclivities, a good deal less earth-bound, and much less adapted to the exigencies of journeying:

> On a gradient of one in one his head swept the ground. To what this
> taste was due I cannot say. To love of the earth and the flowers'
> thousand scents and hues. Or to cruder imperatives of an anatomical
> order. He never raised the question. The crest once reached alas the
> going down again. (29)

The younger self is more interested in the flat landscapes that have
bulked so large in Beckett's most recent prose, and is more given to
speculative hypothesis than the older self: 'We were not in the
mountains however. There were times when I discerned on the
horizon a sea whose level seemed higher than ours. Could it be the
bed of some vast evaporated lake or drained of its waters from
below?' (29).

Difficult as it may be to understand the narrator's lack of interest in
sublime mountain landscape (what 'The End' calls 'the familiar [scene]
of grandeur and desolation'), it obviously has something to do with
the 'erasure' performed at the end of the text. The absence of feature is
what this narrator relishes, because it gives the imagination more to
feed on, and causes the world to vanish: 'It is only fair to say there was
nothing to sweep away. The very flowers were stemless and flush
with the ground like water-lilies. No brightening our buttonholes
with these' (30). In *Imagination Dead Imagine* the 'islands, waters, azure,
verdure' are peremptorily omitted; in *Enough* we see the narrator
presenting a transfigured and semi-fictional world that can be
traversed with comparative ease. In his subsequent writings Beckett
has abandoned the 'old earth' along with the idea of the quest and the
idea of the couple. *Enough* remains fascinating because it offers us the
last tantalizing glimpses of the real world, before we are engulfed by
the imaginary constructs of the texts that follow it. Beckett is well on
the way here to constructing a paradise that need not necessarily be
lost, the paradise of the imagination.

5. *The Lost Ones*

The Lost Ones is an exploratory text written in 1966 in French (first
titled *Chacun son dépeupleur*, the last words of the first sentence, but
finally published under the title *Le Dépeupleur*). The final French title is
(like the English title of *Sans*) a coinage of Beckett's which he found

impossible to translate into English. One reason for the disparity between the French and English titles is doubtless the fact that Beckett could not rely on his English readers catching the allusion to the line of Lamartine's (*'Un seul être vous manque, et tout est dépeuplé'*) which is embedded in the coinage. But it is possible that Beckett also felt, after changing the title of *Sans* to *Lessness* (and thereby advertizing the idiosyncratic linguistic surface of that text), that a simpler and more generally descriptive title was more suited to the material he was translating. For *The Lost Ones* is in many ways the simplest of Beckett's post-*How It Is* prose, the most easily approachable, the least fraught with potholes for the unwary. This is not to say that *The Lost Ones* lacks subtlety, however, for — as critics have not been slow in realizing — it requires as concentrated an attention as any of Beckett's other recent work if its felicities are to be appreciated. *The Lost Ones* reads like an intriguing exercise in openly fleshing out the skeleton of a fiction, in full view of an audience with suspended disbelief, like the Shakespeare of *Cymbeline* or the Yeats of *The Death of Cuchulain*. The very artlessness with which the job is done inspires in a sympathetic reader a kind of tremulous wonder, as if the writer can hardly hope to succeed in seeing his precarious enterprise through to a conclusion. Beckett did indeed abandon *Le Dépeupleur* because he could not see how to bring to an end a world that was going about its business almost without reference to him, and which grew more elaborate and complicated with each attempt he made to describe it, but partially remedied this situation in 1970 by the addition of a final paragraph divorced in time from the events that occupy the main body of the text. And yet it is difficult to feel — despite the intrinsic interest of the final section — that this was an entirely satisfactory strategy, however important it may have been to Beckett (usually, it should be noted, content to abandon works that are slipping out of control). Perhaps the prime reason for the addition was Beckett's realization that his *forte* (even in his new, more abstract manner) was not the plight of a multitude — however many multitudes of readers might identify with it — but rather the plight of an isolated individual, a figure entirely alone in a universe puzzling in the extreme, without the benefit of resources and companions that might explain it, a 'lost one' indeed.

Between his first French drafts and the final published version Beckett dropped the topic headings preceding each section and outlining — in severely abbreviated form — the primary contents of each. He had obviously realized that these titles ('Ladder Law', 'Place', 'Zenith', etc.) were unhelpful and irritating, and interfered with the continuity of the text. The text reads more smoothly without them, if one can speak of smoothness in such an angular piece of prose. *The Lost Ones*, as it stands, for all its unfinishedness, preserves an evenness of tone and coherence of purpose that would only be disturbed by reminders of how atomized its components are. Indeed the more familiar with the text one becomes, the less it seems to be a rehearsal of already established material and the more it resembles a deeply considered, and admirably restrained, exploration of *terra incognita*.

Reading *The Lost Ones* in its proper chronological place among the last works, one is struck immediately by the dispassionate tone, no doubt a reaction to the restrained passion of *Enough*, the work which immediately preceded it. But *The Lost Ones* is actually much closer in subject-matter to *Imagination Dead Imagine*, and ought perhaps to be seen as written in reaction to that work, as *Ping* (according to Beckett) was later composed in reaction to *The Lost Ones*, and *Lessness* in reaction to *Ping*. Beckett has retained, in slightly modified form, the light and heating systems of *Imagination Dead Imagine*, but increased the population of the enclosed space (a cylinder, rather than a rotunda) one hundred fold. The desire to populate a space, resisted since his early days, was obviously something he could resist no longer, not least because he was now dealing with material from which 'all strange' elements could be purged 'away', a world 'all known' as *Ping* would put it. It is this mania for completeness and accuracy which drives Beckett to adopt the pedantically dry and remote voice of *The Lost Ones*, and it is a new confidence in his ability to describe things more fully and more plainly which accounts for the increasingly frequent admissions of emotional involvement which give the text its haunting quality and engage the reader's almost anaesthetized sensibility.

The first section of *The Lost Ones* ('Séjour' in the original French drafts) outlines with exemplary plainness the primary facts of life in the cylinder:

> Abode where lost bodies roam each searching for its lost one. Vast enough for search to be in vain. Narrow enough for flight to be in vain. . . . The light. Its dimness. Its yellowness. Its omnipresence as though every separate square were agleam of the same twelve million of total surface. Its restlessness at long intervals suddenly stilled like panting at the last. Then all go dead still. It is perhaps the end of their

abode. (*The Lost Ones, Six Residua,* London, John Calder, 1978, p. 55: all further references are to this edition.)

It is immediately noticeable, even this early in the text, that whenever a sentence exceeds a very short breath-pause an awkwardness and potential ambiguity (quite foreign to the lapidary clarity striven for) begin to affect the surface of the prose. But at this stage the desire to convey information in as unvarnished a manner as possible proves strong enough to throttle the scepticism, puzzlement and confusion that later bulk much larger. Beckett even becomes quite chatty, or as chatty as his declarative manner will allow him to be:

> Consequences of this climate for the skin. It shrivels. . . . A kiss makes an indescribable sound. Those with stomach still to copulate strive in vain. But they will not give in. Floor and wall are of solid rubber or suchlike. Dash against them foot or fist or head and the sound is scarcely heard. Imagine then the silence of the steps. (55-6)

'Imagine then' is quite without the admonitory tone of Beckett's self-addressed injunctions to 'imagine' the elements of *All Strange Away*; it is as if there is still someone left to address one's remarks to. There is a relaxed informality about most of *The Lost Ones* which co-exists oddly with its moments of *hauteur* or bluntness, but which reflects a new equanimity on Beckett's part, as for instance, in the last sentence of the first section — 'So much for a first aperçu of the abode' (57) — which is signally different from Beckett's irritation at the end of the first paragraph of *Enough* — 'So much for the art and craft' (*SR*, 25). So equable is the prose that there is even a certain blandness about it. But at the point where this threatens to turn into self-satisfaction Beckett promptly punctuates it: 'Such harmony only he can relish whose long experience and detailed knowledge of the niches are such as to permit a perfect mental image of the entire system. But it is doubtful that such a one exists' (57). The studied remoteness of the narratorial voice, less tremulous than that of *Enough* but in its own way quite as personal, allows Beckett the rare opportunity of being both clinically cold and implicitly involved:

> . . . the need to climb is too widespread. To feel it no longer is a rare deliverance. . . . Their solitary attempts to brain themselves culminate at the best in brief losses of consciousness. . . . Woe the body that rashly enters [the tunnel] to be compelled finally after long efforts to crawl back backwards as best it can the way it came. (56, 57)

As the work proceeds the oscillation between dispassionate description and passionate involvement increases to the point where one is no longer certain quite which is which, and one begins to ask oneself whether the former is not in fact a more genuine commitment to the 'lost ones' situation than the latter. But the personal note is kept to an absolute minimum in order that the times where it does intrude may strike with maximum force.

In the second section Beckett introduces for the first time a system of categorizing the inhabitants of the cylinder. The first and second categories prove no problem; there are those 'perpetually in motion' and 'those who sometimes pause' (58). The third category, labelled the 'sedentaries', involves Beckett in finer and more problematic discriminations, and reveal to him not only the folly of his obsession with accuracy but also the first paradox he has encountered in what has seemed to be such an ordered world: 'Paradoxically the sedentary are those whose acts of violence most disrupt the cylinder's quiet' (58). When he moves to the fourth category, the 'vanquished' (as they are later called), they detain him even longer. Beckett is clearly impressed by the way the vanquished are afflicted from time to time by the desire to rejoin one of the categories they have previously been part of, their eyes 'possessed of the strange power suddenly to kindle again' (58) with hope. But he cannot forbear from commenting on how essentially hopeless they (and the members of the other categories) are, and reminding us, in one of the shortest and most decisive sentences in the work, how irremediable and desiccated their existence is:

> And far from being able to imagine their last state when every body will be still and every eye vacant they will come to it unwitting and be so unawares. Then light and climate will be changed in a way impossible to foretell. . . . In cold darkness motionless flesh. (58, 59)

The third section increases the tension of the work by striving to provide a summary of all the information about life in the cylinder that has been offered so far. One begins to become aware of a strange pressure in Beckett's language that is more than simply a longing for scientific accuracy: 'Omnipresence of a dim yellow light shaken by a vertiginous tremolo between contiguous extremes. . . . Corresponding abeyance of all motion among the bodies in motion and heightened fixity of the motionless' (59). There is a desperate quality about these weighty sentences that suggests Beckett is feeling the strain of keeping up the Olympian calm that has marked his enterprise from the beginning. At the same time he contrives to complete an acceptable summary of what has gone before (much fuller than the summaries of material that occupy every third chapter of *Mercier and Camier*) and thereby to extend his investigations of life in the cylinder into areas one would scarcely have believed possible from a reading of the first three sections.

The fourth section (originally titled 'L'Issue' in the drafts, and published separately prior to the publication of a full French text of *Le Dépeupleur*) deals with a topic reminiscent of the ninth of the *Texts for Nothing*: the possibility of a way out. Beckett introduces the idea with a cunning cluster of clichés that cast an ironic shadow over the whole of the subsequent discussion: 'From time immemorial rumour has it or better still the notion is abroad that there exists a way out' (59). The ironic note is maintained by a wry reference to the Romantic poets that Beckett has long had a love-hate relationship with (one recalls here that Lamartine had provided him with a title) and a subtle allusion to the last words of Dante's *Inferno*, reminding us once more of the ninth *Text*, which also ends by referring to them:

> One school swears by a secret passage branching from one of the tunnels and leading in the words of the poet to nature's sanctuaries. The other dreams of a trapdoor hidden in the hub of the ceiling giving access to a flue at the end of which the sun and other stars would still be shining. (60)

By associating these hopes with the fabrications of literature Beckett hints (as later in *Lessness* when talking of the 'blue celeste of poesy') that they are really only a snare and a delusion, and proceeds to demonstrate that such fictions prevent the population of the cylinder from realizing that their predicament is 'issueless'. In the conclusion to this section Beckett increases his irony to the point of outright condemnation, although he cloaks his severity with a tactful withdrawal at the end: 'So much for a first aperçu of this credence so singular in itself and by reason of the loyalty it inspires in the hearts of so many possessed. Its fatuous little light will be assuredly the last to leave them always assuming they are darkness bound' (60).

The fifth section ('Zénith' originally) is the briefest and really only a footnote to the fourth, reminding us of the way a restless idealism has consumed the lost ones and turned them into 'amateurs of myth' (61). The sixth section reverts to more dispassionate appraisal of the complicated 'ladder law' that obtains in the cylinder, and the sentences here are almost without exception longer and more awkward than those we have previously encountered, as if to mirror the complexity of the laws being enunciated. At the same time it becomes clear that a considerable amount of discipline and even violence is needed to prevent the 'abode' transforming itself into 'pandemonium' (63). This is perhaps the last work of Beckett's in which we find the violence that is so evident in *How It Is* or in Molloy's relations with his mother. But one can almost hear the people of the cylinder murmuring resignedly to themselves 'it's our justice' in the manner of *How It Is*, and the absolute obedience of those who are reprimanded is both chilling and strangely charming: 'This docility in the abuser shows clearly that the abuse is not deliberate but due to a temporary derangement of his inner timepiece easy to understand and therefore to forgive' (63). The '*tout comprendre, c'est tout pardonner*' allusion (developed from *How it is*, p. 46 : 'understood everything and forgave nothing') is faintly disturbing, as if man has unjustifiably arrogated to himself the eternal and ubiquitous tolerance of God. But we find the same 'docility' and tolerance operating in the injunction 'not to do unto others what coming from them might give offence' (77). This smacks faintly of the homely ethic of Kingsley's *The Water Babies* but seems to derive from a section of Burton's *Anatomy of Melancholy*[11] (a work Beckett silently quotes from in the poem 'Enueg 1'). Beckett has always been prepared to allude to what Yeats called 'the accumulated wisdom of the world', but perhaps nowhere else has he embedded his allusions so deeply and subtly as in *The Lost Ones*. The glazed surface of the prose effectively prevents our penetrating what lies behind the impassive detachment of the speaker. The rehabilitation of cliché and dead metaphor that Beckett has been engaged in since the days of the trilogy has here been superseded by a prose that seems able to include the tritest elements alongside the most arcane and reduce them all to one enveloping common denominator.

The next three sections are all short and only come to life in the description (section eight) of the 'semi-sages' who 'inspire in those still fitfully fevering if not a cult a certain deference' (64). Beckett has long been fascinated, since his first attraction to Dante's Belacqua, by figures who have abandoned appetite and accepted their condition as 'issueless', and the sentence which ends the eighth section is full of a kind of stunned admiration that the 'semi-sages' have conquered the desire to retaliate that periodically afflicts even the best-intentioned of the other inhabitants of the cylinder. Beckett maintains tension by introducing conclusive and decisive sentences like this — the tenth and fourteenth sections end with utterances of a similar kind — into a work that is sometimes threatened with the 'docility' it is intent on examining. Alternatively Beckett ends a section on a hesitant note, with a sudden alteration of the angle of vision, as for instance in the ninth section: 'Which suitably lit from above would give the impression at times of two narrow rings turning in opposite directions about the teeming precinct' (65).

The tenth section offers more variety than almost any other, oscillating between the 'picturesque detail' (65) of a youngish woman with a baby at her breast and the incipient permutation of the description of how the four categories of inhabitants will in some unthinkable future be reduced to one only: the 'vanquished' (as happens in the fifteenth and final section). However most of Beckett's time in this section is taken up with the 'devouring' eyes that he had first alluded to in *Imagination Dead Imagine*. The fact that Beckett amplifies his account with the one really memorable metaphor in the text is an indication of how important the question of vision has become for him. Embedded in the desiccation which surrounds it, this elaborate metaphor operates with the force of an epic or Miltonic simile, and cannot but remind us of the sand heap referred to in *Endgame* and dramatically in front of us in *Happy Days*:

> Then the eyes suddenly start to search afresh as famished as the unthinkable first day until for no clear reason they as suddenly close again or the head falls. Even so a great heap of sand sheltered from the wind lessened by three grains every second year and every following increased by two if this notion is maintained. (66)

The increased frequency hereabouts of the stock phrase 'if this notion is maintained' (clearly a distant relative of *All Strange Away*'s 'if this maintained') is a measure of how the text has changed in character since the beginning. Beckett is now in the position of asking himself questions — there is another self-addressed question in the eleventh section — and is more and more reliant on retiring from the immediate purlieu of his gaze if he wants to understand the life of the cylinder. The sentence beginning 'An intelligence would be tempted to see . . . ' (66) reminds one of the figure in the first section whose 'detailed knowledge' of this world would allow him to possess 'a perfect mental image of the entire system' and, despite Beckett's disclaimer about the likelihood of this being possible, it is clear that we are in the grip of a very knowledgeable intelligence for much of the time. Beckett actually prefigures the end of *The Lost Ones* — unknown to himself, since it was only completed four years later — by introducing into this tenth section a sense of history that has been signally lacking heretofore: 'But never again will they ceaselessly come and go who now at long intervals come to rest without ceasing to search with their eyes. In the beginning then unthinkable as the end all roamed without respite . . . ' (67). It is clear that Beckett has begun his most epic recent effort *in medias res*, perhaps in the hope that (in the words of 'He is barehead') its history may 'take shape', and only in the final section do we feel that we are, as we have for a long time come to expect of Beckett, at an end.

The eleventh (and second longest) section continues the tenth's interest in eyes, and elaborates on the light which permits the eyes to operate at all: 'the ear finally distinguishes a faint stridulence as of insects which is that of the light itself and the one invariable. . . . the sensation of yellow is faintly tinged with one of red. Light in a word that not only dims but blurs into the bargain' (68). Whilst the synaesthesia that connects sound and vision here is reminiscent of *All Strange Away* (which also makes use of the colour red), it is obvious that the eyes are now in a much more parlous condition:

> . . . the slow deterioration of vision ruined by this fiery flickering murk and by the incessant straining for ever vain with concomitant moral distress and its repercussion on the organ. And were it possible to follow over a long enough period of time eyes blue for preference as being the most perishable they would be seen to redden more and more in an ever widening glare and their pupils little by little to dilate till the whole orb was devoured. (68-9)

Beckett returns to these 'burnt eyes' in the fifteenth and final section in a mood of dispassionate inquiry. But at this point he cannot leave the topic without commenting on his own proclivities and subjecting them to a subtle critique: '. . . the thinking being coldly intent on all these data and evidences could scarcely escape at the close of his analysis the mistaken conclusion that instead of speaking of the vanquished with the slight taint of pathos attaching to the term it would be more correct to speak of the blind and leave it at that' (69). A similar moment of revelation occurs towards the end of this eleventh section when, after dealing with the relationship between light and temperature (less systematized than in *Imagination Dead Imagine*) and postulating 'a single commutator' with a switch that turns them on and off, Beckett makes explicit for the first time what we have long suspected: 'For in the cylinder alone are certitudes to be found and without nothing but mystery' (70). But our wholehearted acceptance of this statement as the premise on which all the conclusions of *The*

Lost Ones depend is affected by the absurd self-confidence of a statement made six sentences previously: 'this is a disturbance analysis makes short work of'. Analysis has always been a mixed blessing in Beckett's work (especially perhaps in *Watt* and *How It Is*) and has usually been more a cause of disturbance than a cure for it. As Beckett states quite categorically in the twelfth section, 'All has not been told and never shall be' (74). Indeed the analysis that forms the basis for *The Lost Ones* seems to suffer a kind of elephantiasis that must have been one of the 'intractable difficulties' which prevented Beckett completing the work to his satisifaction.[12]

The twelfth (and longest) section of *The Lost Ones* is in many ways the dullest, because the exploration of a new subject (the question of queueing for the ladders) does not involve Beckett in any of the tensions and ambiguities that inevitably arise from returning to a subject already dealt with. Only at the end of the section, where an unprecedented cluster of rhetorical questions occurs, do we feel the pressure characteristic of the best parts of *The Lost Ones*. And even here there is a kind of bathos in the evasive and timid withdrawal from the subject of future anarchy: 'Is not the cylinder doomed in a more or less distant future to a state of anarchy given over to fury and violence? To these questions and many more the answers are clear and easy to give. It only remains to dare' (74). The answer to this question and the two questions·that precede it is presumably 'yes'. But such an answer brings into being a dread which is at the furthest remove from the self-satisfied confidence and optimism that dominates *The Lost Ones*. As a prophecy it is actually a good deal less accurate than those of the previous section, since as the final paragraph makes clear, violence and anarchy actually diminish as life in the cylinder becomes subject to greater and greater entropy and gradually rigidifies.

The last three sections are, by contrast, among the most interesting and complex. The thirteenth begins with Beckett apparently on the point of abandoning his empirical approach in order to investigate the effect of the climate on the souls of the inhabitants. But the soul has never been so interesting to Beckett as the body (even the 'soul landscape' of *Watt* is relegated to the addenda) and it is scarcely surprising that the body should remain of primary importance here: 'This desiccation of the envelope robs nudity of much of its charm as pink turns grey and transforms into a rustling of nettles the natural succulence of flesh against flesh' (75). The wryness of tone that characterizes so much of *The Lost Ones* reaches a kind of climax at this point as Beckett concentrates on the rare instances of sexuality in the cylinder: 'The spectacle then is one to be remembered of frenzies prolonged in pain and hopelessness long beyond what even the most gifted lovers can achieve in camera' (75). A similar wryness informs the conclusion to the section, which returns to the question of the periodic lulls that bring all life in the cylinder to a stop. One suspects that the 'vivacity of reaction as to the end of a world' (75-76) is as much Beckett's as the inhabitants', whose emotional attitude to their situation is rarely so clear-cut or so lively. But there is still a real sadness in Beckett's voice at the thought that they have been denied the relief of ending and must re-commence their several quests 'neither glad nor even sorry' (76).

The fourteenth section maintains the thirteenth's emphasis on the physical, but dwells (like the final section) on an individual figure rather than a group. Not even the striking image of the 'mere jumble of mingled flesh' (78) (which is what those queueing for the ladders have become) can compete with the female figure who provides a point of fixity from which others can take their bearings. As in *All Strange Away* the female figure is huddled up in a corner, head bowed, her hands gripping hold of her legs. Her passivity is of the extreme kind that has always fascinated Beckett and is at quite the opposite end of the spectrum from the violence that follows an infringement of the ladder laws. Like her predecessor she is quite unable to resist the close inspection that is basic to the searchers' quests for their lost ones, and in the final section she suffers the most intense and dramatic inspection of all from the last searcher to thread his way towards her.

It remains unclear why Beckett returned to *The Lost Ones* some four years after he had abandoned it. But it has long been obvious that Beckett is obsessively interested in the face-to-face confrontation of two figures, and in concluding *The Lost Ones* he reverts to the situation so memorably dramatized at the end of *Murphy*. Beckett stresses the fact that the most important figure for the last searcher is the first vanquished and finishes this somewhat dehumanised work with a moment of strange tenderness:

> There he opens then his eyes this last of all if a man and some time later threads his way to that first among the vanquished so often taken for a guide. On his knees he parts the heavy hair and raises the unresisting head. Once devoured the face thus laid bare the eyes at a touch of the thumb open without demur. In those calm wastes he lets his wander till they are the first to close and the head relinquished falls back into its place. (79)

The doll-like movements of Mr. Kelly (in *Murphy*) which seem so mechanical and opportunist here give way to a withdrawal so absolute that one cannot but be moved by it. Indeed, when life in the cylinder is finally brought to a halt, one cannot help feeling an immense relief: 'Hushed in the same breath the faint stridulence mentioned above whence suddenly such silence as to drown all the faint breathings put together' (79). The last words, however, referring us back to that 'unthinkable past' when the first searcher 'bowed his head' (63) and became one of the 'vanquished', offer no relief at all. There is a lingering suggestion that 'if this notion is maintained' the world of the cylinder will be 'possessed of the strange power suddenly to kindle again' and thus once again become a place of systematic polity teetering on the edge of anarchy. This is perhaps Beckett's last (and admittedly very tenuous) attempt at the circularity of form that once used to obsess him. Almost all the other late pieces end *in medias res* or in an attempt to erase the reality the text has brought into being. Even in *Lessness*, where the permutations could be continued indefinitely, the last paragraph has a decisiveness that prevents us harking back to the beginning, and the 'unthinkable' futures alluded to at the end of *Imagination Dead Imagine* and *For to End Yet Again* are too unpredictable for us to feel that things will necessarily go on endlessly repeating themselves. It is as if Beckett had realized that circularity of form was as vulgarly plausible as any other concatenation, and determined (since *How It Is*) to write in a resolutely linear way, without regard for the overall neatness of shape that was once important to him. When we recall that *Malone Dies* ends in a clutter of strangulated phrases, *The Unnamable* in utter turbulence, and even *Watt* (despite its formal ending) in a heap of fragments — and how many of the shorter texts have had to be abandoned — it is clear that the circularity of *Molloy* is the exception rather than the rule. Beckett has not changed so radically as to suggest that the future will be different from the past, but he has become less convinced that this will inevitably be the case, perhaps out of fear that we will begin to derive some solace from his pessimism. With a mind like Malone's, 'always on the alert against itself', he has retained the ability to disquiet us more consistently than any other modern writer of comparable stature.

6. *Ping*

Beckett's claim that *Ping* was written 'in reaction to *Le Dépeupleur*'[13] is fully substantiated by the nine variant texts of the French original printed in the appendix to the Fletcher-Federman bibliography. Any doubts we might have about the seriousness of Beckett's enterprise in *Ping* must inevitably be modified in the light of the extraordinarily concentrated labour he expended on this intractable (and in some ways unattractive) material. But it would be mistaken to imagine that all the difficulties in *Ping* can be removed by appealing to rejectamenta, and quite wrong to concentrate our attention on the earlier drafts at the expense of the text Beckett finally elected to publish. Whilst his attitude towards the publication of 'foul papers' seems to have mellowed in recent years, he has remained in principle opposed to the school of thought (espoused, for obvious reasons, by most scholars and academics) that thinks these private evidences of composition should ideally be part of the public domain. (He told me once that he did not even think the publication of Joyce's first version of *A Portrait of the Artist as a Young Man*, *Stephen Hero*, was justified.) Our primary task is to confront *Ping* as published, and not to concern ourselves unduly with how *Ping* came to be made into what it is.

It is immediately clear that Beckett was reacting against the style of *Le Dépeupleur* above all, for there seems to be little commerce between the lugubrious urbanity of *The Lost Ones* and the telegrammatic briskness of the final text of *Ping*. This recoil from the studied artifice of his most allegorical work is manifested as early as the first of the nine variant versions, which preserves more of the detail of *The Lost Ones* than any of the subsequent eight. An intransigent bluntness new to Beckett's work is present at the origins of *Ping*, as the first (French) manuscript version shows:

> Largeur un mètre. Profondeur un mètre. Hauteur deux mètres. Angles droits. Quatre murs cardinaux. Un mètre carré de sol plat. Même chose plafond. Mesures approximatives comme toutes à venir. Pas d'ouvertures. Grand éclairage. Tout est blanc. Pas d'ombre. Des périodes de noir. Grande chaleur. Des périodes de froid. (F. and F., p. 325)

Nothing could be further removed from the fleshier parts of *The Lost Ones* than this bleak rehearsal of rudimentary *aperçus* thrown together without much care for symmetry or resonance. But it is only in the fifth, sixth and seventh versions, where most of Beckett's creative labour is to be found, that the distinctive length and syntax of the published *Ping* make their first appearance.

The reaction that Beckett speaks of was more than a merely stylistic one. He has always, since the book on Proust, considered style to be more a matter of vision than of technique, and the vision of *Ping* is of a very different order from that to be found in *The Lost Ones*. The Olympian *hauteur* of *The Lost Ones* has here been banished in favour of a fractured strenuousness that makes even the myopic tendencies of the earlier text look long-sighted. This is partly the rationale for, and partly the result of, Beckett's conviction that *Ping* is concerned with data which can be said to be 'all known' (*Ping*, *Six Residua*, London, John Calder, 1978, p. 41: all further references are to this edition). But the extreme short-sightedness of *Ping* is so pervasive and disintegrative that for most of the time it seems as if only those things in the immediate vicinity can truly be said to be 'known'. The obsessive repetition that is such a feature of *Ping* — not even the most formulaic areas of *Watt* remotely approach the limited vocabulary of this text — brings certain elements into such prominence that they acquire the status of 'all that can be known'. But habit is as great a deadener here as it was in *Proust* or *Godot* and it is the infrequently encountered elements that stay our dazzled eye and remind us of how unknown and unstable everything beyond the insistently immediate really is.

Beckett's vision in *Ping* resembles that of an artist in collage who juxtaposes items from unrelated areas of experience and renders them all unfamiliar whatever their texture or provenance. And yet *Ping* is finally more of a collision than a collage, in which each lexical item seems to stand on its own and disclaim all contact with its neighbour. The predominantly monosyllabic and disyllabic elements attract our attention as atomized objects in their own right, however much they strive, or are forced, to develop a kind of syntax. Statistical analysis reveals that towards the middle of *Ping* there is a tendency for word-groups to appear in their most elongated version,[14] but such cohesion is really foreign to the mode of *Ping* and does not survive into the last third of the piece. It is impossible to read *Ping* in the consecutive manner in which we read a narrative that is ongoing in its syntax (say, *Ulysses*). It resembles rather a piece of sculpture that we contemplate from outside, attuning ourselves to the shape and texture of the material. It is Beckett's *Finnegans Wake* perhaps, with the important difference that it encourages not poly-valence but absolute mono-valence. *Ping* reflects the impotence and ignorance that Beckett has always carefully distinguished from Joyce's omniscience and omnipotence, and yet it possesses (even for an initiate of Beckettian motifs) a strangeness and opaqueness that prevent it, like the *Wake*, from ever being perfectly apprehensible.

What *Ping* communicates most powerfully is the intrinsic difficulty of seeing anything with the clarity that would be necessary for 'all' to be 'known'. Hence the repetition early in the text of the sentence 'Traces blurs signs no meaning light grey almost white' (41), and hence, too, the inclusion of words like 'haught', 'unover', and 'ping' (41) itself, which are beyond the range of ordinary speech and (especially in the case of the third of these) lack precise connotations altogether. Everything that might serve as a feature that would be interpretable (and thus as a foundation for similar or extended acts of interpretation) is discovered to be too short-lived, or too unprecedented, to be the ground against which other objects might, as in normal spectroscopic vision, figure. Beckett has secreted himself within the white walls of what was once a rotunda and is now a cube, and removed even the skeletal remnants of personality that surfaced occasionally in *Imagination Dead Imagine*.

The sense of human agency combined with miraculous good fortune (which permits the sustained imaginative projections of *Imagination Dead Imagine* to occur) has quite disappeared from *Ping*. There is no longer a being for things to happen to, or an imagination that can organize and synthesize its images. The urbane narrator of *The Lost Ones* has been vanquished as decisively as any of the inhabitants of his cylinder, and a new, and much more radical, impersonality occupies the site left vacant by his absence. (Later, in *Lessness*, an even more extreme impersonality is attempted.) The strange but in some way soothing systems that condition the world of the rotunda and the world of the cylinder are absolutely absent from the cube, where the traces of life are too short-lived for geometrical or arithmetical analysis to prosper. Repeated linguistic assaults on the limited number of features that present themselves are the nearest Beckett can come to insinuating that there is some trace of system somewhere, and the obscure metallic 'ping' (so much more desiccated than the 'ring as in the imagination the ring of bone') is all that remains of what was once a fully automated mechanism.

The persistent reiteration performs the double function of creating a reality and almost in the same breath de-creating it. The strategy of *Ping* is to conjure up the rudiments of a situation and let the formulaic language throttle it, or rather to begin each utterance with what seems to be substantial and to end with indications of absence and vacancy: 'never seen', 'invisible', 'almost never', 'that known not', 'silence within', 'no sound', and most decisive of all (and increasingly frequent towards the end) 'over'. It is as though Beckett were trying to establish a perfect absence by repeated recourse to a mechanism ('ping') and an obsessive image ('bare white body fixed legs joined like sewn') in the hope of wearing out the former and exorcizing the latter. But in each case there is a stimulus towards the kind of delusive hope that kept the 'lost ones' in thrall to their quest, for the bare white body is given eyes and ears and a nose and a head as if it were a real human being, and the 'ping' mechanism activates murmurs that lead Beckett to hope (and fear) that he is 'perhaps not alone' (41) and that there is 'perhaps a nature' (42), human or inanimate, preventing the establishment of a void. The confident assertion that memories of a real and beautiful world 'blue and white in the wind' (44) will no longer trouble him ('that much memory henceforth never' (44), after scores of examples of the more hesitant 'almost never') is undercut by the sudden realization that an eye 'unlustrous black and white half closed long lashes imploring' (44) is gazing back at him and destroying the solitude he has been intent on perfecting. It is clear that the text cannot continue beyond this point without utterly changing its character, for it has been predicated upon the theory that all can be known (and therefore tamed) and it has come upon an item that is so riveting that it must immediately be extinguished. The 'eye of prey' no longer belongs to a dispassionate and scientific observer as in *Imagination Dead Imagine*, but to a being that has taken up the life it has been given and begun to walk (to use the terms of Beckett's poem 'The Vulture'). There is a similar confrontation at the end of *Still 3*, except that there, as befits a mode more tranquil than *Ping* could ever be, there does not seem to be any connection between observed and observer (or indeed between the *aperçu* and the need to bring the text to a halt): 'Size as seen in the life at say arm's length sudden white black all about no known expression eyes its at last not looking lids the ones no expression marble still so long then out'. *Ping* leaves us with no such certainties. All we can set against the horror of the imploring eye is a certain relief that this insistent and rebarbative enterprise can actually be brought to some kind of conclusion. In *Lessness* even this relief is denied us, as the permutations roll on to infinitude and the world dissolves into impalpable 'figments'.

7. *Lessness*

Lessness has not lacked critics to do justice to its formal qualities, despite its forbidding appearance of formlessness. In an age that has increasingly occupied itself with structures and structuration rather than with the paraphrasable content of literature this may be inevitable, and it is not difficult to imagine historians of literature a hundred years hence citing *Lessness* as primary evidence for an Age of Structuralism. One would indeed need to possess exceptional *sangfroid* to deny some connection between an intellectual climate in which the investigation of structures has been powerful and influential and a work dominated by structure composed by a man who has said 'It is the shape that matters'. But at the same time it ought to be remembered that Beckett was enlisted in the ranks of proto-Existentialists little more than a decade ago, and (by virtue of having had many Surrealist friends) as a Surrealist into the bargain. While there can be no doubt that Beckett's work reflects contemporary feeling — and is much illuminated by Structuralist analysis — it seems safer, with this unclassifiable man, to propose that his writing is essentially *sui generis* and better explained in terms of his own private writing career than in terms of the public movements of his time.

Analysis of the structures operating in *Lessness* has inevitably tended to pay little heed to the experience of reading it consecutively. This is a natural reaction to any text that comes close to unreadability, and is a perfectly legitimate critical approach to eminently readable works as well. But it runs the risk of dehumanizing the work and atomizing the artefact into segments or fragments which the work has carefully cemented together. It is invaluable to know the circumstances behind the composition of *Lessness* — the studied randomness that Ruby Cohn has so well described — and helpful to have had identified the six categories into which its material falls. But there is little point in continuing Beckett's permutations and no point at all in contenting oneself with the categories and making no attempt to go beyond them. It is interesting, indeed, that Beckett's own attitude to *Lessness*, as represented by the dustflap to its publication in book form in 1970, underplays the permutative aspect, and stresses rather the 'disorder' that is part of its unfolding:

> *Lessness* has to do with the collapse of some such refuge as that last attempted in *Ping* and with the ensuing situation of the refugee.

> Ruin, exposure, wilderness, mindlessness, past and future denied
> and affirmed, are the categories, formally distinguishable, through
> which the writing winds, first in one disorder, then in another.

The classification of categories here may be a trifle vague in comparison with those of Martin Esslin and Ruby Cohn (each of whom stress different aspects of the fifth and sixth categories) and may seem unduly negative (the first and second categories are usually considered to be 'true refuge' and 'earth', the third 'little body'). But the dustflap notes are certainly the most economical and accurate account of the work we possess, and have the great merit of reminding us of the relationship between *Lessness* and *Ping*, the former written, as Beckett confirmed to Brian Finney, in reaction to the latter.

It has been said by Judith Dearlove, in a sensitive article on the residua, that in *Lessness* Beckett 'creates a work that insists upon being unmade'.[15] But if *Lessness* is to be read at all, we ought to be able to study it without 'unmaking it' unduly. *Lessness* ought not to be accorded a treatment different in kind from that which we give to other Beckett works, especially when it differs only in degree (of difficulty or, if we look at it another way, of simplicity). Although the paragraphs are separated much more decisively than the 'versets' of *How It Is*, they are much more concentratedly related at a deeper level than that of their appearance on the page. The work unfolds, like any other literary artefact, in time and space (its own and ours), however random its composition may have been. It has been noticed, for instance, that the final paragraph performs the role of a conclusion, and also that the first paragraph outlines, in an almost impeccable introductory manner, the skeletal situation later paragraphs will 'flesh out' or, as one might say, de-flesh. No-one would want to claim that *Lessness* exemplified the Aristotelian theory that a work has a beginning, a middle and an end. But it preserves the vestiges of them and consists literally (like *Finnegans Wake*) of nothing less.

The work begins in a mood of great relief that at long last after so many false refuges the true refuge of ruins has been constructed. There is 'no sound no stir' and on all sides an endlessness that makes the earth and sky seem as one. The 'only upright' that disturbs this featureless scenario is a little body with a beating heart. But the box of *Ping* no longer encloses it and no light beckons with the promise of an exit. The first paragraph ends with a strange confidence that at last a truly 'issueless' condition can be contemplated (*Lessness, Six Residua*, John Calder, 1978, p. 47; all further references are to this edition).

The second paragraph confirms this vision by elaborating upon it. The ruins are dispersed in such a way that they are indistinguishable from the elements they once defined themselves against. The 'sheer white blank planes' of *Ping* are 'gone from mind' (47) like figments, as if they never had been. In such a changeless world 'the passing hour' (47) can only be a dream.

But, as if 'the passing hour' has been suddenly revivified by being mentioned, the third paragraph quickens into life and anger, and insinuates a sense of history that has been previously conspicuous by its absence: 'He will curse God again as in the blessed days . . .' (47). Only the reiteration that all has gone from mind preserves the feeling of absence that Beckett is intent on creating.

The fourth paragraph contents itself with restatement, adding only the fact that the little body is 'locked rigid' (47) as the rain once more descends. The fifth admits no new material, except a faint suggestion that the ruins are again 'upright' and more distinct than the little body. The sixth oscillates wildly between assertion and denial, restoring the little body to its eminence and speculating on its ability to come to life despite the desiccation which surrounds it. But with relief the paragraph concludes by stressing the impossibility of this ('No sound not a breath . . .', 48).

The paragraphs begin to lengthen here as if life is indeed a possibility. Without abandoning the oscillation of the sixth paragraph, Beckett concludes for the first time in the work with an unqualified assertion. The sentences beginning 'Never but . . .' (48) seem at this point incapable of carrying out the work of erasure they have been invented to perform. The little body seems assured of life, however miminal: 'He will live again the space of a step' (just as Beckett lived 'the space of a door / that opens and shuts' in a poem of 1948). In this event, the 'endlessness' will be a form of confine 'over him' (48).

The burgeoning of life continues through the eighth paragraph, where the little body is suddenly seen to be 'overrun' (48) as if by termites. The splitting asunder of the true refuge is like the opening of a pod, except that it scatters ruins rather than seeds. It is as if we are reliving the moment when the initial situation came into being, and there is a sense of wonder at such an extraordinary occurrence that quite astounds 'the light of reason' (48).

The ninth paragraph dispenses with denials, except to remind us (twice) that all has 'gone from mind' (48) and, as it were, come to body.

This means that 'unhappiness will reign again' (48) and also means that light will once again construct a refuge to enable the little body to endure its plight with equanimity: 'Face to white calm touch close eye calm . . .' (48).

The tenth paragraph begins with a reminder that the need for a refuge can only be satisfied by blacking out the real world and developing an imaginary one where life exists more passionately ('this wild laughter these cries', 49). The imagination offers clarity and penetration, and transfigures everything with its radiance ('Head through calm eye all light white calm . . .'). The dawn and dusk of everyday existence are revealed as figments that the imagination, 'dispeller of figments' (49) renders real.

The final paragraphs of the first half of the text, the eleventh and twelfth, explore the refuge of the imagination. The 'heart will beat again' and 'he will go on his back face to the sky open again over him' (49). In the event of encountering another ('Face to calm eye' like Murphy confronting Mr. Endon) the imagination will have to recede, account itself a fiction ('the blue celeste of poesy') and leave the little body a 'little void' (49). The 'light of reason' (which could not be dimmed even in the *Texts for Nothing*) will dissipate the imaginative vision.

The little body now has to come to terms with a new impoverishment, 'issueless' because the imagination seems to have been defeated. 'Issueless' began by meaning 'beyond dispute' but has come to mean 'inescapable from' and 'without progeny'. The promise regarding future life made by the fourteenth paragraph is destroyed by the brusque 'figment' that opens the fifteenth (49). Refusal to accept the featurelessness that is a consequence of the defeat of the imagination is futile. The sixteenth paragraph insists upon the 'little void' and stresses that 'the passing light' was just a figment to distract attention from the 'changelessness' (50).

But the next two paragraphs contrive to bring something into being once again (as in the eighth). There is 'no relief' from this compulsion evidently. The cries and wild laughter of the imagination offer a world that is at least alive, however featureless it may otherwise be. But it is not a world that lasts. It is as ephemeral as the beam of light from a lighthouse ('long short', compare *Still 3* and the lighthouse in *Texts 1* and *5* of *Texts for Nothing*). The blackout that begins the twentieth paragraph (50-1) reminds us that the truest refuge of all is to face up to the 'issueless predicament of existence'. In a final bid to disprove this Beckett presents for the first and only time in the work sentences from each of the six categories (50-1).

The attempt is clearly a failure. There are only two more affirmations after this, among a welter of assurances that all is gone from mind. And yet the little body survives this buffeting to dominate the final paragraph, dispelling all other figments (the entire scenario in fact) in an act of erasure like that which ends *Enough*.

Reading a work like *Lessness* consecutively testifies to the fact that our minds cannot be as vigilant as computers. We are a prey to habit, as Beckett stated long ago. Faced with a mass of repeated elements in which no clear subordination of one to another is established, we find ourselves more drawn to some elements rather than others, and only notice some elements the second time around, when those that first intrigued us have receded, or relinquished hold on us. It seems to me that reading *Lessness* in this way makes it a more inexhaustible text than the more conventional approach which 'unmakes' it. There seems to me no reason why we should allow ourselves to be hidebound by the known circumstances of composition — the random selection and combination of a limited number of units. It is an eminently Beckettian paradox that, to analyze the *Texts for Nothing* accurately, we have at each point to bring to bear our knowledge of what precedes and succeeds it, whereas to get the most out of *Lessness*, a text for being, we have to revert to a 'naive realist' linear approach.

8. *Still, Sounds, Still 3*

Still (1973) is neither clinical like *The Lost Ones* nor confessional like *From an Abandoned Work*. It lacks the diagnostic spirit of the short texts of the 1960s, but it more than makes up for it by the manner in which it presents experience for its own sake. It is a splendid simulacrum of the mind quietly communing with itself on the subject of something always on the point of being engulfed by the element it inhabits. The stuttering syntax dramatizes the way the eye adapts itself to states of darkness desirable in that they offer a refuge but disturbing in that they are like the darkness of real being. Beckett is admitting here that complete stillness (short of what Mr. Rooney in *All That Fall* would call 'fully certified death') is impossible to achieve because the mind persists in investigating its perceptions long after the body has ceased to move. The speaker in *Still* has learnt from the mistakes of his predecessors and become less demanding of his surroundings, more content to move slowly between the two positions he especially favours, either seated at the open window facing south or standing by the western window in the gathering gloom. But his mind cannot rest; and the more he concentrates, the more turbulence he uncovers:

> Quite still again then at open window . . . though actually close inspection not still at all but trembling all over. Close inspection namely detail by detail all over to add up to this whole not still at all but trembling all over . . . even the hands clearly trembling and the breast faint rise and fall. (*Still* in, *For to End yet Again and Other Fizzles*, London, John Calder, 1976, pp. 19-20)

From here on the whole impetus of the text is towards the climatic moment when the head, seeking relief from its distress, reposes in the hand and a stillness of mind and body can be temporarily reconstituted. It is symptomatic of Beckett's new tranquillity that this action is accomplished without any of the urgency or dislocation of earlier texts. At the end of the piece the syntax, momentarily ruffled by the 'trembling', regains the quiet declarative power of the opening sentences:

> All quite still again then head in hand . . . as the hours pass lesser contacts . . . with the faint stirrings of the various parts as night wears on . . . Leave it so all quite still or try listening to the sounds all quite still head in hand listening for a sound. (21)

Still, as its conclusion shows, is a far cry from the wild and whirling words of *Ping*. It is perhaps as subtle and compelling in its language as any of Beckett's most recent prose. It demonstrates at every point that Beckett has surrendered at last to the musical properties inherent in language rather than regarding them as incidental beauties he can well do without. He is said to have relinquished English because he could not help writing poetry in that language, but in returning to English in *Still* he has written a poetic text that far exceeds even the best of his poetic efforts. In this serpentine and, as it were, short-sighted prose, each element seems to blend effortlessly and imperceptibly into the next without Beckett losing the muscular energy that has always been his hall-mark. The concentration on sound patterns — alliteration ('quite quiet', 'western window', 'no more movable imaginable') assonance ('window . . . afterglow', 'closing as it goes', 'normally . . . valley'), near homonyms ('some . . . same', 'head . . . hand'), clusters of consonants ('upright wicker chair with armrests . . . stare', 'no such thing the further shelter') — is achieved without our finding them merely precious or exquisite, and the self-critique that has always been present in Beckett is again at work here keeping the emotions under control. The tendency to write blank verse that surfaced uncomfortably at certain moments in the *Texts for Nothing* is here reserved for the moment of greatest intensity: 'till midway to the head it hesitates / and hangs half open trembling in mid air' (21); the temptation to take refuge in the extreme form of patterning, permutation (resisted with difficulty in *Enough* and *Ping* and acceded to in *Lessness*) is here cut short with a dismissive 'etc.' at the one point where it threatens to take over the text (21). If a fascination for repetition remains at the heart of *Still*, it is not because the repeated elements are, as in *Ping*, impedimenta to be circumvented, but because they offer the optimum way of bearing witness to the abiding truth of individual perceptions and expressing the viability of the desire to be still. The atomization of language that occurred in *Ping* has been abandoned in favour of a prose that seems intent on exploring the potentialities of its own idiosyncratic syntax. Beckett avoids excessive pathos and excessive dryness by finding at last the 'syntax of weakness' which he spoke about in 1962, a syntax that operates on our sensibilities by insinuation rather than assertion, by its infinite suggestibility rather than by its vehement rigour.

Still, like all great literature (and unlike *Ping*), creates the taste by which it is to be enjoyed. It is the most satisfying of Beckett's prose texts since *How It Is*. It does not require of a reader that he should be familiar with every other item in Beckett's *oeuvre*; it only requires him to keep his sensibility, in particular his aural sensibility, receptive. It is true that anyone who knows their Beckett well will be reminded, at the beginning of *Still*, that the sudden brightness before sunset is a phenomenon to which Beckett has alluded before, in *From an Abandoned Work*: 'Nice fresh morning, bright too early as so often . . . The sky would soon darken and rain fall and go on falling, all day, till evening. Then blue and sun again a second, then night' (*SR*, 11, cf. *TN*, 30), and in the splendid opening of *Watt* (which also describes Mr. Hackett feeling the arm-rests of 'his' seat in the manner of the speaker of *Still* and *As the Story Was Told*:

> These northwestern skies are really extraordinary, said Goff, are they not.
> So voluptuous, said Tetty. You think it is all over and then pop! up they flare with augmented radiance. (*W*, 13)

Likewise anyone who has read the opening of *Murphy*, with the eponymous hero strapped in his wicker-chair gazing out of the window, can hardly fail to observe the connection between *Murphy* and the situation described in *Still*. There is also a close verbal connection between the conclusion of *Still* ('Leave it so . . .') and the beginning of the third of the *Texts for Nothing* ('Leave all that, I was going to say leave all that . . .'). But none of these analogues are essential to the comprehension of *Still*, except insofar as they serve to confirm one's feeling that Beckett has become less tormented and less violent in forty years of writing. *Still*'s ability to hold us spellbound derives directly from its containing within itself the reasons why it is so and not otherwise.

Still is certainly the nearest Beckett has come to the condition of tranquillity he has been seeking for so long. *For to End Yet Again* is a much more turbulent text, as is only to be expected of a piece that finds it necessary to return to the landscape of ruins and the vain 'dream of a way in space with neither here nor there'. It is indeed characteristic of Beckett's restlessness and his refusal to be seduced by his own imaginings that in the texts which immediately followed *Still*, *Sounds* and *Still 3*, we should see Beckett subjecting his new language to the kinds of strain we normally associate with him.

In *Sounds* the speaker is listening for a sound not because he hopes for something from it (as in *How It Is*) but rather because he wishes to devise a strategy for abolishing its existence. If he can establish the total absence of sound, as in *Still* he has established the total absence of vision, he will be able to convince himself that he has effectively ceased to exist, that he has been 'dreamt away'. [16] As in *Still*, Beckett is torn between the belief that he has achieved his desired aim and a troubled awareness that he has not done so:

> But mostly not for nothing never quite for nothing[17] even stillest night when air too still for even the lightest leaf to carry to sound no not to sound to carry too still for even the lightest leaf to carry the brief way here and not die the sound not die on the brief way the wave not die away . . . (*Essays in Criticism*, XXVIII, no. 2, April 1978, p. 155; all further references are to this printing).

The curious interlude that follows this admission, describing how the figure leaves the summerhouse and goes out to a tree (doubtless the beech tree 'in whose shade' the speaker of *Still* was 'once quite still'), dramatizes how precarious and short-lived the stasis of *Still* can be. But *Sounds* reaffirms Beckett's belief in the possibility of stillness and stasis in its third and final section, [18] which returns us to the refuge of the summerhouse and concentrates on the most decisive proof of all that the speaker has not been 'dreamt away' — the phenomenon of breathing:

> sigh it all out through the mouth that sound then fill again hold and out again so often once sigh upon sigh no question now some time past but quiet as when even the mother can't hear stooped over the crib but has to feel pulse or heart. (156)

It is a moment of great tenderness, like that describing the mother crouched over the praying boy of *How It Is*, or the conclusion of the first of the *Texts for Nothing*. It is more poignant even than the moment in *Still* when the narrator perceives the 'faint rise and fall' of his breast. Beckett seems to have realized sometime in the late 1960s (when he composed *Breath*) that the sound of breathing was an even more important matter than the sound of voices. But whereas *Breath* concentrated on the insistent presence of life, *Sounds* manages to convince us of the almost total absence of life:

> Leave it so then this stillest night till now of all quite still head in hand as shown listening trying listening for a sound or dreamt away try dreamt away where no such thing no more than ghosts make nothing to listen for no such thing as a sound. (156)

The extreme quietness of this conclusion, largely a matter (as in *Still*) of syntactical poise and adroit management of cadence, convinces us that tranquillity can be reconstituted, even after the body has felt compelled to leave its refuge. If it is true, as the narrator assures us, that 'worse than none the self's when the whole body moves', we can content ourselves by reflecting that, when the body is once again still, the self can once again be something.

The very brief *Still 3* returns us to the wicker-chair of *Still* and shows Beckett following the premises of *Still* and *Sounds* through to their conclusions. All activity has ceased, all inquiry has been abandoned, all categories have been destroyed:

> not listening again in vain quite yet while the dim questions fade where been how long how it was. For head in hand eyes closed as shown always the same dark now from all hours of day and night. No nightbird to mean night at least day at least or so faint perhaps mere fancy. . . . Or Mother Calvet[19] with the dawn pushing the old go-cart for whatever she might find and back at dusk. Back then and nothing to tell but some soundless place and in the head . . . (156-157)

It would seem, as much from the tone of what the speaker says as from the utterances themselves, that the protagonist has reached a more complete and fulfilling absence than was possible in either of the previous *Still* texts. But at this point he finds that the problem of the imagination has not been solved so much as shelved. The second half of *Still 3* presents the turbulent world of the imagination, as agonized and fragmentary as the world Beckett dramatized in *Play* (1963): '. . . faces on off in the dark sudden whites long short then black long short then another so on or the same' (157). Faced with this unexpected horror Beckett tries at once to apply the wisdom of stillness discovered in *Still* and *Sounds*: 'say back try saying back from there head in hand as shown' (157). But all he can accomplish in *Still 3* is the perception of a figure mummified to the point of disappearance: 'Size as seen in the life at say arm's length sudden white black all about no known expression eyes its at last not looking lids the ones no expression marble still so long then out' (157). It clearly gives the speaker considerable satisfaction that this mummified figure possesses a life and features that are nothing to do with him. But perhaps his greatest satisfaction derives from the fact that the tranquillity achieved in *Still* and *Sounds* has been shown to be possible even in the world of the imagination.

   Sounds and *Still 3* are clearly of a piece with *Still* in the way they re-establish tranquillity when tranquillity has been seriously threatened. But in these two pieces the surface of the prose is much more ruffled by the turbulence it throws up, and *For to End Yet Again* is more turbulent still. In each case Beckett adapts his 'syntax of weakness' in the light of new aims and new problems, but perhaps only in *Still* can he be said to have found the calm he has spent a lifetime searching for.

9. *As the Story Was Told*

In Beckett's most recent prose the tranquillity and tremulousness that co-exist so compellingly in *Still*, *Sounds*, and *Still 3* are less evenly distributed, and the emphasis reverts to those things that are less 'calmative' and curative, though quite as inexplicable as the miraculous stillness that has enabled the creative mind to discover a temporary refuge. In the text Beckett offered to the publishers of a memorial volume for his friend the poet and dramatist Günter Eich (*Günter Eich zum Gedächtnis*, Frankfurt, Suhrkamp Verlag, 1975, pp. 10-[13]) entitled *As the Story Was Told*, the summer-house of *Still* has

given way to a less accommodating hut that epitomizes the return of
the constricted space so dominant in Beckett's work since the 'vast
tracts' of *How It Is* rotted down to the corridors of 'He is barehead'.
The summer-house retains, however, an almost talismanic value:

> It reminded me strongly of a summer-house in which as a child I used to
> sit quite still for hours on end, on the window-seat, the whole year
> round. It had the same five log walls, the same coloured glass, the same
> diminutiveness, being not more than ten feet across and so low of ceiling
> that the average man could not have held himself erect in it, though of
> course there was no such difficulty for a child. At the centre, facing the
> coloured panes, stood a small upright wicker-chair with arm-rests, as
> against the summer-house's window-seat. I sat there very straight and
> still, with my arms along the rests, looking out at the orange light.
> (*R.U.L. MS* 1396/4/14; all further references are to this copy)

This detailed re-creation of a revered object is not, like Krapp's,
indulgently nostalgic; the speaker here is voyaging through stranger
seas of thought than were available, at the flick of a switch, to Krapp.
Although the speaker is deprived of Krapp's shuffling mobility and
sustaining victuals, there is more equanimity in his voice than Krapp
can muster. The speaker of *As the Story Was Told* has achieved the
'ablation of desire' that Beckett long ago (in *Proust*) recommended, but
he is dependent, in a much more fundamental way than Krapp, upon
some agency outside himself that will provide him with answers to the
questions that most concern him. The relationship between the
speaker and the nameless interpreter is of the vaguely reassuring kind
that we find at the beginning of *Molloy* and in the middle of 'Horn
came always', with the protagonist largely passive, but rousing
himself periodically from torpor in an attempt to exert some control
over his predicament:

> As the story was told me I never went near the place during sessions. I
> asked what place and a tent was described at length, a small tent the
> colour of its surroundings. Wearying of this description I asked what
> sessions and these in their turn were described, their object, duration,
> frequency, and harrowing nature. I trust I was not more sensitive than
> the next man, but finally I had to raise my hand. I lay there quite still for
> a time, then asked where I was while all this was going forward.

The raised hand of this selective interlocutor is obviously designed to
keep the world of tribulation as far as possible at arm's length, in order
that the more appealing (and more lawless) world of memory and
imagination may be induced to replace it. The conditions for doing so
are, at first sight, extremely propitious, since the speaker is as far

away from the 'sessions' as he could reasonably expect to be:

> In a hut, was the answer, a small hut in a grove, some two hundred yards away, a distance even the loudest could not carry, but must die on the way. This was not so strange as at first sight it sounded when one considered the stoutness of the canvas and the sheltered situation of the hut among the trees. Indeed the tent might have been struck where it stood and moved forward fifty yards or more without inconvenience . . .

The canvas within which the session is taking place may lack the bone-like impermeability of the 'little fabric' that dominated *Imagination Dead Imagine*, but the distance between tent and hut is sufficiently large for all sound to disperse before threatening the speaker's solitude. Beckett is a good deal more absolute here than he is in *Sounds*, where an analogous desire for silence is manifested, but where the syntax leaves one uncertain of its attainment: 'But mostly not for nothing . . . even stillest night when air too still . . . for even the lightest leaf to carry the brief way here and not die the sound not die on the brief way the wave not die away'. It is in the knowledge that nothing can disturb his meditations that the speaker in *As the Story Was Told* can call up the summer-house that once meant so much to him; but this freely associative manner would not have been possible without the external agency of his informant. 'Lying there with eyes closed in the silence', the two necessary preconditions of imaginative projection satisfied (no sound and no vision), the 'sessions' can be momentarily forgotten.

But only momentarily, as the amusing synaesthetic blunder 'at first sight it sounded' is no doubt intended to prepare us for. The hut and the tent are in much closer contact than the distance between them would suggest. The figure in the hut is revealed as the recipient of reports from the sessions, and reacts to the interruption with a violence that destroys not only the court of assize but also the figure who has been (unknown to us) arguing his case before it:

> . . . as I watched a hand appeared in the doorway and held out to me a sheet of writing. I took and read it, then tore it in four and put the pieces in the waiting hand to take away. A little later the whole scene disappeared. As the story was told me the man succumbed in the end to his ill-treatment, though quite old enough at the time to die naturally of old age.

The speaker retains his equanimity throughout, and seems quite unconscious of the connections between his arbitrary destruction of the sheet of writing and the consequences of his act. So he returns to the stillness that matters most to him and imagines that the story he has been told has been similarly destroyed by his violent act.

But the last two sentences, as often in late Beckett, add complications. The speaker reverts to his dependence on an external agent and is reminded of his inadequacy with respect to what *Text 5* calls 'that obscure assize where to be is to be guilty':

> But finally I asked if I knew exactly what the man — I would like to give his name but cannot — what exactly was required of the man, what it was exactly that he would not or could not say. No, was the answer, after some hesitation, no, I did not know what the poor man was required to say, in order to be pardoned, but would have recognized it at once, yes, at a glance, if I had seen it.

This conclusion, with its doleful double 'no' like those at the end of *Imagination Dead Imagine* and its frenetic and quiveringly hopeful 'yes' balanced against them, is as impressive a moment as any in Beckett's writings of the 1970s. The separation between what Eliot called 'the man who suffers' and 'the mind which creates' is unbridgeable and absolute. The written word is not, for Beckett, a medium that can absolve the crime of being, and nor is the spoken word. If there were such things as pardons to be had, they could only be 'seen' and might only be imaginary (since the text has conclusively demonstrated, like most of the late Beckett texts, that seeing is imagining). We are left with only a helpless, and by now almost perfunctory, sympathy to shore against the ruins of this sad conclusion.

10. *La Falaise*

In the same way as *As the Story Was Told* is related to the three *Still* texts which precede it, so *La Falaise*, a text written in 1975 as a *témoignage* for a Bram van Velde exhibition (originally titled simply 'Pour Bram') is related to *For to End Yet Again* which — though only published in 1975 — had occupied Beckett since at least 1971, the date of a short piece of prose titled *Abandonné* which is closely related to it. Beckett's *témoignages* have become, over the years, less an outward appraisal of the art object in front of him and more a way of dramatizing his most initmate concerns in a different way. The 1966 text to accompany an Arikha exhibition is utterly different in style and theme from the art criticism of the 1940s. *La Falaise*, like the Arikha piece, is dense and brief, and full of the motifs of the 1970s.

The density of the published text (in *Celui qui ne peut se servir de mots*, Montpellier, Fata Morgana 1975) is the result of a typically Beckettian reduction of more sequential material, achieved by removing paragraphs and jettisoning irrelevant details. An early version begins briskly but without much vigour:

> La falaise se dresse couloir de craie à quelques kilomètres de la fenêtre. Elle a l'air fait par l'homme.
> Quatre mètres de haut sur deux de large la fénetre s'élève loin du sol dans un lieu inconnu. (R.U.L. MS 1396/4/34)

Beckett reduces this ruthlessly 'Fenêtre entre ciel et terre on ne sait où. Elle donne sur une falaise incolore' (R.U.L. MS 1396/4/40). Especially interesting here is the omission of the notion that the cliff has 'a man-made look' about it, which Beckett stresses again later in the first version. The skeletal prose of the published text would indeed sort oddly with this reassuring detail, which distracts us from the more important business (for Beckett) of articulating, as in *Imagination Dead Imagine*, the spatial constraints on the object: 'La crête échappe à l'oeil où qu'il se mette. La base aussi. Deux pans de ciel à jamais blanc la bordent . . . D'oiseau de mer pas trace. Ou trop claire pour paraître'. The only human element in the text is the eye of an unnamed observer who is seeking to find human features where it can, but who is forced to abandon the idea and allow the imagination to take over:

> Enfin quelle preuve d'une face? L'oeil n'en trouve aucune où qu'il se mette. Il se désiste et la folle s'y met. Emerge enfin d'abord l'ombre d'une corniche. Patience elle s'animera de restes mortels.

In *Proust* Beckett quoted Horace[20] on the *amabilis insania* basic to the creative mind (*PTD*, 91), but there is nothing very lovely about this madness. All the imagination can conjure up is a heap of human remains from which it selects a single skull for scrutiny. This is seen, in both versions, less as a *memento mori* than as a necessary strategy designed to bring the text to an end, although the first version preserves more of the imaginative enterprise that is involved: 'Un dernier sursaut fait paraître pour finir un seul crâne entier sur les cinq ou six que valent tant de débris' (early version); 'Un crâne entier se dégage pour finir' (published version).

The eye-sockets of this skull preserve traces of the old gaze ('l'ancien regard') that has always fascinated Beckett, and are presumably distant relatives of the eye which earlier closed in order to allow the imaginative mechanism to function properly. In the final sentences of *La Falaise* this eye recurs as if the imagination has reached a terminal point and can proceed no further. At the same time the imaginative transformation of the cliff into a skull means that the original object of perception is less stable and substantial than it was and disappears from time to time ('par moments'). This means that when the eye which has been seeking solace from the exterior world supplants the defeated imagination, there is effectively nothing for it to fix on. It can only do one of two things: 'Alors l'oeil derrière la vitre d'aller chercher dans les blancs lointains ou bien de se détourner de devant tant de rien' (early version); 'Alors l'oeil de voler les blancs lointains. Ou de se détourner de devant' (published version). Beckett leaves us in little doubt that both these activities are equally pointless once the imagination has ceased to function. The 'blancs lointains' can only be imagined and turning away from the scene solves nothing at all. *La Falaise* reaffirms, in its rudimentary and programmatic way, that the imagination is the only consoling element in Beckett's late prose, however fitful and skull-like its projections may be.

11. *For to End Yet Again*

If *La Falaise* may be seen as a text without any real dimension in time, it is abundantly clear that this is not the case in *For to End Yet Again*. The skull called up in *La Falaise* is 'pour finir' pure and simple; the sepulchral skull in *For to End Yet Again* is invoked 'pour finir *encore*' (as the original French title has it). If *La Falaise* might be categorized as an 'odd' among Beckett's prose 'ends and odds', *For to End Yet Again* is very obviously an 'end', despite the suggestion in the title (and at the end of the piece) that to 'end' for good and all is an impossibility. *For to End Yet Again* is an examination of the mechanics of beginning and ending in which the desire to achieve the latter is continually frustrated by the compulsion to inaugurate the former. It is no accident that the first sentence in the text should begin with the desire to end, and end with the compulsion to begin: 'For to end yet again skull alone in a dark place pent bowed on a board to begin' (*For to End Yet Again and Other Fizzles*, London, John Calder, 1976, p. 11; all further references are to this edition).

The 'beginning' in question is a good deal more skeletal and uncertain than Molloy's 'beginning' at the outset of *Molloy*. 'Beginning' is now less a matter of winding oneself up for a long and unruly narrative than a question of waiting for the quotidian world to recede and an imaginative construct to supervene: 'Long thus to begin till the place fades followed by the board long after. For to end yet again skull alone in the dark the void no neck no face just the box last place of all in the dark the void' (11). It is clear that this 'box last place of all' is related to the cube in *Ping* which has 'fallen over backward' in *Lessness*, clear too that a severely dehumanized world is in the process of struggling into being. (In *Abandonné*, Paris, Editions Georges Visat, 1972, Beckett concentrates on 'une main ouverte poignet ceint du fil d'argent doigts recourbés comme pour fondre' in a manner that recalls *How It Is* and reasserts the presence of a human agency.) The contorted syntax reflects the difficulty of beginning a new imaginative enterprise:

> Place of remains where once used to gleam in the dark on and off used to glimmer a remain. Remains of the days of the light of day never light so faint as theirs so pale. Thus then the skull makes to glimmer again in lieu of going out. There in the end all at once or by degrees there dawns and magic lingers a leaden dawn. (11)

Dawn has always been for Beckett (since 'Alba' in *Echo's Bones*) a time of sadness and frustration because it returns him to the light of day, which is never (as the occulted syntax here hints) as illuminating as the hours of darkness. But at this point we are not being asked to think of an actual dawn (a 'dispeller of figments' as *Lessness* has it) but rather of an imaginary and 'magic' dawn that is indistinguishable from dusk. In a strategy the reverse of that in *Still* (controlled by an effort of imagination rather than the result of natural processes), a landscape emerges from the gloom, as barren and as devoid of colour as the landscape of *Lessness*: 'By degrees less dark till final grey or all at once as if switched on grey sand as far as eye can see beneath grey cloudless sky same grey' (11). The gloom reveals its past: 'Sand pale as dust ah but dust indeed deep to engulf the haughtiest monuments which too it once was here and there' (11). But it also asserts its presence: 'There in the end same grey invisible to any other eye stark erect amidst his ruins the expelled' (11-12). It is clear that this figure is much closer to extinction than its avatars, the 'I' of the novella, 'The Expelled', and the 'he' who in *Lessness* is the prey of an infinitely resurrectible future. But even this scene of rigidity and engulfment cannot endure. The imagination cannot rest content with the scene of stasis it has conjured up as a source of solace: 'First change of all in the end a fragment comes away and falls. With slow fall for so dense a body it lights like

cork on water and scarce breaks the surface' (12). Beckett identifies
this 'first change of all' in the 'last place of all' as a necessary pre-
condition of the end continuing; he does this by means of one of those
puzzling syntactical *non sequiturs* that are habitual in the late prose:
'Thus then the skull last place of all makes to glimmer again in lieu of
going out' (12). The glimmering and the change are indissolubly
connected. But the sentence is not the summary it seems to be so
much as the stimulus to conjuring up a second image. (Interestingly
enough, it is at the corresponding point in *Abandonné* that Beckett was
forced to abandon the work in 1971.)

This second image, of two white dwarfs with a litter, is as full of
movement as the first was static. There is even an obscure harmony in
the reciprocal actions that these new arrivals are engaged in:

> Let him [who follows] veer to the north or other cardinal point and
> promptly the other by as much to the antipode. Let one stop short and
> the other about this pivot slew the litter through a semi-circle and
> thereon the roles are reversed . . . From time to time impelled as one they
> let fall the litter then again as one take it up again without having to
> stoop. (12-13)

Beckett's use of 'Let' here reminds us of his fascination in recent years
with the imperative mood, but it seems here to reflect the experimental aspect of the imaginative enterprise which (as in *Imagination
Dead Imagine* and several of the dramas) finds expression in geometric
terms. Beckett is clearly impressed by the activities of the two white
dwarfs despite deciding that the litter they are carrying is only 'the
dung litter of laughable memory' (13). It is the whiteness of the dwarfs
which makes them stand out from the surrounding greyness and it is
this whiteness which impels the observer to make an act of interpretation that poses further imaginative problems:

> Grey dust as far as eye can see beneath grey cloudless sky and there all at
> once or by degrees this whiteness to decipher. Yet to imagine if he can
> see it the last expelled amidst his ruins if he can ever see it and seeing
> believe his eyes. Between him and it bird's eye view the space grows no
> less but has only even now appeared last desert to be crossed. (13)

The viewpoint of the observer has suddenly altered from 'seen from
above' (which brings to mind the stance of *The Lost Ones*) to 'close
inspection' (which is the hallmark of *Still*). But the 'expelled' seems
strangely reluctant to traverse the 'last desert' and confront the
diaphanous dwarfs in a way that would bring them into focus. He
recognizes that their actions are as timeless and 'immemorial' (13) as

his own are time-bound and private. All he can do therefore is to attempt to decipher them, recognize his inadequacy and disappear:

> Long lifted to the horizontal faces closer and closer strain as it will the eye achieves no more than two tiny oval blanks. . . . Last change of all in the end the expelled falls headlong down and lies back to sky full little stretch amidst his ruins. . . . Eagle the eye that shall discern him now mingled with the dust beneath a sky forsaken of its scavengers. (14)

The 'last change of all' involves the 'expelled' in a stasis more enduring than any heretofore, a stasis analogous to death but not a perfect death. Where previous Beckett figures have taken refuge in closing their eyes, the 'expelled' is freed at last from the quotidian world and can gaze forever on a world of magical beauty and order:

> Breath has not left him though soundless still and exhaling scarce ruffles the dust. Eyes in their orbits blue still unlike the doll's the fall has not shut nor yet the dust stopped up. No fear henceforth of his ever having not to believe them before that whiteness afar where sky and dust merge. Whiteness neither on earth nor above of the dwarfs as if at the end of their trials the litter left lying between them the white bodies marble still. (14)

This airless, cloudless world is neither real nor fictional, and yet it possesses a substantiality that makes it, like the normal world, a prey to the process of erosion. The truly perfect absence, Beckett reminds us, is only a dream: 'dream of a way in a space where neither here nor there where all the footsteps ever fell can never fare nearer to anywhere nor from anywhere further away' (15). The only thing Beckett can do to prevent himself becoming utterly desolate is 'to end yet again' in the manner that has become characteristic of him, aware that it may be necessary to begin again at a later date. He refuses himself the consolation of thinking that the dream world of the imagination is more real than the harsh world that condemns him to oscillate between ends and beginnings. He finally faces the prospect of another end beginning with as much equanimity and fortitude as he can muster:

> No for in the end for to end yet again by degrees or as though switched on dark falls there again that certain dark that alone certain ashes can. Through it who knows yet another end beneath a cloudless sky same dark it earth and sky of a last end if ever there had to be another absolutely had to be. (15)

For to End Yet Again is perhaps the most difficult of all the difficult late texts of Beckett, and yet the language Beckett uses is as musical and rhythmical and emotional as anything in his more accessible earlier work. He seems to have made himself master here, as in *Still*, of infinite nuances within a framework of scrupulous meanness. But he is more lyrical than Joyce. Here is infinite riches in a little room for anyone prepared to puzzle their way through to a conclusion. One is gratified that the text reminds its readers that they need not, in doing so, think they have come to an end. For in returning to the text they will discover something they have not noticed before, puzzle their heads about the space-age feel of the text (white dwarfs are burnt-out stars, and the eyes are said to possess 'orbits'), and will have, like Beckett, to begin, *ab initio*, yet again.

Notes

1. Beckett's first collection of poems was called *Echo's Bones and other precipitates*, Paris, Europa Press, 1935 and the story of Echo and Narcissus in Ovid's *Metamorphoses* has remained central to Beckett's writing.
2. L. Harvey, *Samuel Beckett, Poet and Critic*, Princeton, Princeton University Press, 1970, p. 441.
3. L. Harvey, *op.cit.*, p. 249.
4. A reporter in the *Times* for 27 January 1965 writes: 'Mr Beckett is at present finishing a novel called *Fancy Dying*', which obviously refers to *All Strange Away*.
5. W. Stevens, *The Necessary Angel*, New York, Knopf, 1951, p. 22.
6. Quoted from 'Assumption', *transition*, 16-17 (June 1929), p. 268.
7. B. Finney, *Since How It Is*, London, Covent Garden Press, 1972, p. 10.
8. The phrases are not parallel in the French text *Assez*.
9. See B. Finney, *op.cit.*, p. 27. The unpublished 'J.M. Mime' is a more probable source, as Peter Murphy pointed out to me.
10. R. Cohn, *Back to Beckett*, Princeton, Princeton University Press, 1973, pp. 243-47.
11. R. Burton, *Anatomy of Melancholy*, Everyman edition, p. 166. I owe this discovery of source to Peter Murphy.
12. Beckett's own description, at the head of *The Lost Ones* material he gave to the Reading University Beckett Archive, MS 1396/4/45.
13. B. Finney, *op.cit.*, p. 11.
14. See E.B. Segrè, 'Style and Structure in *Ping*', *Journal of Modern Literature*, vol. 6, no. 1 (February 1977), p. 139.
15. See J. Dearlove, 'The Residual Fiction', *Journal of Modern Literature*, vol. 6, n. 1 (February 1977), p. 117.
16. The description of the 'dreaming back' situation in Yeats's *A Vision* must have been familiar to Beckett, who knows his Yeats well.

17. Clearly an oblique critique of the *Texts for Nothing*.
18. The manuscripts show that Beckett (as often) conceived the piece in three sections and then conflated them. See R.U.L. MS 1396/4/45 to 1396/4/52
19. A figure also mentioned in the second of the *Texts for Nothing* (*Texts for Nothing*, p. 12).
20. The quotation is from *Odes*, iii, 4, but Beckett most probably first encountered it in Burton's *Anatomy of Melancholy*, ed. cit., p. 71.

Ends and Odds in Drama

Ends and Odds in Drama

1. Not I

A discussion of *Not I* should begin with the scalding intensity and overpowering nature of the play as a theatrical experience. For whatever themes underlie this breathless monologue, echoing particularly motifs found in *The Unnamable*, they are subordinate to the bold visual imagery and to the stream of sound that Beckett hoped would 'work on the nerves of the audience, not its intellect'.[1] For attention is focussed, and, in a fine performance, held, by a number of strongly positive visual elements, conceived and situated by the author in very precise spatial terms, and by qualities of vitality, surprise, dramatic contrast, rhythm and balance.

One of the most striking features of *Not I* is, of course, the stark nature of its visual components. The strange pairing of a tall, standing, djellaba-clad figure, Auditor, and an illuminated Mouth brings together two images that contrast sharply with each other in terms of shape, size and mobility. For while Mouth scarcely gives the impression of pausing even to gasp for breath, Auditor remains silent and still throughout, except for the four occasions when its arms are raised and allowed to fall back to its sides. Theoretically, the movements made by the figure of Auditor ought to provide a measure of relief from the intensity of concentration demanded by the verbal outpourings of Mouth. In practice, difficulties in lighting the figure at all adequately have meant that this duality of focus has proved to be something of a dramatic weakness.

A lot of errors or misapprehensions have crept into discussions of the play's visual imagery and it is, therefore, perhaps worth being as precise as possible on this point. The known facts are as follows. In a letter postmarked 30 April 1974, Beckett wrote 'Image of *Not I* in part suggested by Caravaggio's *Decollation of St John* in Valetta Cathedral'.[2] But this must be set alongside the image of the djelleba-clad 'intense listener' seen supposedly in Tunis, if Hume Cronyn and Jessica Tandy have been reported correctly.[3] In fact, Beckett was in Morocco for a month in February to March 1972, returning to Paris on 13 March, only a week before he began the composition of *Not I* on 20 March. He had visited Valetta in Malta some three months earlier.[4] The inspiration was, therefore, of much more recent date than the Tunis visit, which occurred at the time of the Nobel Prize award in October 1969.

The question remains of the stage at which these two separate images entered into the composition of the play and of their relationship with each other and with the finished work. It has been pointed out that 'the author's attention through the early [manuscript] stages of the play was neither on the image of the speaking lips nor the silent enigmatic listener, but on the flow of words'.[5] This conclusion is based on evidence that the first two typescripts do not include the stage directions containing the two images and that the first holograph has them written in only apparently at a later date.[6] But Beckett may have concentrated on the text, simply because that was what remained to be written, the two visual elements being clearly imprinted in his mind before he set pen to paper. Certainly when the stage directions do come to be written in as marginal additions, it is with considerable confidence and clarity of conception and formulation.

The only real uncertainties discernible in the visuals of *Not I*, once they *are* written down, concern the exact height of Mouth above the stage and the corresponding height of Auditor. Mouth is first described as being 'at a convenient level', then on the same typescript (the second) this handwritten direction is crossed out and changed to 'an unnaturally high level', before, with a further change, it finally comes to rest 'about 8 feet above stage level'.[7] MOUTH is named in this capitalized form from the outset; the lighting is as in the printed text; even the invisible microphone is included. Moreover, whatever difficulties arose later in the course of staging the play with respect to the figure of Auditor, in the manuscript versions it is envisaged with great clarity and is presented with scarcely any hesitation.

Even with all this information available, relating the play to its apparent sources is no less fraught with difficulties than is usually the case. For the existence of the 'Kilcool' manuscript, referred to earlier, dated 1963, with its woman's head alone illuminated in the surrounding darkness, is enough to suggest that an element closely related to Mouth had already been in Beckett's mind for many years. Moreover, the dominant inspiration for the work, partly perhaps visual as well as verbal, seems to lie in *The Unnamable*, which Beckett himself referred to as a major source.[8] For there is, after all, far more than a mere pronominal preoccupation in the following passage from *The Unnamaable*:

> Two holes and me in the middle, slightly choked. Or a single one, entrance and exit, where the words swarm and jostle like ants, hasty, indifferent, bringing nothing, taking nothing away, too light to leave a mark. I shall not say I again, ever again, its too farcical. I shall put it in its place, whenever I hear it, the third person, if I think of it. (*TN*, 358)

For Mouth's account seems to arise from the concentration into a few moments of a life made up, like the one described in *The Unnamable*, of 'three things, the inability to speak, the inability to be silent, and solitude, that's what I've had to make the best of' (*TN*, 400). All one can say with any degree of certainty is that the Caravaggio painting, together with the waiting Moroccan figure, focussed Beckett's attention upon a relationship of rapt attention involving an impassive witness and a human head, which became at an early stage a Mouth.

Everything about Auditor's role is ambiguous, its sex, its costume, and the nature of its interest in Mouth's monologue. Even the significance of the raising of the arms, which is explained clearly enough in the author's note as 'a gesture of helpless compassion' (*Ends and Odds*, London, Faber and Faber, 1977, p. 12; all further references in this entire section are to this edition) appears far more enigmatic in performance. When Beckett's American director, Alan Schneider, questioned Beckett as to whether Auditor was a death figure or a guardian angel, the author shrugged his shoulders, lifted his arms and let them fall to his sides, leaving the ambiguity wholly intact.[9] For many critics Auditor evoked the cowled figure of a monk listening to a confessional or 'a huge, silent Druidic figure'.[10] It might also have called to mind the hooded figures of Dante and Virgil witnessing the suffering of the damned in Botticelli's illustrations to Dante's *Inferno* or Goya's etching *The Disparate of Fear* (*Disparate de Miedo*). Most clearly in the intensity of its interest and the silent helplessness of its gestures, Auditor embodies the watching, listening and 'auditing' functions of an audience, while at the same time it supplies the observer or the witness to another's presence and suffering that for so long has seemed indispensable to Beckett's stage world. After being suppressed for technical reasons in the French première in 1975, the role of Auditor was given greater prominence when it was revived in Paris, also directed by Beckett in April 1978. At the end of this production of the play, Auditor covered his head with his hands in a gesture of increased helplessness and despair, as if unable to bear any longer the torrent of sound.

The reduction of the woman's presence to that of a lighted Mouth remains, however, the most startling dramatic image of the play. Yet this image appears quite so powerful only because of the feverish anguished nature of the spoken text. A calmer, more leisurely and more coolly reasoned script would have provided none of the excitement that is generated by this unusual fusion of image and sound.

The balance of these various visual and auditory elements can, however, easily be disturbed by what the director or the actors bring to the play. Even the size of the building in which it is performed can affect quite radically its success or its failure. If the theatre is too large (like the main auditorium in the Théâtre d'Orsay in Paris, for example) Mouth becomes little more than a distant speck of light in the darkness, and the human dimension which is needed to confer life and emotion on the text is lost. If, on the other hand, the theatre is too small, Auditor appears obtrusive and the image of Mouth becomes too precisely anatomical. Although *Not I* can clearly be powerful theatre, it is still extremely fragile.

Mouth's statement takes the form of a fragmented, staccato piece of prose in which all its phrases are disassociated one from another. No sentence is ever completed, even though the sense of the parts and of the whole remains at a reading perfectly intelligible. The text seems, in fact, far more demented than it actually is. But the impression of verbal confusion is just as important as the pattern that binds together these swirling fragments of experience. For in the same way that the life narrated by Mouth has been characterized by division, isolation and absence, so the syntax of the narrative reflects severance rather than conjunction and suggests confusion rather than understanding.

But this fractured syntax does not simply arise from a series of failures on the part of the narrator's memory, nor does it derive from the random revelations of the sub-conscious, like so many Surrealist 'stream of consciousness' texts. Instead, it seems to be transmitted from some undefined source, another voice perhaps, prompting, interrupting, and correcting Mouth in her account. In *The Unnamable*, the narrator states that such a voice:

> issues from me, it fills me, it clamours against my walls, it is not mine, I can't stop it, I can't prevent it, from tearing me, racking me, assailing me. It is not mine, I have none, I have no voice and must speak, that is all I know, it's round that I must revolve, of that I must speak, with this voice that is not mine, but can only be mine, since there is no one but me, or if there are others, to whom it might belong, they have never come near me. (*TN*, 309)

The voice that we actually hear in *Not I*, already at one remove from the 'I', gradually pieces together, apparently through various shards of information offered to it from this unknown source, the strange elements of the situation in which 'She' had found herself. At the same time this voice reveals the virtual absence of real existence that had made up her apology for a life. Beckett is himself reported as having said 'I heard "her" saying what I wrote in *Not I*. I actually heard it'.[11] In this way Mouth too becomes, like the writer, both a receiver and a transmitter, in its latter role literally an organ of emission, an orifice spewing out words coming from she knows not where. The brain has been severed from a 'body machine' which includes the organs of speech, and is unable to initiate, direct, or halt the hectic flow of words.

The suggestion has been made that the spoken text might derive from or be prompted by Auditor, Mouth 'checking with Auditor to make sure she's got it right'.[12] Auditor is also envisaged as possibly representing the 'shadow' or *alter ego* of Mouth. The same critic goes on to suggest, plausibly enough, that Mouth's avoidance of the first person singular is the symptom of a disconnected psychological state in which consciousness of an individual self cannot be maintained. Yet however illuminating a Jungian type of analysis might at first appear to be, if taken by itself, it leaves several important elements of the drama unexplored. For instance, Mouth's firm rejection of the 'I' may be seen as a fierce and deeply human judgement on the desolation and solitude of the barren life that she is forced to recount rather than being a mere restatement of it. Moreover, dramatically much of the force of the text derives from the failure of the third person device that

Mouth employs to distance herself from the life and from the central experience of the play, the audience becoming increasingly aware that displaced narrative text and theatrical reality have come together to form a strange and unsatisfactory amalgam. There is also the danger that too precise an adoption of Jungian concepts and terminology might destroy the fundamental dramatic ambiguity of the relationship that exists between Mouth and Auditor. For the essential factor here seems to lie precisely in the deliberate uncertainty that surrounds the origins of Mouth's words.

Speaking of the image of Mouth, the drama critic of *The Times* wrote that 'in isolation it could be any bodily orifice'.[13] And certainly Beckett displayed no trace of displeasure as, watching the BBC television version, he realized that Mouth had the appearance of a large, gaping vagina.[14] In the text, the wild stream of words is expressly linked by Mouth with excremental discharge, 'nearest lavatory . . . start pouring it out . . . steady stream . . . mad stuff . . . half the vowels wrong' (19), just as in *How It Is* the word and the fart have come to be equated. This form of verbal diarrhoea has occurred on several occasions in the course of her past life to the woman whose story is being related; usually it has been in association with winter and darkness. But the uncontrollable urge to pour out words has also become a part of the extraordinary event around which the whole play revolves, when, wandering in the field, 'She' had suddenly found herself plunged into darkness. The verbal discharge overheard by the Auditor and the audience is, therefore, both an attempt to probe, describe, even explain various features of that event, while being itself an important element in that experience. The further analogue of the writer who is exploring an experience of which the act of writing is a crucial part is once again clear enough.

Taken as a whole, the form of *Not I* might, at first, seem merely to confirm the likely truth of Beckett's comments to Harold Pinter: 'I was in hospital once. There was a man in another ward, dying of throat cancer. In the silence I could hear his screams continually. That's the only kind of form my work has'.[15] *Not I* probably comes indeed as close as Beckett has ever done to reproducing the searing screams of human suffering. Michael Billington in his review of the play aptly compared the image of Mouth with the screams of a Francis Bacon cardinal.[16] And yet, in spite of the verbal chaos out of which the intelligible text emerges and to which it quickly returns, that text is far from being as chaotic as some critics have supposed. The play

has, in fact, a basic form that is relatively coherent, extremely original
and theatrically compelling.

The situation is of an apparently fictional narrative, situated at first
at several removes from the spectator, which gradually assumes its
reality and its relevance *as one experiences it*. The account dictated by
Mouth begins as if it were about to be the biography of a lonely,
loveless, unnamed woman. But biography is quickly foreshortened
to bring together cradle and tomb: 'nothing of any note till coming up
to sixty when . . . what? . . . seventy? . . . good God! . . . coming up to
seventy . . .' (13). Biographical narrative has just as quickly to give
way to a fragmented description of the actual experience when the
woman 'found herself in the dark' (14). From this point on 'life scenes'
alternate with an account of the various elements of that experience
and provide poignant examples of the woman's earlier speechlessness,
isolation and distress, relating in this way her present plight to her
past life. There is something more pathetic, more human and more
disquieting about a situation in which precise memories of a
supermart, a court-room, or 'Croker's Acres' — a real place in Ireland
near Leopardstown racecourse — are set alongside a stark analysis of
the strange limbo world in which 'She' now finds herself. Numerous
interruptions and minute breaks in the flow of the text all preceded by
'what?' (almost thirty in number) ensure that there is constant
movement from one level of time to another and from concern with
the experience itself back to the identity crisis occasioned by it. The
constant interruptions contribute also in a major way to the growing
bewilderment, exasperation and desperation of a spoken text in which
the compulsion to express is counter-balanced by confusion as to why
this compulsion should be felt and uncertainty as to what has to be
said in an effort to draw things to a close. As the various elements of
the situation in which 'she' is found are explored — the buzzing, the
beam of light, the flickering activity of the brain, and, finally, the
stream of words with its accompanying movements of lips, cheeks,
jaws, tongue and the 'mouth on fire' — the subject of the narrative and
the Mouth-narrator, strangely reduced but, nonetheless, theatrically
there, come together into a partial, though incomplete, concurrence.
In this way what began merely as a piece of rapidly delivered
narrative text is transformed into the compelling, yet remarkably
disquieting discovery that Mouth and 'She' can no longer be kept
apart and that the experience being recounted is virtually synonymous
with the experience being observed. Consequently, the spectator is

himself brought into a direct confrontation with the force of Mouth's own anguish. And the source of that anguish is two-fold. On the one hand, Mouth has to face up to the full horror of a life that seems to have been bereft of everything — love, communication, significance — and finds that she is unable to do so. On the other hand, she must still go on searching (perhaps even endlessly) for something that would make some sense out of this barren experience, or at least bring it all to an end. Finding nothing in the present situation that will do either, Mouth's text doubles back on itself, as she finds herself drawn once again into narrative. But she goes back into the *same* narrative with the *same* elements that are unlikely ever to secure a solution or an ending. And the concern throughout for accuracy in the words used, with its consequent qualifications, cancellations and corrections, leads nowhere except back into the same unsatisfactory set of words. The fragment of text heard by the audience is not then part of a linear structure. It is a circular eddy of sound which could presumably go on recurring indefinitely. 'I think I know what it is', the narrator wrote in *The Unnamable*, 'It's to prevent the discourse from coming to an end, this futile discourse which is not credited to me and brings me not a syllable nearer silence' (*TN*, 309).

In the course of this swirling mass of sound, on several occasions Mouth falls back on clusters of memory fragments that, by the end of the play, have come to sound like a virtual litany of solitude. Like Winnie in *Happy Days*, Mouth seeks comfort from familiar phrases, which can, however, provide her with no kind of permanent release. Some of these phrases have been rescued from a loveless upbringing in a waif's home; others are associated with her experience as an old woman in the field, when the light had suddenly gone out and pastoral had been transformed into disturbing nightmare. 'God is love . . . tender mercies . . . new every morning . . . back in the field . . . April morning . . . face in the grass . . . nothing but the larks' (19). The phrases 'God is love' and 'new every morning' were attributed by Beckett to the First Epistle General of John, 4, viii ('He that loveth not knoweth not God; for God is love') and to the Lamentations of Jeremiah, 3, xxiii ('They [the Lord's mercies] are new every morning').[17] But these Biblical phrases are familiar to a Christian (or a former Christian) because they also occur in several well-known Protestant hymns.[18]

At one level, these phrases are invoked in a vain attempt to 'tell how it was . . . tell how it had been', or 'where all else fails these fragments momentarily fill the void'.[19] But their resonance extends well beyond their immediate function. Adding a note of wistful nostalgia and a lyrical quality to an otherwise skeletal text, these 'automatic Christian pieties', interwoven, as Irving Wardle pointed out,[20] with 'harsh Satanic laughter' at the notion of the existence of a merciful God, stand in bitterly ironic contrast to the loneliness, distress and anguish of the life sketched in by Mouth. April, T.S. Eliot's 'cruellest month', with its ironic suggestions of Spring, light and fertility, is also the crucifying month. And throughout *Not I*, Mouth's way of presenting the past life she describes and of accounting for her present Purgatorial state is in terms of a whole cycle of sin, guilt, and purgation that is derived from a guilt-ridden Christian upbringing. And yet the Christian sequence can never be completed to include repentance and amendment, let alone redemption. For what is there for which she could repent? And what could she conceivably amend? Only the possibility that she is being punished unjustifiably for the original sin of being born remains unrefuted. For this is a point of view for which, at least since *Proust* in 1931, Beckett has had the greatest sympathy.[21]

What does seem certain is that Mouth must go on searching for some thoughts or some words that might perhaps bring release from, or at last an ending to, this strange form of purgatory. The theme is, of course, familiar from the novel trilogy, and particularly from *The Unnamable*, where a total, unbroken silence had been sought: 'I want to go silent. Not just as now, the better to listen, but peacefully, victoriously, without ulterior object. Then it would be a life worth having, a life at last. My speech-parched voice at rest would fill with spittle, I'd let it flow over and over, happy at last, dribbling with life, my pensum ended, in the silence. . . . There at last is a fair picture of my situation' (*TN*, 312). In *Not I*, unbroken silence, 'sweet silent as the grave' (16) and *quietas* seem just as remote as they had ever been.

When first performed in New York, London and Paris, *Not I* received wide critical acclaim. Critics were, of course, impressed by the virtuoso performances of Jessica Tandy, Billie Whitelaw, and Madeline Renaud in this most demanding of roles. But they responded above all to the boldness and the stark simplicity of the play's visual imagery, as well as to the overwhelming nature of its torrent of sound. There are a number of other characteristics of *Not I*, however, that, although less easily discerned, are just as important to its final dramatic impact.

Moments of actual comedy are rare in *Not I*, being confined largely

to the orphaning of the little girl at the opening of the play: 'he having
vanished . . . thin air . . . no sooner buttoned up his breeches . . . she
similarly . . . eight months later . . . almost to the tick' (13). Yet, on the
other hand, it hardly seems accurate to define the dominant tone of
the play as one of pathos. For there is a fundamental and rather
grotesque form of incongruity that serves to blunt the pathos and keep
the attention of the audience firmly focussed on the detail of Mouth's
text. Winnie's virtual monologue in *Happy Days* had been saved from
sliding into sentimentality partly at least by her persistent efforts to
understand and come to terms with the strange conditions of her
deprived existence by bringing to bear on them a set of rather limited,
and genteel, reasoning habits. Mouth applies to an even more
extraordinary situation a homely kind of logic and an attempted
precision of language. Such efforts to understand and define her
strangely reduced circumstances inevitably fail, and, like Winnie,
Mouth seems quite aware of this failure, commenting 'vain reasonings'
(15), 'vain questionings' (16). In *Happy Days*, Winnie's efforts had
seemed touchingly human and, in the first part of the play at least,
comic too. In *Not I* the dramatic situation has become so drastically
deprived — rather like a third act of *Happy Days* — and the speed and
tension are so great that humour appears completely out of place.
There are, in fact, several points in the monologue where the
incongruity between the appalling nature of the situation and
Mouth's efforts to get its measure in words stretches *almost* to the
point of comedy: 'she did not know . . . what position she was in . . .
imagine! . . . what position she was in! . . . whether standing . . . or
sitting . . . but the brain — . . . what? . . . kneeling? . . . yes? . . .
whether standing . . . or sitting . . . or kneeling . . . but the brain — . . .
what? . . . lying? . . . yes . . . whether standing . . . or sitting . . . or
kneeling . . . or lying' (14). Yet on such occasions the spectacle of the
would-be rational mind thrashing about to get its bearings and assert
itself in a whirlpool of inexplicable experiences is more likely to arouse
a mixture of fascination and horror than humour. For there is only
time to grasp a sense of anxiety and desperation rather than to isolate
the elements at work in such an incongruous situation and register the
gap between them. Later in the play with the discovery that 'words
were coming' and the even 'more awful' thought that 'feeling was
coming back', the text becomes more frantic still and the tone more
pained and more desperate.

As was suggested earlier, contrary to common belief, Beckett is extremely conscious of the different factors that an audience brings to a play and is adept at manipulating such factors to create new, and extremely vital, sources of dramatic interest and tension in the absence of conventional plot and characterization. In the most general way, the audience's role is perhaps best defined by its twin character- istics of spectatorship and intellectual curiosity and judgement. It might seem at first that in *Not I* Beckett was merely providing a puzzle for the rational mind by combining surprising visual images, a hesitant, and yet probing text, and an extremely unusual dramatic situation. In fact, he goes much farther than this by establishing correspondences between the audience and elements within the play. The parallel between the watching figure of the Auditor and one aspect of the spectator's role has already been mentioned. But the mind of the spectator outside the play, seeking to understand and explain what is going on, also has its echo within the drama in the form of the rational mind of Mouth, struggling to make sense of what is happening to it.

The real originality of *Not I* seems to lie, however, in the way in which the spectator is gradually drawn into a novel and unusually complex form of relationship with the dramatic situation. It was suggested earlier that he was brought into a direct confrontation with Mouth's anguish by gradually discovering that the experience being observed was virtually synonymous with that being narrated. Does this mean, then, as one critic has suggested, that the spectator's involvement becomes, as the play proceeds, a totally direct and sensory one? That '*Not I* makes us aware of the agonizing limitations of seeing, hearing and speaking'?[22] It is certainly tempting to see the impact of the play in sensory, even in visceral terms. For it is certainly true that in watching *Not I* visual and aural senses come to be directly involved. The spectator's situation also resembles that of Mouth, as he strains to hear and focus on the minimal image, as well as trying to understand what has happened and is happening to her. And yet if the spectator does seem to be drawn in this way into active involve- ment with the drama, he never loses his separateness or his judge- ment. Indeed this judgement is implicitly relied upon to balance the tensions that are drawing the narrated and observed experiences together and those that are trying to keep them apart. For the events observed are not entirely synonymous with those narrated. Mouth screams and we register the screams; but she apparently does not. The beam, she tells us 'ferrets around'; but the spotlight does not.

Mouth speaks of a face moving and of eyelids opening and closing and of tears being shed; but of all this we see nothing. In fact, it is essential that this convergence should be incomplete. For Krapp and for Winnie, words were beginning to run out. But the essence of Mouth's drama is that they have returned. So since she must speak, Mouth desperately needs to keep the narration and her own self apart. For if they ever came fully together, she would, in the words of *Text 7*, need to report herself as 'missing and giving up' (*TFN*, 36). As it is, she is caught up in a cyclical structure, repeating the same phrases perhaps endlessly, but at least with a possibility, however remote, that some outlet might at some point be found: 'hit on it in the end . . . think everything keep on long enough' (19) are therefore key phrases as Mouth nears the end of the fragment that we hear.

2. *That Time*

That Time was described by Beckett as a 'brother to *Not I*'[23] and it is related to the earlier play in a number of different ways and on several different levels. The relationship is, of course, to be seen at its closest in the visual image: the head of an old man, the Listener, suspended in the darkness, ten feet above stage level, compared with that of Mouth placed at a slightly lower level in *Not I*. In this respect the common roots of both images may be found in the 1963 'Kilcool' manuscript.[24] Beckett has returned in *That Time* to the image of an entire human head, male rather than female. The initial image is a powerful one and is envisaged as such from the outset. If there is any doubt concerning the stage at which the visuals evolved in *Not I*, the same may not be said of *That Time*. From the first holograph draft, dated Ussy, 8 June 1974, the 'Listener' is described as an 'Old man (sitting) in dark. Facing front, a little off centre. Face alone lit faintly. Very white, long white hair standing on end'.[25] The inspiration is clearly pictorial, probably a William Blake engraving, and most likely his representation of the Listener's fellow sufferer, Job. Added at the side of the manuscript are the directions 'face about 8' above stage level, podium in consequence'. The only query concerns whether the old man's head should be framed by a white pillow. By typescript five, the decision has been made: 'no pillow',[26] although it may be noted in the light of the discussion of the visual images of *Not I* that none of the preliminary stage directions are repeated in any of the intermediary manuscripts.

Both *That Time* and *Not I* (and *Footfalls* after them) gradually uncover a whole lifetime of solitude, desolation and distress. Both plays also have a number of more specific features in common. The man whose three stories are recounted and who is addressed by the voice as 'you' has, like Mouth, consistently shrunk from acceptance of the first person singular ('did you ever say I to yourself in your life', (*EO*, 25), refusing to acknowledge, as the old woman in *Not I* had done earlier, that the sorry figure whose barren life was being narrated could possibly be himself. Further, in both plays, the main protagonist seeks to isolate himself or herself from the external world and from other people. In *That Time*, the old man seeks a refuge in silence, as Mouth had done before him, until once again he feels compelled to pour out words, just as he did when he was a child. Even this sudden impulse to verbalize unites the two figures of Mouth and the Listener as members of the same closely knit family.

Yet the concurrent representation of different stages of the same person's life has more in common with *Krapp's Last Tape*, in which although only two distinct, and dissonant voices are actually heard — that of Krapp at thirty-nine and at sixty-nine years old — a third and younger version of himself in his twenties is alluded to contemptuously by the middle-aged Krapp as 'that young whelp'. In *That Time*, the voice refers to three earlier periods in the protagonist's life: 'The B story has to do with the young man', Beckett has explained, 'the C story is the story of the old man and the A story that of the man in middle-age'.[27]

But the voice itself remains one and the same throughout. This confers an uneasy unity on the various, apparently disparate sequences of memory fragments which surface from their different levels of time. For, although the voice emanates physically from three separate points in the darkness, it is quite natural that it should be accepted as a 'voice in the head' and readily associated — as well as identified in the stage directions — with the wandering mind of the old Listener. The second person form of address provides, however, a degree of narrative distance and a form of displacement which would not have been present, if the memories had been recounted in the first person singular. The theme of separation, yet closeness of relationship is already anticipated, then, by the way in which the voice is separated from but is, nonetheless, related to the protagonist. The choice of the second person also allows for the natural use of direct questions which produce an indecisive, quickly modulating flow of words and introduce a feeling of life and movement into the text. The confusion of impressions which constitutes an integral part of each story seems, moreover, to arise in this way not only as a consequence of the uncertainty of memory, but also to spring directly from the 'alien' quality of those three former selves, who have been brought together here to figure in this carefully structured 'trio for a single voice'.

The old man's listening head is not itself entirely silent, for his breathing can be heard 'audible, slow and regular' (23). As a result, there are four distinct focal points of sound compared with only one visual point of reference. In having the voice come from three loudspeakers, placed on both sides and above the Listener's head, Beckett has harnessed to the theatrical situation the stereophonic principle of separating sounds by means of their physical location. As a result, the play demands an intense and sustained effort of concentration. Yet with a collective, as distinct from an individual, listening experience, such a form of concentration can only too easily be broken — by the coughs or fidgets, for instance, of one's neighbours, whose eyes, like one's own perhaps, may need rather more than Beckett has allowed them to retain interest and attention. Certainly movement in the present is drastically reduced: the old man opens and closes his eyes only four times and, at the end, he breaks into a grin, 'toothless for preference' (30).

That Time is divided into three parts by two median pauses, in the course of which the Listener opens his eyes, bringing him back to the bleak situation in which he was discovered at the opening of the play. The effect is to refocus attention on the somewhat harrowing physical actuality of the old man's breathing presence. It has been suggested that these breaks in the flow of the voices occur when something has been revealed in the texts that should only have emerged at a later point.[28] The manuscripts confirm that this was not really the case and that the breaks are determined less by content than by timing and length of text. They also seem to follow a change in the normal sequence of the voice patterns. Placed where they are, in fact, the play has come to be divided into three parts of equal duration, and, since the pauses are induced on each occasion by a different text (if one includes the terminal silence, that is by B, A, and C respectively), the effect of the first two breaks may be regarded as one of arriving at a false, unsatisfactory conclusion. This is then followed by a fresh resurgence of memories, which produces yet another set of balanced variations, until a further abnormal sequence occurs.

The finished pattern is a relatively complex one. The physically separated trio of recorded voices, A, B, and C, each makes twelve statements, or memory fragments, providing 36 statements or 'versets'[29] in all. The order is as follows:

I	ACB	ACB	ACB	CBA	(*Silence*)
II	CBA	CBA	CBA	BCA	(*Silence*)
III	BAC	BAC	BAC	BAC	(*Silence; smile*).

It is worth pointing out that it was only in the fifth typescript version that Beckett arrived at this particular detailed pattern and that the final combination of three in each part was the last to be determined.[30] It was also only in the course of writing the play that he moved away from his original conception of a more limited number of interruptions, with a correspondingly longer text for each section, to the present more fragmented and more complex text. He also abandoned his early idea that one voice should actually interrupt another, provoking resistance so that a degree of overlap would inevitably occur. Instead, he settled for a smooth transition or flow from one voice to another, though one which would be easily perceptible.

The repetition of a dominant pattern in each part — ACB in part one, CBA in part two and BAC in part three — also provides a continuous, if varied, thematic flow, disturbed only by the abnormal set of variations at the end of the first two parts and broken by the two median silences. The third and last part differs in that the final combination, BAC, instead of changing its order, repeats yet again the pattern of the three preceding sets of statements. While avoiding, as one critic has pointed out,[31] the closed globular form of construction that would have resulted from yet another rearrangement of the elements (that is ABC), suggesting that the voice might go on revolving indefinitely in its permutations of memory, the final retention of pattern leads to a conclusion which is structurally more satisfying and thematically more conclusive. It is also clear that the final combination, BAC, has reestablished and maintained a natural order of progression in the man's life from youth (B) through advanced middle-age (A) to old-age (C).

It is not, however, because of the preservation of this formal patterning that the old man smiles before the final fade-out and curtain. In the light of his earlier unresponsiveness and in the context of the closing words of the play ('come and gone no one come and gone in no time gone in no time', 30), the smile comes as a considerable dramatic surprise. Enigma remains, in fact, an essential part of the dramatic effect, just as it did at the end of *All that Fall*, or of *Happy Days*, where one was uncertain as to whether Willie wished to touch, kiss or kill his wife. Is it here simply a smile of satisfaction at the restoration of these old times? A smile of relief and contentment that at last all the torment is nearly over? A wry reflection on the insignificance of the individual human existence in the context of infinity? Or a smile indicating that even capitulation to the void can still be endured with serene acceptance? Whatever interpretation one adopts — and my own combines the attitudes expressed in the last two questions — the smile remains a startling human response, very different in kind from the earlier, more passive opening of the eyes, or the snatching at the breath of life.

If the structure of the play recalls the combinatory art of some seventeenth-century mathematician, the text itself is in no sense lacking in emotional depth, resonance, or range of theme. The 'moments of one and the same voice' (22), A, B and C, recount scenes which possess their own shifting moods and individual themes. But what needs to be stressed most of all is that, although all of the three texts were written out in full, separately and consecutively (mostly in June 1974), the different fragments are experienced sequentially, either in the theatre or on the printed page. It would, then, be pointless merely to separate threads that have been so intricately woven together. For the early drafts show that Beckett spent considerable time in getting what he termed the 'continuity' right. This involved him not only in realizing the pattern for the fragmented experience just described, but also in working out a sequence in which one part of the text reflects upon, as well as follows another, either by association or by contrast. In discussing the three different sets of statements, therefore, neither the flow of the text nor the intercutting of the various fragments can be ignored. A more valid approach is to consider first of all how recurring images interrelate to express, develop, or modify certain dominant themes or moods. For the images in the play are not static, they evolve as the situation in each story unfolds, changing their shape and their resonance as they come to be affected by other surrounding images.

In his critical study, *Proust* (1931), Beckett had quoted Proust's remark: 'But were I granted time to accomplish my work, I would not fail to stamp it with the seal of that Time, now so forcibly present to my mind, and in it I would describe men, even at the risk of giving them the appearance of monstrous beings, as occupying in Time a much greater place than that so sparingly conceded to them in Space, a place indeed extended beyond measure, because, like giants plunged in the years, they touch at once those periods of their lives — separated by so many days — so far apart in Time' (*PTD*, 12). The protagonist of *That Time* also touches upon periods of his life which are far removed from each other in time. He is, like Proust's creatures — in Beckett's almost exclusively pessimistic reading of Proust at least[32] — another of Time's 'victims and prisoners' (*PTD*, 12-13), but Beckett's man has little of the giant about him. He is overwhelmed by Time, which not only deforms ('we are not merely more weary because of yesterday, we are other', *PTD*, 13), but sweeps him along on a tide which makes the past appear remote, uncertain, and illusory, and the individual human life seem like the fleeting disturbance of a still, silent, indifferent world, a diminutive ripple on the surface of infinite Time.

'Old scenes' from widely separated moments in the old man's life emerge and flow into one another. The young man, together at first with his love, and then alone in the same settings; the middle-aged man returning once again alone, to rediscover 'Foley's Folly', the ruin where he used to hide when a child; the huddled, solitary figure of the old man seeking shelter in the Portrait Gallery, the Post Office or the Library. These are the basic situations depicted and developed in the three stories of A, B and C. And as he looks back on this past, contemplating these various 'old times', the voice repeatedly uses the words 'that time' as it attempts to isolate, capture, identify and savour certain of these moments snatched from the grip of Time.

Yet, even as he recalls it, the past escapes him. It is slippery and elusive, and the way into it through memory is notoriously unreliable. So the process can only operate by a series of statements, which are promptly followed by questions, doubts, qualifications, or cancellations. Memories, which at first are put forward as firm realities, are soon found to be problematic or erroneous ('took the eleven to the end of the line and on from there no no trams then all gone long ago'. 23). But, more fundamentally, the past will not be treated as if it were a butterfly to be caught in a net, pinned down for display, and lovingly contemplated. For once the attempt has been made to capture it in words, the memory of 'that time' simply melts away, or changes its shape and its nature, or again is transformed by another and rather different 'that time'. In *Krapp's Last Tape*, memories could at least be isolated one from another — partly because of Krapp's methodical, mechanical way of recording them. But in *That Time* they flow one into another and become almost impossible to differentiate, losing their sharpness and their individual quality in the relentless flow of Time.

What sets out as if it were going to be the nostalgic evocation of a search for childhood experience or an elegiac recreation of a scene of two lovers, portrayed, like Romeo and Juliet, 'vowing every now and then you loved each other' (23), becomes contaminated by contact with the surrounding memories of that 'other time' when 'it was always winter, that time in the Portrait Gallery' (23). But such memories also contain the seeds of their own transformation or disintegration with images of ruination, solitude, desolation or death: in A's statements for example, the 'grey day', 'the ruin where you hid as a child', 'the old rails all rust', 'all crumbling away'; in B's story, the lovers set physically apart, sitting together at each end of the 'long low stone like millstone', which, like the 'marble slab' in the Portrait Gallery in C's story, carries the menace of a death image. As these situations are developed, so the images of isolation, dehumanization, decline and death increase. What had begun in A's statements as a search for a childhood experience of solitude returns full circle, at the end of his day-long visit, to that same solitude, but with the added desire to get 'to hell out of it all and never come back' (30). The young man's (B's) story moves from vows of love and idealized togetherness through images of pollution, disintegration and death ('facing downstream into the sun sinking and the bits of flotsam coming from behind and drifting on or caught in the reeds the dead rat it looked like', 26) to end in a solitary acceptance of the void, 'a great shroud billowing in all over you' (29). The old man's (C's) memories of seeking shelter in the Gallery, the Post-Office, or the Library end with the dust ('whole place suddenly full of dust', 30). This conclusion inevitably evokes the passage of time, decay, death and nothingness and recalls the Biblical image of the human flesh as dust and Macbeth's 'all our yesterdays have lighted fools / The way to dusty death'. Within Beckett's own work, the image echoes specifically Clov's words in *Endgame* 'I love order. It's my dream. A world where all would be silent and still and each thing in its last place under the last dust' (*EG*, 39).

Perhaps most crucially, man emerges in the play as a solitary figure in the face of the 'monster Time', retreating from a life which appears unreal, impermanent and transient. Several static tableaux emphasize the fragility and transiency of the life of the individual by setting images of a more permanent, unpeopled, petrified world alongside others of absence, irreality, fragility and death: the child on the stone in the ruin; the man huddled on the doorstep in the old green greatcoat handed on from his father; the lovers who at first resemble figures in a still-life composition, but later come to be described as 'no better than shades' (26). In the Portrait Gallery, the old man gazing at the portraits of the dead is suddenly surprised to find his own reflection looking back at him, as if he were already one of them himself. But this realization of the inevitable fact of death, although described as a 'turning point', does not in itself provide the start for any positive response to the 'absurd', as it did, for example, with such horrific results, in Camus's *Caligula*. Instead, though important, it is only one of many so called turning points in the man's life ('always having turning points and never but the one the first and the last', 26). For nothing is able to change the fundamentally intolerable nature of life, once it has been set in motion. 'You're on earth', Hamm had commented in *Endgame*, 'There's no cure for that!' (*EG*, 44).

Temporal and spatial extension is accorded to the lifetime of the individual by depicting the protagonist at different moments in time and space. But that lifetime is itself set in the context of the aeons of Time by a whole series of images evoking life in the womb, birth itself ('curled up worm in slime when they lugged you out and wiped you off and straightened you up', 26), as well as the reflections of the past generations in the 'portraits of the dead black with antiquity and the dates on the frames in case you might get the century wrong' (26). So when A expresses his total disorientation and absence of any sense of identity, it is against a backdrop of infinite time and infinite space ('not knowing where you were or when you were or what for place might have been uninhabited', 28), repeating exactly Krapp's phrase concerning 'absence'. The ambiguity of the title means that it should be read both as 'that time' and as 'that *Time*'. Beckett had great difficulty in rendering this play into French for the recurring phrase 'that time' clearly means at once 'cette fois' (or 'la fois où') and 'ce Temps'. His title *Cette fois* was, as he put it, a 'recognition of the impossibility of capturing both senses'.[33]

As so often with Beckett's writing, the text acquires a greater resonance because of the Biblical nature of some of its images, words and phrases. In *That Time*, such echoes serve to extend the temporal sweep of the play back from Beckett's old man through Jesus Christ and Lao Tse, the founder of Taoism ('that old Chinaman long before Christ born with white hair', 25) to an apparently casual, but certainly not accidental, allusion to the first man God created: 'not knowing who you were from Adam no notion who it was saying what you were saying'(26).

But Biblical echoes are both generalized in their reference, invoking a Job-like feeling of desolation and distress, and more specific. In directing the play in Berlin, hardly surprisingly, Beckett alluded to the Bible as the source of the phrase 'the passers pausing to gape', Klaus Herm, the actor, supplying the precise reference to Saint Luke.[34] But if this passage, which continues 'quick gape then pass on pass on pass by on the other side', undoubtedly echoes the story of the Good Samaritan (St Luke, X, 30-35), it also picks up, whether consciously or not on Beckett's part, the phrase used in the Book of Psalms 'they gaped upon me with their mouths' (Psalm 22). And this same psalm may have supplied Beckett with a number of the images that are most deeply embedded in the text of *That Time*. 'Tottering and muttering all over the parish till the words dried up and the head dried up and the legs dried up whosoever they were or it gave up whoever it was' (27), not only recaptures the style of the Authorized version of the Bible, with its repetitiveness and its unusual 'whosoever they were' construction, but may well also echo the images of physical paralysis and decay found in the laments of King David: 'My strength is dried up like a potsherd; and my tongue cleaveth to my jaws; and thou has brought me into the dust of death' (Psalm 22, 15). One might be tempted to see the phrase 'curled up worm in slime' as reminiscent also of the Psalmist's words 'But I am a worm, and no man: a reproach of men and despised of the people' (Psalm 22, 6-7). But, as used by Beckett, the image is foetal and primeval, bringing together both birth and man's distant origins billions of years ago in the mud.

In each panel of the fragmented triptych that makes up *That Time*, the central protagonist seeks to isolate himself as much as he can from others and from the outside world. Ultimately, too, he finds that he is separated from his own Self, the existence of which can possess for him no firm reality. As a child, in A's story, he would slip away to hide in the ruin, for there among the rubble and the nettles 'no one came'. This account develops in parallel with that of the same man returning in late middle-age to seek out once again the same isolated spot. Near the end of the play, however, the two stories converge as, unable to reach the ruin and realizing that, after all, place has no significance, the older man reverts to his childhood isolation, shutting himself off completely from the passers-by. Earlier, he had already deliberately cut himself off from communicating with anyone, opting never to utter 'another word to the living as long as you lived' (27). C's account tells how, as an old man, he would slip into various public buildings 'when no one was looking' (a phrase repeated on each occasion) not only to find shelter but also to savour solitude, stillness and silence. In the Portrait Gallery, for example, sound is minimal, the silence being broken only by the shuffling, phantom-like tread of the odd attendant and by the old man muttering to himself. In the Post-Office, the look of others is reversed, as the old man for once takes note of his fellow-men. But this look serves only to reinforce his own sense of non-existence, as he notices their eyes 'passing over you and through you like so much thin air' (29). Even though apparently together, the two lovers in B's account always sit or lie in the sand, 'parallel like on an axle-tree' (26).

An important motif in all three accounts is the attempt, even the need, to make up the Self, just as life itself comes to be equated with a work of fiction that has to be invented, a common theme in Beckett's prose fiction: 'making it all up on the doorstep as you went along making yourself all up again for the millionth time' (29). These inventions are used partly to provide a series of 'old tales' to keep out the void and partly to create a form of surrogate existence for the protagonist. Life-scenes, uncertain memories and fictional creations become then indistinguishable and the whole status of the 'real', especially the reality of the Self, appears blurred and indeterminate.

Synonymous with this need to make up his own life is the practice, adopted first by the child but followed later by the grown man, of filling in the silence by creating several voices, all of which are fragments and figments of a Self which can be neither isolated nor defined. This sophisticated form of ventriloquism is a verbal substitute for a sense of identity, a dialogue between parts of a self which will never come together to form a whole. It provides a form of consolation, but no solution to the fundamental fragmentation that it reflects. And the wheel has, of course, come full circle. For in his old age — perhaps even on his death-bed — the Listener continues to seek for some vicarious comfort from his own voices, as he listens to himself 'drooling away', still striving to 'make up' his life, even as he approaches its end.

There is clearly a temptation to regard Beckett's play as being concerned merely with a strange, disturbed personality. Indeed, the characteristics just described — the desire for isolation, the severance of social relations and the withdrawal of communication with others, the creation of a surrogate self and a multiplicity of voices — may be regarded as ways of dealing with the threats of, to use R.D. Laing's terms, the 'engulfment', 'implosion' and 'petrification' that form part of the experience of some psychotics.[35] Images used to express fears associated with psychosis occur in this play as they do in many others by Beckett. The Biblical sounding preoccupation with the 'drying up' of words, head and legs, for example, like Winnie's desire in *Happy Days* for the 'happy day to come when flesh melts at so many degrees' (*HD*, 16), may be seen as a recurrent psychotic image of consuming fire, just as the conversion of the Other and (as a kind of self-defence) the Self into 'a thing, a mechanism, an *it*, being petrified' is a common enough experience among psychotics. Beckett uses the 'ontological insecurity' of his old man, however, not to highlight mental instability but to reflect upon painful aspects of existence and, primarily, to present a concentrated image of human isolation in a world that is hurrying about its business, ignoring the signs of decay, disintegration and death with which it is surrounded. Unlike Hamm's mad engraver in *Endgame*, Beckett's protagonist in *That Time* knows that the end of the world has not yet arrived. Yet he dissociates himself from life with as much enthusiasm as if such an end were 'devoutly to be wished'.

A sequential view of the text of *That Time* reveals then a number of central themes and common images. Yet the use of a three-fold text permits a much wider and more varied spectrum of moods, tones and colours than would have been possible with a single narrative thread. For each of the three accounts is given its own physical setting, its own season of the year, even its own light, as well as its own range of incidents and images.

The setting for the memories of A is the protagonist's former home town with its grey, desolate landscape in which everything — the disappearance of the trams, the closure of the 'Doric terminus of the Great Southern and Eastern' (27) (Dublin's Old Harcourt Street station) — prevents him from reaching his destination, the isolated 'ruin where you hid as a child'. The mood is one of deprivation and self-isolation, as the older man seeks out a place cherished only for the solitude that he could find there. As he sits on the doorstep in the pale sunlight, he falls back into a state of virtual non-existence, lifted briefly out of space and time, but, unlike Proust's Marcel, finding no miraculous 'essential statement of reality' in the rediscovery of the past, either through voluntary or involuntary memory. Indeed his morning urgency to find the Folly comes to be matched only by his evening desire to escape from these old scenes of his past. The people he encounters there merely 'gape at the scandal . . . drooling away out loud' (29). So much for the fond remembrance of things past!

B's memories appear at first to stand in marked contrast with both of the other two accounts. The setting is rural wth an Impressionist landscape of sunlight, blue sky and 'wheat turning yellow'. The mood is nostalgic, quiet and elegiac, as the two lovers sit, contentedly it would seem, on the stone at the edge of the little wood. Yet the confusion, which dominates all the different sets of memories in this play, extends here to the emotions, as the lovers sit in a daze in which almost all movement, symptomatic of life, has been removed. The atmosphere is created primarily by a series of negatives, 'all still no sign of life not a soul abroad no sound' (24).

The lovers are described in fringe situations, at the edge of the wood, on the towpath of the canal, or lying on the sandy beach gazing up at the sky, poised between the various elements in a state of suspended animation. The imagery is almost entirely inanimate and both the natural setting and the objects or figures within it are defined in terms of general outline and statuesque quality rather than of life and movement.

It soon becomes clear that this intense scene of pure love, unsullied by physical contact, though first presented directly as a remembered moment, is in fact being looked at from a point in time at which it had long since been recognized as past and the memory of it consequently diminished. Four different time levels are linked in this one reminiscence: the idealized love scene itself, the same scenes but with the man now alone, the time when the memory of those scenes provoked tears, and the time when even the tears have dried up. Though the love scene itself has become equated with 'just another of those old tales to keep the void from pouring in on top of you' (25), the memory of the love vows registers movingly in the theatre: 'then in a whisper so faint she loved you hard to believe you even you made up that bit' (29). Nonetheless, the impact of such an emotional statement is ambiguous, for doubt has been cast upon the reality of even that key memory. So confusion reigns as memories shift and change and the impression given is that even the love expressed may have been more of an aspiration than an actuality. B's account ends, however, not with the memory of a love that may once have existed or may have been fictional — for, as events recede, the two converge — but with the apparent failure of the creative imagination and the acceptance of the void: 'When you tried and tried and couldn't anymore no words left to keep it out so gave it up there by the window . . . gave up for good and let it in and nothing the worse a great shroud billowing in all over you on top of you' (30). If the tone of sadness that has dominated the account remains at the end, it is accompanied by a more mellow note of acceptance akin to that found in some of Beckett's recent prose fragments.

The setting for C's account is once again that of the city, with the protagonist 'shivering and dripping', seeking shelter from the cold and the rain in the Portrait Gallery, the Post Office and the Library 'always winter then endless winter year after year as if it couldn't end' (*EO*, 27-28). The mood is more sombre still in this account and the sense of isolation more intense for being experienced in places normally frequented by others. Confusion is centred here primarily upon things of the mind and the issues raised are more clearly meta-physical in nature. Yet these issues are not stated in terms of actual philosophical questions. Various recounted experiences — catching sight of his own reflection in the Portrait Gallery, trudging around the parish 'making it up that way', noting how he seemed not to exist for others and, finally, listening to the message of the dust — all reveal radical human uncertainties: uncertainty as to the identity of his Self, uncertainty concerning his actual existence, and uncertainty as to purpose and direction, except towards inevitable death. Yet the closing image of the dust extends much further than the death of individuals (his mother, 'the lot you the last', (24)) to evoke the passing of generations, even whole civilizations. It also invokes the essential brevity and transience of all human life: 'what was it said come and gone was that it something like that come and gone come and gone no one come and gone in no time gone in no time' (30).

Such a discussion of themes and imagery might seem to imply an excessively turgid, depressing text. The truth is quite different. For the writing has a stark, desolate beauty and a sense of life and movement (even the occasional flash of dry humour, 'the Public

Library that was another great thing free culture far from home', 28)
that gives it a vivid, memorable quality. The text impresses partly
through its sharp precision of visual detail: 'the white hair pouring
down from under the hat' (29); 'in the old green holeproof coat your
father left you' (28); the small child reading his picture book 'among
the giant nettles' (25); the glider passing overhead as they lay in the
sand like 'the two knobs on a dumbbell' (27); talking to yourself 'till
you were hoarse' (25); 'sitting at the big round table with a bevy of old
ones' (30). An equally precise concern for rhythm and balance characterizes the language as much as it does the overall shape. The ruin
which began life in the manuscripts as 'Maguire's Folly' ends it as
'Foley's Folly' for the sake of the sound. And 'that made you twist
round to see' becomes 'had you swivel on the slab' partly for the
same reason. Small interjections like 'whose else' inserted into the
sentence 'with your arms round you whose else hugging you for a bit
of warmth to dry off' (24) introduce minute touches of irony or
ambiguity into an already extremely dense text.

But the text is saved from seeming contrived or artificial by the
apparent spontaneity and fragmentary nature of the speaker's
statements, as he is allowed to roam apparently freely, prompting,
questioning or negating what the mind dredges up. Surprising
though it may seem, Beckett's recent miniature dramas appear less
self-consciously 'artful' than Harold Pinter's plays on related themes,
Landscape, *Old Times* and *No Man's Land*.

It is partly perhaps the delicacy of *That Time* as a piece of writing
which makes it less satisfactory in the theatre than on the printed
page. For in the theatre subtleties tend to become submerged in the
general flow of words. And the impact of that flow is inevitably less
striking in *That Time* than in *Not I*. Beckett was very much aware that
That Time lay 'on the very edge of what was possible in the theatre'.[36]
In a holograph note written during its composition, he wrote: 'To the
objection visual component too small, out of all proportion with aural,
answer: make it smaller on the principle that less is more'.[37] He seems
to be alluding here to Giordano Bruno's philosophical principle of
identified contrarieties already outlined with great clarity by Beckett
in the 'Dante . . . Bruno. Vico . . Joyce' essay of 1929.

> There is no difference, says Bruno [but the words are Beckett's],
> between the smallest possible chord and the smallest possible arc, no
> difference between the infinite circle and the straight line. The maxima
> and minima of particular contrarieties are one and indifferent. Minimal

heat equals minimal cold. Consequently transmutations are circular. The principle (minimum) of one contrary takes its movement from the principle (maximum) of another. Therefore not only do the minima coincide with the minima, the maxima with the maxima, but the minima with the maxima in the succession of transmutations. Maximal speed is a state of rest. The maximum of corruption and the minimum of generation are identical: in principle, corruption is generation. (*OE*, 6)

Yet Beckett recognizes that there is a world of difference between philosophical principle and theatrical practice. He is acutely aware that if the principle is not applied with great care and tact, it can work against him. This, it seems to me, is exactly what happens in *That Time*. For however beautifully written or finely structured the play undoubtedly may be, the disproportion between the visual and aural elements is surely too great for a resounding success in the theatre.

3. *Footfalls*

Beckett began to write the short play, *Footfalls*, in Berlin on 2 March 1975,[38] a little less than a week before the opening night of his now famous production of *Warten auf Godot* at the Schiller-Theater. The first manuscript draft consists of only two and a half pages. This includes most of the opening dialogue between the old mother and her daughter (who was called Mary in the first draft), together with an early version of the mother's monologue, which is very different from that printed in the published text. By the Autumn the Royal Court Theatre's plans for a Beckett seventieth birthday season for the coming April and May in London were well advanced. These plans included an evening of 'shorts', for which *That Time* was already written. With this in mind, Beckett returned to work on his earlier draft of a play written especially with the actress, Billie Whitelaw, in mind. On 1 October[39] he added a 'sequel' (called then an 'Appendix') to what he had already written, recast the mother's speech later that month, and then worked almost continuously on the play in Paris until early November, when he felt sufficiently satisfied to announce that it was completed,[40] although it was to be modified later in several minor respects in the course of the three productions which Beckett has directed.

Two alternative titles, *Footfalls* and *It all*, were assigned to the first version, but *Footfalls* soon emerged as the right one. For Beckett insists that the image of the woman pacing relentlessly up and down is central to the play. 'This was [my] basic conception . . . ', Beckett commented, 'the text, the words were only built up around this picture'. 'If the play is full of repetitions, then it is because of these life-long stretches of walking. That is the centre of the play, everything else is secondary.'[41] The woman, renamed May, a diminutive, of course, of Mary, but with an added ironic suggestion of Spring (and yet another of Beckett's characters with the 'M' siglum) paces up and down across the stage in nine[42] 'clearly audible rhythmic' steps, revolving 'it all' in her mind. Her pacing punctuates, or accompanies, the words in each of the three sections or stages of the play in which she appears. Moments of frozen immobility alternate with this pacing and an intricate interplay of movement and speech is envisaged from the earliest stage. But what is also clear from the manuscripts is that this central, and only visible, pacing figure, itself dimly lit, was conceived from the outset in relation to the surrounding darkness; it was also accompanied by another essential element in the drama, the mother's voice emanating from the darkness. In other words, the play was visualized in terms of a composite, and specifically theatrical image, sound and silence, repeated movement and total stillness, faint — and steadily diminishing — light and complete darkness supplying the various contrasting elements that were to be organized into a miniature and delicate drama which appears every bit as mysterious as the strange spectral figure of May herself.

After the première in London in May 1976, many critics confessed themselves intellectually baffled by this elusive little play. Yet, in one sense, the feeling of bewilderment helped at least to focus critical attention upon some of the features of the play that are most crucial to its dramatic impact: the shocking image of the woman, May, dressed in a worn grey tattered, trailing wrap, her face skeletal, her hair grey and dishevelled, and her bony hands clasped tightly across her body, grasping her shoulders in a gesture of isolation and distress; the remorseless nature of the slow, rhythmic pacing; the subtle interplay of light and darkness; the different voice levels, that of the mother coming from the back of the stage and amplified, that of the daughter coming from the front of the stage and live; the gradual fading away of the chimes, the light, and the footfalls, and, finally, the disappearance of the ghostly presence of May herself; and the stark patterning of verbal echoes in the mother's account of the daughter's strange life and in the story recounted later by the daughter. Everything in the writing, and in the London production directed by Beckett, seems, in fact, to have been shaped to evoke feelings of distress, strangeness and mystery, a sense of inexplicable seeking, and yet the distillation of absence and loss. This does not, of course, mean that elements of the play which might, at first, have appeared tantalizingly obscure, do not later fall into much sharper and clearer focus. What it does mean is that, for many spectators, the play could succeed in the theatre at a level which involved the senses and the emotions rather more than it did the intellect. In fact, the reason inevitably seeks for explanations for this unusual phenomenon, as the sight, sounds and rhythms of a woman's determined pacing are revealed. Yet only enough information is offered to add to the resonance of the image and not enough to destroy the sense of mystery that pervades the entire play.

The pacing, although never really explained, acquires, nonetheless, a strange form of justification. Partly this arises from its very obsessional quality and partly from the mother's own words, which present May's solitary pacing as representing the externalization of an inner anguish. So, as well as pacing out the eternal round of time, May appears to be seeking to resolve something that cannot ultimately be resolved. For the enigmatic 'it all' which she constantly revolves in her 'poor mind' is linked quite clearly to her own life in particular, to the point when 'it all' began, and to life in general. Beckett explained to Charlotte Joeres, the actress who played the part of the mother at the Schiller-Theater Werkstatt in 1976, that she interrupts herself in the sentence ' "In the old home, the same where she — (*Pause.*)" and continues "The same where she began" because she was going to say " . . . the same where she was *born*". But that is wrong, she hasn't been born. She just began. It began. There is a difference. She was never born'.[43] In *All that Fall* (1957), Mrs. Rooney recounted how she once attended a lecture given by one of those 'new mind doctors':

> I remember his telling us the story of a little girl, very strange and unhappy in her ways, and how he treated her unsuccessfully over a period of years and was finally obliged to give up her case. He could find nothing wrong with her, he said. The only thing wrong with her as far as he could see was that she was dying. . . . The trouble with her was that she had never really been born. (*ATF*, 33-34)

This story derives from a lecture given by the psychologist, C.G. Jung, in the mid-thirties, which Beckett attended while he was staying in London.[44] It should be remembered that Beckett had a slight personal link with Jung, in that James Joyce's daughter, Lucia (who was in love with Beckett), was Jung's patient at the end of 1934.[45] May in *Footfalls* is Beckett's own poignant recreation of a girl who had never really been born, isolated and permanently absent, 'as though May were standing on the side-lines',[46] distant and totally encapsulated within herself.

And yet immured as she is within herself, at times May can and does speak. Indeed, just as her pacing expresses her own inner torment, so, as for Mouth in *Not I*, words become her means of attempting to tell obliquely 'how it was'. The words that she invents, however, in the third part of the play, evoke only a double representation of her own pseudo-existence — the strange life of an unhappy girl who had never really been. For she appears first in the fiction, as the ghost whose 'semblance' we see pacing in front of us, 'a faint tangle of pale grey tatters' (*Ends and Odds*, London, Faber and Faber, 1977, p. 36; all further references are again to this edition); then again, in the final story, she materializes as yet another image of herself, in the shape of Amy (appropriately enough an anagram of her own name, but also, in the normal English pronunciation 'ay-me' or in French 'ami'), who was unable to observe the strange, ghostly figure walking in the church at Evensong, because she too was 'not there'.

Repetition, parallels, and balance evidently play a crucial part in this play. The pacing persists throughout, relating a concrete, dramatic reality — which may itself be that of a ghostly nonexistence — both to the woman's past life as it is recounted by her mother, and to the phantom presence which may be seen walking in the transept of the church. Similarly, each part ends with a reiteration of the daughter's obsessional concern with revolving, or telling, 'it all'. The third part repeats exactly the words which conclude the opening dialogue, but both voices now issue from the mouth of the same woman. The Amy of the story has replaced May, but she repeats the same words spoken earlier by the mother and the daughter.

It is worth looking in a little more detail at the various phases of the play's development in order to see what effects such repetitions and parallels achieve. In the first tableau, the opening words of the play, the repeated 'Mother', summon a voice out of the darkness, as if May were herself conjuring a ghost back from the past. And the voice answers from the darkness, as if this were indeed true. But the mother also seems able to relate to the stage presence of her daughter, counting the steps as she paces and responding to her questions like an aged relative whose present sufferings might conceivably be alleviated. For the subject of the dialogue is a precise evocation of human concern, May's questions suggesting both realistic actions and objects for the easing of suffering. The scene is, in fact, clearly that of a 'dying mother' and is referred to as such by Beckett in a manuscript note.[47] But what could easily have been full of human pathos becomes more neutral, less stark and harrowing, yet more mysterious, because of its ritualistic quality and strange fusion of past and present time. Repetition and balance play, then, an important part in shaping a liturgy of suffering in which not only age and illness are evoked but, as the following extract reveals, life itself is indicted as a Passion to be lived through and wished away:

> M. What age am I now?
> V. And I? (*Pause. No louder.*) And I?
> M. Ninety.
> V. So much?
> M. Eighty-nine, ninety.
> V. I had you late. (*Pause.*) In life. (*Pause.*) Forgive me again. (*Pause. No louder.*) Forgive me again.
> M. What age am I now?
> V. In your forties.
> M. So little?
> V. I'm afraid so. (34)

The mother's monologue which makes up the second section seems to be addressed to the watching audience ('But let us watch her move, in silence', 35) and is unheard by the daughter, with whom she now has no contact. In Beckett's own German and French productions, May whispers or mouths words to herself, illustrating the mother's answer to her own question 'Does she still sleep? . . . Still speak? Yes, some nights she does, when she fancies none can hear' (35). The exact status of the voice and its invisible owner remains mysteriously ambiguous. It bears witness to the strange presence that we too observe. But it is the voice of a ghost, seeing but herself unseen. The mother's voice has its own idiosyncrasies of vocabulary and phrasing, which are later adopted by the daughter in the 'sequel'. The mother also poses some of the questions that the spectator may himself be asking: 'Where is she, it may be asked', 'But this, this, when did this begin?', 'Does she still sleep, it may be asked' (35). But the answers are more likely to deepen the mystery than solve it. We learn from the mother, for instance, that the place in which she is seen pacing up and down is the old home, that the strip upon which she walks was once a carpeted pile, and that, when she sleeps, 'she bows her poor head against the wall and snatches a little sleep' (35). It is disconcerting to realize, then, that May sleeps on her feet facing the wall, which is the front of the stage and through which we observe her. In this way, the invisible fourth wall of the naturalistic theatre takes on a new, and most unusual dimension. As the time sequence is uncertain in the first part, so, in this second part, the physical location too becomes dubious and mysterious.

The principal 'event' of this section represents a development in the strange biography which is being recounted and it clearly came as a surprise to the mother, who is at once here narrator and biographer. For, suddenly, the daughter had announced that the motion of her pacing was in itself not enough and that she needed to *hear* the sound made by her feet on the floor. The carpet has not therefore simply been worn away as a result of her pacing, as one might at first have surmised. It had been expressly removed to allow the evidence of her own pacing to be heard. No explanation for this request is offered. It is simply described as a crying need.

The third part of the play consists of May's 'epilogue', partly composed already, but for the most part invented as she goes along. Before this, however, she adds a 'sequel' to her mother's account, in which an undefined 'she' (presumably herself, the 'I' being as unacceptable to her as it was to Mouth in *Not I*), returns to haunt the church, slipping in through a locked door and standing stark still or pacing up and down, as we have seen May herself doing throughout the play. Only the absence or presence of sound seems in fact to differentiate her account of what occurred in the church from what we have witnessed of her own behaviour. Yet even sound, which in the theatrical sense is real and audible, is at another level uncertain and unverifiable: 'No sound. (*Pause.*) None at least to be heard' (36), which is echoed by a phrase in the poem 'neither', written some time after *Footfalls* (indeed during the Berlin rehearsals of the play), 'unheard footfalls only sound'.[48]

In this third stage of the play, the ghost walks in the church, 'up and down, up and down, his poor arm' (36). The manuscripts and type-scripts of the play reveal quite clearly how this particular image developed. Entering the church by the 'South door' (which became the 'North door' in performance and in the collected volume, *Ends and Odds*, Beckett commenting that South gave too warm an idea, for 'Everything is frost and night'[49]), in the first manuscript, the figure paced up and down 'the corresponding transept'. This becomes in the first typescript the 'corresponding arm' — the church being built, of course, in the shape of Christ crucified on the cross — which, in typescript 2A, is again changed to 'his poor arm'.[50] The change not only introduces a further element of mystery. It confers a sense of human pathos on the passage, and, if the allusion is picked up, it also adds a religious dimension to the suffering evoked in the text.

May goes on to invent a story in which the only two characters are again a mother, Mrs. Winter, and her daughter, Amy. The chief common link between this story and May's own biography is that the girl, Amy (called Emily in the first drafts) also claimed not to have been there, when the strange apparition had been observed by her mother during Evensong. But there are other parallels between the two sections. The question 'What do you mean, Amy?' (37), for instance, picks up the earlier 'What do you mean, May?' (35), and expressions like 'the child's given name' appear in both parts, as well as the verb 'fancy' used to mean 'suppose' by both mother and daughter. In performance, it was also found that phrases like 'Not enough?' and 'Not there?' could be spoken so as to sound like direct echoes from the previous section. The technique of handling dialogue in narration is also similar in both cases, the name of the character speaking being given on every occasion.

But what is the purpose of such intricate parallelism? First, the dominant verbal repetitions clearly echo the revolving motions of the woman whom we see in front of us. The form of the play, therefore, becomes that of a series of circular revolutions, moving from one phase of absence to another, gradually fading away into less and less sharp definition and moving towards silence, stillness and deepening darkness. There are, in fact, four stages to the play, the fourth consisting of an empty stage, where there is 'no trace of May' (37). By reading through the earlier drafts, which are looser, less taut, and less meticulously shaped than the finished text, it is also possible to see how much more compelling the play becomes as a result of these parallels and echoes, which confer aesthetic pleasure, as well as lending wider resonance to the play.

For every element in *Footfalls* is part of a total choreography of sound, light and movement. As Walter Asmus's production notes show, Beckett was anxious as a director to make the lighting and sound levels as much a part of the formal patterning as was the verbal text. So the chimes of the bell which separate and frame each section died away in seven seconds, and the light came up and faded away also in seven seconds; the light and the bell become respectively dimmer and softer as the play proceeded. There is no doubt that in all of Beckett's work as a playwright and as a director what has been called the 'echo principle' is merely part of a way of conceiving of the text rather like a musical score, in which phrases, notes and rhythms are picked up and restated, sometimes in the same form, sometimes with variations, whether slight or intricate. It matters relatively little whether these echoes are consciously perceived by the spectator or not. They register unconsciously and confer shape and strength on a work which inevitably appears lacking in the interest derived from conventional narrative or delineation of character.

In *Footfalls*, however, the many parallels and repetitions, together with the analogies which exist between the mother and daughter in both the drama itself and the story which is set into the drama, serve also to create a play in which we can never be quite sure of what we are looking at or to what we are listening. We realize, perhaps only *after* the play has ended, that we may have been watching a ghost telling a tale of a ghost (herself), who fails to be observed by someone else (her fictional *alter ego*) because she in turn was not really there. So Beckett's ghost story, which probably has its roots in a fusion of the image of a woman pacing (perhaps, it has been suggested in Deirdre Bair's biography, Beckett's own mother)[51] and the account of Jung's girl patient who 'had never really been born', assumes the form of a complex set of variations on appearance and dramatic reality. For since, as we have seen, even the mother's voice may simply be a voice in the mind of a ghost, everything may be regarded as illusion in this little play. And yet it is an exceptional achievement on Beckett's part to have made the strange amalgam of absence and suffering created by these various levels of ghostly representation seem so tangibly real.

It might appear, as with the protagonist of *That Time*, that, in May, Beckett was presenting an extreme case which could possess little general significance. And yet, although the play begins with a specific and very human mother/daughter relationship and appears to narrow down to focus upon one woman, in fact its echoes reverberate much more widely. For May, though virtually absent from life herself, seems in her constant pacing to be both sharpening and questioning its pain and its suffering. This apparent paradox is achieved by the repetition of phrases such as 'your poor lips', 'your poor mind' (34) and the more resonant 'his poor arm' (36), but also by the force of a stark statement like 'she would halt, as one frozen by some shudder of the mind' (36). Perhaps more crucial, however, in this respect is the evocation of the expanded version of the closing prayer of Evensong, taken from the second book of Corinthians, chapter thirteen, 'The love of God, and the fellowship of the Holy Ghost, be with us all, now and for evermore. Amen'. In the London production, the final 'Amen' was pronounced as two syllables, 'Ah-men', just as the earlier 'Sequel' had been pronounced 'Seek well'. In this way the play absorbs into itself much wider associations. There are, in fact, signs that, in the course of writing the play, Beckett developed the figure of May as a tormented soul, in the world but not of it, suffering every day from 'some shudder of the mind'. For the associations with religion and with Christ's Calvary are in no way accidental. The pacing along 'his poor arm' has already been mentioned but the game of 'lacrosse' is adopted for the religious association of the pun, and, when translated into French, the game became significantly 'ce jeu du ciel et de l'enfer'.[52]

Among human beings, May is exceptional in Beckett's terms only in the undiluted concentration of the 'rounds' of her distress. Seven or nine, the figure is uneven, as she paces out the days of the week, or the months of gestation, after which, in Beckett's stern vision, suffering is handed on from mother to daughter. If Jung's girl patient has haunted Beckett for so long, it is because she epitomized for him a permanent sense of existence by proxy, of being absent from true being. And if, in discussing May's posture in the course of directing the play in Berlin, Beckett used a term with strongly Sartrian associations 'being for itself', it is, I think, not only because this expressed admirably the girl's isolation, but because it also focussed upon a constant feature of life on 'this old muckball' (*KLT*, 17). But with this 'an intuition of a presence, embryonic, undeveloped, of a self that might have been but never got born'.[53] The *être manqué* is not, then, simply May but Man in general.

4. *Theatre I*

First published in French as *Théâtre I* in *Minuit 8* (1974), this slight but interesting fragment of theatre reads as if it might have bolted from the same stable from which *Endgame* had already emerged with more dignity and to considerably more success. The relationship between A, a blindman, seated on a folding-stool and scraping a fiddle, and B, a one-legged cripple, confined to a wheelchair and pushing himself along by means of a pole, seems to represent a point prior to a state of interdependence such as that in which Hamm and Clov are found. In this case, the mutual needs rapidly become clear and the advantages of a symbiotic relationship seem obvious, in theory at least: B would offer A company and access to food — corned beef and potatoes — and would act as his eyes; A would push B about in his wheelchair and tuck his rug around his feet (or his foot since he only has one!). But when put into practice, however tentatively, the theory conspicuously fails to lead to any satisfactory state of companionship. For there is in A and B the same juxtaposition of contradictory impulses and the same striking ambivalence of behaviour that was present in the relationships of Estragon and Vladimir and of Hamm and Clov. Irritability and the desire to help follow one another in rapid and apparently random succession. B even strikes A with the pole, after the latter has begun to wheel his chair about, commenting when the blow has been struck: 'Now I've lost him. He was beginning to like me and I struck him. He'll leave me and I'll never see him again. I'll never see anyone again' (64).

In fact, although the theatre fragment was written after the French *Fin de partie* (*Endgame*), it is much closer to this play in time than its dating in *Ends and Odds* as 'circa 1960' might suggest. It is now clear that it was first written in English and not in French, in a different and longer version entitled *The Gloaming*, the manuscript of which is dated December 1956 (Reading University Library, MS 1396/4/6; all further references are to this R.U.L. MS, followed by a page reference). This situates it between *Fin de partie* and the English translation, *Endgame*.

The similarity with *Endgame* may be one reason why Beckett did not attempt to develop the play further and why he only published it at a much later date among the 'odds'. On occasions too Beckett's short play seems to come much too close for comfort to John Millington Synge's *The Well of the Saints* (with the blind Martin Doul feeling the light of the day) and to W.B. Yeats's *The Death of Cuchulain* (Yeats's blindman feeling Cuchulain's body as A does B's in *Theatre I*, starting with the feet). Yet there is a certain macabre and inconsequential humour and a stark, memorable quality to parts of the dialogue that is characteristically and uniquely Beckettian: 'B: Day . . . night . . . (*Looks.*) It seems to me sometimes the earth must have got stuck, one sunless day, in the heart of winter, in the grey of evening' (66). Several passages make one suspect, however, that Beckett may have sensed that the dangers of repetition or self-parody were too great to allow him to complete or release the play earlier; e.g. 'A: Have you only one leg? B: Just the one. A: And the other? B: It went bad and was removed' (65-66).

Hardly surprisingly, the early draft of *Theatre I*, *The Gloaming*, included further reminiscences of *Endgame* that were to be removed in the French version, as well as a number of passages that look forward to Beckett's later dramatic writing. The song from *Watt* that Clov sung, for example, in the American production of the play directed by Alan Schneider, 'Bid us sigh on from day to day / And wish and wish the soul away', is included in the text of *The Gloaming*. And B's loaded query, 'Have you your wits about you, Billy, have you still some of your wits about you?' (62) anticipates Winnie's similarly phrased question to Willie in *Happy Days*.

Beckett had only finished writing *All that Fall* in English for the BBC some three months earlier, and the cripple in *The Gloaming* has inherited several of the blind Mr. Rooney's characteristics, his tetchiness, his occasional dry wit ('Why don't you walk round in a spiral? Have you no system?', R.U.L. MS, 14), as well as his tendency towards stasis: 'But no man was ever less on the look out than I. Why I just sit there in my black shed without moving . . . Then from one dawn to the next, my only sign of life is to take out my watch, wind it up and put it away again. Otherwise I might just as well be . . . you know. (*Pause.*) Well perhaps not quite' (R.U.L. MS, 5).

But the fact that the two characters should possess so little that is their own is only one of several problems associated with this text. The end of the published version contrives an artificial, suspended situation, as A wrenches the pole from B's grasp as an angry reprisal to his taunting. The possibilities remain open again, apparently, as they did in *Endgame*. And yet because the situation remains a hypothetical one, the final frozen tableau of the *Theatre I* fragment can possess none of the resonance of the earlier play's concluding scene.

It is, of course, an inevitable consequence of Beckett's vision that ending and endings should be difficult. And here, as so often in Beckett's manuscripts, several possible endings are envisaged or attempted. *The Gloaming* version resolves the suspended moment with the pole being given back to the cripple and with the blind man returning with difficulty to his stool and his fiddle, paving the way, it might appear, for a *da capo* conclusion. Yet further dialogue, omitted in the published text, re-opens the possibility of a relationship with the renewed question: 'Is there nothing I can do for you, Billy?' (R.U.L. MS, 16), the blindman's reply taking the form of an unattainable wish to return to a scene of his youth. Inevitably, this merely leads to another rather weak *impasse*. And although the final speech looks forward to the lingering contemplation of a lyrical moment akin to that with the girl in the punt in *Krapp's Last Tape*, written just over a year later, at the time it probably seemed too sentimental (and perhaps even too personal) for Beckett to allow it to stand in this context as an ending to the play:

> Bring me back to the hot summer evening out in the Bay with my father in the little rowboat, fishing for mackerel with a spinner. To the time when it was still time. "Do you remember what they look like?" "Yes, father, all blue and silver". (R.U.L. MS. 16)

Instead, elements of the personal experience have emerged elsewhere in Beckett's published work, but depersonalized and transformed: 'Yes, I'm here for ever, with the spinners and the dead flies, dancing to the tremor of their meshed wings, and it's well pleased I am, well pleased, that it's over and done with, the puffing and panting after me up and down their Tempe of tears' (*TFN*, 32).

5. *Theatre II*

Although this discarded piece of theatre is dated 'circa 1960' in *Ends and Odds*, a manuscript draft from two years earlier exists in Trinity College, Dublin, Library.[54] This situates a first version, written in French and different from that eventually published in 1976[55], as between the English plays *Krapp's Last Tape* and *Embers*. Visually, indeed, the play takes Krapp's zone of light and divides it into two, focussing on two tables and chairs (with a reading-lamp on each table), placed symmetrically on either side of the stage. The two speaking characters, A and B, are in a sixth floor apartment to investigate the temperament and past life of a third person who is present on stage but remains totally silent throughout, silhouetted against the night sky and clearly on the point of throwing himself out of the window.

Theatre II has a number of affinities with the unpublished *Eleuthéria*:

the central theme of suicide; the discussion concerning a silent character (present in *Eleuthéria* in another part of the split set); an emphasis on separate stage 'territories'; the use of lamps to mark out these areas and to separate light and dark; and in spite of a basically serious subject-matter, a surface lightness of tone and a delight in parody. But as an investigation or interrogation play it may be compared with the second *Pochade radiophonique* (*Radio II*), where the pain of the subject is also treated with indifference or even mockery.

The task of the two investigators in *Theatre II* seems to be to check the books of a person before he kills himself, providing testimonies from others or 'confidences' from the subject himself in an apparent attempt to help him to decide whether he should or should not do this. But the lineage of the two figures, A and B, whose names emerge from their dialogue as Morvan and Bertrand, is very much the vaudeville background of Estragon and Vladimir. For they indulge in sharp, lively repartee like members of a music-hall or cinema screen comic duo: 'Finches, pinhead' (83), 'Don't whinge, Morvan, that will get us nowhere' (78), 'you'd be the death of me, if I were sufficiently alive' (83); they talk like stage Welshmen or Scotsmen 'no, Morvan, look you' (81) and 'oh you bonny wee birdie' (83); they get involved in a misunderstanding about a 'heirless' or 'hairless' aunt; and they decide that a running 'gag' with the reading-lamps going off and coming on again 'has gone on long enough' (78).

But again, like Estragon and Vladimir, they are not only vaudeville characters. A series of small, inconsequential remarks confers on them enough individuality to endow them with a surprising degree of dramatic life. A (Bertrand) is more practical, better organized and more knowledgeable; B is more nervous, hot-tempered and prone to use oaths and four-letter words and, although less sensitive than A, he is capable of graphic turns of phrase, as when he comments on the excellent chance of C killing himself by jumping from the sixth floor: 'He has only to land on his arse, the way he lived. The spine snaps and the tripes explode' (72). A and B are bound together by mutual needs but again this symbiotic relationship is as subject to irritability and impatience as that of Estragon and Vladimir had been.

The surface lightness of tone derives partly from the lively banter of this administrative duo. But it also owes a lot to word-play and stylistic parody. Witnesses who provide comic depositions concerning the subject C's unhappy life have names carefully chosen for their associations: Mr Peaberry, the market-gardener who gives evidence concerning C's knowledge of national epics; Mr Swell, the organist at Seaton Sluice, who rhymes his contribution like Swift; Mr Moore, the light comedian whose address is given as 'c/o Widow Merryweather-Moore at All Saints on the Wash!'; and C's wife, whose name, Aspasia, is that of a famous Greek courtesan, but who is 'button designer in residence, in the Commercial Road East'. C's name, Croker, is ironically appropriate and is one to which Beckett has shown some attachment.[56] The depositions themselves parody several different styles: legalistic syntax and phraseology, applied incongruously to the withholding of sex; 'literary' English contributed by 'Mrs Darcy-Croker, woman of letters'; advertising jargon; and a descriptive account of C as he sat 'scrutinizing a lump of dogshit' (75) provided by Mr. Feckman, a 'certified accountant and friend for better and for worse' (76).

Notwithstanding these many instances of word-play and linguistic parody, the fragment still manages to strike an authentic note of genuine suffering. For the by-play with the lamp, B's concern only to find the main verb in C's confession, and his apparent indifference to the isolation and suffering evoked there do not entirely erase the pain contained, for example, in this summary of a youth of regular absconding:

> Aged ten, runs away from home first time, brought back next day, admonished, forgiven. (*Pause.*) Aged fifteen, runs away from home second time, dragged back a week later, thrashed, forgiven. (*Pause.*) Aged seventeen, runs away from home third time, slinks back six months later with his tail between his legs, locked up, forgiven. (*Pause.*) Aged seventeen runs away from home last time, crawls back a year later on his hands and knees, kicked out, forgiven. (79)

Later there are several rather moving allusions to suffering, waste and death that possess a characteristically Beckettian note of ambiguity. The bird which A and B hear singing so beautifully is singing with its mate dead in the same cage. Concerning the beauty of the bird's plumage, A comments 'And to think all that is organic waste! All that splendour!' (83). At the very end, A's inspection of C's face, which remains invisible to the audience, provides a moment of unbroken pathos.

For a variety of reasons *Theatre II* is more successful than any of the other theatre fragments that I have so far read. It has a lively, varied, even at times sparkling dialogue from two sharply drawn characters. A variety of incidents focusses on the same central issue of suffering and pain. It has a relatively wide intellectual and emotional range and blends tragi-comic elements together smoothly. In the end it remains, however, a fragment, twice as long as *Footfalls* but clearly lacking its sense of completeness. On the other hand, it is difficult to envisage it being extended successfully. Everything seems after all to have been said concerning C. And a series of related investigations would almost inevitably involve repetition of theme and perhaps treatment.

Looking back at these two theatre fragments from the late 'fifties after the miniature dramas of the 'seventies focusses attention on the basic differences that exist between them. In the main, *Theatre I* and *Theatre II* look back to *Waiting for Godot* and *Endgame* rather than forward to the later plays. *Theatre II* might seem to anticipate *Play* in its use of parody. But setting the parody of everyday language in a strange limbo world is of a different order of imaginative conception from the more banal depositions of the theatre fragment. Perhaps only one image remained impressed on Beckett's mind to recur later in *That Time* and the television play, *Ghost Trio*: the man, perhaps about to die, who has an enigmatic smile on his face.

Beckett's work in the theatre after *Play* has differed fairly drastically from that found in these two fragments. He has focussed more recently on simple, stark, fraught situations, on an extreme concentration and economy, and on a musical style of patterning of motifs. Reduction in the number of characters, reduction of the human body to a part rather than the whole, and reduction in other elements involved has not meant a similar reduction in density or in emotional power. In the miniatures of the 'seventies indeed, this density and power derives partly from the juxtaposition or confrontation of different time states, and partly again from establishing an unusual relationship between the material of the play and the audience watching. A comparison of the dramatic 'Odds' (*Theatre I* and *Theatre II*) with the 'Ends' (*Not I*, *That Time* and *Footfalls*) emphasizes therefore the essentially innovatory quality of Beckett's recent writing for the theatre. Exactly how successful as pieces of theatre these miniatures will eventually be judged to be is difficult to predict. I have already suggested serious misgivings about *That Time* in performance. Yet although the canvas is smaller than in *Waiting for Godot* or *Endgame*, *Not I* and *Footfalls* seem to possess some of the resonance of the earlier plays as well as having their own sources of dramatic interest and strength.

Notes

1. Beckett to Jessica Tandy. Quoted in E. Brater, 'The "I" in Beckett's *Not I*', *Twentieth Century Literature*, 20, no. 3, July 1974, p. 200.

2. Letter to J. Knowlson, postmark 30.iv.74.

3. The account of this visit is given in E. Brater, 'Dada, Surrealism, and the Genesis of *Not I*', *Modern Drama*, XVIII, no. 1, March 1975, p. 50.

4. These dates are established by Beckett's correspondence with J. Knowlson. D. Bair, *Samuel Beckett. A Biography*, provides a similar framework, pp. 621-3.

5. S.E. Gontarski, 'Beckett's Voice Crying in the Wilderness: the Emergence of *Not I*', paper given to Modern Language Association of America Congress, December 1976.

6. The entire set of holographs and typescripts are in Reading University Library, R.U.L. 1227/7/12/1 to 1227/7/12/7. The stage directions are also inserted into the second typescript by Beckett as holograph additions.

7. The three changes are made on R.U.L. MS 1227/7/12/3.

8. At rehearsals of the play at the Royal Court Theatre in London, January 1973; subsequently, Beckett has directed several people who inquired into the origins of *Not I* to *The Unnamable*.

9. E. Brater, 'Dada, Surrealism, and the Genesis of *Not I*', p. 57.

10. *Time*, 11 December 1972, p. 122. Richard Roud likened Auditor to a priest at confessional in *The Guardian*, 24 November 1972.

11. D. Bair, *op. cit.*, p. 622.

12. E. Brater, 'The "I" in Beckett's *Not I*', p. 197.

13. I. Wardle, *The Times*, 17 January 1973.

14. The writer was present at the BBC film studios in Ealing when Beckett first saw a preview of the television version.

15. D. Bair, *op. cit.*, p. 528.

16. *The Guardian*, 17 January 1973.

17. These sources were written into the French translation (*Pas moi*) deposited in Reading University Library.

18. For example, 'Come let us all unite and sing / God is love' (Howard Kingsbury); 'God is love: His mercy brightens' (John Bowring); 'New every morning is the love / Our wakening and uprising prove' (John Keble).

19. B. and J. Fletcher, B. Smith, W, Bachem, *A Student's Guide to the Plays of Samuel Beckett*, London, Faber and Faber, 1978, p. 200.

20. *The Times*, 17 January 1973.

21. 'The tragic figure represents the expiation of original sin, of the original and eternal sin of him and all his "socii malorum", the sin of having been born', *Proust and Three Dialogues with Georges Duthuit*, p. 67.

22. E. Brater, 'The "I" in Beckett's *Not I*', p. 199.

23. Letter to J. Knowlson, 24.ix.74.

24. Trinity College, Dublin MS 4664, pp. 10-13.

25. R.U.L. MS 1477/1.

26. R.U.L. MS 1477/6.
27. W.D. Asmus, 'Rehearsal notes for the German première of Beckett's *That Time* and *Footfalls* at the Schiller-Theater Werkstatt, Berlin (directed by Beckett)', *Journal of Beckett Studies*, no. 2, Summer 1977, p. 92. This is certainly the way in which Beckett envisages the three stages (i.e. BAC), not as, on the basis of the statement from A 'and the white hair pouring out down from under the hat', the recent *A Student's Guide to the Plays of Samuel Beckett*, pp. 203-4 maintains as the order of seniority, BCA.
28. A. Libera, 'Samuel Beckett's *That Time*', forthcoming in the *Journal of Beckett Studies*.
29. The term 'verset' is used by R. Cohn in 'Outward Bound Soliloquies', *Journal of Modern Literature*, vol. 6, no. 1, February 1977, pp. 17-38.
30. R.U.L. MS 1477/1 to MS 1477/10. Typescript 5 is MS 1477/6.
31. A. Libera, *op. cit.*
32. The pessimism of Beckett's reading of Proust is shown clearly in S. Rosen, *Samuel Beckett and the Pessimistic Tradition*, New Brunswick, Rutgers University Press, 1976, pp. 137-152.
33. Conversation with J. Knowlson, 3.xii.78.
34. See W.D. Asmus, *op. cit.*, p. 93.
35. See R.D. Laing, *The Divided Self. An Existential Study in Sanity and Madness*, Harmondsworth, Penguin Books, 1965, Chapters 3, 'Ontological Insecurity'; 4, 'The Embodied and unembodied self' and 6, 'The false-self system'.
36. Conversation with J. Knowlson prior to the production of *That Time* in May 1976.
37. R.U.L. MS 1639.
38. Holograph manuscript, R.U.L. MS 1552/1. First page dated 2.3.75.
39. Holograph manuscript, R.U.L. MS 1552/1; the second page is dated 1.10.75. The second draft of the mother's monologue is dated 25.10.75.
40. Letter to J. Knowlson, dated 7.xi.75.
41. W.D. Asmus, *op.cit.*, pp. 83, 85.
42. In *Footfalls*, London, Faber and Faber, 1976, May paces seven steps across the stage, but this was corrected in the Royal Court performance to nine steps, to give greater width. The Faber text was set before the production in May 1976. In *Ends and Odds*, London, Faber and Faber, 1977, the text is amended to nine, although an error has crept in on p. 33, where the steps are mistakenly left as seven. In the French première of *Pas*, with Delphine Seyrig as May, at the Théâtre d'Orsay (11 April 1978) nine steps were also adopted.
43. W.D. Asmus, *op. cit.*, pp. 83-4. In the first typescripts, reference is made to 'a general practitioner named Haddon. Long past his best' for whom her birth was 'his last mess' (R.U.L. MS 1552/2).
44. W.D. Asmus, *op. cit.*, pp. 83-4.
45. See R. Ellmann, *James Joyce*, New York, Oxford University Press. 1959, pp. 689-693.
46. W.D. Asmus, *op. cit.*, p. 87.
47. R.U.L. MS 1552/1.

48. 'Neither' was written to be set to music by Morton Feldman in September-October 1976. Beckett himself terms it a 'text'. It is published in the *Journal of Beckett Studies*, no. 4.
49. W.D. Asmus, 'Rehearsal Notes', *op. cit.*, p. 85.
50. Typescript 2 is R.U.L. MS 1552/3 and 2A is R.U.L. MS 1552/4.
51. D. Bair, *op. cit.*, pp. 10-11.
52. *Pas suivi de quatre esquisses*, Paris, Les Editions de Minuit, 1978, p. 11.
53. L. Harvey, *Samuel Beckett, Poet and Critic*, Princeton, New Jersey, Princeton University Press, 1970, p. 247.
54. Trinity College Dublin MS 4661, a holograph in French of 33 pages.
55. *L'Herne*, Samuel Beckett, no. 31 (1976), pp. 15-23.
56. Cf. Croak in *Words and Music* (1962) and Croker's Acres in *Not I*. The latter was apparently a real place near to Leopardstown Race Course in Ireland. Croker was, according to Beckett, the name of an American millionaire whose horse Joss won the Derby. *A Student's Guide to the Plays of Samuel Beckett*, p. 200.

A Poetics of Indigence

A Poetics of Indigence

Despite having lived, since the war, in an intellectual atmosphere that has been dominated by criticism and the theory of criticism, and despite being often reminded that the creative writer is the most imaginative of critics, we have allowed a corpus of criticism by one of our most outstanding creative writers to come into being without our taking cognizance of it. The purpose of this chapter is to examine the critical writings of Samuel Beckett and to demonstrate that they are quite as remarkable and challenging as any of the more canvassed critical theories to have claimed our attention in recent years. This is easily the most neglected area of Beckett's *oeuvre*, as I pointed out some years ago,[1] and yet it presents as compelling a profile and as dense a character as that more accessibly offered by his fiction or his drama. For all its idiosyncrasy and obliqueness, Beckett's criticism, like all the best criticism, has made a permanent contribution to the psychology of creativity.

Beckett has possessed from the start a temperament deeply suspicious of system-building, whether in philosophy or religion or literature: 'I can't see any trace', he has been quoted as saying, 'of system anywhere'. At the same time Beckett has also believed that a unit or item within this non-system may possess a quality that the whole does not possess: 'it is the shape that matters', he told Harold Hobson, *apropos* four sentences of Augustine. There may seem to be a contradiction here, but it is the kind of contradiction that is basic to Beckett's thinking and it provides a useful *entrée* into Beckett's achievement in criticism. Beckett has made no attempt to systematize his aesthetic thinking, and yet if we follow him patiently, from his first such utterance to his most recent, a discernible shape begins to emerge. To reconstruct Beckett's theoretical position from the disparate utterances that suggest he has no theoretical position at all may seem like flying in the face of the de-constructive impulse that is everywhere present in his critical writing. But it remains the only way to bring into the foreground ideas which are partially obscured by the fact that Beckett is mostly discussing other artists than himself and only very occasionally coming out into the open to present his own feelings.

Beckett is uninterested in theorizing because he is uninterested in absolutes. The world discloses itself to him as a purgatory in which the only absolute is 'the absolute absence of the Absolute' (*OE*, 22). He is a determined enemy, therefore, of those who propose unduly neat solutions to complicated problems, or who rely excessively on the accepted modes of simplifying one's problematic relationship with the world. In his first published essay ('Dante . . . Bruno. Vico . . Joyce', 1929), Beckett takes Vico to task for being seduced by the 'neatness' of his theory about the relationship between Philosophy and Philology, and Croce for taking the line of least resistance and turning Vico into a mystic. In a similar way he criticizes Curtius (in his first book) for waxing excessively paradoxical about Proust.

Beckett's stress in 'Dante . . . Bruno. Vico . . Joyce' falls on the empiricism of the four writers concerned, and on their belief in 'poetry' as against 'metaphysics'. Beckett invokes the 'practical roundheaded' Vico as the first thinker to discuss poetry both imaginatively and with scientific precision. Vico attracts Beckett because he gives full value to the individual and particular item without scanting its claims to universality and perfect intelligibility, whilst at the same time reminding us that intelligible things cannot, and ought not to be, explained away. The greatest art, Beckett claimed in the serious conclusion to a spoof lecture, is both 'perfectly intelligible' and 'perfectly inexplicable'.[2] It communicates by means of metaphor and image but preserves a strangeness about it that makes it difficult, at times impossible, to read in any meaningful sense. Beckett reveals in the essay that, for him, there is a lugubriousness about the alphabet that is markedly inferior to 'the savage economy of hieroglyphics' (*OE*, 15). The alphabet belongs to the 'monodialectical' world which Beckett is intent on removing himself from; the hieroglyphic enables him to keep faith with the dualism that has been basic to his thinking for fifty years. For the hieroglyphic is not only a perfect marriage of form and content — which Beckett has to keep together to satisfy his empiricist and pragmatist tendencies — it is also sufficiently alive to suggest the 'furious restlessness' and 'flux' within the form — which satisfies Beckett's abiding sense of 'the absolute absence of absolutes'. Beckett stresses the 'inevitable clarity of the old inarticulation' and is intent on suggesting that Joyce's *Work in Progress* has a similar clarity, despite its forbidding surface. The real enemy, in Beckett's opinion, is 'interexclusiveness', which requires one to separate out elements that are one and indivisible. 'Structure' is therefore not so much an external framework or skeleton as an internal intertwining, a living thing. Beckett admires Vico, like later Structuralist critics, because he has laid bare the transformations that make language inexhaustible. But at the end of the essay Beckett ventures into a more personal account of the creative process, without benefit of Vico or Joyce, or, for that matter, Dante and Bruno. The artist, for Beckett, is a figure who, by virtue of being 'partially purged' of an interest in the outside world, becomes the 'partially purgatorial agent' revealing to the inhabitants of the world that absolutes are absolutely absent from their purgatorial lives. This is a far cry from the four writers Beckett has been discussing, and reads like a manifesto for Beckett's subsequent literary career.

In the critical writings that followed this sudden outburst, Beckett drops the purgatorial overtones, but continues to explore the relationship between the artist and the outside world. At the same time, in his book on Proust (1931) Beckett develops the ideas of the essay on *Work in Progress* in a manner that leaves us in no doubt as to his personal interest in what he is saying. It is amusing to find Beckett later claiming (in an essay of 1945) that the 'apodictic'[3] propositions of conventional criticism prevent one from recognizing the personality that lies behind the remarks, since the propositions in *Proust* certainly do not suffer from this disability and are as 'apodictic' as anyone could wish.

In the essay on Proust Beckett reiterates and extends the ideas of clarity, inarticulation and hieroglyph that are at the heart of the earlier essay. Proust is praised, as Joyce had been, for making no attempt 'to dissociate form from content' (*PTD*, 88) and praised also, again as Joyce had been, for apprehending the world 'metaphorically' (*PTD*, 88). As far as Beckett is concerned Proust's world of 'intrinsic flux' (*PTD*, 17) is akin to the 'furious restlessness' of Joyce's. When Beckett speaks of 'the two dynamisms without synchronisation' (*PTD*, 17) in

Proust's book, he is not so much describing the nature of human relationships in Proust as the relationship between the writer and the objects that are the material for his art. Throughout *Proust* Beckett concerns himself with this relationship, stressing that the object becomes a 'source of enchantment' (*PTD*, 23) only when perceived in its singularity[4], and that the artist (or subject) must slough off the merely contingent superfluities that occlude an object's realness. If we remember how deeply impressed Beckett had been by Vico's ability to preserve the individuality and universality of each particular item, it will come as no surprise to find Beckett praising Proust for his interest in the 'concrete' (*PTD*, 79) and his achievement of an 'ideal real' (*PTD*, 75).

But what is new in Beckett's attitude is a profound interest in the mechanics of the relationship between subject and object. The object possesses, for Beckett, an 'ideal impermeability' (*PTD*, 57-8); reality, therefore, can only be 'hermetic' (*PTD*, 74). The imagination 'cannot tolerate the limits of the real' (*PTD*, 74) but is fascinated by the hermeticism of the real. Only the magical perception of the artist allied to the immense labour of the artisan can penetrate the impenetrable, and 'trace' the 'hieroglyphics' (*PTD*, 84). By virtue of 'inspired perception' (*PTD*, 84) the enigmatic can be made oracular; the actual can be seen to be the inevitable: 'one real impression' (*PTD*, 14) and 'one adequate mode of evocation' (*PTD*, 14-15) work together with the 'cruel precision' (*PTD*, 27) of a camera. (Compare the 'savage economy' of the Joyce essay.) But it is not merely inspiration that distinguishes Proust and artists like him from those 'realists' who (like the 'book-keepers' of the Joyce essay and the 'chartered recountants' of the Jack Yeats essay of 1936[5]) 'worship the offal of experience' (*PTD*, 78) and produce the 'penny-a-line vulgarity of a literature of notations' (*PTD*, 76): the primary distinguishing factor is the capacity for hard work.

There is a great gulf fixed for Beckett between the object as it really is and the object as art makes it seem:

> Proust respects the dual significance of every condition and circum-
> stance of life. The most ideal tautology presupposes a relation and the
> affirmation of equality involves only an approximate identification, and
> by asserting unity denies unity. (*PTD*, 69-70)

(Beckett hints here that art is, ideally, tautologous but, in practice, disunified.) It is precisely because of its absolute disjunction from life that art may be said to possess a 'brightness' (*PTD*, 76) that makes us turn to it for illumination. But this is not illumination in the religious sense, however much Beckett stresses the patience and purity of the artist. The artist is more like a negative mystic than a canonized saint: 'The artist is active, but negatively, shrinking from the nullity of extracircumferential phenomena, drawn in to the core of the eddy' (*PTD*, 65-6). (In the 1932 'Poetry is Vertical' manifesto[6], which Beckett signed, the artist is involved in 'mantic' activity, however, divinely mad, prophetic.) To rely on the exercise of the will, or on 'the vulgarity of a plausible concatenation' (*PTD*, 81-2) is, as with a mystic, to deprive oneself of one's innate powers and to hamper one's inspiration. The work of art is dormant within the artist's self, and can only be discovered when he penetrates the *'gouffre'* (*PTD*, 31) that stands between his habitual response to the world and his renewed awareness of it. If this makes the practice of art seem dangerously self-contained, it is clear that this does not trouble Beckett: 'The artistic tendency is not expansive, but a contraction. And art is the apotheosis of solitude. There is no communication because there are no vehicles of communication' (*PTD*, 64). Beckett admires Proust not for his capacity to apprehend the correspondences between the self and the unself — which he inevitably associates with Baudelaire and the Symbolists — but rather for his ability to construct a self irrespective of the claims of the unself. Hence he labels Proust's enterprise as 'autosymbolism' (*PTD*, 80), to show that it is a logical development from Baudelaire, but quite different from what Baudelaire achieved.

When Beckett speaks, at another point in the essay, of Proust's 'intellectual animism' (*PTD*, 36), he is obviously seeking to align Proust with the primitive animism that Vico had exposed as the basis of language. But it is clear that the hieroglyphics of art (as traced by Joyce and Proust) are far from primitive and are 'intellectualised' to a very high degree. It is symptomatic of Beckett's increasingly cerebral attitude to creativity that we should hear almost nothing in the essay on Proust about the 'direct expression' that was basic to the Joyce essay, and much more about the problems of perception that make all expression indirect. Joyce's directness is such that Beckett is largely content to quote him; Proust's obliqueness involves Beckett in the business of translation. It reflects Beckett's altered view of art when he approves Proust's claim that 'the duty and the task of a writer . . . are those of a translator'. Although Beckett states that 'the germ of the Proustian solution is contained in the statement of the problem itself', it is clear that the problematics of art are beginning to bulk larger than the solutions. Whereas the first essay begins with a cavalier warning about 'the neatness of identifications', the second begins with a tight-lipped recognition that 'the Proustian equation is never simple'. In the critical writings of the 1930s Beckett gradually comes to realize that the equations are more complex than even Proust imagined.

Beckett's next major published critical pronouncement occurs in the essay on the poet Denis Devlin that appeared in *transition* in 1938. But between 1930 (when he was writing *Proust*) and 1938 (when he had taken upon residence in Paris after 'years of wandering'[7]), Beckett's poetics had undergone a profound and dramatic change. A contributory cause was the failure to complete his first full-length prose work, *Dream of Fair to Middling Women* (begun 1932), but his secession from academic life — he left Trinity College in 1931 — was also an important factor. Beckett had begun to realize that his ideas were too heterogeneous and advanced to flourish in an academic atmosphere and had made the decisive step of becoming a writer rather than an academic. He had spoken with passion in *Proust* of 'the infinite futility — for the artist — of all that is not art' and resolved to attempt something a little less infinitely futile.

In the event Beckett found he had exchanged one form of futility for another. *Dream* got held up in what he was later disposed to think of as the *'limae labor'* stage (*MPTK*, 153), and was in any case, more an apologia for the kind of literature he would ultimately write than literature in its own right. It was, however, a cutting-loose on Beckett's part from the Joyce and Proust who had meant so much to him up to this time. In *Dream* Beckett speaks of the writer P. (pretty obviously Proust) who is indifferent to *'l'extase du décollage'* and indicates that he is not going to follow Cézanne and the Cubists into collage but rather that he is going to exploit instead the *décollage* of an art work that is haphazard to the point of extinction. *Dream* is not a piece of Surrealist automatic writing, but it is certainly a piece of erratic and self-indulgent writing, without any of the painstaking artfulness of Joyce or Proust. 'The only unity', Beckett writes in *Dream*, 'in this story is, please God, an involuntary unity'.

In one sense at least, *Dream* satisfied what Beckett had always seen as a *sine qua non* of the art work; it possessed the 'furious restlessness' of *Work in Progress*, and the 'flux' of *À la recherche du temps perdu*. It is clear that the apophthegm in *Proust* which Beckett silently purloined from Francesco de Sanctis — *'Chi non ha la forza di uccidere la realtà non ha la forza di crearla'* — has come to mean more and more to him by the time of *Dream*. But the power to create reality, to keep his characters 'one and indivisible' proves quite beyond him, and he can only make a virtue of necessity when he find them 'described, but not circumscribed . . . stated, but not summed'.

In *Dream* Beckett wages war on the forces of mechanization that immobilize the object in an artificial stasis, and tries desperately to achieve the kind of relativism he had admired in Proust, shorn of Proust's 'torment of clarifications' that he had never much liked.[8] Musical form seems to offer a way out. But the musical analogy that ended *Proust* is now seen to be a Symbolist pipe-dream. Nothing would be nicer, Beckett writes, than to join everything up nicely, with the formal elegance of a sonata, but the written word and the musical phrase are of different and irreconcilable orders, the latter as 'intelligible' and 'inexplicable' as one could wish for, the former neither intelligible nor inexplicable. The 'cenotaphs of indivisibility' that Beethoven could construct from a 'blizzard of electrons . . . threatening to come asunder' are not, in Beckett's opinion, a possibility for the literary artist.

Literature is revealed in *Dream* as an inferior art, an art of poverty. The 'magic' of which he had spoken so openly and encouragingly in *Proust* is revealed as a spell which, far from creating a living thing, immures its products in a 'chloroformed world'. What Beckett seems to be seeking is an art that gets beyond words to the silences between them:

> 'I shall write a book', [Belacqua] mused . . . 'where the phrase is self-consciously smart and slick, but of a smartness and slickness other than that of its neighbours on the page . . . The experience of my reader shall be between the phrases, in the silence, communicated by the intervals, not the terms of the statement . . . his experience shall be the menace, the miracle, the memory of an unspeakable trajectory.'

Despite continual mockery by Beckett, it is clear that he treats Belacqua's programme seriously, however much claptrap it may contain. Beckett is aware of the absurdity of what he is saying, just as he will later be in his much terser exchange with Georges Duthuit, but he intends the ideas to be taken seriously, and repeats them in simpler terms a moment later:' "If ever I do drop a book . . . it will be ramshackle, tumbledown, a bone-shaker, held together with bits of twine, and at the same time, innocent of the slightest velleity." '
Dream, alas, is far from 'innocent of the slightest velleity'; only fifteen years later, in *Molloy*, did Beckett achieve a really imaginative and

overpowering presentation of the 'incoherent continuum' that *Dream* is always talking about.

It is symptomatic of Beckett's change of emphasis that we should find him (in 1936, reviewing a Jack B. Yeats novel) observing of its technique, 'The moments are not separate, but concur in a single process: analytical imagination'. But it is also quite clear that it is not so much the single process as the discontinuities in Jack Yeats's prose that impress him most. Discontinuity allows Yeats, in Beckett's opinion, to abolish the dichotomy between fiction and truth and create a world of 'imaginative fact' which possesses the 'mobility' of the real world and the 'autonomy' of the created, artificial world. Beckett's respect and admiration is clearly for those writers who, in integrating the disintegrative tensions of the creative process, contrive to remind us of those tensions in the finished product. This is why Beckett speaks so highly of 'the disruptive intelligence, exacting the tumult from unity' in an O'Casey review of 1934, and admires the way O'Casey 'discerns the principle of disintegration in even the most complacent solidities'.[9] But he does not honour O'Casey with the ultimate accolade. Only in talking of Jack Yeats does he use the phrase he had previously used only of Proust: Jack Yeats's novel presents 'the "ideal real" . . . so obnoxious to the continuity girls'.

Beckett nowhere defines what exactly he means by the 'ideal real'. But he indicates very clearly what the 'ideal real' does not involve. Symbolism of the Baudelairean variety keeps the real and the ideal apart; 'there is no symbol' in Jack B. Yeats. 'There is no satire' either, because even the best satire (Swift's for example) drives a wedge between the abstract and the concrete. Best of all, 'there is no allegory, that glorious double-entry, with every credit in the said account a debit in the meant, and inversely' (cf. *PTD*, 79-80). The 'ideal real', in short, comprises a 'single series of imaginative transactions' which will not permit us to separate out the constituent parts. Not until the 1940s did Beckett abandon the idea that the art work could in some mysterious way disguise the labour that had gone into its making.

'Les deux besoins' dates from around 1938 but is much more important than any of the published journalism of the 1930s. There is much in the essay that stems from his earlier utterances, in particular the belief that art is a mysterious activity which cannot possibly be appreciated by everyone. 'In the enthymemes of art', writes Beckett grandly — surreptitiously reminding us that art has a logic of sorts —

'it is not premisses that are lacking but conclusions'. Beckett extends this idea by suggesting that the artist is involved in questions without answers, 'rhetorical questions without an oratorical function'. The impulse towards art originates in a 'hell of irrationality' that can only be tempered by 'the series of pure questions' which constitute the art work. Beckett raises, in this connection, the spectre of the Greek figure Hippasos who demonstrated to the Pythagoreans the incommensurability of side and diagonal in a square, a figure he again alludes to in *Murphy* (begun 1935) (*M*, 26). Hippasos attracts Beckett because he is a disinterested figure ('neither a fascist nor a communist' is Beckett's way of putting it), unimpressed by the consoling fictions of Pythagoras and only concerned with the truth. But Hippasos also provides Beckett with a basis for his own excursion into geometry, a six-pointed star shape made up of two interpenetrating triangles (or six peripheral triangles surrounding a central hexagon). Although Beckett's notebooks are crammed with calculations and geometric constructs of various kinds, Beckett rarely permits himself the shorthand of a diagram in his published work and realizes here that his diagram requires a lengthy gloss before it can be said to be intelligible. It is in glossing this diagram that the two 'needs' of the title are related to the question of vision that dominated *Proust*.

The 'need to need' and the 'need of which one has need' are as incommensurable as the side and diagonal of Hippasos. But they are brought into contact by the artistic 'conscience' which, properly exercised, offers the artist not only an 'entry into the void of having seen' but also an 'exit from the chaos of wanting to see'. It would be pleasant to dismiss this severely structured diagram as fantastic and absurd if it did not offer us clear proof that Beckett was seeking to formulate a poetics that would enable him to create something more truly individual than *Dream* could ever have been. The two inter-penetrating triangles are an attempt on Beckett's part to express the centrifugal and centripetal tensions that make the artistic impulse so puzzling and contradictory. The hexagon at the centre is the enclosed and slightly forbidding precipitate of the 'creative autology' that the artist has engaged in. The image of the star is a perfect exemplification of the theories adumbrated in *Dream*, and reminds us (as the essay on Denis Devlin will do more forcibly) that the art work, however obscure it may be, illuminates our muddled and amorphous lives. In 'Les deux besoins' we see Beckett shifting, despite his diagram, from the art work that is the product of incommensurable tendencies to the artist who finds himself the prey of incommensurable desires. Beckett is much less concerned after this with describing the finished product, the precipitate, and concentrates instead on the process of making, the experiment.

The 'Denis Devlin' review of 1938 looks a lot less eccentric when the argument of 'Les deux besoins' and the Jack Yeats review have been taken into account. Beckett tightens up his formulations here, notably in the suggestion that art has always been 'pure interrogation, rhetorical questions less the rhetoric'. Even the moments of what seem like rhetorical flourish — 'Art is the sun, moon and stars of the mind, the whole mind' — have the effect of reminding us how mentalized and cerebral the artistic enterprise is for Beckett. Beckett states categorically here, for the first time publicly, that 'art has nothing to do with clarity, does not dabble in the clear and does not make clear' and reminds us that the artist is alone: 'With himself on behalf of himself. With his selves on behalf of his selves'. The opposition is no longer between two related needs within the artist, however, but between the artist's need and the public's need. Beckett at first suggests that a distinction between these two needs ought not to be necessary, but he ends up decisively supporting the one and pouring scorn on the other:

> As between these two, the need that in its haste to be abolished cannot pause to be stated and the need that is the absolute predicament of particular human identity, one does not of course presume to suggest a relation of worth. Yet the distinction is not perhaps idle. . . . On the one hand . . . the art that condenses as inverted spiral of need . . . whose end is its own end in the end and source of need. . . . And on the other . . . the morbid dread of sphinxes, solution clapped on problem like a snuffer on a candle, the great crossword public . . .

Beckett sees these two categories as necessary and unavoidable polarities, and compares them to the 'symbiosis' of Dives and Lazarus who, even in death, 'did not cease to be divided'. But his patience with those who suffer from a 'morbid dread of sphinxes' is clearly wearing rather thin, and this 'symbiosis' is given pretty short shrift in the critical writings of the 1940s.

Almost all Beckett's critical writing since 'Denis Devlin' has been on painters and painting rather than writers and writing, and it is clear that Beckett felt the need to develop his ideas in a context that was not already literary in orientation. Of Beckett's two related essays on the van Velde brothers[10], the second is very much the better, although neither is as concise and compelling as any one of the three Duthuit dialogues. The title of the first essay (from a story which surfaces again in *Endgame*, 21-2) reminds us that the artefact, however imperfect, is more important than the world which condemns it. The 'symbiosis' of the 'Denis Devlin' essay has broken down, and the artist and his world are irremediably at odds. At the same time the critic's ability to express his feelings about art has diminished almost to the point of disappearance, and there is an atmosphere of uncertainty that is quite different from the relative confidence of 1938.

There remains on Beckett's part, however, a hankering after the 'ideal real' which he now finds exemplified in the paintings of Bram van Velde: 'it is exactly by idealising [extension] that he has been able to realize it objectively, with a purity without precedent'. Geer van Velde, by contrast, is 'entirely oriented towards the outside, the hurly-burly of things in the light'. In Bram's case the object submits to being changed by the artist; in Geer's the object inflicts change on the artist. Beckett is still thinking dualistically here, and at this point in time has no wish to decide in favour of one approach rather than the other. In the second essay he even states that the two attitudes are allied to one another 'as rest is to exertion'. But in the second essay Beckett makes it clear that, whichever alternative is adopted, the object resists being represented anyway, which virtually forces him to abandon his speculations as to whether the subject dominates the object or *vice versa*. The subject is now seen to be as much an obstacle as the object. In Geer's case, Beckett suggests that he resolves his predicament by 'engulfing' the external world with its own externality; in Bram's case, Beckett suggests that he resolves his predicament by retiring into the confinement of his inner world. Both painters remain passive in relation to their material, in a mood of what Beckett might perhaps call 'humanistic quietism'.[11] It is, in fact, the absence of a relationship between self and unself (the absence of an object to which the painter plays the role of subject) which is 'the new relationship and the new object'. Art has not been liberated from the object, but rather 'liberated from the illusion that there exists more than one object of representation, perhaps also of the illusion that this unique object *can* be represented'.

Beckett's haphazard formulations in these two essays form the basis for his severely logical stance in the *Three Dialogues*. Beckett reveals himself here as someone who, without deriding those artists who have 'enlarge[d] the statement of a compromise' (as almost all, in Beckett's view, have done), nevertheless prefers an art that makes no pretension to expression and relishes its own inability to conquer its 'insuperable indigence'. The purity of Bram van Velde's achievement derives from the absolute absence of the kind of 'predicament' that gave Rilke 'the fidgets' and makes Masson 'wriggle':

> [Bram] van Velde is the first whose painting is bereft, rid if you prefer, of occasion in every shape and form, ideal as well as material, and the first whose hands have not been tied by the certitude that expression is an impossible act. (*PTD*, 121)

The absence of any consideration of Geer van Velde indicates that Beckett has openly chosen one *empêchement* rather than the other. This prevents him developing a dualism comparable to that found in the two essays in French. But his dualistic tendencies remain well-served by returning to the question of the artist's relationship with his material: 'if the occasion appears as an unstable term of relation, the artist, who is the other term, is hardly less so. . . . The objections to this dualist view of the creative process are unconvincing'. The 'new relationship and the new object' of 'Peintres de l'empêchement' have disappeared; there is now no object and no relationship. Beckett's tone at the end of the third dialogue has a bitterness that indicates he is not only criticizing Duthuit, but also castigating his own timidity in his previous essays on Bram van Velde:

> I know that all that is required now, in order to bring even this horrible matter to an acceptable conclusion, is to make of this submission, this admission, this fidelity to failure, a new occasion, a new form of relation, and of the act which, unable to act, obliged to act, he makes, an expressive act, even if only of itself, of its impossibility, of its obligation. I know that my inability to do so places myself, and perhaps an innocent, in what I think is still called an unenviable situation, familiar to psychiatrists. (*PTD*, 125-6)

This represents a kind of terminus in Beckett's poetics, beyond which there seems to be nowhere he can go. It is his most radical and intransigent statement of what is, indeed, as Duthuit says, a 'fantastic theory', 'a violently extreme and personal point of view'. But for all its eccentricity, it preserves a certain logic, like most of Beckett's other ideas about the creative process. At the beginning of his career he was stressing how irrational was the compulsion to create, and how turbulent the surface of the artefact was likely to be. The interrogative aspects have now diminished, and the purity of the artistic motive has been removed from the foreground. But the need to create remains at the centre of his thinking. The 'ideal real' has had to be abandoned as a fiction; but, with the reduction of 'les deux besoins' to one and the re-interpretation of 'need' as 'obligation', there remains something concrete and practical at the heart of the Beckett aesthetic. We may seem to be a long way from the 'roundheaded' Neapolitanism of Vico, but we are still concerned with the 'economy of hieroglyphics'. And it is clear that Beckett would say of Bram van Velde, as he had said of Joyce twenty years before, that his painting 'is not *about* something: *it is that something itself*'. Despite his fondness for dualisms, Beckett still believes that art is 'a single series of imaginative transactions'.

Beckett's ideas in the *Three Dialogues with Georges Duthuit* are so radical that it should not surprise us if he has not dramatically developed his poetics since 1949. Writing on the paintings of his friend Henri Hayden in 1952 Beckett adopts once again the para-doxical mode of the *Three Dialogues*, the 'ideal real' having given way to the 'irréelle' and 'inactualité' of Beckett's post-Trilogy situation. The only vestige of his pre-war poetics to survive in the Hayden essay is his fondness for a subtle humour, a *risolino* that he finds in Ariosto and Jack B. Yeats. [12] Otherwise all is paradox and uncertainty, with the nagging suspicion that what looks like order is really disorder: 'Etrange ordre des choses, fait d'ordre en mal de choses, de choses en mal d'ordre'. What Beckett most admires in Hayden, as in Bram van Velde, is his ability to remain calm amid so much disorder and to wait 'sans espoir', in an attitude of resignation, for the art work, the 'chose faite', to emerge. No wonder Beckett calls Hayden's *oeuvre* 'imper-sonnelle', produced as it is by a 'double effacement', effacement of the subject that makes and effacement of the object that is made. To produce an art work at all under such conditions moves Beckett to wonderment and admiration, and there is none of the flippancy and savagery that is the hall-mark of his reviews of the 1930s.

In a *hommage* to the paintings of Jack B. Yeats, published in 1954, Beckett stresses that it is not the critic's role to provide 'reassuring notes on these desperately immediate images'. [13] All a critic can do is 'bow, wonder-struck' at the way Yeats has submitted to 'what cannot be mastered' and produced a 'great internal reality which incor-porates . . . nature and void, everything that will cease and everything that will never be'. It is the 'urgency' with which Yeats has worked, the 'magic' of his craftsmanship, the 'violence of need' which un-leashes such vibrant images. Like Hayden, Yeats has acquired the technique of presenting us with an 'unparalleled strangeness' that makes him seem scarcely human: 'The artist who stakes his being comes from nowhere. And he has no brothers'. Indeed, whereas in 1945 Yeats's paintings '[brought] light, as only the great dare to bring light, to the issueless predicament of existence'[14] by 1954 it has become clear to Beckett that Yeats is: 'sending us back to the darkest part of the spirit . . . [and] permitting illuminations only through that darkness'. The hint that illumination is still possible, after Bram van Velde's demolition of expressiveness, is the first indication that Beckett is emerging from the poetics of the *Three Dialogues*. Without ceasing to admire Bram van Velde, Beckett began to see, in the late 1950s, that there might be an exit from the predicament he had once considered 'issueless'.

By 1961, as an interview with Tom Driver demonstrates, Beckett was obviously feeling that he need not remain lodged in the '*impasse*' of which he had spoken to Israel Shenker in 1956. It remains important for Beckett to testify to the disorder he sees everywhere ('The only chance of renovation is to open our eyes and see the mess'[15]). But even more important now is the order that 'admits the chaos and does not try to say that the chaos is really something else'. Form therefore 'exists as a problem separate from the material it accommodates', a distinction which the Beckett of 'Dante . . . Bruno. Vico . . Joyce' would have found himself quite unable to make. The form, and the consternation behind it, are still seen in terms of problems rather than solutions. Whereas in the *Proust* essay the problem contained the solution within it and in the dialogue on André Masson the solubility of Masson's problems robbed them of their 'legitimacy', in the interview with Tom Driver the discovery of a form that will not falsify 'the mess' can only take place outside 'the mess'. The art object will not, as Beckett seemed to think in the 1930s, disguise the chaos and call it something else; this can only happen if the statement of a problem contains its own solution. In the 1960s Beckett knows that the chaos must be allowed to exist in its own right, 'accommodated' by the form but not contained within it.

In a short text written to accompany an exhibition by the Israeli artist Avigdor Arikha, dated December 1966, Beckett explores still further the relationship between the form and the mess:

> Siege laid again to the impregnable without. Eye and hand fevering after the unself. By the hand it unceasingly changes the eye unceasingly changed. Back and forth the gaze beating against unseeable and unmakable. Truce for a space and the marks of what it is to be and be in face of. Those deep marks to show.[16]

The 'without' has now become 'impregnable' (and hence 'unseeable' and 'unmakable') in a way that the 'hermetic' reality of the *Proust* essay was not. This is not just a matter of 'empêchement' but is, rather, conditioned by a total loss of faith in the artist's ability to penetrate the 'unself'. It remains important for Beckett that the artist should, after a suitably tranquillizing 'truce', record to the best of his ability the evidence — the wounds — of 'what it is to be and be in face of'. But the 'unself' remains impregnable, however expert the eye and hand of the artist. The subject-object dichotomy is now quite irrelevant; Beckett's main concern here is with the absolute isolation of the artist. The form is finally much less important than the mess. One is tempted to think that it was ever thus, for Beckett.

To study the changing configuration of Beckett's critical opinions over fifty years is to become aware of how subtle and original a thinker Beckett can be on the subject of art and artistic activity. He has not always argued his ideas with the clarity and rigour that would attract a professional aesthetician. But when he has felt the compulsion to express himself in a more discursive manner, he has always written cogently and stimulatingly. There are commentators who tend to hypostatize Beckett's ideas as they were at the time of *Proust* or at the time of the *Three Dialogues*, and who have thereby contrived to suggest that little change is to be observed since the late 1920s. Given the inaccessibility of much of the material, this was perhaps unavoidable. But it has prevented Beckett's criticism gaining the currency it deserves, and diverted attention away from a body of work that is substantial, intelligent and coherent. To call this body of work a 'poetics' may seem somewhat grandiose; but it is perhaps the only way of suggesting to others that it is worth their consideration. To call it a 'poetics of indigence' may seem to highlight one idea at the expense of many others; but it is perhaps the only word that can encapsulate the obsession with 'need' and 'poverty' that has been at the heart of Beckett's thinking through such a long and distinguished career.

Notes

1. In my *Samuel Beckett*, London, Henley and Boston, Routledge & Kegan Paul, 1976, p. 13.
2. 'Le Concentrisme', Reading University Beckett Archive, MS 1396/4/15. Later used again in *Proust*, p. 92.

3. 'La peinture des van Velde ou le monde et le pantalon', *Cahiers d'Art*, 20-21, 1945-46, p. 350.

4. Watt's experience with the singular visit of the Galls is rather different, however.

5. 'An Imaginative Work!', *Dublin Magazine*, XI, n.s. July-September 1936, p. 80.

6. *transition*, 21, March 1932, pp. 148-9.

7. Beckett's own description, in the poem 'Gnome', *Dublin Magazine*, IX, n.s., July-September 1934, p. 8.

8. Quoted from 'Le Concentrisme' (see note 2).

9. 'The Essential and the Incidental', *The Bookman*, LXXXVII, Christmas 1934, p. 111.

10. For details of the first, see note 3; the second is in *Derrière le Miroir*, 11 and 12, June, 1948, pp. 3, 4 and 7.

11. The title (possibly not Beckett's own) of a review in *Dublin Magazine*, IX, n.s., July-September 1934, pp. 79-80.

12. *Hayden*, by Jean Selz, Geneva, Pierre Cailler, 1962, pp. 40-1. Cf. the Jack Yeats review of 1936 (see note 5).

13. Translation (by Ruby Cohn) of 'Hommage à Jack B. Yeats', *Les Lettres Nouvelles*, II, April 1954, pp. 619-20 in *Jack B. Yeats: a centenary gathering*, ed. Roger McHugh, Dublin, 1971, pp. 75-6.

14. 'MacGreevy on Yeats', *Irish Times*, 4 August 1945, p. 2.

15. L. Graver and R. Federman, *Samuel Beckett: the Critical Heritage*, p. 218.

16. Beckett's English translation of *Pour Avigdor Arikha*, Paris, Galerie Claude Bernard, 1967. Published in Victoria and Albert Museum catalogue, February-May 1976.

Beckett and John Millington Synge

Beckett and John Millington Synge

On a number of occasions Samuel Beckett has expressed his deep admiration for the plays of John Millington Synge. A request in 1956 for an appreciation of George Bernard Shaw as a playwright elicited from Beckett the following wry response: 'I wouldn't suggest that G.B.S. is not a great playwright, whatever that is when it's at home. What I would do is give the whole unupsettable apple-cart for a sup of the Hawk's Well, or the Saints (Synge's *The Well of the Saints*) or a whiff of Juno, to go no further'.[1] Beckett recalls that he saw most of the Synge revivals at the Abbey Theatre in Dublin in the 1920s[2] when he was reading Modern Languages at Trinity College, where Synge had also been a student some thirty years earlier. What have been termed the four 'shanachie' plays[3] (*Riders to the Sea*, *The Shadow of the Glen*, *The Tinker's Wedding* and *The Playboy of the Western World*), as well as, perhaps a little more surprisingly, in view of its concluding note of triumph, *Deirdre of the Sorrows*, must be added to *The Well of the Saints* as plays that Beckett knows well and greatly admires; all of them are in his personal library.

There is, of course, much in Synge's background that would attract Beckett and draw them together: similar origins in middle-class Anglo-Irish families from South County Dublin; a personal link through the painter and writer, Jack B. Yeats, who spent a month with Synge in 1905 visiting Connemara and Mayo, illustrated Synge's *The Aran Islands*, and whom Beckett met several times from 1931 until Yeats's death in 1957; links with France and Germany and a mutual interest in Continental literature — Synge translated, among others, poems of Villon, Walter von der Vogelweide, and

Leopardi, all poets admired by Beckett.[4] But, above all, Beckett would have been impressed by Synge's qualities as a writer and a dramatist, his imaginative strength, his blend of humour and pathos deriving from a tragi-comic vision, his clear-sighted pessimism and yet his vitality and courage, as well as his bold experimentalism in creating a rich, idiosyncratic language for the theatre.

Yet it has been claimed that there is more than mere affinity between these two Irish authors and that, as a playwright, Beckett owes something of a debt to Synge.[5] This influence, which must have been sensed by many theatre-goers, has been alleged by a number of critics, but, until recently, it remained unconfirmed and it has not yet been explored in any great detail.[6] Now, in answer to a somewhat bold question relating to the most profound influences that he himself acknowledged upon his dramatic writing, Beckett referred me specifically to the work of J.M. Synge.[7] Such an acknowledgement is relatively rare with Beckett and the nature and extent of his debt is therefore all the more worth pursuing.

First of all, there are a number of fairly obvious, surface similarities between the dramatic worlds of Beckett and Synge. Estragon and Vladimir wait in vain for Godot to arrive on a lonely road by a tree set in a barren landscape similar to that found in Synge's *The Well of the Saints*, where the weather-beaten, blind couple, Martin and Mary Doul, grope their way on to the stage and sit wearily on a heap of stones, trying, like Hamm in *Endgame*, to feel the light of the sun. In *The Tinker's Wedding*, the younger couple, Michael Byrne and Sarah Casey, have made their camp by the roadside, and, like Estragon in *Waiting for Godot*, they sleep in, or by the side of, a ditch. All of these low-life characters (who speak, nonetheless, at times in the language of the poet that Estragon says he once was) are searching for something that will transform their lives from drab monotony to wonder, beauty or significance — a miraculous cure for blindness in *The Well of the Saints*, marriage in *The Tinker's Wedding*, or a saving Godot in *Waiting for Godot*. Beckett's play also has characters who, like Christy in *The Playboy of the Western World*, gnaw at turnips or sit clutching chicken-bones in their hands. Such common features of barrenness of setting, harshness of environment and simplicity of situation can, of course, be found in the work of other dramatists, such as W.B. Yeats's *At the Hawk's Well* or *Purgatory*, which we can be certain that Beckett knew well,[8] or again Strindberg's *Dream Play* or *To Damascus*, which Beckett insists he did not.[9] Yet, however bleak the setting or harsh the life that we witness Beckett's characters enduring in their stage-world, they react with a courage, resilience and humour that brings them much closer in spirit to Synge's Irish peasant-folk than they are to Strindberg's The Stranger or even to Yeats's Old Man.

In terms of atmosphere too, Beckett's plays, sometimes perhaps in spite of appearances, are closer to the plays of Synge than they are to those of Strindberg, or for that matter Chekhov and Ibsen. If the tramps in *Waiting for Godot* evoke the geography of the French provinces (the Pyrenees, the Vaucluse, the Macon country), the world that they inhabit, their lineage and the less easily defined 'feel' of the characters — in the French as well as in the English text — is unmistakeably Irish. And so Anouilh's view of *Waiting for Godot* as an unusual hybrid, 'the *Pensées* of Pascal played by the Fratellini clowns'[10] needs to be extended to include a number of genes inherited from Synge's beggars or tinkers.

The world that is depicted in Beckett's radio play, *All that Fall*, is specifically Irish and, although the characters are, on the whole, more solidly middle-class, they recall in several ways Synge's own highly voluble creations: Christy, the dung-carrier, directly by name, and Maddy Rooney, indirectly, by her imaginative vitality and her verbal inventiveness. Even *Endgame* which, initially, appears to be radically different from Synge's theatre has, nonetheless, some of the heavily claustrophobic atmosphere which is found in *Riders to the Sea*. The natural features of sea, sky, shore, rock and storm which dominate Synge's play still preoccupy Hamm and Clov but appear extremely remote from their closed inner 'soul-scape', as if they belong to another world removed in space and time. In Beckett's radio play, *Embers*, these same natural elements are organized in such a way that, again, Synge may be brought to mind but, since they occur within the skull of the main character, Henry, the differences are probably more striking than the similarities. In Beckett's most recent television play . . . *but the clouds* . . . (1976), although the title is taken from W.B. Yeats's poem 'The Tower', the main male protagonist is very much a Synge character, coming back into his sanctum 'having walked the roads since break of day, brought night home' (*EO*, 53).

Beckett's characters resemble Synge's most of all, however, in that they are splendid, compulsive talkers, creating out of apparently static situations a dialogue — or, perhaps more impressively, a monologue — that fixes the attention by means of rhythm and image as well as by the human life that is evoked there and the resonant, universal themes that are touched upon, often in a very oblique manner. In Beckett, however, this very Irish ability to spin words *ex nihilo* is much more self-conscious than it is in Synge and the status of words in Beckett's plays has become more uncertain, as they reflect an unsureness of self, convey something of the alien nature of others, or express a fleeting, and painful, awareness of the mysterious nature of reality. More frequently though, words are used as a shield to protect man from a reality that he can face up to only with reluctance and that his reason finds inexplicable. Estragon and Vladimir are extremely conscious of their reliance upon words to hold the silence at bay: 'That wasn't such a bad little canter' (*WFG*, 65) comments Estragon, after they have managed to inject some life into a flagging dialogue with a snatch of desperate repartee. When Hamm states in *Endgame* that what is keeping them there is 'the dialogue', he is expressing more than a mere theatrical truth, in a play in which words, which are necessary both to keep them going and perhaps, conceivably, to find some ending to their suffering, are, like everything else, in dreadfully short supply. Winnie in *Happy Days* is a true descendant of the Playboy of the Western World, as one critic has already described her, [11] in the sense that the 'gift of the gab' enables her to transform a mysterious, painful reality into an illusory, yet comforting, world of words. Yet, as we have seen earlier, Winnie is also aware, fitfully at least, of how language functions for her as habit; sorrow and pain are therefore allowed to creep into her speech from time to time as she recognizes the alternative to her smoke-screen of words, a terrifying combination of enforced silence and an undying consciousness. Alone with his tape-recorder, Krapp too depends upon words, in his case a few words, recorded many years ago in an attempt to capture a significant, but already past, experience, but which still mean more to him than any of the words that he can now use to describe an empty, disastrous present.

It has been suggested that the example of Synge's own closeness to self-parody helped Beckett to develop in his fiction and in his plays a deliberate self-consciousness so that, in Katharine Worth's words, 'his Molloys and Malones have the gift of the gab and can tell a gallus story with the same lilt and gusto as Christy Mahon, making it seem as large as life and twice as natural. But they parody themselves in the same breath, have an ear permanently cocked for the overdone phrase, the false note, the bit of romantic excess'. [12] Certainly Christy's account of how he killed his 'da' has a note of histrionic self-consciousness that looks forward to Pozzo's over-inflated rhetoric or to Hamm's and Winnie's deliberately self-conscious story-telling: 'With that the sun came out between the cloud and the hill, and it shining green in my face. "God have mercy on your soul", says he, lifting a scythe, "or on your own", says I, raising the loy.'[13] Yet it seems far more likely that the self-consciousness and self-parody found in Beckett's writing resulted from a close acquaintance with fictional works like Sterne's *Tristam Shandy* or Diderot's *Jacques le fataliste*, or even Joyce's own highly self-conscious, elaborate linguistic construct, *Finnegans Wake*. It probably also arises out of a critical attitude towards language that is part of the intellectual heritage of the Anglo-Irish writer and that, in its most radical form, springs from Beckett's personal meditation on the functions and inadequacies of language, prompted largely by Fritz Mauthner's critique of language,[14] a study which Beckett is said to have read aloud to James Joyce in the late 1930s.[15]

Hardly surprisingly, one finds a number of interesting thematic parallels betwen Beckett's and Synge's plays. Most fundamental perhaps is the sense of a profound rift between God and man and between the ideal and the actual, which is almost as strong in Synge as it is in Beckett. The ending of Synge's *Riders to the Sea*, for example, provides as bitter an indictment of the orthodox view of God as a beneficent protector as does Winnie's own intolerable plight in *Happy Days*, where her Miltonic greeting to the day, 'Hail holy light', contrasts ironically with the searing heat that beats down so inexorably upon her. Further, in her aspiration to gravity-free flight and the contrasting cruel reality of her burial in the earth, Winnie is not far removed in her longings from Nora Burke in *The Shadow of the Glen*, who feels herself torn between the pull of a firmly rooted, conventional, stultifying existence and the impulse towards a fuller, freer, less inhibited mode of living. Yet what in Synge had seemed at least dramatically realizable — after all Nora does leave with the tramp at the end of the play and Maurya in *Riders to the Sea* finds some measure of acceptance and peace — has become in Beckett yet another deceiving element in a totally unacceptable form of botched creation. For, in Beckett's plays, images of freedom, lightness and joy find their reflection in a kind of muted yearning and melancholic nostalgia, although, of course, dramatically the status of the image remains ambiguous. One might compare, for example, from this point of view, the tramp's words in *The Shadow of the Glen*

Come along with me now, lady of the house, and it's not my blather you'll be hearing only, but you'll be hearing the herons crying out over the black lakes, and you'll be hearing the grouse, and the owls with them, and the larks and the big thrushes when the days are warm, and it's not from the like of them you'll be hearing a talk of getting old like Peggy Cavanagh.[16]

with Hamm's speech in *Endgame*, in which the many qualifications and the conditional tense express an unrealizable yearning: 'If I could sleep I might make love. I'd go into the woods. My eyes would see . . . the sky, the earth. I'd run, run, they wouldn't catch me' (*EG*, 19). In the shorter plays particularly, Synge showed that he was as acutely aware as Samuel Beckett was of the passage of time, its debilitating effects, and the all-pervading presence of death. Nora Burke asks Michael Dara in *The Shadow of the Glen*, for example,

Why would I marry you, Mike Dara? You'll be getting old, and I'll be getting old, and in a little while, I'm telling you, you'll be sitting up in your bed — the way himself was sitting — with a shake in your face and your teeth falling, and the white hair sticking out round you like an old bush where sheep do be leaping a gap.[17]

Comparing this with such macabre (yet realistic!) passages in Beckett's plays as Hamm's 'But we breathe, we change! We lose our hair, our teeth! Our bloom! Our ideals!' (*EG*, 16) or with Mr Tyler's bitterly comic line in *All that Fall*, 'What sky! What light! Ah in spite of all it is a blessed thing to be alive in such weather, and out of hospital' (*ATF*, 11) it will not seem at all surprising that Robin Skelton should regard *The Shadow of the Glen* as 'the precursor of much black comedy, and the true forerunner of *Juno and the Paycock* and *Waiting for Godot*'.[18] How very 'Beckettian' Synge can appear is well illustrated by a speech from *The Well of the Saints*, in which the dark words of Martin Doul, the blindman temporarily cured by the Saint, foreshadow the sad portrayal of a suffering world found in Beckett's *All that Fall* or the more apocalyptic vision of Hamm's 'mad' painter and engraver in *Endgame*,

That's great sights, holy father . . . What was it I seen my first day, but your own bleeding feet and they cut with the stones, and my last day, but the villainy of herself that you're wedding, God forgive you, with Timmy the smith. That was great sights maybe . . . And wasn't it great sights seeing the roads when north winds would be driving and the skies would be harsh, and you'd see the horses and the asses and the dogs itself maybe with their heads hanging and they closing their eyes.[19]

It is not, of course, that Beckett has taken over ideas, attitudes, or even phrases from Synge's theatre — although occasionally he makes explicit, and almost certainly deliberate, allusion to the latter's plays. It would indeed be very strange if there were not such resemblances and thematic parallels between two writers who share so much by way of background, heritage and interests and who have in common, above all, an essentially tragi-comic vision of human life. In analyzing some of the closely related elements in Synge and Beckett — an anarchic irreverence of thought, a revelling in the grotesque and the macabre, an intellectual and spiritual extremism that declines compromise and cannot isolate the light from the dark, the grave from the gay, life from death — Alec Reid has clearly defined where these two writers differ and yet where they converge:

> Synge, recognising the inevitability of the dark, still defies it by seeking exultation, responding when he can to the primitive and the wild. Beckett, turning from such emotional response, drives his intellect to the creation of a world where there is nothing left to lose. The contrast, however, is more apparent than real, since both are facing up to the same conclusion — that man, for all his reason and aspiration, will age and die like the beast in the field and must suffer as well.[20]

It seems to me, however, that Beckett may well owe to Synge rather more than has been generally recognized. Aesthetically, one of the most satisfying features of Synge's theatre is, in Una Ellis-Fermor's words, that 'dramatic intensity invariably finds poetic expression' there.[21] It is not, of course, simply that an apparently regional speech is elevated to a poetic level in Synge's plays, but that many basically poetic (and musical) devices are exploited dramatically to arrive at a text characterized by density, ambiguity, resonance and multiplicity of levels, both intellectual and emotional. In putting forward the view that it is in this particular direction above all that Beckett may owe his greatest debt to John Millington Synge, it is important to state several things very clearly. Firstly, I have no authorial backing for such a view; secondly, Synge's texts were certainly not alone in indicating to Beckett an approach that he might follow in his own theatre; finally, and most important, once the route was signposted for him, Beckett quickly made it his own, developing and transforming whatever dramatic techniques he may have adopted.

This aspect of Beckett's debt can perhaps be best discerned by looking at several related tendencies in Synge's theatre. One of the most striking characteristics of Synge's plays is a tendency to transform the local, the particular, the everyday, and the trivial into the universal, the momentous, the memorable and the archetypal, while still preserving the original, local, more superficial level. In terms of basic plot, *Riders to the Sea*, *The Shadow of the Glen*, *The Tinker's Wedding* and *The Well of the Saints* all dramatize incidents and situations that have their source in Irish folk-tales or anecdotes. Yet they acquire much of their dramatic strength from the fact that they transcend the purely local and assume a much wider relevance and resonance. *The Shadow of the Glen*, for example, evolves beyond the story once recounted by Pat Dirane to Synge to link up with the classical tale of the widow of Ephesus. More significantly, the essential dramatic conflict of this play is between, on the one hand, passion, impulse, dream and a yearning for freedom and awareness, and, on the other hand, security, confinement, habit, materialistic satisfaction and self-satisfaction. Again, *Riders to the Sea*, however localized it might at first appear, is in fact a universal drama which refers 'not only to Irish history and folklore, but also to a world of archetypal symbolism'.[22] *The Playboy of the Western World*, which shocked some early critics by seeming to cast a slur upon the Irish peasantry, clearly uses at least dramatically credible responses to a boy who has murdered his own father to explore the interplay between illusion and reality, word and deed, poetry and existence.

The transformation of local source material in Synge's plays is effected, however, not so much by modifications of plot as by the nature of the language, imagery and symbolism of the plays. In *The Shadow of the Glen*, for example, we encounter a tramp who can request a 'sup of new milk' and accept instead, more gratefully, a whisky but who, by the resonance and allusiveness of his own rich, highly imaginative talk, can make the everyday and the trivial express much deeper fears and feelings, themes and thoughts.

> I was passing below on a dark night the like of this night, and the sheep were lying under the ditch and every one of them coughing, and choking, like an old man, with the great rain and the fog . . . Then I heard a thing talking — queer talk, you wouldn't believe it all, and you out of your dreams, — and 'Merciful God', says I, 'if I begin hearing the like of that voice out of the thick mist, I'm destroyed surely'. Then I run, and I run, and I run, till I was below in Rathvanna. I got drunk that night, I got drunk in the morning, and drunk the day after — I was coming from the races beyond — and the third day they found Darcy.[23]

In this speech, image, rhythm and repetition, as well as imprecation and idea, concur to express first a disquiet, then a panic that, for all its precise localized setting, has a universal psychological relevance, as well as an ambiguity that arises out of the apparent casualness of its religious echoes, Patch Darcy being presented here, and at several other points in the play, as if he were a Christ-like martyr figure.

Yet it is clear that, as with Christy Mahon in *The Playboy of the Western World*, the 'Christ analogue' is simply one of a number of associations that, as we shall see, are not confined to madness or martyrdom.[24] To overstate any of these parallels, echoes or associations means not only that one is distorting a dramatic character but also, I think, misunderstanding Synge's intentions in the drama. For the poetic and dramatic density which makes for the success of some of Synge's plays lies principally in a thematic and tonal patterning that works partly through oblique allusion[25] and partly through asymmetrical repetition and repetition with variation. Quite often the allusiveness of Synge's dramatic text is relatively overt, the thematic or tonal link being easily percieved — not necessarily a defect, of course, in a direct medium like the theatre. Synge's colour symbolism, for instance, in *Riders to the Sea* is fairly obvious, the sacrificial rites associated with death being evoked by allusions to the red mare and the red sail and by the visual presence on stage following the drowning of Bartley of the keening women dressed in red petticoats. Death is reflected too in the ominous verbal image of the black hags flying on the sea, by the black cliffs and the allusion to the pig with black feet, while the white boards are visible throughout the play waiting for the body of one of Maurya's sons for whom they are to provide a shining white coffin. Bread and holy water also obviously function as symbols of life.

In the same play, however, several recurring images evoke certain rather less obvious parallels with classical, as well as Christian, myths; the sea, for example, brings death to the entire family of a woman who is as ill-fated as Euripides's Phaedra and plays a part as great as Poseidon did in the death of Hippolytus. The failure to obtain nails when the white coffin-boards were purchased surely recalls the nails by which Christ was transfixed to the Cross. In *The Shadow of the Glen* the sexual aspect of Nora Burke's predicament is expressed by a variety of images that suggest abandonment, unbridled passion, and yet the need for sexual subjugation. Only Patch Darcy who died mad seems to have been enough of a man to control the mountain ewes with which Nora is obliquely compared. And, by comparison, her would-be love, Michael, unwittingly concedes his own manly inadequacies and failure by using the same image.

It's no lie he's telling, I was destroyed surely . . . They [the ewes] were

that wilful they were running off into one man's bit of oats, and another
man's bit of hay, and tumbling into the red bogs till it's more like a pack
of old goats than sheep they were . . . Mountain ewes is a queer breed,
Nora Burke, and I'm not used to them at all.[26]

Thematic and tonal patterns are often established in Synge's plays by
the repetition of certain key images, words or phrases. In *The Shadow
of the Glen*, for example, the slightly varied phrase 'it's too lonesome
you are', 'a lone woman', 'in a lonesome place' reveal Nora Burke's
psychological and sexual deprivation as well as her social isolation in a
spot where the contrasts of light and dark, and hill and glen evoke life
or death, renewal or capitulation. Again physical and spiritual death
are linked by such phrases as 'in the dark mist', 'when the mist is
down', 'in the evening of the day' and 'when night falls'. This may be
contrasted with the explicit juxtaposition of light and dark, up and
down, warmth and cold that occurs in *The Tinker's Wedding* when
Sarah Casey taunts Michael with a potential elopement with 'Jaunting
Jim',

> It's yourself you'll be calling God to help, in two weeks or three, when
> you'll be waking up in the dark night and thinking you see me coming
> with the sun on me, and I driving a high cart with Jaunting Jim going
> behind. It's lonesome and cold you'll be feeling the ditch where you'll be
> lying down that night, I'm telling you, and hearing the old woman
> making a great noise in her sleep, and the bats squeaking in the trees.[27]

It is a tribute, of course, to Synge's craftmanship that his patterning of
images and symbols, use of echo and allusion and repetition of word
and phrase to express important themes, feelings, moods or myths
rarely result in the plays appearing contrived or stylized. Instead,
they produce a living dramatic text which, largely because of
its suggestiveness and ambiguity, operates on several levels
simultaneously.

Anyone closely familiar with Samuel Beckett's theatre will
recognize that some of the features which have just been (somewhat
artificially) separated in Synge's dramatic writing are important
characteristics of Beckett's dramatic style also. 'Beckett has succeeded',
wrote H.A. Smith of the early plays, 'in *fusing* the ordinary and the
poetic and in establishing an ironic counterpoint between a surface
triviality or banality and overtones which are infinitely varied in their
power of suggestion and often vast to the point of [being] cosmic in
their implication'.[28] 'Nothing to be done', announces Estragon as he
struggles to remove his boot at the opening of *Waiting for Godot*, and
the whole play proceeds to show how appropriate this statement is to

man's bewildered position in the unverse. A single gesture, or a piece of apparent horseplay, too, can enrich the play enormously with its suggestiveness or its ambiguity of reference: Estragon, standing on one leg and imitating the tree, will recall for many, for example, in his pathetic query 'Do you think God sees me?' (*WFG*, 76) a martyred Christ (with whom he has compared himself all his life), as well as echoing John Donne's question in his poem, 'The Cross', 'who can deny mee power and liberty / To stretch mine arms and mine owne Cross to be?'.[29] The multiplicity of levels which is found in the text of *Waiting for Godot* is very striking and has already been much discussed by critics, some of whom have been led astray by focussing upon several of the associations or overtones at the expense of the sense of the play as a whole: one thinks, for example, of what has been made of the tree being 'couvert de feuilles' (in the French text) and having 'four or five leaves' (in the English version), as well as elaborations of the kind of association that I have just made. For *Waiting for Godot* is a play that strives above all to avoid definition. Uncertainty, ignorance, and impotence emerge in hundreds of questions that receive no answer and are reflected in numerous images of powerlessness, decline or circularity. In this context, ambiguity, suggestiveness and diversity of meaning are therefore crucial factors in depicting man as, in Beckett's own words, a 'non-knower and non-can-er'[30] eking out an existence that he experiences most sharply as suffering and cannot even begin to comprehend. 'I suppose this — might seem strange' comments Winnie in *Happy Days* '— this — what shall I say — this what I have said — yes — were it not . . . that all seems strange (*Pause*.) Most strange. (*Pause*.) Never any change. (*Pause*.) And more and more strange' (*HD*, 34).

Even in a play like *Krapp's Last Tape*, where the light and dark emblems are organized in such a way that, while functioning naturally enough, they provide a coherent, basically Manichean, intellectual infra-structure, no solution is offered to the fundamental conflict with which the play is concerned. For Krapp, having aspired at thirty-nine to an intellectual reconciliation of spiritual and sensual, remains at seventy torn by the demands of the flesh (as his need for women has diminished so his addiction to booze and bananas has increased), and, more crucially, he finds his earlier pretensions, aspirations and claims ludicrously inappropriate.

Of all Beckett's characters, Winnie in *Happy Days* would seem to be the most at home with the 'surface triviality and banality'. And yet her virtual monologue holds the attention by making half-remembered literary quotations, biblical echoes or half echoes, and, more frequently, jarring or ironic juxtaposition confer upon a living, seemingly commonplace, speech a complexity of verbal texture. So in this context the final words of the *Gloria*, 'world without end, Amen', resound with appalling irony and apparently insignificant phrases such as 'sleep for ever — marvellous gift' acquire an unusual resonance. Most of the major philosophical problems that have preoccupied man through the ages are also touched upon by Winnie at some point in the play, raised obliquely, even at times without her seeming to notice, but never, of course, solved. In Beckett's radio play, *Embers*, the dominant mood is conveyed by words and phrases that, by themselves, have relatively little resonance: 'old men', 'great trouble', 'white world', 'not a sound', 'fire dying'. Yet used repeatedly or in juxtaposition one with the other, these word-clusters jointly give a density to the text and allow the listener to be held, and perhaps moved, by the complex asymmetrical verbal patterning and by the kaleidoscopic variations of level and tone. As a glance at almost any of Beckett's plays from *Waiting for Godot* to the most recent *That Time* and *Footfalls* reveals, certain forms of repetition and repetition with variation, used differently from play to play, are favoured by Beckett to establish both broad patterns of cyclical recurrence (as in the repetition of the entire triangular dialogue in *Play*) and smaller eddies within a whirlpool that he depicts as never quite managing to suck man down to total extinction.

Most, if not all, of the common elements discerned in the plays of Beckett and Synge — multiplicity of levels, allusiveness, ambiguity and repetition of image, word and phrase — could, of course, be traced in the work of other dramatists or could have been transposed from the arts of music or painting. One thinks, for instance, of analogies that have been drawn between some of Beckett's methods of dramatic composition and musical form: a statement of theme, followed by multiple, highly elaborate variations, played upon it by various instruments,[31] the reprise *da capo*, as it was used by Haydn, and changes from the major to the minor key, the latter being an analogy that Beckett made himself in one of his production note-books.[32] His great curiosity concerning problems of composition in painting and his interest in compositional techniques in music (as well as his accomplishment as a pianist) are too well known to make such transpositions at all implausible. In earlier drama, Racine, on whose plays Beckett lectured while on the staff of Trinity College, Dublin, had already shown in *Phèdre* how images of heat and cold, light and darkness, could be used to express shifting psychological and emotional states. Chekhov had provided many discreet examples of the use of ambiguity and the creation of multiplicity of levels of significance.

It is the concurrence, however, of all these various elements in Synge and Beckett and the ways in which they are handled by the two dramatists that leads me to suggest that Synge's success in exploiting these devices dramatically to produce a dense, allusive, 'poetic' text proved to be an inspiration to Beckett when he came to write for the stage and for radio. To say this is not, of course, to identify Beckett's and Synge's individual use of these devices. A full comparative study would be needed to examine these differences adequately. But a few general points might usefully be made by way of conclusion.

First, although there are, as we have seen, a number of thematic affinities between the plays of Beckett and Synge, the wider themes of Beckett are more metaphysical than those of Synge, who tends to express mainly psychological fears, impulses, conflicts and emotions. Secondly, the 'poetry' of Beckett's drama tends to arise more commonly out of balance, rhythm and the evocative associations of relatively ordinary words, as well as from striking, highly imaginative dramatic images, rather than from the more colourful, sometimes more overtly lyrical language of Synge's drama. Thirdly, if Synge employs a surprisingly wide range of allusions to classical myths, Celtic folklore and Christian and pagan rites and beliefs, Beckett's own allusions, parallels and echoes are often more oblique as well as more erudite. An ambiguity, already present in Synge, has been more fully developed by Beckett; yet it is not used in the plays as the younger Beckett would have used it, with exhibitionistic brilliance and devastatingly learned wit. Instead, just as the mature Beckett is drawn to the image rather than to the symbol, so his handling of allusion and ambiguity is both more controlled and more subtle. It is sometimes felt that Beckett delights in allusion and ambiguity merely because it represents a rich source of dramatic interest, even tension. It seems to me rather that when it is combined, as it is in Beckett with a drastic simplicity of dramatic situation and issue, ambiguity is also a means of expression ideally suited to depict a world which eludes definition and reduction to system of any kind. If a number of the dramatic methods adopted by Beckett may seem therefore to be intellectual and sophisticated, the basic attitudes which they strive to express stem from emotional responses, from feelings of despair, sorrow, disorientation, compassion, and yet courage, humanity and resilience. In the past, attention has tended to be focussed upon the emotional affinities and points of divergence between Beckett and Synge. To suggest that Beckett owed Synge the dramatist a further debt for the seeds at least of elements found in his dramatic style is not to deny this deeply human affinity. Nor does it do any disservice to Beckett to indicate that plays of the imaginative power and originality of *Waiting for Godot*, *Endgame*, *Krapp's Last Tape* or *That Time* had part of their source in Beckett's own response to the 'compressed density',[33] rich allusiveness and tragi-comic blend of the theatre of John Millington Synge.

Notes

1. J. Knowlson, *Samuel Beckett: an Exhibition*, London, Turret Books, 1971, p. 23.
2. Letter to the author, 17.xii.1970.
3. R. Skelton, *The Writings of J.M. Synge*, London, Thames and Hudson, 1971, p. 56.
4. For a discussion of these authors in the context of Beckett's work, see J. Pilling, *Samuel Beckett*, chapter 5.
5. See, for example, R. Skelton, *op. cit.*, p. 172; Katharine Worth in the introduction to *Beckett the Shape-Changer*, London and Boston, Routledge and Kegan Paul, 1975, p. 5, asserts that Beckett is 'very much in tune with Synge and often echoes him', see also pp. 4, 5 and 8. A weak essay by B. Hibon, 'Samuel Beckett: Irish tradition and Irish creation' in *Aspects of the Irish Theatre*, Lillie, Editions Universitaires, 1972, compares *Waiting for Godot* with *The Tinker's Wedding* with respect to the characters and the situation presented.
6. The fullest discussion that I have come across so far is Alec Reid's most interesting article 'Comedy in Synge and Beckett' in *Yeats Studies*, no. 2, 'Theatre and the Visual Arts A Centenary Celebration of Jack Yeats and John Synge', eds. R.O'Driscoll and L. Reynolds, Shannon, Irish University Press, 1972, pp. 80-90.
7. Letter to the author, 11.iv.1972.
8. See Katharine Worth, 'Yeats and the French drama', *Modern Drama* 8, 1966, pp. 382-391. It is worth recalling what W.B. Yeats said of Synge's dramatic simplicity: 'perhaps I was Synge's convert. It was certainly a day of triumph when the first act of *The Well of the Saints* held its audience, though the two chief persons sat side by side under a stone cross from start to finish', 'An Introduction for my Plays', 1937, in *Essays and Introductions*, London, Macmillan, 1961, p. 528.
9. In spite of Beckett's strong disclaimer, Anthony Swerling still finds that 'there is hardly an element, theme, fact or condition of *Godot* and *Fin de Partie* which is not to be found or paralleled in Strindberg's theatre', *Strindberg's Influence in France, 1920-1960*, Cambridge, Trinity

Lane Press, 1971, p. 111. I can only say that I consider this to be as absurd as it would be to make any similar claim for Synge's influence on Beckett. Beckett confirmed that he had neither seen nor read Strindberg's *The Dream Play* before writing *Waiting for Godot* (letter to the author, 11.iv.1972).

10. Jean Anouilh in *Arts-Spectacles*, 400, February 27-March 5 1953, p.1.

11. K. Worth, *Beckett the Shape-Changer*, p. 8.

12. K. Worth, *Beckett the Shape-Changer*, p. 5.

13. *J.M. Synge: Collected Works*. Volume IV, Plays, Book II, ed. Ann Saddlemyer, London and New York, Oxford University Press, 1968, p. 103.

14. On Mauthner and Beckett, see Edith Kern, *Existential Thought and Fictional Technique: Kierkegaard, Sartre, Beckett*, New Haven, Conn., Yale University Press, 1970, p. 238; D.H. Hesla, *The Shape of Chaos, an Interpretation of the Art of Samuel Beckett*, Minneapolis, University of Minnesota Press, 1971, p. 234 note 18 and J. Pilling, *Samuel Beckett*, pp. 127-129.

15. Richard Ellmann, *James Joyce*, New York, Oxford University Press, 1959, pp. 661-2.

16. *J.M. Synge: Collected Works*. Volume III, Plays, ed. Ann Saddlemyer, London and New York, Oxford University Press, 1968, p. 57.

17. *J.M. Synge: Collected Works*. Volume III, Plays, p. 51.

18. R. Skelton, *The Writings of J.M. Synge*, p. 63.

19. *J.M. Synge: Collected Works*. Volume III, Plays, p. 141.

20. A. Reid, 'Comedy in Synge and Beckett', p. 88.

21. *The Irish Dramatic Movement*, London, Methuen, 1954, 2nd ed. revised, p. 163.

22. R. Skelton, *The Writings of J.M. Synge*, p. 43.

23. *J.M. Synge: Collected Works*. Volume III, Plays, p. 39.

24. The analogy with Christ is fully discussed in Hugh Maclean, 'The Hero as Playboy', *University of Kansas City Review*, XXI Autumn 1954, pp. 9-19; Howard Pearce, 'Synge's *Playboy* as Mock Christ', *Modern Drama*, VIII, December 1965, pp. 303-310; and Stanley Sultan, 'A Joycean Look at *The Playboy of the Western World*,, *The Celtic Master, Being Contributions to the First James Joyce Symposium in Dublin*, Dublin, Dolmen Press, 1969, pp. 45-55.

25. I use the word 'allusion', although I share Malcolm Kelsall's view that there is no 'sustained referential scheme' in Synge's plays, see *The Playboy of the Western World*, ed. M. Kelsall, London, Ernest Benn, 1975, p. xxi. See on this subject also R. Skelton, *The Writings of J.M. Synge*, pp. 119-121.

26. *J.M. Synge: Collected Works*. Volume III, Plays, p. 47. An article that deals more fully with Synge's verbal repetitions (and oppositions) is Seamus Deane's 'Synge's Poetic Use of Language', *J.M. Synge Centenary Papers 1971*, ed. Maurice Harmon, Dublin, Dolmen Press, 1972, pp. 127-144. I came across this piece after completing this chapter.

27. *J.M. Synge: Collected Works*. Volume IV, Plays, p. 11.

28. 'Dipsychus among the Shadows' in *Contemporary Theatre*, Stratford-upon-Avon Studies, no. 4, London, Arnold, 1962, p. 157.

29. John Donne, *Poetical Works*, ed. Herbert J.C. Grierson, Oxford University Press, 1971, p. 303.
30. Israel Shenker, 'Moody Man of Letters', *New York Times*, 6 May 1956.
31. See John Spurling's chapter, 'Son of Oedipus' in J. Fletcher and J. Spurling, *Beckett: a Study of his Pays*, pp. 72-77.
32. Schiller-Theater MS production notebook, *Das letze Band*, R.U.L. MS 1396/4/16.
33. M. Kelsall, ed., *The Playboy of the Western World*, p. xviii.

Beckett and Kleist's essay
'On the Marionette Theatre'

Beckett and Kleist's essay 'On the Marionette Theatre'

Beckett's admiration for Heinrich von Kleist's 'Über das Marionetten-theater', written in 1810, emerged clearly in October 1976 during rehearsals of the first production on BBC television of his recent television play *Ghost Trio*, for a programme of three plays consisting of *Not I*, *Ghost Trio* and . . . *but the clouds* . . . , called collectively by Beckett 'Shades'. While discussing various possible ways in which the man in the room in *Ghost Trio* might move from his stool to the door, the window, the mirror and the pallet, then back again to his stool, and the different ways in which he might raise his arm to open the door or the window or drop his head, Beckett referred the actor, Ronald Pickup, and subsequently myself, to several aspects of Kleist's essay on the marionette theatre, above all to the advent of self-consciousness and loss of harmony in man and yet to the value of economy and grace of movement. Beckett seemed most impressed by the vivid quality and striking force of Kleist's examples. But he was not simply using these examples to illustrate what he himself was trying to achieve in *Ghost Trio*. There was no doubt in the mind of anyone present that Kleist's essay also expressed memorably some of Beckett's own deepest aesthetic aspirations. I shall try to suggest later some of the reasons for this sympathy, even to some extent this identity of approach. Beckett shows little enthusiasm for the rest of Kleist's work, yet the essay on the marionette theatre fascinates him greatly. If, on the little evidence available, there is no justification for speaking of actual influence, there is much common ground to be explored between Kleist's essay and Beckett's own ways of thinking about art, the theatre and life. The present brief chapter is intended as no more than a first, modest glance at a relationship that will undoubtedly attract much further attention.

Kleist's essay on the marionette theatre has long been well-known to German readers. As Idris Parry pointed out recently,[1] its admirers range from Thomas Mann (whose *Doktor Faustus* saw the essay given as prescribed reading to Leverkühn, who had made a pact with the devil in return for the creative impulse) to Rilke who, in 1913, spoke of 'this master work', and to Hugo von Hofmannsthal, who, in 1922, wrote that Kleist's essay was 'the most perceptive piece of philosophy since Plato'. It has been much less well-known, however, to an English reading public, although, as a respondent to Professor Parry pointed out,[2] several English translations are in existence, from one printed in Gordon Craig's *The Marionette* in 1918 to Parry's most recent one published in the *Times Literary Supplement*. Beckett's friend, Eugene Jolas, also translated it into English in *Vertical* (1941) — unknown, it would appear, to Beckett. But Beckett assured me in any case that he had read the essay in the original German.

In this essay, Kleist compared the movements of the human dancer with those of the marionette, which, one of the speakers maintains, are superior to those of the human figure because:

> They are not hindered with the inertness of matter, the quality most resistant to dancing, because the lifting power is greater than that which keeps them down . . . The puppets need the floor only to touch and enliven the swing of their limbs by momentarily retarding their action. We need the floor only to refresh ourselves from the strain of dancing, a moment which is not really dancing and with which we can do nothing but show it as little as possible.[3]

According to Kleist's speaker, puppets possess therefore a mobility, a symmetry, a harmony and a grace greater than any human dancer can ever have. For, inevitably, they are totally lacking in self-awareness, hence affectation, which destroys natural grace and charm in man. One of the parts of the essay which particularly impressed Beckett concerns the advent of self-consciousness and its effects on the natural charm of man. Kleist's speaker tells the following story:

> I bathed, about three years ago, with a young man who at that time possessed extraordinary charm. He might have been about sixteen, and only indistinctly could one see the first traces of vanity caused by women's favours. We had recently seen in Paris 'The youth drawing a thorn from his foot'. The copy of this statue is well known and is present in most German collections. A glance he cast in a large mirror, while putting his foot on a stool to dry it, reminded him of this statue. He

> smiled and told me of the discovery he had made. I had had the same
> idea but, either to test the strength of his charm, or to damp his vanity a
> little, I laughed, and replied that he saw ghosts. He blushed and lifted
> his foot again to prove it, but the experiment failed, as could have been
> foreseen. Confused, he lifted his foot three, four, perhaps even ten
> times. In vain he was unable to produce the same movement again. On
> the contrary, his movements now had such a comical element that
> I could hardly refrain from laughing. From that day, so to speak from
> that moment, an inconceivable change occurred in the young man. He
> began to stand before the mirror for days, and lost one charm after
> another. An invisible and inconceivable power had come like an iron net
> about the free play of his gestures, and after one year there was not a
> trace of his charm which before had delighted the eyes of his
> companions.[4]

This discovery of self represents, of course, a Fall. Self-consciousness separates man from the world, even from his own Self since,
essentially, the very consciousness of self means that he is perceiving
himself as Other. Disunity, disharmony, and fragmentation
therefore enter, where once there was natural harmony, symmetry
and grace. Parry expresses the Kleistian formula in the following way:
'I think, therefore I am aware of myself, and if I am aware of my *Self* I
must know I am a separate entity, aware of and therefore separate
from my surroundings; but true knowledge is complete, connected,
indivisible, so separation into subject and object, self and surroundings, means distance from knowledge, consequently uncertainty
and doubt. Man, the thinking animal, is in Rilke's phrase from the
Duino elegies, "opposite and nothing but that, and always opposite" '.[5]
For the culprit, as with the Biblical Fall, is knowledge, which, in man,
is necessarily incomplete and imperfect. Man is, therefore, a creature
permanently off balance. He lacks the unity, harmony, symmetry
and grace that characterizes the puppet. For in Robert Helbing's
words, 'Symbolically, marionettes represent beings of innocent,
pristine nature. They are members of only one world responding
"naturally" and "gracefully" to divine guidance. This is under-scored
by their apparent weightlessness . . . They represent a state of grace, a
"paradise lost" to man, whose conscious and wilful "free" self
assertions make him self-conscious'.[6]

Kleist also recounts the remarkable tale of a fencing bear, which
Beckett specifically quoted when speaking of the nature of movement
in *Ghost Trio*. This concerns an expert fencer who, having beaten a
young man (also a talented fencer), is taken to fight with a bear. The
fight proceeds along the following unusual lines:

'Thrust, thrust', Baron G said, 'and try to strike him'. After I had recovered from my astonishment, I lunged at him with the rapier, and the bear parried the pass. I tried to deceive him with feints, the bear did not move. I attacked him afresh with skill momentarily inspired. I should have surely struck a man's breast. The bear made only a short movement with his paw and parried the pass. I was now almost in the same situation as the young Baron [his former opponent]. The bear's seriousness intervened to upset my composure. I made alternate passes and feints. I dripped with sweat. In vain; the bear not only parried all my passes like the first fighter in the world, he did not accept my feints; no fighter on earth could have done that. Eye to eye, as if he could read my mind, he stood raising his paw ready for battle, and when my passes were not really meant he did not move.[7]

The bear represents, again symbolically, the creature without knowledge, who is able, therefore, to respond naturally and unselfconsciously to the thrusts of the fencer and is not deceived by his false passes. Further, in parrying the actual thrusts, the bear does what he has to do to avoid being struck with strict economy and with the maximum of grace.

At the end of the essay, Kleist draws a striking conclusion from his previous exposition of the unavoidably 'fallen' state of man. 'We see', he wrote, 'that the darker and weaker is Reflection in the organic world, the more apparent Grace becomes, shining and ruling. But as the intersection of two points, from the one side of a point, after passing through the infinite, returns suddenly to the other side; or, the image of a concave mirror after moving into the infinite appears suddenly again, near and before us; so, when Knowledge has gone, so to speak, through the infinite, Grace returns again, appearing at the same time, most purely in the structure which has either no knowledge, or an infinite knowledge, to wit: in a marionette or in a God.

' " Therefore, we must eat again of the Tree of Knowledge to return to a state of innocence?" I said, a little distracted.

"Indeed", he answered, "that is the last chapter in the history of the world." '[8]

This anti-intellectual, almost visionary conclusion looks forward, then, to a time when knowledge might be total and indivisible. 'The two ends of this circular world join in Paradise as the grace of God and the grace of the puppet, which submits exclusively to natural law. Spiritual and physical grace are one. The dance of these marionettes stands for all unaffected responsive gesture[s]; it is form drawn without effort from the flow of life, visible music.'[9]

It would, of course, be quite misguided to attempt to read Beckett's recent plays as if they represented some kind of commentary on Kleist's essay. Clearly they are nothing of the kind. And yet the essay appears to throw some light on aspects of several of the plays which might at first appear to be a little puzzling. In *Ghost Trio*, for instance, the male figure (F) acts as if he were *virtually* a puppet, turning his head sharply whenever he thinks 'he hears her' and moving around the room, as if he were being controlled by the woman's voice, which issues what are, ambiguously, either commands or, more likely, anticipations of actions. The movements of his hand, as he pushes open the door or the window, and the movements of his head, as he bows it in front of the mirror, are all slow, deliberate, highly economical, and extremely graceful. In Beckett's own version of *Ghost Trio*, directed by him for Süddeutscher Rundfunk, these movements were even slower and seemingly less of this world than in the BBC version directed by Donald McWhinnie. At rehearsals for this latter production, Beckett stressed that when the man looks up from the pallet to the mirror, it should be in a smooth, unbroken, graceful movement. And like the bear in Kleist's story, in fact, the man makes only the smallest of movements necessary in order to perform what he wants or is guided to do.

There are then, in *Ghost Trio*, two completely different types of movement, the sustained and the gentle contrasting with the abrupt and the jerky. For Beckett's man in the room is still, in spite of everything, a creature bound to a world of matter, not quite the still-life figure that at first he appears to be. Nor is he yet completely free from affectation, as his look into the mirror indicates, or totally indifferent to the world of the non-self, as his responses to stimuli either from outside or from within his own mind suggest. It would appear, however, that, as Beckett's man comes ever closer to a state of stasis — and F in this play spends most of his time totally immobile, listening to the recording of Beethoven's 'Ghost Trio' though not, it would seem, himself controlling its appearance and disappearance — his movements appear to be approaching at least the grace, economy and lack of self-consciousness that Kleist had described as possible for the marionette but impossible for the human dancer.

May in the slightly earlier *Footfalls* is scarcely part of this world, sharing only in its pain and its suffering. She is at once an apparition and a fiction. Totally self-contained in her movements Beckett refers to her, as we have seen, as 'being for herself'. This encapsulation

within herself means that she is insufficiently aware of the outside
world to possess any real affectation. She has indeed 'never been
really born'. But in spite of her absence from the world, like the
dancer she still touches the ground, if less and less noticeably as the
play proceeds through its four stages. The sounds made by her feet
might then be interpreted as an attempt to assert some form of
presence in an alien world of matter, giving concrete, auditory
expression to the anguish that her pacing externalizes. In this way,
her request to 'hear the feet, however faint they fall' (*EO*, 35) — for
motion is not enough for May, she must hear the sound — takes on an
interesting significance in the light of Kleist's essay.

Beckett has always been interested in shape in an art-work, as in
ideas. But, in recent years, he has also placed increasing emphasis on
severe restraint and economy of movement and gesture both in his
writing and in his directing. I should like to suggest that, in this
respect, he is extremely close to Kleist's marionette essay.

One of Beckett's friends from the 'twenties, Bill Cunningham, who
accompanied him from time to time to plays at the Abbey Theatre in
Dublin, recalled on a recent Telefís Eireann radio programme that
when Beckett saw the famous actor, Michael Dolan, in September
1924, playing the part of a modern Job in T.C. Murray's *Autumn Fire*,
he remarked 'how much his [Dolan's] hands came into expressing his
feelings, when, as a man who was maimed and stricken, he had all
these tragic occurrences falling upon him'. Martha Fehsenfeld reports
how moved Beckett is said to have been by the gestures made by
Madeleine Renaud's ageing arms, as she acted Winnie in *Happy Days*.
In almost any of Beckett's plays from *Krapp's Last Tape* onwards, and
in all of his own productions, one finds a meticulous concern for the
power of small gestures or movements; for example, Martin Held's
arms folded across his body and clutching his upper arms, in Beckett's
own production of *Krapp's Last Tape* at the Schiller-Theater in Berlin
in 1969, or Billie Whitelaw performing the same gesture in *Footfalls* in
1976. Or, again, one thinks of Krapp's slow, lingering glance back to
look for death lurking in the darkness surrounding him or the gesture
of cupping his hand as an accompaniment to his account of the
moments spent with the girl in the punt. In *Happy Days*, attention
centres on the most minute gesture of Winnie's hands, face, mouth or
eyes. For it is not grandiose gestures which have attracted Beckett —
there are hardly any which would qualify for that epithet in the whole
of Beckett's theatre — but restraint, economy, grace and musicality of

gesture and movement. These were all terms which Beckett used concerning the movements of the man in the room in *Ghost Trio* and they have been invoked on numerous occasions by the author while directing his own plays.

In Beckett's recent writing for the theatre and for television, minimal movements and slow, graceful gestures figure not as the residue of a wider repertory of gestures, as has often been supposed, nor simply as ways of achieving stark dramatic effects. They appear rather as intimations (though necessarily imperfect ones) of a state of grace, harmony, economy and beauty akin to that discovered by Kleist's speaker in the movements of the marionette and glimpsed perhaps most clearly by Beckett in music itself. If one thing is clear about Beckett's recent work as a playwright *and* as a director in the theatre, it is that he conceives movements as 'visible music' and choreographs an entire production so as to blend sound and silence, movement and stillness into a tight, musical structure.

Actors have been telling us for years how musical Beckett's texts are and how, once the rhythms of his dramatic language (visual as well as verbal) have been captured, acting his work begins to seem a little less difficult. Beckett's own Schiller-Theater production of *Waiting for Godot* in 1975 illustrated how quite lengthy stretches of dialogue possess their own internal rhythms, cadences, changes of pitch, tone and key and how they are related in the text (and could be related in a fine production to passages which precede or follow them). 'Producers', Beckett said to Charles Marowitz as early as 1962, 'don't seem to have any sense of form in movement. The kind of form one finds in music, for instance, where themes keep recurring. When, in a text, actions are repeated, they ought to be made unusual the first time, so that when they happen again — in exactly the same way — an audience will recognize them from before.'[10] Beckett's Berlin production of *Waiting for Godot* admirably demonstrated this sense of 'form in movement', shaping speech, gestures and movements into a precisely organized, musically balanced, and aesthetically satisfying work. Beckett's production notebooks — for *Krapp's Last Tape*, *Endgame* and *Happy Days* all, like *Waiting for Godot*, done with the Schiller-Theater company in Berlin — show how important musical concepts and parallels are to him as a director. He is concerned, for example, in the *Krapp's Last Tape* notebook that the voices of the younger Krapp, recorded on tape, and the older Krapp who is preparing his last live recording should be carefully distinguished one from the other by musical pitch. When working with Jean Martin on the same play at the Récamier theatre in Paris in 1970, Beckett aimed to confer a rhythmical quality on Krapp's pacing.[11] In *Footfalls*, the pacing of May and her stark gestures were not only rigorous and yet extremely economical, they were also rehearsed with meticulous concern for sound, visual effect and rhythm. In his own production at the Royal Court Theatre in May 1976, Beckett stressed that the aim was not to perform the play in a realistic or psychological manner, but to do it musically. Finally, in *Ghost Trio*, while explicitly linking what he was doing with Kleist's 'fencing bear', Beckett sought to add a musical precision to an economy and grace of movement that resulted in a strangely haunting performance.

It is not at all surprising, of course, that Beckett should have been so strongly attracted to Kleist's essay. For trapped as he is by his own consciousness of self, Beckett's man yearns to escape from the limitations of his mortal state. *Krapp's Last Tape* is a play about a desire for harmony that is never achieved. For Krapp aspires, yet fails, to rise above divisions in which he is inextricably caught up. Man emerges, in fact, in all of Beckett's plays as permanently off-balance, and divided between the worlds of sense and spirit. Reading of Kleist's dancer, one is inevitably reminded of Winnie in *Happy Days* whom Beckett described, we may recall, as a 'weightless being' who was 'being cruelly devoured by the earth'.[12] She too is divided between spirit and matter, seeking (and again failing) to free herself from her entanglement with being, which slowly takes on the form of an entombment. Beckett's own dualism may have its origins in Cartesian divisions of mind and body and may come extremely close at times to Gnostic ways of thinking about matter and the desire to escape from its clutches, but his sense of the disaster of self-consciousness in man (and the inadequacy of the human intellect to arrive at any form of salvation) finds an unusually faithful echo in Kleist's remarkable essay.

Notes

1. *Times Literary Supplement*, 20 October 1978, pp. 1211-1212.
2. *Times Literary Supplement*, 27 October 1978, p. 1260; letter from George Speaight.
3. Heinrich von Kleist, 'About the Marionette Theatre', translation by Cherna Murray, *Life and Letters Today*, vol. 16, no. 8, Summer 1937, p. 103.

4.   'About the Marionette Theatre', p. 104.

5.   I. Parry, 'Kleist and the Puppets', *Times Literary Supplement*, 20 October 1978, p. 1212.

6.   R.E. Helbing, *The Major Works of Heinrich von Kleist*, New York, New Directions, 1975, p. 36.

7.   'About the Marionette Theatre', pp. 104-5.

8.   'About the Maionette Theatre', p. 105.

9.   I. Parry, *op. cit.*, p. 1212.

10.   *Encore*, March-April 1962, p. 44.

11.   Interview with Jean Martin, 3 December 1978.

12.   Quoted in Ruby Cohn, *Back to Beckett*, p. 190.

Select Bibliography

ABBOTT, H.P.: *The Fiction of Samuel Beckett. Form and Effect*, Berkeley, University of California Press, 1973.

BAIR, D.: *Samuel Beckett. A Biography*, New York, Harcourt Brace Jovanovich, 1978.

CALDER, J., ed.: *Beckett at Sixty. A Festschrift*, London, Calder and Boyars, 1967.

CANARIS, V.: *Samuel Beckett. 'Das letzte Band'. Regiebuch der Berliner Inszenierung*, Frankfurt, Suhrkamp Verlag, 1970.

COE, R.N.: *Beckett*, Edinburgh and London, Oliver and Boyd, 1964.

COHN, R., ed.: *Samuel Beckett, a Collection of Criticism*, New York etc., Rutgers University Press, 1962.

COHN, R.: *Back to Beckett*, Princeton, New Jersey, Princeton University Press, 1973.

COHN, R., ed.: *Samuel Beckett a Collection of Criticism*, New York etc., McGraw-Hill Inc., 1975.

DUCKWORTH, C., ed.: Samuel Beckett, *En attendant Godot*, London, Harrap, 1966.

ESSLIN, M.: *The Theatre of the Absurd*, Harmondsworth, Penguin Books, 1968.

ESSLIN, M., ed.: *Samuel Beckett. A Collection of Critical Essays*, Englewood Cliffs, New Jersey, 1965.

FINNEY, B.: *Since 'How It Is.' A Study of Beckett's Later Fiction*, London, Covent Garden Press, 1972.

FEDERMAN, R.: *Journey to Chaos : Samuel Beckett's Early Fiction*, Berkeley and Los Angeles, University of California Press, 1965.

FLETCHER, B.S. AND J., SMITH B. and BACHEM W., eds.: *A Student's Guide to the Plays of Samuel Beckett*, London and Boston, Faber and Faber, 1978.

FLETCHER, J.: *The Novels of Samuel Beckett*, London, Chatto and Windus, 1964.

FLETCHER, J.: *Samuel Beckett's Art*, London, Chatto and Windus, 1967.

FLETCHER, J. and SPURLING, J.: *Beckett. A Study of his Plays*, London, Eyre Methuen, 1972.

GONTARSKI, S.E.: *Beckett's Happy Days. A Manuscript Study*, Columbus, Ohio, Ohio State University Libraries, 1977.

GRAVER L. and FEDERMAN, R.: *Samuel Beckett : the Critical Heritage*, London, Henley and Boston, Routledge and Kegan Paul, 1979.

GUICHARNAUD, J.: *Modern French Theatre from Giraudoux to Genet*, New Haven, Connecticut, Yale University Press, 1967.

HAMILTON, K. and A.: *Condemned to Life. The World of Samuel Beckett*, Grand Rapids, Michigan, W.B. Eerdmans, 1976.

HARVEY, L.: *Samuel Beckett, Poet and Critic*, Princeton, New Jersey, Princeton University Press, 1970.

HESLA, D.: *The Shape of Chaos. An Interpretation of the Art of Samuel Beckett*, Minneapolis, University of Minnesota Press, 1971.

JANVIER, L.: *Pour Samuel Beckett*, Paris, Éditions de Minuit, 1966.

KENNER, H.: *Samuel Beckett. A Critical Study*, new edition, Berkeley and Los Angeles, University of California Press, 1968.

KENNER, H.: *A Reader's Guide to Samuel Beckett*, London, Thames and Hudson, 1973.

KERN, E.: *Existential Thought and Fictional Technique : Kierkegaard, Sartre, Beckett*, New Haven, Connecticut, Yale University Press, 1970.

KNOWLSON, J.: *Samuel Beckett : an Exhibition*, London, Turret Books, 1971.

KNOWLSON, J.: *Light and Darkness in the Theatre of Samuel Beckett*, London, Turret Books, 1972.

KNOWLSON, J., ed.: Samuel Beckett, *Happy Days / Oh les beaux jours*, London and Boston, Faber and Faber, 1978.

MERCIER, V.: *Beckett/Beckett*, New York, Oxford University Press, 1978.

MOROT-SIR, E., HARPER, H. and McMILLAN, D. eds.: *Samuel Beckett. The Art of Rhetoric*, Chapel Hill, North Carolina, Department of Romance Languages, 1976.

PILLING J.: *Samuel Beckett*, London, Henley and Boston, Routledge and Kegan Paul, 1976.

REID, A.: *All I can manage more than I could*, Dublin, Dolmen Press, 1968.

ROBINSON, M.: *The Long Sonata of the Dead. A Study of Samuel Beckett*, Hart-Davis, 1969.

ROSEN, S.: *Samuel Beckett and the Pessimistic Tradition*, New Brunswick, New Jersey, Rutgers University Press, 1976.

WEBB, E.: *Samuel Beckett : A Study of his Novels*, London, Peter Owen, 1970.

WEBB, E.: *The Plays of Samuel Beckett*, London, Peter Owen, 1972.

WORTH, K., ed.: *Beckett the Shape-Changer*, London and Boston, Routledge and Kegan Paul, 1976.

ZILLIACUS, C.: *Beckett and Broadcasting. A Study of the works of Samuel Beckett for and in Radio and Television*, Abo, Abo Akademi, 1976.

Index

Index of Beckett references

290

General Index

292

OTHER GROVE PRESS DRAMA
AND THEATER PAPERBACKS

CRITICAL STUDIES